ELKIN MATHEWS

Elkin Mathews, c. 1912. Elkin Mathews Archives, Reading University.

ELKIN MATHEWS

Publisher to Yeats, Joyce, Pound

James G. Nelson

THE UNIVERSITY OF WISCONSIN PRESS

The University of Wisconsin Press
114 North Murray Street
Madison, Wisconsin 53715

3 Henrietta Street
London WC2E 8LU, England

5 4 3 2 1

Printed in the United States of America

Library of Congress Cataloging-in-Publication Data
Nelson, James G.
Elkin Mathews : publisher to Yeats, Joyce, Pound/James G. Nelson.
320 pp.   cm.
Includes bibliographical references and index.
1. Mathews, Elkin, 1851–1921. 2. Yeats, W. B. (William Butler),
1865–1939—Publishers. 3. Joyce, James, 1882–1941—Publishers.
4. Pound, Ezra, 1885–1972—Publishers.
5. Publishers and publishing—Great Britain—Biography.
6. Literature publishing—Great Britain—History.
7. Authors and publishers—Great Britain—History.
I. Title.
Z325.M385N45   1989
070.5'092—dc20
[B]   89-40265
ISBN 0-299-12240-9   CIP
ISBN 0-299-12244-1 (pbk.)

CONTENTS

ILLUSTRATIONS

ILLUSTRATIONS

In his preface to *The Oxford Book of Victorian Verse* (1912), the well-known critic Arthur Quiller-Couch paid tribute to Elkin Mathews and John Lane—"My especial helpers among publishers of recent verse"—men who, as he observed, "at first in conjunction, of late years separately—have done so much to keep alive the fire of poetry in England." In *The Early Nineties: A View from the Bodley Head* (Harvard UP, 1971), I detailed the means by which Mathews and Lane as partners in the little bookshop and publishing firm in Vigo Street, London, known as the Bodley Head created a vogue for poetry which influenced literary developments both in Britain and America during the early nineties. In what I conceive of as a complement to that book, the present work chronicles the publishing career of Mathews from the time of the dissolution of the partnership with Lane to his death in 1921.

Although John Lane's career as a publisher has been recorded in books such as J. Lewis May's *John Lane and the Nineties* and in numerous articles and other accounts, Mathews' endeavors to sustain the cause of poetry at a time when modern literary currents were beginning to flow have received less attention. Mathews is often singled out as among that courageous little band of small publishers around the turn of the century who, in the words of Robert Scholes, "had a direct hand in the shaping of new literature," but he is overshadowed in the publishing history of the times by his former partner and has never been given his due as a publisher who, by affording young writers an opportunity to publish their work, encouraged many of them who became significant figures in the development of modern poetry. It is my purpose in this book, therefore, to fill this lacuna in publishing history by providing the reader with a detailed account of Mathews' achievement as a publisher and the means by which he sought to attain his goals. In particular, I stress the role he played in the literary careers of his most important authors, devoting separate chapters to W. B. Yeats, James Joyce, and Ezra Pound. In my view no history of the rise of modern literature is complete without an account of Mathews' role in keeping "alive the fire of poetry" during the early years of this century, and no publishing history of our age is sound which does not acknowledge his efforts, in the words of Robert Bridges, "to publish poetry cheaply," thereby affording young poets a publishing opportunity while supplying the clientele for poetry an affordable source of quality verse.

After Mathews' death in 1921, the bulk of his library, containing many of his publications, was sold at a three-day auction during April 1922 conducted by the well-known firm of Messrs. Hodgson and Company. Since it had been Mathews' habit to file much of his correspondence with his authors in his personal copies of their books, the dispersal of his library has made it difficult and time-consuming to bring together the records necessary to a history of the firm. Fortunately, the books and documents retained by Mathews' widow, Edith, made their way in 1966, through the generosity of his daughter, Nest Elkin Mathews, to the archives of the Library of the University of Reading, whose Keeper of Archives and Manuscripts, Dr. J. A. Edwards, made my task easier by providing me with his kind assistance and advice on a number of occasions.

Other persons who generously gave of their time to facilitate my researches and to whom I owe my gratitude are Robert J. Bertholf, Curator of the Poetry/Rare Books Collection, State University of New York at Buffalo Library; Patricia Willis, Curator of American Literature, Yale University Library; Anthony S. Bliss, Rare Book Librarian, University of California, Berkeley; Stephen Corey, Special Collections Librarian, University of San Francisco Library; Donald D. Eddy, Librarian, Department of Rare Books, Cornell University Library; Cathy Henderson, Research Librarian, Harry Ransom Humanities Research Center, University of Texas, Austin; Sara S. Hudson, Assistant Curator, Library Manuscripts, Huntington Library; Donald Kunitz, Head, Department of Special Collections, The Library, University of California, Davis; Bernard Meehan, Keeper of Manuscripts, Trinity College Library, Dublin; C. G. Petter, Archivist Librarian, University of Victoria Library; C.D.W. Sheppard, Sub-librarian, the Brotherton Collection, University of Leeds Library; Lola Szladits, Curator, the Berg Collection, New York Public Library; and Marjorie G. Wynne, Research Librarian, Yale University Library.

In addition, I wish to thank those who kindly answered my inquiries and provided me with illustrations and other materials: Professor William M. Murphy of Union College, Schenectedy, New York; Barbara Kaye (Mrs. Percy Muir); Dr. Lawrence Rainey, Yale University; Dr. John Kelly, St. Johns' College, Oxford; and Warwick Gould, Royal Holloway and New Bedford College. Needless to say, my gratitude also goes to my many friends and colleagues who have afforded me over the course of my researches invaluable counsel and encouragement, among them those who read portions of my manuscript and gave me the benefit of their expert knowledge: Professor Jerome Hamilton Buckley of Harvard University, Dr. G. Krishnamurti of the Eighteen Nineties Society, Dr. Philip Kent Cohen, Mr. Mark Samuels Lasner, Mr. Charles Cox, and Professor Phillip Herring of the University of Wisconsin. For reading the entire manuscript and tendering me their valued advice I thank my former colleague at the University of Wisconsin and now Vice President of the John Simon Guggenheim Foundation, New York, Dr. G. Thomas Tanselle; Professor Joseph Wiesenfarth of the University of Wisconsin; and Dr. Ian Fletcher. I also thank Mr. Cuthbert Mathews, Elkin Mathews' nephew; his daughter, Elizabeth Lydia Mathews; Audrey Mathews Griffin (Mrs. Charles Griffin), Mathews' niece; and her daughter, Rosamund Griffin, for sharing with me their knowledge of their kinsman. My greatest debt of gratitude, of course, is owed to Mathews' daughter, Nest, who made available to me the books, documents, photographs, and other materials about her father which she still retains. Through my visits with her in her home and through our correspondence, she has provided me with invaluable information and has been an unfailing source of inspiration. I also wish to thank Carolyn Moser who edited the text and Kathy Dauck and Mary Ann Ford for typing the manuscript.

For permission to quote from unpublished manuscripts and other copyright materials I am indebted to Miss Nest Elkin Mathews (Elkin Mathews letters and documents); Mrs. Nicolete Gray and the Society of Authors, on behalf of the Laurence Binyon Estate; Curtis Brown Ltd., on behalf of John Child-Villiers and Valentine Lamb as literary executors of the estate of Lord Dunsany; Anne and Michael B. Yeats (Lily Yeats letters and diary and Jack B. Yeats letters); Oxford University Press (W. B. Yeats letters); New Directions Publishing Corporation, agents, for the Trustees of the Ezra Pound Literary Property Trust; the Society of Authors for the estate of James Joyce; Mr. Roger Lancelyn Green (Gordon Bottomley letters); Mr. Peter Newbolt (Sir Henry Newbolt letters); Mr. Merlin Holland (Oscar Wilde letters); Mr. Brian Read (Arthur Symons letters); and the Directors of William Clowes Ltd. (business documents of the firm).

For permission to quote from unpublished manuscripts and other materials in their collections, I thank the following libraries: Harley K. Croessmann Collection of James Joyce, Morris Library, Southern Illinois University; Cornell University Library; Beinecke Rare Book and Manuscript Library, Yale University; Harry Ransom Humanities Research Center, University of Texas at Austin; Houghton Library, Harvard University; Brotherton Library, University of Leeds; the Elkin Mathews Archive, University of Reading; Special Collections Library, Columbia University; Princeton University Library; The Poetry/Rare Books Collection of the University Libraries, State University of New York at Buffalo; Huntington Library, San Marino, Calif.; William Andrews Clark Memorial Library, University of California at Los Angeles; Bancroft Library, University of California at Berkeley; Special Collections and Archives, Margaret I. King Library, University of Kentucky; National Library of Ireland; Berg Collection and the Rare Books and Manuscripts Division, New York Public Library; Trinity College Library, Dublin University; Bodleian Library, Oxford University; Special Collections Library, University of Delaware; Special Collections Library, University of Victoria; Library of Worcester College, Oxford University; and the British Library.

For permission to reproduce certain illustrations in this book I thank Miss Nest Elkin Mathews (photo of Elkin Mathews c. 1912; Mathews' account of sales for Ronald Firbank's *Odette d'Autreverne*, 1904; Mathews' letter to J. M. Synge, 20 Jan. 1905; drawings by Edith Elkin Mathews); Anne and Michael B. Yeats (pencil drawing of Elkin Mathews by John Butler Yeats; chalk drawing of Elkin Mathews by Jack B. Yeats); and Collection of American Literature, Yale University Library (front cover and title page of Jean de Bosschere's *Twelve Occupations*).

I am also grateful for permission to reprint in Chapters 2, 3, and 4, and Appendix A revised versions of articles first published in *Papers of the Bibliographical Society of America, Journal of Modern Literature, James Joyce Quarterly,* and *Journal of the Eighteen Nineties Society.*

Finally, I would like to thank the organizations which have supported my research with funds so generously given: the Research Committee of the Graduate School of the University of Wisconsin, the National Endowment for the Humanities, the American Council of Learned Societies, the American Philosophical Society, and the Bibliographical Society of America.

ELKIN MATHEWS

CHAPTER ONE

Elkin Mathews, His Life and Career:

An Overview

ELKIN MATHEWS' claim to our attention derives largely from the fact that his career in publishing coincided with the transition from Victorian to modern literature, a period which literary historians date from about 1880 to 1920. Numerous publishers, large and small, were in business during those years, but what makes Mathews unique is the role he played in encouraging new poets at a time when the various currents leading to modern literature were beginning to flow. Although the fortunes of poetry were on the decline, Mathews, who thought of himself exclusively as a publisher of belles lettres, had the desire and the ability to support young poets who otherwise might never have found an audience for their innovative steps toward a transformed and revitalized poetic. During his more than thirty years as a publisher, from 1887 to 1921, he brought out books and periodicals central to the Decadent and Symbolist movements of the nineties; published the work of authors in the forefront of the Celtic movement; and issued numerous books by Ezra Pound expressive of those ideas so seminal to poetry in the teens, ideas often opposed by the so-called Georgian poets whom Mathews also published. A list of some of his most significant publications reads like a roll call of books crucial to the rise of modern literature: Oscar Wilde's *Salome*, Arthur Symons' *Silhouettes*, W. B. Yeats's *Wind Among the Reeds*, Kenneth Grahame's *Pagan Papers*, John Masefield's *Ballads*, Ezra Pound's *Lustra*, and Richard Aldington's *Images of Desire*. Moreover, he published

3

such significant first books as Lionel Johnson's *Poems*, J. M. Synge's *Shadow of the Glen and Riders to the Sea*, Vincent O'Sullivan's *Poems*, James Joyce's *Chamber Music*, Lord Dunsany's *Gods of Pagāna*, Ronald Firbank's *Odette d'Antrevernes*, W. W. Gibson's *Urlyn the Harper*, Bliss Carman's *Low Tide on Grand Pré*, F. S. Flint's *In the Net of the Stars*, and Eleanor Farjeon's *Pan-Worship*, as well as A.E.W. Mason's first novel, *A Romance of Wastdale*, and Nancy Cunard's first book of poems, *Outlaws*. And although Mathews' claim to fame rests primarily on his role in the rise of modern literature, he also deserves attention for the tasteful design and format of his books which—especially during the nineties—were important to the evolution of the modern book, and for the intelligent use he made of both innovative and original book designers and illustrators such as Charles Ricketts, Walter Crane, H. P. Horne, Selwyn Image, Aubrey Beardsley, S. H. Sime, Pamela Colman Smith, James Guthrie, and Jack B. Yeats.

Charles Elkin Mathews was born 31 August 1851 in Gravesend, downstream from London on the Thames, where his family for generations had been engaged in shipbuilding, shipping, and other related enterprises, one of his ancestors (a friend and correspondent of Samuel Pepys) having once held the important position of Clerk of the Check. Like his second cousin, the poet Edwin Arnold, the future publisher received his early schooling at Gravesend before his father, Thomas George (listed on Mathews' marriage certificate as a timber and slate merchant), tiring of commercial life, moved with his wife, Frances Elkin, and his family of three sons and six daughters to the village of Codford St. Mary in the Vale of Wylye on the edge of Salisbury Plain in Wiltshire. Here, in a house known as "The Poplars," the reserved, bookish father led a quiet life, his income supplemented from time to time by his well-to-do father-in-law. In this pleasant rural seat, Elkin, like all his siblings, was allowed to follow his own inclinations, which were antiquarian and literary. In reply to a reporter's question in 1906 as to how he came to select his profession, Mathews replied: "I have been a collector of old poets and *belles lettres* all my life and, therefore, when the time came for me to choose a vocation, it seemed natural that I should turn my hobby to a practical use."[1]

Having learned accounting from his older brother, Thomas George, Mathews followed him to London, where in his mid-twenties he entered the workaday world in the employ of Mr. Charles John Stewart of King William Street, the Strand, who was known as "the last of the learned old booksellers." Following his apprenticeship, Mathews managed Peach's well-known library at Bath for several years before returning to London, where he found employment in the firm of the Messrs. Sotheran in Piccadilly. Ambitious to go into business for himself, Mathews, in 1884, with the £125 he had acquired from an uncle, chose to open an antiquarian and general bookshop at 16 Cathedral Close in the old west-country town of Exeter, which, as he later stated, "seemed to lend itself to the nature of the work upon which I had decided to embark."[2] "An admitted expert by this time of ancient tomes of many periods," the young bookseller, according to one account, "began not only to deal but to publish," intent on realizing some day his long-cherished ambition to become the Edward Moxon of his time.[3] As he later observed, "I always felt very strongly that if one was unable to achieve distinction in letters oneself, the next best thing was to be the means of giving to the world the work of others more generously endowed."[4] To this end, in 1887 Mathews joined several other local booksellers in publishing a little volume entitled *We Donkeys on the Coast of Devon*, another in a series of books relating the spring rambles of their rather formidable author, Miss Maria Susannah Gibbons, who traveled along the byways of rural Devon via donkey tandem. Using the imprint of C. Elkin Mathews, Mathews was also in the process of publishing several other books of local interest when in the summer of 1887 he vacated his premises in Exeter and established himself in business in London.[5]

Mathews' decision to leave Exeter was based in part on his realization that "a native was already in possession of the field, and his monopoly of the good book-buyers was not to be assailed,"[6] and in part on his decision to form a partnership with a young man by the name of John Lane whom he had met through his brother Thomas George, Lane's superior at the Railway Clearing House in London. Lane, himself an avid book collector who aspired to the role of bookseller and publisher, had seen in Mathews a means of attaining that end and sought to persuade his friend that setting up shop in London with himself as silent partner would be advantageous. Mathews with some reluctance at length agreed and, through Lane's agency, leased premises at 6b Vigo Street (between Regent Street and

Mathews' shopfront at 6b Vigo Street as it appeared in an ink drawing, c. 1891

the Burlington Arcade). Here, in what one of its habitués later referred to as "a funny little shop, almost the smallest in London, in
which there was hardly room to turn round, the walls crowded with
shelves and piled up with books from floor to ceiling," Mathews
opened for business on 10 October 1887.[7]

Having associated his business in Exeter with the name of its native
son, Sir Thomas Bodley, the founder of the famed library at Oxford,
Mathews brought the association along with him when he came up to
London, anxious no doubt to link his new shop in Vigo Street with
the name of the celebrated book fancier. Since Robert Dunthorne, the
shop's previous occupant, had decorated his "Cabinet of Fine Arts"
with a sign designating it "The Rembrandt Head," Mathews and Lane
decided to replace it with one bearing the physiognomy of Sir

Thomas Bodley, thereby christening their new shop "The Bodley Head."

Although of necessity he continued to be primarily an antiquarian and general bookseller, Mathews, having had a taste of publishing at Exeter, came to London determined to enlarge these activities. With Lane's support, he looked for some niche in publishing in which he might modestly invest. Unfortunately, poetry (to which he was predisposed) was in a state of decline, the field, after the heyday of the great Victorians, largely left to the so-called minor poets and poetasters. The two young entrepreneurs recognized, nevertheless, the increasing demand for and rising value of the privately printed, limited edition book—for example, the delightfully quaint little volumes of verse which Dr. C.H.O. Daniel gave his family and friends and distributed to a few subscribers at Oxford[8]—and shrewdly saw the commercial possibilities inherent in such books. Aware that the appeal of the limited edition book lay beyond mere quality of content, that its charm resided in its rarity, its fine paper and typography, and its tasteful format (all of which set it apart from the cheap, mass-produced book characteristic of Victorian publishing), Mathews and Lane needed nothing more than the catalytic effect of the personable, dashing, and ebullient young Richard Le Gallienne to launch what came to be known as the Bodley Head book.

Le Gallienne, who had arrived in London from Liverpool shortly after Mathews had returned to London, quickly insinuated himself into a number of the literary coteries, especially those composed of young poets and artists eager to generate new literary and artistic currents. Soon on friendly terms with such notables as Oscar Wilde and W. B. Yeats, Le Gallienne met Lane, who in turn introduced him to Mathews. Years later Mathews recalled the early impact of the young poet: "I think I met Mr. Richard Le Gallienne first in 1888. 'Narcissus' as he was soon to be called had just quitted the banks of the Mersey for those of the Thames. He had already privately printed in Liverpool some 'vain amatorious verses.' Neither Byron nor Shelley looked the poet more than he did, and with his poetical sentiment for beautiful things in life and art he quickly caught the public fancy."[9] Sharing the partners' love of old tomes and their delight in the limited-edition book—later expressed in his celebrated essay, "Limited Editions, a Prose Fancy"—Le Gallienne himself (as Mathews suggests) had already privately printed a collection of verses entitled *My Ladies' Sonnets* in a limited edition which included fifty large-paper copies numbered and signed by the author. With Le Gallienne's book before him and his first-hand expertise in producing such books at his service, Mathews published the first Bodley Head book in March 1889, not surprisingly Le Gallienne's second book, *Volumes in Folio*. Mathews advertised the book in the *Athenaeum* and elsewhere as a new volume of "Verse de Libricité," earning himself a reprimand from his old friend Dr. Alexander Grosart, who, as the publisher later recalled, "had misread libricité for lubricity."[10] Reflecting in both its title and contents its author's and its publisher's love for old and rare books, *Volumes in Folio*—in almost every way a

An early publisher's device for the Bodley Head, c. 1890

8

companion volume to *My Ladies' Sonnets*—with its blue-gray "antique boards," its imitation vellum spine with raised bands, its Van Gelder handmade paper, and its tastefully designed title page lettered in red and black, was worthy of being the first of those books which over the next several years were to bring fame to the quaint little shop in Vigo Street and for it the title of Parnassus. As *Volumes in Folio* was followed by such beautiful books as Ernest Radford's *Chambers Twain* (1890), Walter Crane's *Renascence* (1891), Arthur Symons' *Silhouettes* (1892), John Gray's *Silverpoints* (1893), John Addington Symonds' *In the Key of Blue* (1893), Francis Thompson's *Poems* (1893), and Wilde's *Salome* and *The Sphinx* (1894), Mathews and Lane created a vogue for poetry daintily packaged which brought about what the periodical press proclaimed a "golden age" and dubbed "the remarkable poetical renascence of the early nineties."

The question, of course, is, how did Mathews and Lane make the combination of minor poet and handsome book pay? They did so by effective production practices which cut the cost to a minimum. For example, Mathews and Lane employed larger-than-usual type sizes (above ten-point) and more leading than normal between lines, creating an effect Ada Leverson once jokingly described as the tiniest rivulet of text meandering through the very largest meadow of margin. This habitual use of a relatively little text per book, of course, substantially reduced the cost of typesetting. Moreover, the partners printed their editions on remainders of fine paper which they bought at far below the normal price. In addition, they negotiated agreements which paid their authors at best a modest royalty only after production costs had been paid, and among other things, limited the editions to the number of copies the poetry market would bear— usually between 300 and 600 copies.[11] Through these means, Mathews and Lane were able to sell the Bodley Head book at something less than the five shillings normally charged at the time for a book of poetry and still make a good profit. Consequently, by January 1892 Lane had taken rooms in fashionable Albany and, having relinquished his job at the Railway Clearing House, had ceased to be a silent partner and had come into the business full time. And by 1893, Mathews, who had lived with his brother's family at Woodburn House, 154 Greenlanes, Stoke Newington, London, was able to establish a residence of his own at 1 Blenheim Road, Bedford Park, where he lived for the next few years with his five maiden sisters, next door to the painter John Butler Yeats and his family, which included his young but increasingly prominent son, the poet William Butler Yeats, and his younger son, the artist Jack.

Dating from the mid-seventies, Bedford Park was, as Nikolaus Pevsner has observed, "the earliest of the planned garden suburbs" and was, at that time, as Yeats later described it, "a new enthusiasm: the pre-Raphaelite movement at last affecting life."[12] Situated along curved streets shaded by carefully preserved old trees, the detached, semidetached, and terrace houses of Bedford Park were typified by such picturesque architectural features as "Dutch gables or tile-hung gables, much use of decorative tiles, white window casements, white little oriels, cosy porches, etc."[13]—all bespeaking the suburb's origin in the Aesthetic movement. Although its newness had worn off by the nineties, the community, as one of its historians has said, was still inhabited by "artists, poets, academics, journalists, actors, and cultivated members of the professional classes."[14] Among the prominent residents Mathews came to know especially well were, of course, the senior Yeats, through whom he met Frederick York Powell, the Icelandic scholar and Oxford professor whom Mathews later singled out for a special tribute: "It was a fortunate thing for me that I went to live in Bedford Park about 1893. There mainly through the Yeats family I got to know the late Professor York Powell . . . and to him I owed much literary help and advice."[15] It was to Powell, also, that Mathews owed his well-known rebus (later used as the publisher's device for his Vigo Cabinet series), designed one evening at 1 Blenheim Road

Publisher's device designed as a rebus by F. York Powell and John Butler Yeats and often used by Mathews on his title pages

with the assistance of John Butler Yeats.[16] One other neighbor appears to have been especially close—Dr. John Todhunter, whom Mathews had known earlier as a member of the Rhymers' Club and whose *A Sicilian Idyll* he had published in 1890. Mathews later published Todhunter's volume of poems, *Sounds and Sweet Airs* (1905), and the posthumous *Essays* (1920). Despite a rather unpleasantly argumentative wife, Todhunter was a hospitable man whose Bedford Park home was often the scene of notable gatherings, some of which were recorded in memoirs and other autobiographical records such as the diary of "Michael Field." This diary affords us a glimpse of the Mathewses as well as of another well-known Bedford Park personality, the anarchist Sergius Stepniak, the author of *Underground Russia*: ". . . to spend the evening with Dr. Todhunter. 'Toddy' is glad to see us . . . We meet Stepniak and his wife . . . Elkin is there, with a procession of virgin sisters with eyes that shine like tin plates."[17]

On at least one occasion, Mathews and his sisters themselves contributed notably to the busy social whirl of Bedford Park, which, we are told, included "costume conversazione, or *tableaux vivantes* or fancy dress balls."[18] Occasioned by the tercentenary of Izaak Walton's birth, the celebration was distinguished by a delightful card of invitation designed, drawn, and hand-lettered by Jack Yeats, which read:

SAINT IZAAK'S DAY.

(August 9, 1593 – August 9, 1893)

Mr & Misses Elkin Mathews

at Home

Wednesday: August 9th 8. to 12.30.

1. Blenheim Road

Bedford Park. W.

R . S . V . P .[19]

A mark of Mathews' esteem for his "patron saint," the famous author of *The Compleat Angler*, the affair was chronicled in the *Publishers Circular* and, of course, in the *Fisherman's Gazette*, which proclaimed the "at home" "a brilliant success."[20]

At the time of the "at home," Mathews was, according to J. Lewis May (who served his apprenticeship under Mathews and Lane), "a

11

neat, dapper, little man, rather fussy and old-maidish in his ways." In his early forties, the man May describes "was clean-shaven, with a bald globular head much too large for his body."[21] Though verging on caricature, May's impression of Mathews as a Humpty-Dumptyish sort of figure with a small torso and large head is borne out by a later description by the poet Henry Newbolt, who likened his publisher to "a big-headed big-eyed timorous boy,"[22] which exactly describes the Mathews John Butler Yeats portrays in his fine pencil drawing of December 1893. The high, full forehead and rather prominent eyes of the balding Mathews which created the characteristic impression are even more apparent in the distinctly less idealized, more realistic crayon drawing by Yeats's son Jack; dating from July 1894, it portrays a morose young man, the Mathews increasingly annoyed by Lane at work and vexed by domestic infelicities at home.[23]

Amused by his neighbor's domestic situation, John Butler Yeats (who had plenty of domestic troubles of his own) often indulged in a bit of fun at Mathews' expense in letters to his daughter, Lily.[24] These letters, nevertheless, provide significant glimpses of the Mathews of the Bedford Park years, glimpses which reveal a somewhat parsimonious, uncharacteristically ill-tempered man presiding over a household of rather highly strung, helpless women who in their dress and behavior approximated that view of the aesthetic female given consummate expression in Gilbert and Sullivan's *Patience* and George du Maurier's cartoons in *Punch*.[25] For instance, in a letter to Lily written on a Sunday in January 1896, Yeats related an event incidental to a meeting at his home of the Calumet Conversation Club, to which he, Mathews, and about a dozen other Bedford Park residents belonged. It seems that when Yeats's daughter Lolly and his wife went next door to spend the evening with the Mathews sisters, "the noble Elkin," preparing to leave to attend the meeting, "*first of all lowered the gas*," the sisters not daring to "put it up when he had departed. After a time," commented Yeats, "when he gets too old to go racketing about and must sit by the chimney corner what a time they will have."[26]

Several weeks later when the Calumet gathered at 1 Blenheim Road, Yeats again found material to amuse Lily. Aware while he wrote that Mathews was entertaining his intended, the artist Edith

Elkin Mathews, December 1893. Pencil drawing by John Butler Yeats, signed and dated. Collection of Michael B. Yeats.

Elkin Mathews, 2 July 1894. Chalk drawing by Jack B. Yeats. Elkin Mathews Archive, Reading University.

Calvert, Yeats gleefully anticipated Mathews' discomfiture:

> At this present moment in blissful forgetfulness of everything Elkin is gazing on his fiancée. Were he to look at his card, he would be very much astonished. He will be more astonished when half an hour hence 13 or 14 pipes (as you used to call them) all very thirsty walk in and ask strong drink. Lolly was in and is quite sure none of them know it is his Calumet but that it is to be all young lady.[27]

Fortunately, Mathews was not so absent-minded as the elder Yeats had anticipated, for in his next letter to Lily he wrote:

> I am glad you liked the story of the Calumets. However little Elkin was much wiser than we supposed. He was quite ready (or nearly so) to receive our distinguished company. He was not *quite* ready—since the first two Calumets on arriving found a guest having his supper. It was Fairfax Muckley (a decorative artist) whom Elkin had asked, as Fairfax supposed, to supper. Fairfax being a very sensible man insisted on his supper, and, as the girls told me, absolutely declined to *hurry* it.

Continuing with his account of the evening, Yeats went on to complain that despite a good deal of talk,

> our chairman [Mathews] being a muff, it was all between individuals till at last I whispered my disgust into the ears of Fox Bourne and Benson— and Benson in his sweetest tones said, "Mr. Chairman, please Mr. Chairman," and then we all together began shouting "Mr. Chairman." It took some time I can tell you before we roused Elkin to a consciousness of his dignity and his duties. However, I was sleepy, and besides I was much depressed and disappointed at Elkin not being caught napping.[28]

If Mathews' situation at home was unsatisfactory, his position at the Bodley Head was even less satisfactory. Since Lane had come into the business full-time, the partners found themselves working increasingly at cross-purposes, with Lane prone to involve himself and the firm with authors and artists about whom Mathews had grave objections on moral grounds. For instance, Mathews had become more and more uneasy about Wilde's association with the Bodley Head. Not only had the author of *Salome* and *The Sphinx* seduced Edward Shelley, a clerk whom Lane had planted in the firm in 1890 to spy on Mathews, but he had arranged with Lane during the summer of 1893 for the Bodley Head to publish his *Portrait of Mr.*

15

W.H., a story about Uranian love.[29] Inevitably the partnership became untenable, and Mathews viewed his deliberate exclusion from the dinner in April 1894 in celebration of the publication of the first number of the *Yellow Book*—the sensational new Bodley Head quarterly edited by Henry Harland and Aubrey Beardsley—as the final in a series of provocations and affronts engineered by Lane. As he explained it in a letter written some months later,

> The Editors of the *Yellow Book* gave a dinner to the contributors & Lane alone represented the firm. I only heard about this dinner by accident— Lane never volunteered any information about it until I taxed him. I learned afterwards that many *asked* where *I* was—and that when Lane was asked to speak for the publishers—he with the boldest effrontery said that he deeply regretted the unavoidable absence of his partner— and that he was not present to join in the general enthusiasm and so on.
>
> As a matter of fact I could have attended the dinner with the greatest ease in the world; I had *absolute* leisure that evening, and there was not the slightest colour for him to make such a statement. He had evidently represented to the Editors that he alone was the partner interested in the working of the *Yellow Book,* and they did not take the trouble to act otherwise.[30]

After a struggle between Mathews and Lane over the firm's authors, "Parnassus," as the *Athenaeum* observed, was divided into two peaks, with the partnership dissolved on the last day of September 1894.[31] Mathews remained in the premises at 6b Vigo Street, while Lane, taking the Bodley Head sign with him, moved to new quarters opposite in Albany. Observing some months later that "the *Bodley Head* is fast becoming identified with fiction of a very modern character— made up emotion and no morals," Mathews reconciled himself to its loss and determined to conduct his own business along the lines of the early Bodley Head by continuing to publish belles lettres, by which he meant "essays, poetry, drama, and that higher fiction in which the educated classes may be supposed to take an interest."[32]

Continuing to support the so-called Decadents, Mathews brought out Lionel Johnson's *Poems* in 1895 and Ernest Dowson's book of short fiction, *Dilemmas,* in the same year. Moreover, he published numerous volumes of poetry over the next several years which in their format, binding design, illustrations, and letterpress carried on the early Bodley Head tradition of beautiful books—for example,

Publisher's device designed by Louis Fairfax-Muckley appearing on the title page of many of Mathews' lists of "Books and Belles Lettres"

Selwyn Image's *Poems and Carols* (1894), designed with a title page by H. P. Horne; R. D. Blackmore's *Fringilla* (1895), with binding design and illustrations by L. Fairfax Muckley; May Probyn's *Pansies* (1895), with cover design and title page by Minnie Mathews (the publisher's sister); W. B. Yeats's *Wind among the Reeds* (1899), with binding design by Althea Gyles; and Gordon Bottomley's *The Gate of Smaragdus* (1904), designed in the mode of Charles Ricketts by the author with illustrations by Clinton Balmer.

Meanwhile, Mathews in 1894 had fallen in love with a woman thirteen years his junior, Edith Laura Calvert, whose father, Charles Anthony Calvert, had once held the prestigious post of secretary to the Colonial Bank (now Barclay's) and whose ancestry was linked with the famous family of Calverts who founded Maryland.[33] Having rid himself of Lane, the publisher (now seriously contemplating marriage) sought to rid himself of his sisters, and set about relocating them. The sisters, reluctant to leave an environment so perfectly suited to their aesthetic sensibilities, decided on a house in Flanders Road on the southern edge of Bedford Park. But as Lolly Yeats wrote her sister, Lily, Mathews objected strenuously, wanting them farther

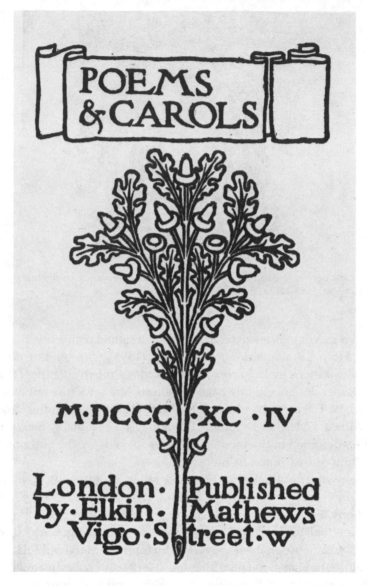

Title page of Selwyn Image's *Poems & Carols* (1894), one of Herbert P. Horne's celebrated title designs

off.[34] His manueverings were at length successful, and Mathews married Edith Calvert on 16 July 1896 in the parish church of St. George's, Tufnell Park, London. Launched in a marriage which proved both happy and enduring, Mathews—whom Lily Yeats once describes as a "cross little man"—regained his characteristically kind and genial

Cover of R. D. Blackmore's *Fringilla* (1895), designed by Louis Fairfax-Muckley

Title page of May Probyn's *Pansies* (1895), designed by Mathews' sister Minnie Mathews

manner, proving to be an ideal companion to his wife and a pleasant-natured, sincere, and loyal friend to the many authors and artists whom he published.[35]

Mathews' marriage and the subsequent birth of a daughter, Nest, in July 1897 led to his making something of a specialty out of children's books, a very popular genre at the turn of the century. Although he had brought out Mrs. Arthur Gaskin's *ABC. An Alphabet* in 1895 and her illustrated edition of Isaac Watts's *Divine and Moral Songs* in 1896 (which eventually sold over 5,000 copies), over the next decade or so, he published a distinguished series of children's books, many of which were illustrated by his wife, who had been trained at the Royal Academy schools. Working closely with her friend, Ada Stow, who wrote the text, Edith Calvert illustrated the very popular *Baby Lays* in 1897 and *More Baby Lays* the following year. In addition to creating delightful Christmas cards in the Kate Greenaway style, Edith also provided the illustrations for Dorothea Goré Browne's *Sweetbriar: A Pastoral with Songs* (1905), Alexandra Von Herder's *The Little Mermaid: A Play in Three Acts* (1905), Agnes Begbie's *Christmas Songs and Carols* (1908), and Margaret Arndt's *Meadows of Play: Verses for Children* (1909). Among Mathews' most notable books for children were those written and illustrated by Jack B. Yeats: his plays for the miniature stage, *James Flaunty; or, the Terror of the Western Seas* (1901), *The Treasure of the Garden* (1902), and *The Scourge of the Gulph* (1903), and his stories, *The Bosun and the Bob-Tailed Comet* (1904) and *A Little Fleet* (1909). Although Mathews' books for children were ordinarily advertised along with his other publications in his catalogues and announcements, on occasion he issued attractive lists adorned with illustrations and headed "Little Books for Little Folks Published for Elkin Mathews at His Shop over against the Albany in Vigo Street, London West."

Having moved from 1 Blenheim Road to the nearby 13 Addison Road in 1898, Mathews, seeking to provide a quieter, less socially demanding environment for Edith, who was in frail health, moved with his family in 1903 to a house called "Russettings," Shire Lane, in the Hertfordshire village of Chorleywood. This was to be the publisher's home until his death in 1921. Here he often entertained close relatives, friends, and, on occasion, authors—the young Ezra Pound among them. According to Cuthbert Mathews, the publisher's

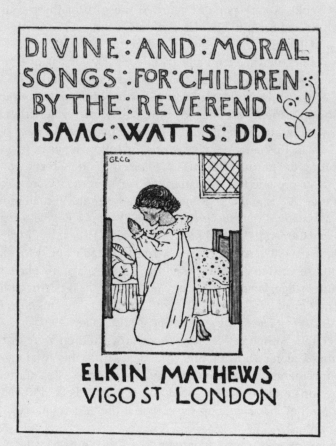

Front cover of the prospectus for Watts's *Divine and Moral Songs* (1896)

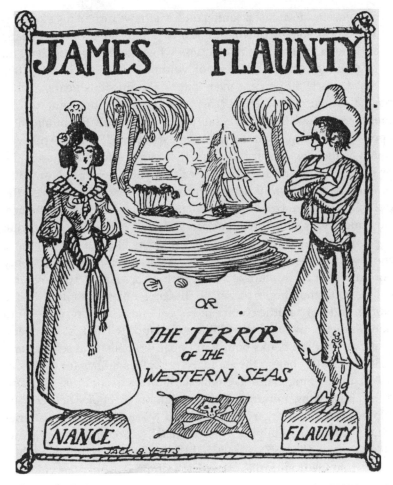

Title page by Jack B. Yeats for *James Flaunty,* one of his "Plays in the Old Manner"

nephew and godson, Mathews "was a genial and jovial host given to relating incidents and contacts made during his daily activities and closing with a characteristic chuckle."[36] When not entertaining guests, he loved to pore over the many old volumes and other objets d'art in what was known as the "book-room," which contained Mathews' collection of "Waltoniana" and his most valued and best-loved antique, the ornately carved oak hanging cupboard which once had belonged to Izaac Walton.[37]

23

His domestic life at last a settled one, Mathews turned his attention to the major problem confronting him as a publisher: finding means to continue to publish poetry at a time when there was little demand for it. Although the publication of volumes of poetry had in 1895 increased nearly 50 percent over that of the previous years, a phenomenal rise attributed by at least one journal "to the fame of fortunes made in Vigo Street," the sale and consequently the publication of poetry had declined during the last years of the decade.[38] And even though as the new century dawned there were efforts to change the low estimate of poetry held by the reading public—Henry Newbolt's founding of the *Monthly Review*, for example—nothing revived the kind of interest in verse typical of the early and middle nineties. Consequently, as Newbolt later observed, "In 1900 it was vain to look for poetry in the 'serious' reviews. . . . Papers like the *Spectator* and *Saturday Review* were genuinely interested in verse, but could only afford room for a few stanzas at a time. In short, a poet, whatever his quality, could not hope to gain a hearing unless he published a volume, and he had little chance of his volume being accepted—until Elkin Mathews invented the Shilling Garland."[39] The first of several significant series of books bound in paper wrappers and selling for a single shilling (far below the standard rate of 5 shillings for a book of poetry), the Shilling Garland enabled Mathews to continue his tradition of publishing minor poets. In addition to books of verse by Laurence Binyon, Margaret Woods, and Mary Coleridge, the series included Stephen Phillips' *Christ in Hades* (1896) and Henry Newbolt's *Admirals All* (1897), attractive little books which propelled their authors into the front ranks of poetry. Comprising only ten volumes, the Shilling Garland series was followed by a far more ambitious one in 1900 dubbed the Vigo Cabinet series, which over the first two decades of the new century ran to nearly a hundred and fifty volumes, a veritable panoply of belles lettres reflecting many of the movements of poetry and including works by W. B. Yeats, J. M. Synge, James Elroy Flecker, Arthur Symons, Harold Monro, John Masefield, and Richard Aldington. Professing himself to be "a great believer in the series," and having asserted on one occasion that "there is certainly no better medium for pushing a book by a new writer,"[40] Mathews during the course of his career introduced several

more series of books—the Satchel, the Savile, and the Burlington—
which ran concurrently with the long-term Vigo Cabinet series.

Through these series and other more conventional means, Mathews was able to provide young poets with a forum from which they
could be heard. As a result, the little shop in Vigo Street continued to
be what it had been in the early nineties, "a west-end Mecca of poets,
young and old."[41] As such, it was sought out by many of those men
and women who since have become celebrities of early-twentieth-
century literature—among them Ezra Pound, F. S. Flint, Maurice
Hewlett, W. H. Davies, Marianne Moore, Harriet Monroe (who was
introduced to Mathews by May Sinclair), Ford Madox Hueffer, T.
Sturge Moore, as well as the patron of Irish letters, the New York
lawyer, John Quinn.

Unfortunately, at the close of 1912 Mathews was forced to vacate
his "well-known haunt for lovers of *belle-lettres*" as a result of a desire
on the part of his landlord, the Royal Geographic Society, to seek
more spacious quarters. Consequently, the society sold its premises,
which contained the Vigo Street shop, to new owners, who then set
about rebuilding the entire block. Mathews found a new home for his
business at 4a Cork Street, several blocks away, near Bond Street.
Although the new premises were "larger and more convenient," as
one of the announcements read, visitors to the Cork Street shop
found Mathews in much the same surroundings as those in Vigo
Street. When Sylvia Beach was collecting books prior to opening
Shakespeare and Company in Paris, she passed through London and,
as she later recalled,

> On the way to the boat train. I stopped in Cork Street at the little
> bookshop of the publisher and bookseller Elkin Mathews to order my
> Yeats, Joyce, and Pound. He was sitting in a sort of gallery, with books
> surging around and creeping up almost to his feet. We had a pleasant
> talk, and he was quite friendly. I mentioned seeing some drawings by
> William Blake—if only I could have something of Blake's in my shop!
> Thereupon he produced two beautiful original drawings, which he sold
> to me for a sum that, according to Blake experts who saw them later, was
> absurdly small.[42]

Although J. Lewis May pitied Mathews—"It must have been a
wrench leaving that place in Vigo Street"—the publisher appears to

Mathews' shopfront at 4a Cork Street

have been none the worse for the move, having, as he sought to assure his customers, "greater convenience for your inspection of my stock of publications, and my Collections of Old Books, Prints and Autographs."[43] That the shop in Cork Street continued to attract young poets seeking a publisher is borne out by Herbert Read, who in his autobiography wrote about his introduction to Mathews:

When, in January, 1915, I joined the Army, I was posted to a battalion stationed in Dorset. I had to travel via London and arrived in that city for the first time in my life. I carried, besides my military baggage, a large bundle of poems, and at King's Cross I told the taxi-driver to go to Waterloo via Cork Street. All I knew about Mr. Mathews was that he had been publishing the kind of poetry I was interested in: I had no introduction to him nor any means of obtaining one. However, he received me very kindly in the back of his shop and undertook to consider the publication of my poems if I would pay a reader's fee, which I willingly did.[44]

Read's *Songs of Chaos* was but one of many books Mathews published during the course of World War I despite the fact that he, like other publishers, faced many difficulties: shortages of labor among printers and binders, shortages of paper, and increased production costs. As Mathews complained to Lord Dunsany in a letter of 1916, since the war began, "composition, printing, paper, binding have gone up tremendously and I shall probably have to pay double for the production of the plates [what I paid] before the war."[45] Shipping costs, especially that of freight overseas, also greatly increased, as did the risk, complicating cooperative publishing efforts between English and American publishers. For example, in 1916 Laurence Binyon attempted to work out an agreement between his American publisher, Houghton Mifflin, and Mathews for the publication of his book *The Cause*. In a letter to Ferris Greenslet of Houghton Mifflin, Binyon wrote that Mathews favored publishing the book in England rather than buying sheets of the American edition because, as Binyon observed, he is "depressed by the extortionate cost of freight." Binyon, however, felt differently. Citing the fact that "paper and printing and binding are in such a bad way here from shortage of labour as well as high prices," he was of the opinion that it would be better for Greenslet to print the volume in an America still untouched by the war.[46]

Confronted with such problems, Mathews was forced to raise the price of his books as well as to sacrifice the quality of materials in them. Furthermore, his problems were augmented from an unexpected source: on the evening of Tuesday, 29 June 1915, a devastating fire broke out in the bindery of Matthew Bell and Company in Cursitor Street, Chancery Lane, where the publisher stored his unbound stock. Through the agency of fire, smoke, and water, many of Mathews' publications, including the unbound sheets of Pound's translation of the *Sonnets and Ballate of Guido Cavalcanti*, of which Mathews had sold bound copies since 1913, were destroyed.[47] That the fire represented a considerable loss to Mathews can be gathered from a letter to Henry Newbolt in which the publisher, having apprised the author of the loss of "nearly half the stock" of *Goodchild's Garland*, went on to observe: "Unfortunately many other of my publications perished at the same time."[48] Nevertheless, he was able to do his part in the war effort not only by continuing to cope with the demands the war made on him, but by publishing over forty volumes of war poetry, a popular genre, of course, at the time.[49] Some of the more notable books included *Invocation: War Poems and Others* (1915), the first of several volumes by Robert Nichols, who (though forgotten today) became the most popular poet during the later years of the war,[50] and the first of Laurence Binyon's volumes of war poems, *The Winnowing-Fan: Poems of the Great War* (1914). *The Winnowing-Fan* contained "For the Fallen," the "one poem by a civilian," according to Bernard Bergonzi, "that has had more than a passing fame,"[51] and includes the familiar lines which have been engraved on war memorials throughout the British Empire:

> They shall grow not old, as we that are left grow old:
> Age shall not weary them, nor the years condemn.
> At the going down of the sun and in the morning
> We will remember them.

Among Mathews' most popular volumes of war poetry was one of curious note, *A Prisoner of Pentonville* (1919), written by a conscientious objector under the pseudonym "Red Band," whose verses were compared favorably by critics with Wilde's "Ballad of Reading Gaol." Also there were several by W. W. Gibson: *Thoroughfares* (1914), *Battle* (1915), and *Friends* (1916); Alexander Robertson's *Comrades* (1916); and the prolific Cicely Fox Smith's four books celebrating the war at sea, *The Naval Crown: Ballads and Songs of the War* (1915), *Fighting Men* (1916), *Small Craft* (1917), and *Songs and Chanties, 1914–1916* (1919).

Although the war intervened, Mathews' major achievement during the Cork Street years was his continued fruitful relationship with Ezra Pound, who, having tried his luck with the ill-fated Swift and Company and the American firm of Small, Maynard, returned to Mathews for the reissue of *Personae and Exultations* and *Canzoni and Ripostes*, Ezra Pound's poems, volumes 1 and 2, in May 1913. *Cathay* then followed in 1915 and, in 1916, *Lustra* (after what Pound later referred to as the "long and comic" history of the controversy over its publication), in the famous unabridged edition of 200 copies in September and the regular, "emasculated" edition in October.

Looking back over Mathews' publishing career of some thirty-four-odd years, one must concede that his love of poetry, his commitment to belles lettres, and his attachment to the minor poet earned him many successes and, indisputably, the place of honor Robert Scholes assigns him among that handful of "small publishers who were so influential in British literary developments around the turn of the century," those courageous "men who had a direct hand in the shaping of new literature."[52] Nevertheless, Mathews' rejection of both Joyce's *Dubliners* (in 1907 and again in 1913) and T. S. Eliot's early poems (in 1917) suggests that he ultimately was unable to embrace the modernist idiom he had helped to shape. His publication of Pounds's *Lustra* in 1916 marked a limit beyond which he—then in his

Device by Arthur J. Gaskin for front cover of Mathews' "Catalogue of Publications," c. 1910

mid-sixties—was unprepared to go. And although he brought out his last book of Pound's poetry, *Umbra*, in 1920, it was nothing more than a collection of Pound's early poems, a memorial, so to speak, to the Pound Mathews genuinely liked and approved. By the last year of his life, an observer of the publishing scene commenting on Mathews' latest list of new books (which included a volume of Lionel Johnson's reviews and critical papers, Stanley Casson's *Rupert Brooke and Skyros*, and several books of verse by now long-forgotten poets), remarked: "Mr. Elkin Mathews goes his quiet, unperturbed and unpretentious way through the land of *belles lettres* as if never a Futurist had threatened to ravage the fair country with horrid war."[53] The victim of a brief bout with pneumonia, Mathews died on 10 November 1921 at his home in Chorleywood.[54] According to one summing-up of his life and career, Mathews

> was a gracious personality with a touch of old-world courtesy about him. Without and within, his premises in Cork Street were redolent of a more leisurely, a more bookish age than ours. To stand in his book-lined shop and look along the dark passages into his back room and see him seated at his high desk, silhouetted against the window, was to be transported into the eighteenth century and catch something of the sensation Goldsmith and Shenstone must have had when they called on their booksellers. It was a pleasant oasis in a too-restless modern world and he harmonized pleasantly with his surroundings.[55]

Among the encomia in letters of condolence received by his widow, those Mathews would have appreciated most were Alfred Perceval Graves's reference to his "manly sympathy with young authors" and Pound's assertion that Mathews "had been much more of a friend than a publisher."[56] Although Mathews never achieved the fame and the wealth of some other publishers of his day, he did, nevertheless, merit the fine tribute the poet Edward Thomas once paid him, describing him as "not only poor but honest—a wonderful combination of virtues especially in a publisher."[57]

CHAPTER TWO

Publishing Poetry Cheaply:
Elkin Mathews' Serial Publications

THE SHILLING GARLAND SERIES

ONE OF THE means Elkin Mathews employed to publish belles lettres during those lean years which stretched from the later nineties through World War I was the so-called "series," a sequential publication of books sharing not only the same design and format but also a loosely similar focus. Mathews, who was of the opinion that "there is certainly no better medium for pushing a book by a new writer," consequently proved through the years to be (as he once confessed to a reporter) "a great believer in the series," producing no less than five: the Shilling Garland, the Vigo Cabinet, the Satchel, the Savile, and the Burlington series. Of these the two most notable were the Shilling Garland and the Vigo Cabinet series, each in its own way a significant venture in publishing.[1]

Although Mathews had undertaken the publication of H. P. Horne's Diversi Colores series (so named for Horne's own beautifully designed little book of verse, *Diversi Colores*, published in 1891) and had issued Selwyn Image's *Poems and Carols* as the second volume of the series in late 1894, Horne's departure for Italy in 1895 effectively brought that series to a close. Consequently, it was not until Mathews decided to bring out the Shilling Garland series in 1895 that his career as a publisher of a series actually began. Composed of ten slender booklets of verse written for the most part by young, relatively un-

31

known poets, and published over a period of some three years between December 1895 and December 1898, the Shilling Garland
series developed out of an idea which originated with Laurence
Binyon, a young poet who earned his living as an assistant in the
Prints and Drawings department of the British Museum. Since taking
his B.A. at Oxford in 1890, Binyon had published poems in the
beautifully designed and produced journal of the Century Guild, the
Hobby Horse, which in the early nineties had been issued from the
Bodley Head. Probably as a result of this connection, Mathews and
Lane had published Binyon's first book of verse, *Lyric Poems*, in 1894.

Despite his initial successes, Binyon, like many young poets, was
frustrated by the current publishing practice which, based on the
"dogma," as Binyon later wrote, "that those who bought poetry at all
would just as soon give 5/– as any smaller sum," virtually shut out the
new poet from a publishing opportunity and the young poetry reader
(who, Binyon argued, was in the majority) from the pleasure of pur-
chasing a book of verse. Consequently, Binyon developed the idea of
commencing a series of shilling volumes of new poetry which would,
in effect, circumvent the current practice. To this end, Binyon approached Mathews in 1895 and having conjured up all his powers of
persuasion, "with the utmost difficulty" prevailed on him "to start a
series of shilling books of new verse."[2] Mathews' hesitation to launch

Publisher's device on verso of the back wrapper of the Shilling Garland books,
originally designed by Louis Fairfax-Muckley as a tailpiece for Blackmore's *Fringilla*

such a venture can readily be understood, since major commercial publishing firms of the day held the view that any first edition—whether written by a young or old, known or unknown person—cost so much to produce initially that a low price was an impossibility. As late as 1910, when the House of Murray timidly ventured into the series business with the announcement of its "New Shilling Library," it included only volumes on which "the prime cost has been covered and some test made" of their "capacity of sale in large numbers." Only then, Murray held, is it prudent "to issue an edition at a price that leaves but a slender margin over its paper and printing cost." Mathews by deciding to implement Binyon's idea was therefore flying in the face of the collected wisdom of the industry, which while it admitted the proposition "that good literature should be published at a price within the reach of everyone," agreed with Murray's position on the economics of publishing shilling books.[3] Binyon was encouraged in his views by his friend and mentor Robert Bridges, the future poet laureate, who believed that the shilling series would set "the example of publishing poetry cheaply."[4] So close were the ideas of Binyon and Bridges as plans developed that the two appear at one point to have contemplated doing the series together, each supplying the copy for alternate numbers. But Binyon seems to have had second thoughts, writing Mathews in the summer of 1895 to say that he had "no wish to appear as a kind of satellite to Bridges, much as I like and admire him: and if we two ran a series together, it would perhaps give that impression." Binyon then went on to propose to the publisher an arrangement by which he would "bring out a certain number of poems in shilling parts (supposing the 1st is successful): and if Bridges likes, he can start a parallel series of his own. He agrees at any rate to provide copy for one part. But I think it would be best if the covers were different, and the two series (supposing Bridges continues his) quite independent of each other. Of course, the same type and format could be used."[5]

By late August, Binyon's idea for two parallel series had been discarded in favor of a single series edited solely by himself, commencing with an initial number featuring his poems followed by a second number contributed by Bridges. Bridges continued to be an active participant in formulating policy, conveying his views to Mathews through Binyon, especially as they concerned himself, his reputation, and his contribution to the series. For instance, once it had been decided to include other authors in the series, Bridges asked that an agreement be drawn up in writing "with the stipulation that the choice of writers for the series" remain with either Bridges or Binyon.[6] This apparently was important to Bridges; he did not relish having his name associated with poets of whom he did not approve. As W. B. Yeats later observed, Bridges had become "the patron saint" of a literary movement which numbered among its adherents not only Binyon, but such other young poets as Stephen Phillips, Mary E. Coleridge, and Henry Newbolt, as well as the older Richard Watson Dixon.[7] By bestowing his patronage through Binyon on his chosen few, Bridges was responsible for the Shilling Garland's Oxford aura, which critics were quick to discern in the fact that all seven Shilling Garland authors besides Bridges—Binyon, Phillips, Coleridge, Newbolt, Dixon, Manmohan Ghose, and Margaret Woods—had close ties to Oxford and that four of the seven, like Bridges (and perhaps through his agency)—Binyon, Coleridge, Woods, and Dixon—were authors of books privately printed by Dr. C.H.O. Daniel, the provost of Worcester College, on his hand press at Oxford.[8]

As the plans for the new series developed, Binyon, having chosen the type and the paper, turned his thoughts to the format, which he visualized in terms of a little anthology of verse entitled *Primavera* to which he had contributed in 1890 along with three other Oxonians— his cousin Stephen Phillips, Manmohan Ghose, and Arthur S. Cripps. Later referred to as "the little Oxford forerunner of the 'Shilling Garland,'" it prefigured the format of the new series in its size (7" X 4⅜") as well as in its typically Century Guild design and ornamentation.[9] This design was the creation of Selwyn Image, the friend of both Mathews and Binyon, who later designed and drew the wrapper ornament for the Shilling Garland series: a long stem with leaves and blossoms usually printed in black, standing horizontal and centered, along with a distinctive hand-lettered title.

Among the first notices of the coming venture in new poetry was one appearing in the "Literary Gossip" column of the *Athenaeum* for September 7, 1895: "Mr. Elkin Mathews proposes to issue at intervals a series of shilling volumes of poetry, beginning in November. The first volume, 'London Poems,' will be by Mr. Laurence Binyon, and the second by Mr. Robert Bridges."[10] Another reference to the new series appeared a week later in the "Notes and News" column of the *Academy* and reflects Mathews' initial decision to name the series "The Splendid Shilling," as he later wrote in a draft of his reminiscences, "to commemorate the lines—"

> Happy the man who void of cares and strife
> In silken or in leathern purse retains
> A Splendid Shilling.[11]

Informing readers that the publisher meant "to issue occasionally slim volumes of poetry by writers of distinction," the statement continued: "The modest price justifies the name by which the series will be known—namely, 'The Splendid Shilling,' after the title which Milton's nephew, John Phillips, gave his poem."[12] Binyon, however, had increasing doubts about the title, informing Mathews in mid-September that "the more I consider the *Splendid Shilling* title the less I like it. Everybody who saw the [Daily] Chronicle paragraph or who hears of the title, is puzzled by it. That is surely a thing to avoid. I think it was a mistake to drag in Phillips' poem, as that has nothing whatever to do with us and only leads people astray from the fact I want to emphasize that the books are priced at a shilling.[13] Although York Powell, Mathews' Bedford Park neighbor and adviser, thought the "Splendid Shilling" as a title was "quite all right and knocked off in red pencil suggestions towards advertising it, . . . a certain distinguished poet," Mathews later wrote, "expressed the wish that it should be known as the 'Shilling Garland', and the Garland it became."[14] Since Binyon's views often reflected those of Bridges, his objections to Mathews' series title may have been those of his mentor If so, Bridges was probably the "distinguished poet" mentioned by Mathews and the "poet of eminence" referred to in rumors which surfaced in the press about the change in the title of the series. Reflecting the change, Mathews' announcements in November referred to the series as the "Shilling Garland," and despite the fact that it, in the opinion of one commentator, suggested "cheap obituary wreaths," it was allowed to stand.[15]

Meanwhile, Mathews, who had made arrangements to publish three books jointly with the new American firm of Way and Williams —William Sharp's *Ecce Puella*, Roden Noel's *My Sea and Other Poems*, and Percy Hemingway's *The Happy Wanderer*—was negotiating with

Monogram used on the verso of a blank page at the back of William Sharp's *Ecce Puella* (1896)

the Chicago firm to copyright the Shilling Garland series and sponsor its publication there.[16] In expectation of arranging some sort of deal with Way and Williams, Mathews, in the autumn of 1895, held up publication of the first number of the Shilling Garland, Binyon's *First Book of London Visions*, which he had hoped to bring out in November in time for it to profit from the Christmas buying season. Unfortunately, no word from Way and Williams had been forthcoming by 19 December, when Binyon, by then on the verge of desperation, wrote Mathews:

> I hope you will have heard from Chicago to-day. But in any case I propose that you issue the book to-day, even if W and W [Way and Williams] offer to copyright the series, which I don't expect. Should they make the offer, they can have the rest of the series.
>
> As I suppose I am the person who will lose by not being copyrighted, I have less hesitation in proposing this. It seems better than continually disappointing people: and if you don't hear to-day, this plan will not necessitate waiting for next mail.[17]

Accordingly, Mathews published Binyon's *First Book of London Visions* without further delay. Containing twelve poems which filled 32 pages, the fragile little book was distinctive and tasteful in its reddish-brown paper wrappers, which bore Selwyn Image's bold, modernistic, hand-drawn sans serif lettering and design in black, quite similar to the title page he had provided Binyon's 1894 *Lyric Poems*.

The series was warmly received by reviewers. The earliest response, that which appeared in the "Reviews" column of the *Publishers' Circular* for 18 January 1896, informed readers that Binyon's "pamphlet . . . begins the series of new poetry at popular prices which is to be known as the 'Elkin Mathews' Shilling Garland,'" and went on to profess itself "doubly grateful" not only for Binyon's poems but for a "'lively sense of benefits to come' in succeeding blossoms of the garland."[18] "The Literary Lounger" in the pages of the *Sketch* for 5 February, reported that Binyon "leads off in Mr. Elkin Mathews' new poetical series—bearing the doubtfully poetic name of 'The Shilling Garland.'" Despite his criticism of the series title, the reviewer was of the opinion that Binyon's poems were "genuine things cut out of the heart of London life," and concluded by hoping that the poet "has 'London Visions' enough to fill a great many more of Mr. Mathews' 'Shilling Garlands.'"[19] Heading its review "A Notable No. 1," *Bookselling* for March awarded kudos to Elkin Mathews, who, it observed, "has had many happy ideas from the time he started the little mecca on Vigo Street, which will figure largely in the future history of literature in the late nineteenth century." Moreover, it continued, "one does not remember any better notion than this of shilling volumes— or pamphlets—of new poetry."[20]

However welcome the series might have been to reviewers, the fact that the Shilling Garland was a good value impressed the commentators most. For instance, in "Our Monthly Parcel of Books" section of the *Review of Reviews*, it was observed that

> the pursuit of the "new poet" is fraught generally with considerable expense. Slim volumes published at five shillings apiece (with no discount!) seems to be the usual form. But for once I can send you a little book by a young writer who puts no such high estimate upon his power of attraction, Mr. Laurence Binyon's "First Book of London Verses" [sic] (Mathews) is issued at the low price of a shilling, and at that price certainly deserves to be bought by every lover of verse, and every reader who takes any interest at all in the production of the younger men.[21]

And as succeeding volumes in the series appeared, reviewers continued to recommend them. The poet and critic Norman Gale opined, in reviewing Stephen Phillips' *Christ in Hades and Other Poems* (Shilling Garland no. 3), that "lovers of a good bargain should not let such an opportunity slip."[22] Similarly, the reviewer of the same volume for the *Saturday Review* urged his readers to buy not only because the poetry was excellent but because the purchase demanded "no larger expenditure than a shilling."[23]

Not only was the Shilling Garland series generally welcomed by reviewers and its aims and values appropriately noticed and praised, but Binyon's lead-off volume, *First Book of London Visions*, also was, on the whole, well received. Vying with William Ernest Henley, Oscar Wilde, Arthur Symons, and others in capturing the ambiance of the city in short, impressionistic vignettes, Binyon was approvingly perceived by one reviewer as "a poet student of London life, who does not think his dreams of beautiful things and thoughts too super-fine to keep company with actualities."[24] Referring to him as "an impressionist word-painter" whose poems are "mainly harmonies in grey and other sad tones," the critic for the *Publishers' Circular* found "sufficient freshness" in Binyon's poetry to enable him to look forward to a second book of London visions.[25]

As a result of the initial reception both of the series and its first "garland," Mathews and Binyon might well have thought the new venture in poetry well-launched, and so it seemed. But various problems soon arose which are reflected in the correspondence between the principals. For example, in January 1896, soon after Binyon's *London Visions* had appeared, Mathews was contemplating the publication of a volume of poetry in the Shilling Garland written by a person by the name of Strange.[26] Binyon, however, recommended that Strange's poems be published in some other "form than the Garland," giving as his reason the fact that he did not find them equal to the poems of A. C. Benson (a young don at Eton whose early volume, *Poems*, had been published by the Bodley Head in 1893), which Bridges believed were not "up to the Garland standard." Binyon found Strange's verse, though promising, technically immature "and wanting in concentration."[27]

Shortly after, Binyon was also at odds with Mathews over the publisher's proposal to add a volume of Frederick Wedmore's prose to the series, despite Wedmore's celebrity as an author and art critic. Binyon wrote:

> I have been thinking over Wedmore, but confess I still object. 1. To advertise the series as poetry, & then go off into prose at the 4th or 5th number seems to me unfair to subscribers & likely to create an injurious

impression of a medley & a lower standard. 2. Think of the inundations of prose-people we shall have. Poets are bad enough already.

I had a confidential talk with A. W. Pollard this morning. He has had much experience in editing & publishing of "series," & he thinks it would be a fatal mistake to introduce Wedmore. Why can't you publish his affair at a shilling separately? I can't see what advantage it would get by being in the series.

Evidently in an effort to circumvent any further proposals of this sort by Mathews, Binyon concluded:

My advise is that no one more be even entertained at present, till it's known what kind of a success we shall have. Else it may be you will be burdened with all sorts of useless copy. Why not say you are full up till July, & cannot consider anybody for six months? Life won't be worth living if one is to be nibbled at by several poets a week.[28]

Intended for publication soon after Binyon's *London Visions*, Bridges' Shilling Garland volume (so eagerly awaited by Binyon and Mathews) was greatly delayed, posing a far more serious problem for them to overcome. In November, Bridges had not been certain whether he could get his ode for the Purcell commemoration celebration done in time to publish it as the second number, so he suggested that his contribution appear in the announcements for the forthcoming series as *New Poems by Robert Bridges*.[29] Then, in January, Bridges, having gotten Richard Watson Dixon's consent to publish a selection of his poems as one of the Shilling Garland numbers, was "in no humour" to work up "his own things"; instead, Binyon informed Mathews, he "wants to copy out Dixon's and have them issued as No. III before his own No. II—if necessary with a notice of delay." Clearly worried, Binyon inquired of Mathews: "Will this damage the interests of the series? If not, I suppose we must humour his perversity. It is very vexing. If such arrangement would harm trade prospects I will represent this to R.B."[30] Whether or not Binyon so represented the matter to Bridges, the poet got his manuscript of the ode and other new poems to Mathews in early February, but again the publication of number 2 was delayed, this time because Bridges belatedly made his own arrangements with Way and Williams to publish an edition of his Shilling Garland number in America.[31] Since this meant that the book had to be set up in type and printed in the

United States and copies deposited in the Library of Congress in order to secure copyright, publication in England had to be postponed. Apprehensive lest the momentum of the series be lost through such a hiatus, Binyon advised Mathews to bring out Stephen Phillips' *Christ in Hades and Other Poems* (by now chosen as the third volume of the series) "quite soon, say in ten days' time" and further urged the publisher to

> get the papers to insert a paragraph saying No. 2 is delayed for unavoidable reasons, naming an exact date for its appearance, and at the same time say something of Phillips (I wrote a skeleton paragraph for Lewis [probably J. Lewis Hind, editor of the *Academy*] the other day) and recall attention to the Series. I think this better than dilly-dallying with No. 2, as it will be 3 months after No. 1 if we wait for R.B. No doubt we shall lose something: but on the other hand we gain an opportunity for recalling attention to the Garland.

Frustrated, presumably, by the unwillingness of Way and Williams to expedite the publication of Bridges' poems in the United States, Binyon concluded: "It's vexing (America seems always vexing): but I think you will probably take the same view as I do: and if so we shall, I believe, pull through all right."[32]

Since Phillips' book was already at the printers, there is no apparent reason why Binyon's advice could not have been followed. However that may be, two days later there appeared in the "Notes and News" column of the *Academy* the following announcement: "*Christ in Hades*, by Mr. Stephen Phillips, will immediately follow Mr. Robert Bridges' volume in the 'Elkin Mathews Shilling Garland.'"[33] I suspect that Mathews, perhaps afraid of offending Bridges, decided to risk the consequences of delay. As a result, the Shilling Garland's second and third volumes—Bridges' *Ode for the Bicentenary Commemoration of Henry Purcell, with Other Poems* and Phillips' *Christ in Hades and Other Poems*—appeared almost simultaneously in mid-April.[34]

Bound in tan paper wrappers, Bridges' book of verse offered as its chief attraction the "Ode to Music" written as text for Hubert Parry's cantata performed at the Leeds Festival and the Henry Purcell Commemoration in London during 1895, the bicentenary year of the great seventeenth-century composer's death. It was preceded by a "Preface" on the musical setting of poetry and an "Analysis" or brief résumé of the ode's ten sections, and was followed by four short poems. Despite the celebrity of its author, the *Ode* was not well-received by reviewers, who throughout the nineties thought Bridges, as one critic expressed it, "too severe a stylist," too "classical for popularity."[35] Sensing that the poet's task had not been wholly congenial and his collaboration with Parry not altogether happy,[36] the reviewer for the *Bookman* felt that the effort at supplying words for music could have better been left to a writer "more facile and of less distinction." Nevertheless, he continued, Bridges "dances gracefully enough in his fetters, and with no little dignity to boot. At the same time it is impossible not to regret that so fine a talent as his should be lavished so—seemingly—laboriously, on a theme so poetically unprofitable as the Purcell Commemoration Ode."[37]

Had the newly launched Shilling Garland series had to rely on Bridges' *Ode* to accelerate its momentum, it might very well have faced its demise, owing to the long delay in the book's publication and its cool reception. Fortunately, the momentum of the series was revived and its prestige enhanced from an unexpected source: the sudden and notable success of Phillips' *Christ in Hades and Other Poems*. The first of the Shilling Garland's two very popular triumphs, Phillips' little book, bound in very pale lavender paper wrappers with design and lettering in dark purple and containing the title poem and four shorter ones, gave a tremendous boost to the series. One of those books of poetry like Byron's *Childe Harold's Pilgrimage* which almost overnight transforms its author into a major poet, *Christ in Hades* projected the very minor Phillips into the forefront of poets writing in the later nineties. Although he had privately printed two little books of poetry, *Orestes* (1884) and *Eremus* (1890), and had published verses in *Primavera* and an entirely revised version of *Eremus* (1894), Phillips had gained little recognition. In fact, when his *Christ in Hades* was announced by Elkin Mathews, his chief claim to fame seems to have been that of an actor whose delivery of the ghost's speech in *Hamlet* at the Globe Theater had won him a call—"a unique distinction," according to the blurb.[38]

Thanks largely to the efforts of Binyon, Phillips' little book of verse received on its debut enthusiastic acclaim from several influential critics writing in some key periodicals. Its success is a signal example

41

of the effectiveness of the practice of "logrolling" in the nineties. Binyon, even before he had written Mathews back in January—"I think Phillips' book should go"—had been endeavoring to enlist the very substantial aid of Sidney Colvin on behalf of his cousin's poetry. Keeping his publisher abreast of his efforts, Binyon wrote Mathews that "Colvin is very enthusiastic about" Phillips "and is getting all his friends to read *Eremus*."[39] After the delay in publishing Bridges' *Ode* materialized, Binyon redoubled his efforts, advising Mathews that "I think I can turn things to account by persuading Colvin that Phillips will stand little chance if he doesn't energetically support him. Have spoken to him of this already, & he says he could get 3 or 4 reviews." Writing Mathews in late February, Binyon reaffirmed his determination to "do my utmost for Phillips' book. I think it a critical time for the Garland, & we must just thrust it down the public mouth. If you see Folkard [the printer], tell him I must have 2 copies of C in H proofs—one to give Colvin, as he may be able to help by having an advance copy."[40] Colvin—who had had a distinguished career as Slade Professor of Fine Arts at Cambridge University and as director of the Fitzwilliam Museum before coming to London as keeper of the prints and drawings in the British Museum (where he was Binyon's superior)—had established his credentials as a critic of literature by writing the volumes on Landor and Keats for Morley's English Men of Letters series. Consequently, as Binyon had hoped, Colvin's favorable opinion of Phillips' book of poems was the key to success.

Colvin appears to have been reluctant to write a review of *Christ in Hades* himself. Phillips was still urging him to do so after several key reviews had appeared and the book's fate still hung in the balance: "If you could possibly find time to write even a few words somewhere I think it would just turn the scale as the poem has received real attention. . . . I hope you will not think I want to bother you, but I am sure that a few words would *just put the poem out of its agony.*" Whether or not Colvin finally acceded to Phillips request—there is no evidence that he did, though he could have written an unsigned review—other letters between the two suggest that he was mainly helpful in securing reviews for the book from other critics. Like Binyon, Phillips was convinced that "it is *reviews* that are wanted," and he was assiduous in courting Colvin, urging him in letters and personal interviews to help in "logrolling" the book. Having thanked Colvin for securing a review in Richard Holt Hutton's *Spectator*, Phillips went on to write:

> The other paper I should much like to get a review in if possible, is the Daily Chronicle. This is, especially for a cheap book, to my mind the most important through its large circulation and coming before very many who do not read the literary journals. Do you think this could in any way be managed? I know that William Archer reviews sometimes for it and he would I think remember me through my *stage* connection. I know that he read Eremus sometime ago. If you should run across him, perhaps you might mention the new poem; and it could be sent to him.[41]

That the assault of the two cousins on Colvin had its desired effect appears to be borne out by the reviews which began to appear soon after the publication of *Christ in Hades*. Highly favorable responses appeared in the *Sketch*, the *Spectator*, and the *Bookman*. Moreover, the *Saturday Review* proclaimed Phillips "a new and powerful individuality, standing quite alone among our younger poets."[42] And Norman Gale, the poet and critic for the *Academy*, asserted that Elkin Mathews, "wandering in search of poets with a shilling's worth of song for sale . . . will certainly travel a considerable distance before he finds a singer to supply him with a better bundle of poems than that delivered into his charge by Mr. Stephen Phillips."[43] The wide and varied praise which the periodical press awarded Phillips over the next few months had its effect. Sales of *Christ in Hades* soared. By late September "a third large edition" was reported by Mathews, who, doubtless taking advantage of Phillips' new celebrity, also announced a volume of "New Poems" by the poet.[44] A fifth printing with additions was advertised in January 1898,[45] and a sixth with additions was listed on the inside front cover of Manmohan Ghose's *Love-Songs and Elegies*, published in April 1898. By then Mathews had lost Phillips to John Lane, who in December 1897 had announced that the Bodley Head was "about to publish, under the simple title *Poems*, a volume containing all the work of Mr. Stephen Phillips to the present time. Mr. Lane has arranged with Mr. Elkin Mathews for the inclusion of the little *Christ in Hades* book."[46]

Phillips' *Christ in Hades* was followed in July 1896 by *Aëromancy and Other Poems* (Shilling Garland no. 4), written by one of the two

43

women represented in the series, Mrs. Margaret Louisa Woods, a novelist as well as poet, and a friend of Dr. Daniel, who had on his small handpress at Oxford privately printed two of her books of verse—*Lyrics* (1888) and *Songs* (1896). As far back as February, Binyon had told Mathews to "announce no. 4 as 'Aeromancy,' & other poems." Although, at the time, the title had struck him as "a little odd," he had concluded that it was "but perhaps none the worse for that." Mentioning that the title poem was "on the bells of Oxford," Binyon observed that he had seen it "and it contains much beauty."[47] Including eight lyrics besides the longer title poem, *Aëromancy* hardly achieved the success of *Christ in Hades*; yet it did merit a second printing and considerable critical notice in some important periodicals. In fact, one reviewer—Norman Gale in the pages of the *Academy*—pronounced *Aëromancy* the best volume so far of the Shilling Garland series, though "forgetful of neither the fragments of excellence in *London Visions* nor the strength and music in *Christ in Hades*." Gale, like other critics, faulted "Aëromancy" for its occasional obscurities, but concluded that the "pamphlet" deserved "the votes, the shillings, and the love of all who wish their shelves to carry the best products of song."[48] Moreover, the reviewers often praised what one termed Mrs. Wood's "exquisiteness of sound painting" exhibited in all the poems, but generally agreed that the shorter lyrics (which some felt were better) would probably be more popular than the title poem.[49]

Although Binyon in February had projected *Aëromancy* as Shilling Garland number 4, there is evidence to suggest that Canon Richard Watson Dixon's *Songs and Odes* (Shilling Garland no. 5) had during the spring of 1896 been thought of as the fourth number. Bridges in an April letter to Mathews spoke of it as number 4, and an announcement in the "Notes and News" column of the *Academy* for 23 May 1896 refers to "the next volume of Mr. Elkin Mathews' 'Shilling Garland'" as Dixon's *Songs and Odes*.[50] Doubtless the lengthy preparations for its publication had something to do with the fact that Mrs. Woods's volume preceded it, as Binyon originally had planned. Preparations were complicated by the fact that Bridges was chiefly responsible for Dixon's Shilling Garland volume. Not only did he select the poems and write a prefatory note (which for some reason was not published), but he also generally saw the volume through the press along with Dixon.

Having been introduced to Dixon by Gerard Manley Hopkins many years before, Bridges not only had influenced the canon but had, as one of Dixon's chief advocates, arranged for the private printing of several books of Dixon's poems by the Daniel Press in the 1880s. Moreover, in the 1890s, he had introduced Dixon to some of the younger poets, several of whom also appeared as Shilling Garland authors: Binyon, Henry Newbolt, H. C. Beeching, Mary Coleridge, Margaret Woods. Though neither a young nor a new poet, Dixon had never been a popular poet, and Bridges, feeling that Dixon's poetry deserved a larger audience, saw the Shilling Garland book as a chance to win for his friend a wider recognition. Although in a letter to Mathews Bridges had predicted that "the great excellence of the best selections" of Dixon's poems would "some day be recognized—and one cannot tell when," Bridges hoped that the publication of *Songs and Odes* would be the time.[51] In his memoir of Dixon, Bridges wrote that he edited the selection with confidence that it would find public acceptance. He was greatly disappointed, however: "The blank result of the one experiment which I confidently did make, when some of [Dixon's] most beautiful lyrics were reprinted in Mr. Elkin Mathews' Shilling Garland, rebuffed me."[52]

Bridges' "experiment" involved selecting some eighteen poems, all but three of them taken from two Daniel Press books, *Odes and Eclogues* (1884) and *Lyrical Poems* (1887).[53] In early April 1896, Bridges had submitted his selection to Mathews along with a letter in which he left to the publisher "the arrangement of the pages" but cautioned him "to keep the order of the poems as I have arranged them."[54] By June, Dixon had returned the proofs of *Songs and Odes* (which both he and Bridges had read) with some corrections, a desire to see the printer insert more space between "headlines and the verses in pp. where the poem is continued to a second page," and a request for a second round of proofs which, having subsequently been sent, were read and returned to Mathews in early August.[55]

Songs and Odes, then, appeared in mid-October 1896. A sign of "the blank result" Bridges spoke of as a consequence of his experiment was a lack of critical response. Although the *Bookman* for October announced that Mathews was soon to publish "a very welcome book of poems by Canon Dixon, whose connection with Rossetti was well-known,"[56] the reviews after the fact were few even if, on the whole, positive. "The merit of some of the contents is very dark to me," wrote the "Literary Lounger" in the *Sketch*. "But," he continued, "there are bursts of originality and of beauty, albeit severe in kind."[57] The one really sympathetic notice appeared in the *Saturday Review* and observed that heretofore Dixon had not "found a wide public for his verse." But, the critic went on to say, "the present shilling book of lyrics . . . shows the author at his best, and should," echoing Bridges' hope, "do something towards procuring him his due rank among living poets. The poems are short and there are not many of them, but they are sufficient to reveal the originality of thought and feeling, the loftiness of attitude, and the fine observation which mark Canon Dixon's work."[58]

Dixon's *Songs and Odes* was followed in December by Binyon's *Praise of Life* (Shilling Garland no. 6). Unlike *London Visions*, which was forward-looking in its impressionistic evocations of the city-scape, Binyon's second contribution to the series was reminiscent of the Romantic poets in its response to nature. Like its predecessor, however, *The Praise of Life* exhibits Binyon's continuing experiments in meter. Reacting negatively to this, the critic for the *Saturday Review* attributed the poet's "tendency to play tricks with the recognized laws of English prosody" to "Mr. Bridges, that learned heretic."[59]

Another of Bridges' protégées, Mary E. Coleridge, writing under the pseudonym Anodos,[60] added *Fancy's Guerdon* (Shilling Garland no. 7) to the series in April 1897. Reluctant to embarrass the memory of her great uncle, Samuel Taylor Coleridge, by publishing her poetic effusions, Miss Coleridge, heretofore known for her prose romances, had at the urging of friends, especially Henry Newbolt and Bridges, at last compromised and allowed a volume of verse, *Fancy's Following*, to be pseudonymously and privately printed by Daniel in 1896.[61] Of the forty-eight poems in that volume, eleven were reprinted in *Fancy's Guerdon*, to which were added seven more from her sizable stock of unpublished pieces. Responding to the new book with a rather abrupt, brusque "Another shilling garland—the seventh," one reviewer compared *Fancy's Guerdon* to some of the previous numbers:

"If it does not rise to the level of the best of Mr. Laurence Binyon's pages, and lacks the distinction of utterance which characterizes Mr. Robert Bridges' contributions to the series, it escapes the grand manner which those who were not impressed greatly by Mr. Stephen Phillips' volume found a little trying."[62] A year after its publication, an announcement in the "News Notes" column of the *Bookman*, almost certainly supplied by Mathews, let drop the identity of the author of *Fancy's Guerdon* in a ploy to revive flagging sales in the light of Miss Coleridge's new romance and the tremendous success of the latest Shilling Garland volume: "Miss M. E. Coleridge, whose novel, 'The King with Two Faces,' is attracting so much attention, is, we believe, the author of a small volume of poems published last year by Mr. Elkin Mathews. The title is 'Fancy's Guerdon,' by Anodos, and the little book is published in the same form as Mr. Newbolt's 'Admirals All.'"[63]

Admirals All and Other Verses (Shilling Garland no. 8), which had appeared in October 1897, some six months after *Fancy's Guerdon*, had become an immediate success despite the fact that its author, Henry Newbolt, a young lawyer, was hardly known to the literary world. No one expected "the little pamphlet of twelve pieces . . . in a blue sugar-paper cover" (as Newbolt later described it)[64] to become one of the biggest success stories in poetry during the decade of the nineties. True, the volume's most famous piece, "Drake's Drum," had greatly impressed Robert Bridges: "It isn't given to man to write anything better than that," he had told Newbolt on first reading the poem. "I wish I had ever written anything half so good."[65] Moreover, it had been proclaimed on its appearance in the pages of the *St. James's Gazette* as one of the best sea songs in the language. Nevertheless, the book's sudden celebrity came as a great surprise. Set off skyward like a rocket by William Archer's glowing review in the *Daily Chronicle*, *Admirals All* required some four printings in a fortnight, a twenty-first by 1905, and a thirtieth by 1910—a total of some 30,000 copies in all.

Born in Staffordshire and educated at Clifton and Oxford, Newbolt had practiced law in London since 1887. Meanwhile he had published a novel about the Napoleonic wars, *Taken from the Enemy* (1892), and a blank-verse tragedy based on the Arthurian stories,

Cover of Henry Newbolt's *Admirals All* (1897). Cover designs for all the Shilling Garland books were by Selwyn Image, who devised a unique lettering for each title.

Mordred (1895), neither of which had gained much attention. Encouraged, however, by the poet and critic Andrew Lang, Newbolt had succeeded in placing a number of poems and ballads in such journals as *Longmans Magazine*, the *Pall Mall Gazette*, the *Spectator*, and the *St. James's Gazette* during 1895–96. Newbolt became acquainted with Robert Bridges in 1894 through the Alfred Waterhouses (Mrs. Bridges' parents) and later found himself a neighbor of Bridges at Yattendon. Naturally enough, he showed some of his poems to Bridges, whose poetical abilities he greatly admired. As a consequence, Newbolt was invited by Binyon to contribute a volume to the Shilling Garland series.[66]

Composed almost entirely of poems celebrating "the sound and splendour of England's war," *Admirals All and Other Verses* can be seen as a part of the "tendency among contemporary verse-writers to return to martial and inspiriting themes, and especially to the maritime glories of England" which one critic had noticed "since the appearance of Rudyard Kipling's *Barrack-Room Ballads* in 1892."[67] Much of its success can be attributed to the rising tide of patriotic feeling attendant upon Queen Victoria's diamond jubilee in 1897 and the jingoism which reached its full with the outbreak of the Boer War in 1899.

That sales of *Admirals All* were unexpectedly brisk from the outset is suggested by Newbolt's account of how one evening shortly after its publication he passed down the Strand on his way home from Lincoln's Inn:

> I stood for a moment or two at the wide entrance, half doorway half bookstall, of the Dennys' shop at the west end of Holywell Street—the "Booksellers' Row" for which the present generation will look in vain. One of the Dennys said the usual "Good evening" to me, and added, "Have you come for your book, sir? You are just in time, we've hardly a copy left to-night." "How many had you this morning?" I asked lightly. "I don't know, but we shall have five hundred tomorrow if we can get them."[68]

Mathews moved quickly to see that booksellers "could get them" by commissioning a second printing soon after publication. He was contemplating a third printing by Friday, 26 November, as a letter from Newbolt indicates: "Many thanks for proof of cover of 2nd ed.

of 'Adm. All' . . . I am glad you are thinking of a third edition."[69] A further indication of the immense popularity of *Admirals All* is the uncharacteristic dispatch with which Mathews moved to follow up the success with the issuance of a larger book of Newbolt's poems bound in hard covers. On Monday, 15 December, Mathews wrote out an agreement to publish such a volume allowing Newbolt "a royalty of 15% on the full published price on all copies sold (counting 13/12) should the price be 5/—. . . the royalties to begin with the first copies sold."[70] This rather handsome offer must not have met with Newbolt's approval, however, for the publisher, determined to hold onto so valuable and highly successful a new client, on the following Monday modified his proposed agreement in another letter so as to allow Newbolt a royalty of 15 percent on all copies sold up to 2,000 and 20 percent afterwards.[71]

Of course, another sign of the book's success was the "chorus of praise" from the periodical press, which "greeted Mr. Newbolt's booklet of patriotic verses."[72] Fortunately the earliest response, which appeared in the columns of the *Daily Chronicle* ("then the most 'literary' of the dailies," to quote Newbolt),[73] was William Archer's very favorable review. However, Archer posed one problem for Mathews and Newbolt by preferring the stanza arrangement of "Drake's Drum" as it had appeared in the *St. James's Gazette* in January 1896. The problem was resolved when Mathews agreed with Newbolt that the stanza arrangement of the popular poem as it stood in the first printing of *Admirals All* should be that of all future printings. Referring to the matter in a letter to Mathews, Newbolt wrote:

> I am glad that you approve the present order of the stanzas in Drake's Drum. It is exactly as I first wrote it, & the alterations both of order & of one or two words, made by the Editor of the St. James's Gazette, were made without consulting me. Both he and the Daily Chronicle reviewer [William Archer] . . . miss the point you mention, viz: that the third stanza "picks up" the first & so rounds off the piece: Moreover the *keynote* is "he's in his hammock" (& not "he was a Devon man") & must be the first note: lastly "Capten art tha sleepin' there below" has no meaning until you get him "in his hammock."[74]

Although there were minor criticisms in otherwise favorable reviews, the critic for the *Spectator* was typical in expressing "the greatest possible pleasure" in noticing "the delightful little collection of bal-lads."[75] As one might expect, reviews often addressed the question of Kipling's influence and Newbolt's handling of the ballad. Typical was the view of one critic who asserted that Newbolt "had done a notable thing. He has managed to write ballads full of ring and go, and full also of patriotic feeling, without imitating Mr. Rudyard Kipling."[76]

All in all, the press viewed *Admirals All and Other Verses* as a worthy and welcome addition to the series. For example, the critic for the *Illustrated London News* observed that the latest Shilling Garland author, Mr. Newbolt, "though in a style entirely different from those who have preceded him, maintains the tradition of the series . . . in his 'Admirals All.'"[77] Expressing perhaps an oblique criticism of the series, another reviewer opined that "the ranks of Mr. Mathews' shilling poets are very sensibly strengthened by the addition of Mr. Newbolt. New poets are not often so vigorous and straightforward as he is. . . . he brings to his task a fine enthusiasm for heroism, a gift of swinging metre, some power of using words, and the true English point of view."[78]

If, as the reviewer says, Newbolt's *Admirals All* was a distinct departure from the verse which the public had come to associate with the Garland, the two final volumes—Manmohan Ghose's *Love-Songs and Elegies* (no. 9) and Binyon's *Second Book of London Visions* (no. 10)—were a return to the quieter rhythms and tones of the lyric in the former and to the impressionist sketches of city life in the latter. Ghose and Binyon had known each other at Oxford and had pub-lished together in *Primavera*. That the two men remained friends is suggested by Ghose's dedication of his Shilling Garland volume "to Laurence, and the Remembrance of Happy Hours." Doubtless it was these ties that led Binyon to invite Ghose's contribution, even though his friend had returned to India after his Oxford days to teach English literature.[79] Though one might expect the verse of an Indian to project something of a foreign flavor, Ghose's lyrics in theme, language, and meter are in every way typical of so much lyricism of the nineties with just a touch here and there of exoticism in a poem like "Myvanwy." Perhaps this is why the book, originally titled *Indian Elegies and Love Songs* in the press announcements,[80] was published during the last week of April 1898 as simply *Love-Songs and Elegies*.

51

Although the *Bookman* informed its readers in March that "Mr. Laurence Binyon will follow Mr. Manmohan Ghose with a 'Second Book of London Visions,'"[81] the last volume of the series did not appear until mid-December 1898, with a title page dated 1899. Bringing the Shilling Garland full circle with his return to the scenes and themes of his *First Book of London Visions*, Binyon in the *Second Book* gave evidence of those poetic powers which had appeared in the first. Combined, these two books formed what Donald Davidson later called Binyon's most substantial contribution to the poetry of the nineties.[82]

Before the last volumes of the Shilling Garland were published, the first volume of *Elkin Mathews' Garland of New Poetry* was issued in 1897. Probably a means of remaindering unsold copies of the series booklets, it contained the first five numbers of the series with, to quote the advertisement, "General Title, Contents, and Wrappers bound in" at the price of six shillings.[83] Since copies exist dated both 1897 and 1898, Mathews, having sold out the first issue of 1897, must have had another bound with a new title page bearing the new date. In February 1899, he issued the second volume, which contained the final five numbers of the series. Both volumes were bound in cloth with a wreathlike garland of flowers and leaves designed by Selwyn Image stamped in blind on the front covers and printed on the title pages.[84]

Meanwhile Mathews had announced his intention to suspend the Shilling Garland series "for a time and (not necessarily superseding it)" to issue annually in the autumn "The Garland of New Poetry: an Anthology of unpublished pieces by various writers."[85] Binyon, who was serving as editor, sent Mathews the manuscript of the anthology in early September 1898, along with a letter in which he discussed his ideas "about get-up of the book." Responding to the publisher's concern that the "matter wouldn't bulk enough," Binyon went on to suggest that "we might put rather less on the page than in the Garland or use a single lead. If you would like," he then proposed, "I would do a design for cover. I give a rough idea on next page. It would look well in yellow or green, or dark green on pale. But I could not afford to do this for nothing. If you like to have it, I will ask 3 guineas payable on publication for it and for the work of editing (which has been considerable), and this I think would be cheap."[86] Although Mathews evidently thought so too, he accepted Binyon's proposal with the proviso that the three guineas be paid in January after he had begun to recoup some of the costs of publishing his autumn list of books. Binyon, however, was not amenable, explaining to Mathews in a revealing letter that

> any odd pound or two will be very useful to me this next month or so; later on I shall not be in such need of cash. The delay makes it no longer worth my while. You will get the editing of this volume, which has meant a good deal of time and trouble to me, for nothing; you have had all my work for the Garland for nothing, besides all the credit: and therefore I cannot but be surprised that you want to have the advantage, and give me the inconvenience of deferring payment of so small a sum. But since you wish it so, the design must be omitted or some one else got to do it.[87]

Unwilling to dispense with Binyon's attractive cover design at so late a date and to appear ungrateful for all Binyon had done, Mathews acquiesced, sending a check to Binyon in the amount of three guineas "for designing cover and editing Garland."[88]

The Garland of New Poetry by Various Writers appeared in December 1898 (during the same week as Binyon's *Second Book of London Visions*) and included new poems by the Shilling Garlanders Laurence Binyon, "Anodos" (Mary E. Coleridge), and Manmohan Ghose, as well as hitherto unpublished verse by Victor Plarr, Selwyn Image, A. Romney Green, Reginald Balfour, and "E.L." (Edith [Mrs. Alfred] Lyttleton, Balfour's sister). Bound in pale blue-gray paper-covered boards with Binyon's typically ninetyish binding design in dark blue, the Garland anthology sold for three shillings and sixpence.

With these efforts of late 1898 and early 1899, the Shilling Garland series came to a close. During the years of its publication, as the *Illustrated London News* affirmed, Mathews had "gained considerable renown for his 'Shilling Garland' series."[89] In the eyes of poets and critics alike, "to attain a place" in the series was "in itself a literary distinction."[90] Although none of the ten books of poetry published in the series possessed the quality critics today demand of major poetry, Binyon's impressions of the urban scene—among the earliest in this mode—remain significant examples of early modernist departures from the Victorian poetic idiom. Moreover, his experiments as well as those of others influenced by Bridges—in particular, Phillips, Dixon, and Newbolt—mark an important effort to break free of the typically Victorian patterns of meter and rhyme. Consequently, Binyon shared with Bridges the jibes of critics who saw these highly conscious, often painstakingly achieved experiments with classical meters as either merely bad workmanship or literary perversity. Similarly, Phillips and Newbolt, popular as they were, failed to escape critical censure for their metrical "indiscretions." Nevertheless, such departures from the Victorian norm mark the Shilling Garland series as typical of the nineties, a period out of which the characteristic poetry and art of the twentieth century emerged. Negligible as some of the poetry admittedly was, the series can be said to have its place in the history of English literature, contributing to the rise of the modern poetic idiom.

The series, more importantly, has its place in the history of publishing because it successfully fulfilled its aims, one of which was to provide a publishing opportunity for new poets. Recognizing the role of the series in helping new poets, E. K. Chambers, reviewing the "Literature of 1896," turned his attention briefly to the minor poets "who may be the major poets of tomorrow," and declared, "to these Mr. Elkin Mathews's 'Shilling Series' is a great boon."[91] Of the eight poets whose work appeared in the ten numbers of the series, two—Phillips and Newbolt—not only became popular and critically acclaimed poets almost overnight but also were launched on poetic careers of real distinction as a result of their Shilling Garland volumes. Though failing to attain anything like the popularity and praise of these two, three others—Binyon, Woods, and Coleridge—gained much-needed attention as well as momentum which carried them forward in their poetic careers.

The other principal aim of the Shilling Garland—to publish poetry in an inexpensive format—also was fulfilled. To liberate books of verse from the thrall of the five-shilling minimum price was, of course, dear to Binyon's heart, and looking back on the Shilling Garland experiment from the hindsight of twenty years, he declared unequivocally that "the idea proved a great success," citing as an example the fact that Newbolt's *Admirals All* sold 25,000 copies.[92] That Binyon was right when he argued that poetry in an attractive but inexpensive format would sell for a shilling is demonstrated by the fact that all but two of the volumes were reprinted at least once, with Phillips' *Christ in Hades* reaching six printings and *Admirals All* thirty.[93] Given the fact that, as Binyon later observed, Mathews made "no large profits," had "small capital and quite inadequate means for distribution on a large scale," these sales must be judged a triumph in the annals of publishing poetry, especially since they came at a time when the major publishers would not "take trouble about poetry because at best the return was small."[94] Mathews' interest in publishing poetry and his willingness to lead the way in securing inexpensive means of publishing young poets of talent, in both the Shilling Garland series and its sequel, the Vigo Cabinet series, must be applauded and accorded the word "success."

THE VIGO CABINET SERIES

The Shilling Garland series had been largely Binyon's venture as well as his idea, with Mathews serving in the capacity of publisher, or what one might call the producer. Respecting Binyon's editorial authority, Mathews had acquiesced in his decisions, finally exercising his own will only toward the end, when he chose to include the poetry of Reginald Balfour and his sister, Edith Lyttleton, in *The Garland of New Poetry by Various Writers* apparently without enthusiasm on Binyon's part. Mathews' increasing impatience with Binyon's editorial control and desire to assert his own may have had something to do with the series coming to a close when it did and with Mathews' failure to carry out the plan to publish *The Garland of New Poetry* annually.

Having been convinced by the success of his first series that there was "no better medium for pushing a book by a new writer," Mathews launched the Vigo Cabinet series in the spring of 1900, which ran to 145 numbers over the next eighteen years and became, as he proclaimed, "the longest series of original contemporary verse in existence."[95] Directed as Mathews alone saw fit, the Vigo Cabinet series in its authors and contents reflected Mathews' own tastes and interests during the first two decades of the twentieth century like nothing else with which he was involved.

The series derived its name from the fact that the little shop in Vigo

𝕰𝖘𝖘𝖆𝖞𝖘 𝖎𝖓 𝕾𝖔𝖓𝖌
𝕭𝖞 𝕸𝖆𝖉𝖆𝖒𝖊 𝕸𝖚𝖗𝖎𝖊𝖑 𝕽𝖎𝖈𝖍𝖆𝖗𝖉

SECOND   CENTURY

LONDON: ELKIN MATHEWS, VIGO STREET, W.

Cover design for the Vigo Cabinet series books

Street had—owing to its size—been referred to as "The Cabinet of Fine Art" by its previous occupant, Robert Dunthorne. Mathews chose as its subtitle "An Occasional Miscellany of Prose and Verse," thus indicating that while its focus would remain on belles lettres, the scope of the new series would be broadened beyond that of its predecessor to include in addition to poetry some drama, short fiction, and essays.

In format the Vigo Cabinet series books, measuring approximately 6⅜ by 5⅛ inches, were shorter and wider than those of the Shilling Garland series, indeed almost square. The books, usually containing 64 pages, were quartos, with gatherings of four leaves, bound in tinted paper wrappers with yapp (or circuit) edges. As in the case of the Shilling Garland series, the color of the wrappers varied from title to title, the choice of color apparently that of each author. Writing his friend J. M. Synge about the format of the series in which the playwright's *Shadow of the Glen and Riders to the Sea* was later to appear, John Masefield sent along "a specimen (it's a grisly thing in its way) which," he observed, "will show you the size and shape of the series. You can choose any colour you like for a cover."[96] The wrapper front was decorated with a design in black depicting Mathews' Vigo Street shop with a banner across the upper-right-hand corner bearing the words "Vigo Cabinet Series." Unlike the design, which was centered,

Publisher's device used on the back cover of the Vigo Cabinet series books and on Mathews' letterhead

57

the lettering of the title and author, also in black, was set flush with the left margin, a departure from typical Victorian publishing practice. The back of the wrapper was decorated with a device built around Mathews' rebus (designed by Frederick York Powell) in black and centered. The inside of the wrappers usually bore current lists of the Vigo Cabinet series books. Although initially available only in paper wrappers selling for one shilling, selected numbers of the series later were issued bound in cloth-covered boards with lettering in gold on the front and spine, selling for one shilling and sixpence. Two numbers appeared in a deluxe edition: W. B. Yeats's *The Tables of the Law and the Adoration of the Magi* (no. 17), which was printed on slightly thicker paper than that of the shilling edition and bound in blue-gray paper boards with buff linen spine, with lettering in black and selling for two shillings and sixpence; and Max Weber's *Cubist Poems* (no. 24),[97] which in addition to its 500 copies in wrappers also appeared in an edition of 100 copies on handmade paper and with a certificate—presumably a certificate of limitation.[98] Although most numbers were not illustrated, several were: for example, Agnes H. Begbie's *Christmas Songs and Carols* (no. 50), embellished with seven drawings by Edith Calvert (Edith Elkin Mathews), and John C. Taylor's *The Northern Sea: A Legend of the Norwegian Fiords* (no. 13), with sixteen illustrations by the author. Moreover, several had frontispieces: K. W. Lundie's *English Echoes from the Quartier Latin: Poems* (no. 5) was furnished with a frontispiece depicting the Sorbonne in black and white, and Alexander Robertson's *Comrades* (no. 36) was enhanced by a frontispiece portrait of the author, who was killed at the Somme in 1916.

Thinking of the Vigo Cabinet series in terms of a popular audience, Mathews sought to choose books whose contents would appeal to the tastes of the general poetry reader. Consequently, the series as a whole is an interesting index to the preferences of the English reading public during the early decades of the twentieth century. Titles such as *Sylvia's Rose and May Moon* (no. 46), *The Dream Merchant and Other Poems* (no. 83), *A Singer of Dreams* (no. 95), *Puck's Flight and Other Poems* (no. 91), *Elfin Chaunts and Railway Rhythms* (no. 20), and *Songs Satanic and Celestial* (no. 15) convey something of the flavor and the scope of the series.

Appearing at a time when the literary editor of the *Academy* observed that "books about the war come into this office with the frequency of shells in a besieged town,"[99] the first Vigo Cabinet book—the Rev. John Huntley, Canon Skrine's little volume of jingoist verse, *The Queen's Highway and Other Lyrics of the War, 1899–1900*, published in late May 1900—was a timely choice to inaugurate

Max Weber's cover design for his *Cubist Poems* (1914)

'TIS THE BIRTHDAY OF OUR KING

Illustration for Agnes H. Begbie's *Christmas Songs and Carols* (1908), by Mathews' wife, Edith Calvert (Edith Elkin Mathews)

the series, given the enormous appetite of the British public for books about the Boer War. And although most of the Vigo Cabinet books, like Skrine's, are of little interest today to anyone other than the historian of popular culture, several are significant landmarks in the annals of literary history, none more so than J. M. Synge's first book, consisting of two one-act plays, *The Shadow of the Glen and Riders to the Sea* (no. 24). Not only was it a milestone in Synge's career, but it was a central book in the Irish dramatic movement. *The Shadow of the Glen and Riders to the Sea* was among the best-selling numbers, with over 5,000 copies sold, and in terms of literary quality was the series'

SEE HOW THE POPPIES NOD, BABY BOY, BABY BOY!

Illustration for Agnes H. Begbie's *Christmas Songs and Carols* (1908), by Mathews' wife, Edith Calvert (Edith Elkin Mathews)

most distinguished production. Among other notable works which appeared in the series were W. B. Yeats's *Tables of the Law and the Adoration of the Magi* (no. 17), and selections from the *Poems of Lionel Johnson* and the later *Some Poems of Lionel Johnson* (both of which, at different times, appeared as no. 34). The series also included John Masefield's important second book, *Ballads* (no. 13); Logan Pearsall Smith's *Songs and Sonnets* (no. 64); Victor Plarr's most ambitious work, *The Tragedy of Asgard* (no. 27), which continued the action of Matthew Arnold's venture into the realm of Nordic mythology, *Balder Dead*; and the first collection of verse by the American artist and

61

student of Matisse Max Weber, *Cubist Poems* (no. 24), inspired, as were his paintings, by primitive and archaic sculptures and written in the manner of expressionist literature.

As a vehicle for new poets, the Vigo Cabinet series, too, had a modest success, including, in addition to Synge's plays, the young Wilfrid Wilson Gibson's first book, *Urlyn the Harper and Other Song* (no. 7), and two of his other early volumes, *The Queen's Vigil and Other Song* (no. 9) and *The Nets of Love* (no. 28), and several other firsts worth mentioning: Harold Monro's *Poems* (no. 37) and James Elroy Flecker's *Bridge of Fire* (no. 45). And, again like the Shilling Garland series, the Vigo Cabinet series was a success in providing the public with belles lettres at a very low price. As a commentator in the *Bookman* in 1903 observed: "It is not long since one of our leading critics declared that the curse of modern poetry lay in the fact that (in his own phrase) it is 'so deadly dear.' Mr. Elkin Matthews [*sic*] seems determined to remove this reproach, and his Vigo Cabinet Series, with their thick paper, excellent printing, and dainty *format* are as cheap as the most exacting and miserly of critics could wish."[100]

Reflecting the movement away from the insularity of the Victorians toward a more cosmopolitan outlook and range of interests on the part of the Edwardians, the series notably produced a relatively large number of translations, ranging from the extant verse of Sappho (no. 65) and the quatrains of Omar Khayyam (no. 53) to the lyrics of the Ruthenian poet Tarás Shevchéncko (no. 86). Among the more interesting as well as significant examples were *Poems in Prose from Baudelaire* (no. 29), selected and translated from *Les Petits Poèmes en Prose* by Arthur Symons, and *Baudelaire: The Flowers of Evil* (no. 66), selected and translated by Cyril Scott.[101] The work of two contemporary German poets, Stefan George and Hugo von Hofmannsthal, was represented in *German Lyrists of To-day* (no. 58), translated by Daisy Broicher, who was responsible for the later *German Lyrics and Ballads* (no. 3). Given the popularity of the great Norwegian dramatist in England during the late nineteenth and early twentieth centuries, it is not surprising to find a selection of *Ibsen's Lyrical Poems* (no. 8) early on among the Vigo Cabinet series translations. Less expected, however, is a book entitled *Under Swedish Colours: A Short Anthology of Modern Swedish Poets* (no. 87), which included the verse of King Oscar II, Viktor Rydberg, and Oscar Levertin, translated into English by

Francis A. Judd with a preface by that well-known interpreter of Scandinavian letters, the critic Edmund Gosse. Enhancing the cosmopolitan aura of the series—though no translation—is A. Yusef Ali's *Mestrovic and Serbian Sculpture* (no. *38*), surely one of the more interesting oddities found among its numbers.

By June 1909, the Vigo Cabinet series reached sixty volumes with the publication of Broicher's *German Lyrists of To-day* (no. 58), *Phantasies* (no. 59) by Gertrude H. Witherby, and *Three Poems* (no. 60) by Charles F. Grindrod—all three, according to the *Publishers' Circular*, "tastefully got up and well printed on good paper."[102] The ever-increasing number of books in the series, in itself a sign of success, prompted Mathews to begin bringing out a selection of them in cloth-bound covers as well as in paper wrappers. According to a brochure which Mathews issued in 1912, when the series reached a hundred numbers, ninety-four titles were still in print—some in second printings—and of these, thirty-seven could be had in both wrappers and hardcovers.

On reaching one hundred numbers, Mathews celebrated the event and commenced what he called the Vigo Cabinet series' "Second Century" with the publication of *The Vigo Verse Anthology* (no. 1) in September 1912. Composed of selections of poems from the first fifty numbers, Mathews' "lyrical anthology"—as he referred to it in his short preface—was an attempt to take advantage of what he saw as "something of a reawakening of the popular interest in current verse," an awakening which, perhaps, owed something to the Vigo Cabinet series itself. In his preface, citing as evidence for the revival of interest in contemporary poetry the recent appearance of "several anthologies of the work of living poets" (the Poets' Club anthology of 1909 no doubt among them), Mathews showed his early awareness of a trend in poetry which was to lead to the publication not only of five volumes of Georgian poetry in the next few years, but to several other important collections of modern verse both in England and America, such as the first Imagist anthology, *Des Imagistes* (1914), and Ezra Pound's *Catholic Anthology* (which Mathews published in 1915).

By 1920 "that famous series of 16 mo. booklets, many of which are exceedingly rare," as one critic observed of the Vigo Cabinet series, had long since grown venerable in the service of belles lettres, with many of its numbers—this critic cited Masefield's ballads, Yeats' stories, and Synge's plays—taking "a notable place in the history of books."[103] Moreover, four numbers reached a second printing—Wilfrid Wilson Gibson's *Urlyn the Harper, and Other Song* (no. 7) and *The Queen's Vigil, and Other Song* (no. 9), John Masefield's *Ballads* (no. 13), and C. Fox-Smith's *Songs in Sail and Other Chanties* (no. 14). Even better sales were achieved by Alexander Robertson's *Comrades* (no. 36), which reached a third thousand, and Synge's *Shadow of the Glen and Riders to the Sea* (no. 24), which, having been published in a first printing of a thousand copies in 1905, went into further printings in 1907 and 1909. A fourth thousand was issued in 1910 and a sixth thousand in 1911. Although the sales of individual numbers in the series were seldom large—a printing (or what Mathews called an edition) generally varying from as few as 250 to an average of 500 copies—total sales ultimately reached approximately 75,000 copies, not a bad record for a series devoted almost entirely to poetry.

OTHER SERIES

His Vigo Cabinet series having reached thirty-two volumes by 1906, Mathews in an interview announced his intention "to supplement it by a fresh venture." "This," he went on to say, "is to be called the Satchel Series, because the size is handy for carrying about."[104] Volumes in the Satchel series had dimensions almost identical to those of the Shilling Garland booklets—approximately 7 by 4⅜ inches—and were available in both a cloth binding and paper wrappers selling for a shilling and sixpence and a shilling, respectively. Issued in a variety of colors, the books of the series were identifiable largely through their format and cover design: volumes bound in cloth were distinguished by two double borders on the front cover within which the title and author's name appeared; the series' device, a satchel bearing the initials "SS," usually (but not always) appeared on the back cover. The series' title page, divided into three separate parts by horizontal lines in red, was enclosed in a single border, also in red, within which the title, author's name, and other pertinent matter appeared in black, a design which was duplicated on the front cover of the paperbound volumes with "The Satchel Series" added above the top border and the back cover being decorated with the series' device.

Among the notable titles of the series—which included seventeen in all—was the initial volume, John Hamilton Reynolds's *The Fancy*, a reprint of the book published by the friend of John Keats in 1820 under the pen name of Peter Corcoran.[105] A cooperative effort on the part of John Masefield, who provided an introduction, and Jack Yeats, who contributed thirteen pen drawings in black and white, *The Fancy*, published in late 1905, was one of the first fruits of that close friendship between Masefield and Yeats which provided the series with another notable volume, Masefield's *A Mainsail Haul*, with a frontispiece by Jack Yeats. Masefield also provided the introduction to E. H. Visiak's first book of poems, *Buccaneer Ballads*, which appeared in the series in 1910, the first of three little books by Visiak whose titles suggest their piratical subject matter: the other two were *Flints and Flashes* (1911) and *The Phantom Ship* (1912). Interestingly, the best-seller of the series was a book whose authorship has been attributed to Mathews himself, *The Views of Christopher*, with a preface by Coulson Kernahan.[106] First published in 1904 and later included in the Satchel series, the popular little book of moral essays written in a seriocomic style, reached "a third thousand" by 1910.

While the Vigo Cabinet and Satchel series were still being published, Mathews began yet another, the Savile series, named for the street, Savile Row (famous for its sartorial establishments), on the corner of which the Vigo Street shop stood. The smallest in format—5 3/16 by 3 7/8 inches—the books, bound in paper-covered boards with the color varying from title to title, sold for a shilling and generally contained 32 pages. Although its first number, Mrs. George Cran's *The Song of a Woman*, appeared in December 1909, the Savile series' claim to fame rests on the fact that its number 7, a volume of verse entitled *The Tempers*, was the first commercially published book by William Carlos Williams, whose friend, Ezra Pound, had gotten Mathews to publish it. Issued in an edition of about a thousand copies, *The Tempers*, bound in cream-colored paper-covered boards with lettering on the front cover and spine in gold, appeared in September 1913 and was reviewed by Pound (in the *New Freewoman*), who saw its nineteen poems as "distinguished by the vigour of their emotional colouring."[107] Besides its literary contents, the appeal of the Savile series book lay in its petite format, which gave it the charm of a miniature book.

Title page of F. P. Osmaston's *Art and Nature Sonnets* (1911), designed by James Guthrie of the Pear Tree Press, shows the wonderful designs used by Mathews. This title was not in any of the poetry series.

Similarly, the distinction of Mathews' last and least-known series, the Burlington, was in its size. Named for Burlington House, the home of the Royal Academy, in whose near vicinity the Vigo Street shop lay, the Burlington book's format was the largest of any of Mathews' series (Imperial 16mo). Bound in cloth, the Burlington book sold for two shillings and a sixpence. Inaugurated in 1911 with the publication of *Sonnets of Lucilla* (first series), the Burlington continued a year later with a second series, the poetic endeavors of Grace E. Tollemache. Several other numbers followed over the years, none of which were in any way distinguished.

By the close of the war, Mathews' zeal for the series appears to have declined; all four of the ongoing ones petered out before his death in 1921. By that time, however, Mathews' series had done their work, having been the indispensable vehicle for the introduction of many new writers, some of whom had attained great distinction in the world of belles lettres. Mathews' series had demonstrated not only that first editions of new writers could be produced inexpensively and in small numbers, but also that they could be done attractively. In format and design, Mathews' series were tasteful and aesthetically appealing, their slight size, spare contents, limited numbers, and even their paper-wrapped fragility giving the individual booklet the aura of preciosity, a quality much prized by the devotees of aestheticism and decadence. It is quite possible that Arthur Davison Ficke's idea of starting "a periodical series of little volumes" by new poets, which led to the founding of the Samurai Press, was inspired by Mathews' Shilling Garland and Vigo Cabinet series.[108] The appeal of Mathews' series is also shown, by the response of the poet Gordon Bottomley, who in the design and format of his own volumes carried the qualities and characteristics of the nineties book into the twentieth century. In 1907, when he was preparing to publish the first of his two volumes of poems entitled *Chambers of Imagery*, he discussed at some length the physical appearance of his book with Mathews, who suggested following the format and design of the Vigo Cabinet series. "If you were to see how many of your Vigo Cabinet Series stand on my shelves," Bottomley replied, "you would, I am sure, feel assured that my appreciation of them is too great for me to require reconciling to them. And if in this instance, I feel to [sic] desire another shape of page, it is the beauty of

Frontispiece of John Masefield's *A Mainsail Haul* (1905), by Jack B. Yeats

Sturge Moore's cover design for Cloudesley Brereton's *Mystica et Lyrica* (1919)

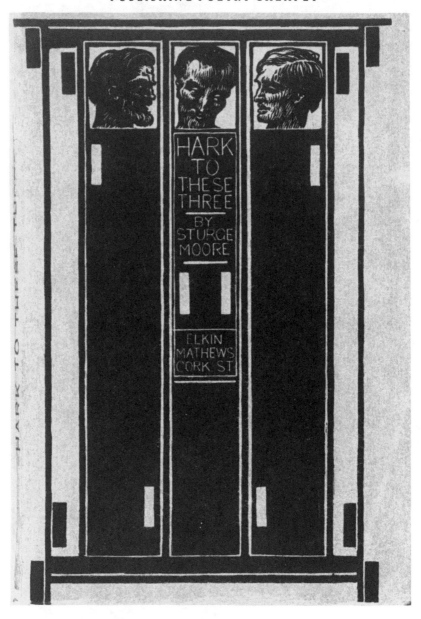

Sturge Moore's cover design for his own book of essays, *Hark to These Three* (1915)

another of your series (the Shilling Garland) that has given me the idea—so that I am hopeful you will not reproach me for my preference."[109] Consequently, both the first and second volumes of *Chambers of Imagery* are similar in size and format to the books of the Shilling Garland, attesting to the series' quality of design and aesthetic appeal.

CHAPTER THREE

Elkin Mathews, W. B. Yeats, and the

Celtic Movement in Literature

WILLIAM BUTLER YEATS

IN 1906, Elkin Mathews in response to an interviewer's question, "Then you have done much to assist the Celtic movement?" replied: "Yes; it has always had my sincerest sympathy. I have followed it from the start with great interest, and am convinced that it is destined to exercise a lasting influence on the national character."[1] Mathews was referring, of course, to the revival of interest in Celtic literature during the late eighties and nineties which had produced such works as W. B. Yeats's *Wanderings of Oisin* (1889) and *The Celtic Twilight* (1893), Elizabeth Sharp's anthology *Lyra Celtica* (1896), and many other books of stories and poems characterized by what one critic has described as "a particular landscape and atmosphere, a vaporous and watery, gray, drearily beautiful natural world, whether in Ireland, Wales, or Highland Scotland."[2] Typified by a strange melancholy and charged with a set of emotions thought to be peculiar to the Celtic race, the literature of the Celtic movement, with its evocation of the distant past, had a special appeal for Mathews, an antiquarian at heart and a lover of Pre-Raphaelite poetry who responded in particular to verse which often amounted to little more than Celtic variations on Rossettian moods and Swinburnean dreams.

Mathews' initial contact with the Celtic movement probably came through Richard Le Gallienne, who having recently come to London from his native Liverpool had lost no time in introducing himself to the literary circles of the capital.[3] In this way, he had come to know Yeats and other Celticists and later to join them in the Rhymers' Club. It was by acting on the advice of the adventurous Le Gallienne that Mathews first came in contact with the Celtic movement in the autumn of 1889. As Yeats reported it to Katharine Tynan, the publisher wrote him "asking for an experimental dozen of Oisin, sale or return of course and promising to advertize me—with press opinions, in his catalogue."[4]

A more significant contact came in January 1891, when Mathews received an invitation from Ernest Radford, a barrister and poet, to attend a meeting of the Rhymers' Club. And despite the fact that Mathews, as Radford observed, did "not rhyme," he often attended meetings of the club during the early nineties, becoming one of the so-called "permanent guests."[5] Unlike the Irish Literary Society, the Rhymers' Club was not tied to any particular literary or political movement; nevertheless, its membership included a sizable contingent of "Celts," among them its founders, the Irishman Yeats and the Welshman Ernest Rhys. Consequently, at its meetings—held either, according to Yeats, "in an upper room with a sanded floor in an ancient eating-house in the Strand called The Cheshire Cheese" or in the homes of various members—Mathews could not help but become acquainted with the proponents of the Celtic movement, who, in addition to Yeats and Rhys, included John Todhunter, Lionel Johnson, T. W. Rolleston, G. A. Greene (the club's secretary), and A. C. Hillier.[6] Mathews was to form lasting friendships with most of these men and was later to publish books by Todhunter, Yeats, Johnson, and Greene. When in 1891, at Yeats's suggestion, the Rhymers compiled and sought to publish an anthology of their poetry, they naturally turned to Mathews, who was gaining attention among the London literati as the publisher of finely printed, handsomely bound and illustrated limited edition books.[7]

The Book of the Rhymers' Club appeared in February 1892 and was followed two years later by *The Second Book of the Rhymers' Club*, both issued from the Bodley Head in small limited editions. Given the largely heterogeneous nature of the Club, neither the first nor the second of these anthologies was an expression of any particular literary or aesthetic mode, yet, thanks largely to Yeats's twelve contributions, both books contained a sizable group of poems meant to promote the Celtic literary movement. For example, several of Yeats's most famous early poems first appeared in book form in these anthologies, among them "The Lake Isle of Innisfree," "A Man Who Dreamed of Fairyland," "Father Gilligan," "The Folk of the Air," and "The Fiddler of Dooney." In addition to these, the Celtic movement was represented in three poems by Rhys—"The Wedding of Pale Bronwen," "Howel the Tall," and "To O.E."—and in two by Johnson: "To Morfydd" and "Celtic Speech." One other, "Arts Lough," was contributed by Greene.[8]

Mathews' ties with Yeats, in particular, were strengthened in 1893 when the publisher moved to Bedford Park, where, as we have seen, he took up residence next door to the Yeats family, which at the time still included the eldest son, Willie. During the years in which they were neighbors in the "arty" suburb,[9] the two families became close friends—one of the Mathews' sisters, Minnie, fell desperately in love with Willie, and Nest, Mathews' young daughter, was handed over the garden wall to be admired by the elder Yeats—and remained on cordial terms throughout their lives.

Although Mathews had sold Yeats's *The Wanderings of Oisin* and had published his poems in the Rhymers' Club books, he was especially anxious to add the increasingly well-known and influential young poet to his list of authors in the late summer of 1894, when, in the wake of the dissolution of his partnership with John Lane, he lost several writers who chose to follow Lane (along with the Bodley Head sign) to quarters opposite Mathews' in Albany. Mathews had strong support among the Rhymers in his battle with Lane over the firm's authors and sought to make the most of this by soliciting books from the club's members. Among several of those who responded positively was Yeats, whose first collected edition of poems was in the process of being published by T. Fisher Unwin. Yeats, anxious to help Mathews, declined Unwin's advice to include his new poetic drama, *The Shadowy Waters*—then, as Yeats thought, near completion—in the collected poems, writing Unwin that he had promised the play to Mathews, who "is a friend & a neighbour & I was glad to give him the book as he thought it would help him in the present crisis of his affairs." "Besides," Yeats continued, "he has a special public I would be glad to get at," suggesting that Mathews' artistically designed and handsomely produced books that appealed to the literati also predisposed the poet to the publisher's plea for help.[10] Mathews at the time courted Yeats by sending him copies of his latest productions—Selwyn Image's *Poems and Carols*, Lionel Johnson's *Poems*, and May Probyn's *Pansies*, for example—in hopes not only of securing his manuscripts for publication but also of obtaining possibly favorable reviews by Yeats in the *Bookman*.[11] Besides *The Shadowy Waters*, Yeats in the summer of 1894 also promised Mathews his new volume of poems, *The Wind among the Reeds*, and was thinking, as he told John O'Leary, of "going in to Elkin Mathews one of these days to arrange for a volume of Irish essays."[12]

Unfortunately for Mathews (who had listed both the play and the poems in his season's announcements in October 1894), Yeats had difficulties with the play and had to set it aside, and the preparation of his first collected edition of poems for Unwin (which included the rewriting of *The Wanderings of Oisin* and the expansion and alteration of *The Countess Kathleen*) preoccupied him through much of 1895, thus delaying work on *The Wind*. Moreover, other projects, including composing and compiling his stories for *The Secret Rose*, which appeared in April 1897, further postponed the publication of Yeats's new poems. That Mathews still expected to publish not only *The Wind* but *The Shadowy Waters* as late as June 1896 is indicated by the fact that he gave Yeats an advance of £4 on the royalties expected to accrue from the sales of both the play and the poems.[13]

It was probably early 1897 before Yeats gave his serious attention to readying *The Wind* for publication. Once he put his mind to it, the book's course was further complicated as well as delayed by an altercation between Mathews and Yeats which also involved Mathews' former partner, John Lane, over the American rights to the book. When the partnership between Mathews and Lane had been dissolved, Yeats had sided with Mathews, promising him the right to publish *The Wind*, which was to include all of his new poems written since 1892. Mathews at that time, it appears, drew up an agreement for the book which he sent Yeats, who, unwilling to sign it, threw it aside among some other papers. As a result, when Lane several years later—probably 1897—sought the American rights to *The Wind*, proposing to Yeats a plan whereby he would print the book through his New York branch of the Bodley Head and supply sheets to Mathews for the English edition, Mathews objected, arguing that the agreement which he had drawn up allowed him to dispose of the American rights. And although in his reply Yeats wrote, "If you are quite confident that American rights were set down in that 'agreement' I will not say they were not," he simply insisted that since he had not signed the agreement—"because I took a different view & did not wish to bind myself in matter of details until it became necessary to do so"—he was free to make, as he wrote,

> the best business arrangement for the American rights I can. They are, as you will see, absolutely in my hands. Mr. Lane has offered me very good terms—the same terms as you give me for England. I have no good reason to refuse them unless I get better. I cannot go to Mr. Lane & say,—as you already know "the American rights belong to me, but I will not give them to you because I will not." I sided with you as against Mr. Lane so far as to give you the ordinary English rights of this book—I cannot do more than that for to me he is simply a publisher who has offered certain terms.

Determined to have his way in the matter, Yeats tried to convince Mathews that "by the arrangement proposed by Mr. Lane, your small profits under the usual arrangement, will be compensated for by the much cheaper rate at which you will get the books. The best American printing, (and I will see that it is the best) is," he argued, "as good as possible." Continuing to placate Mathews, Yeats observed that at the time of the agreement in 1894 the manuscript of *The Wind* contained "some eighteen lyrics, the MS. of which was in your hands for a time. I have now in all some thirty-two or thirty-three lyrics and have added some prose essays of nearly equal importance. We have all, therefore, gained by the delay, at least if we can arrange things amicably as I have no doubt we will."[14]

Mathews under the circumstances had no alternative but to submit, remaining uneasy, feeling, no doubt, that he had reason to be wary of any deal involving his old partner. Nevertheless, at a meeting between the three principals at Lane's office, Mathews went along with Lane's plan to print *The Wind* in America. Out of Lane's presence, however, Mathews once again tried to scuttle the plan, writing under a sense of some urgency to Yeats and advising him not to part with the manuscript of the poems until Lane has come to an agreement in writing with me—as thinking over what he said the other day it may after all seem best to me to print the volume here and *be quite independent of all arrangements with him in regard to the production of the book.* You having agreed to forego £7.10.0 of your American royalties to me to help recoup my losses, has left the way open for him to copyright there—and even if it cost me more at the start—I fancy I should gain in the long run by having no complications with Lane.[15]

Yeats, unfortunately for Mathews, had already mailed part of the manuscript, writing his publisher the following day to express his regrets:

> I am sorry to say that in agreement with the arrangement made by us at Mr. Lane's I posted the first part of the MS. to Mr. Lane on Saturday night. You will remember that I asked you, at Mr. Lane's, if you agreed to the suggestion that I send him the MS.—I was anxious not to do so without your agreement.[16]

The proverbial die having been cast, Lane was free to proceed with his plan for *The Wind,* which called for the printing of the entire first edition at the University Press of H. O. Houghton and Company in Cambridge, Massachusetts, thus enabling Lane to avoid paying the rather formidable American tariff on imported books and thereby being able to offer Yeats a very favorable business arrangement for the American issue. The plan then called for the 500 English sets of sheets (with their specially prepared title page and no colophon) to be shipped to Mathews in London. That Mathews had supervised the artwork, however, led to the odd arrangement of having the binding of *The Wind* originate in England, with Mathews in all likelihood sending brasses and a roll of cloth to Lane's American branch.[17]

Mathews and Yeats had been at odds over the binding for *The Wind* for some time before its publication. Thinking in terms of a book which in its physical appearance would be worthy of its contents and reflect its Celtic subject matter—one, that is, comparable to the kind of books of verse he associated with Mathews—Yeats envisioned his new book of poems with an appropriate cover design and a frontis-piece. For these he chose an artist close to the Celtic movement, Althea Gyles, who had done the cover design for *The Secret Rose.* Much taken with her art during the nineties, Yeats wrote an article about her for the *Dome* in which he referred to "the beautiful lithe figures of her art" as "a beginning of what may become a new manner in the arts of the modern world."[18]

Mathews, however, appears to have opposed the artwork, perhaps in the belief that it was neither profitable nor necessary in the light of a decline in the early nineties' vogue for elaborately decorated books. Thinking in terms of a plain, simple, and inexpensive format for *The Wind* that was more in keeping with his practice as a publisher at the turn of the century, Mathews indicated his reluctance to make use of Miss Gyles's talents in his characteristically indirect way, that is, by simply not replying to her two letters of inquiry as to when her cover design would be required if *The Wind* was to be published in the spring of 1897. Yeats, then, having been appealed to by the artist, presumably settled matters when he advised his publisher: "It will make matters much simpler for us all if you answer her at once."[19]

Although Yeats prevailed in his desire to decorate *The Wind* with Gyles's binding design, Mathews apparently won out in his bid to keep costs down by eliminating the frontispiece: Gyles's pen drawing of Yeats, stylized, in the word of one critic, "as Rosicrucian mage blowing a rose petal."[20] Persisting in his determination to cut costs, Mathews had a proof of the binding design made up in yellow instead of the gilt previously agreed upon. When, however, he dispatched this to Yeats in the autumn of 1898, the poet was appalled and wrote Mathews a spirited letter of protest in which he declared:

First the colour and the cloth won't do. It is a colour I particularly dislike. The colour should be the same dark blue as my "Secret Rose." Secondly the yellow lines won't do. This cover is simply ugly. The lines should be in gold or the cover should be perfectly plain. I thought it was understood that the design was to be in gold. Please either get the design printed in gold or abolish it altogether, letting me know what the block has cost. Surely you must see yourself that it is absurd to print a book of verse of any kind of importance with the same kind of common stuff on the cover that you put on a novel. What you have to consider is whether you can do the things in gold, increasing the price of the book to 5/– if you like, though I should think this unnecessary. If not, print in a perfectly plain blue cover of the same sort as [William] Watson's "Father of the Forest." In either case please let me have another proof. I have the strongest objection to designs printed in yellow or any other colour or in anything except gold. The cover you sent me would do neither of us

78

credit. I believe on the other hand that if you make it a really charming book to look at you will help the book greatly.[21]

Yeats's assumption that his rather blunt letter would bring Mathews around to his way of thinking was—much to his surprise— proven wrong when several weeks later he learned that in speaking of "a perfectly plain blue cover" as an alternative, he had, in fact, given the publisher a perfect out. Mathews—as he had wanted to do all along—then proposed scrapping Gyles's design and bringing *The Wind* out in undecorated paper-covered boards. This, needless to say, provoked another letter in which Yeats admitted: "I should not have suggested the alternative of a plain cover. It would be very unfair to Miss Gyles who has done her work. We are indeed bound to her." "The book," he continued,

> is a good size—over 100 pages—& will have a better sale than either my collected poems or "The Secret Rose"—both which books have covers in gold & the expense of printing these books must have been much greater. I must therefore ask you to print this design in gold. I have written an article on Miss Gyles's work which is being published in the December "Dome" with five illustrations of her work. I think it may attract some attention & I am quite confident that her design will help my work if it is printed in the best way. The print in yellow I condemn absolutely.[22]

Having demanded to see "the new proof of the cover as soon as possible, whether you have decided to print in gold or quite plain,"[23] Yeats shortly received two different proofs, one in dark blue cloth with the design in gold and the other in blue-gray paper-covered boards with the design in black probably similar to the one later used as an alternate binding for the third English printing. Somewhat mollified, Yeats responded to the new proofs in a letter of 2 December 1898: "Many thanks for the cover[;] the gold one is of course the best but the other is really very good. Certainly much better than I expected."[24] Despite the fact that the way now lay open to Mathews to choose an inexpensive binding for *The Wind*, he ultimately ordered the first and second printings (produced simultaneously) bound in the dark blue cloth with Gyles's wraparound design stamped in gilt as Yeats clearly preferred.

It was probably after this debate over the binding for the ordinary issue of the first printing of *The Wind* that Charles Ricketts, the creator of beautiful binding designs for such books as Lord De Tabley's *Poems, Dramatic and Lyrical* and John Gray's *Silverpoints* (both published by Mathews and Lane in the early nineties), suggested to Yeats that *The Wind* also be issued in deluxe form in full vellum with Gyles's design in gilt.[25] The idea appealed to Yeats not only on aesthetic grounds but on economic grounds as well, prompting him then to suggest to Mathews that Gyles's design be printed on vellum copies only,[26] the idea being, as he later wrote, that "people will be all the more glad to buy the vellum copies if the design is not made common by printing it on all copies in some poorer way."[27] In other words, since the vellum copies sold for 12/6 and the ordinary copies for 3/6, it would be to the monetary advantage of both poet and publisher if more vellum copies were sold. Although this idea was not adopted at the time of the first printing, it was one which Yeats persisted in articulating.[28]

Despite Yeats's desire to make a radical distinction between the ordinary and deluxe copies of *The Wind*, the ordinary third printing of 1900 still was issued in dark blue cloth with Gyles's design in gold, as in the first and second printings; however, it was accompanied by an alternate binding style: blue-gray paper-covered boards with Gyles's design stamped in black—a clearly less ostentatious use of the design. It was not until the fourth printing of 1903 that Yeats's idea "to put the design in gold on a few vellum copies and to bind the ordinary copies in plain boards with a paper label" was finally adopted, the ordinary printing of 1903 being issued, according to Allan Wade, "in light mottled blue paper boards with buff linen spine, lettered in black on front cover, with a label, printed in black, pasted on the spine." The printing of 1907, as Wade points out, "is similar but in dark blue paper boards; that of 1911 is similar but in light blue."[29]

Although Mathews had hoped to have *The Wind* out the last week in January 1899, the book was not actually published until April, the first printing consisting of 500 copies.[30] According to Ricketts, only 12 full vellum copies of the deluxe edition were bound out of the 500.[31] As Yeats had argued, Gyles's elaborate wraparound design, composed mainly of reeds and leaves bending in the wind á la art nouveau and rising out of wavy horizontal lines representative of rippling water, made *The Wind* a delightful book to look at. The title at

Cover of W. B. Yeats's *The Wind among the Reeds* (1899), by Althea Gyles

81

the top of the front cover was balanced at the bottom by the author's name rising over a flamelike pattern highly reminiscent of one of Gyles's mentors—both spiritual and artistic—William Blake.

The further history of *The Wind* after its publication in April 1899 centers on Yeats's efforts to free the book first from Lane and later from Mathews for the purpose of consolidating his works in the hands of A. H. Bullen in England and Macmillan in America. As early as 1894, when he was negotiating with Unwin for the publication of the first collected edition of his poems, Yeats had begun to recognize that a collected edition of his works under the aegis of one publisher on each side of the Atlantic would be difficult, realizing even then, as he wrote Unwin, that "my prose & verse is so scattered between Lawrence & Bullen—who have some prose—you & Matthews [*sic*] that a collected edition is far off. I can but keep the way clear for it & have accordingly made such arrangements with both Matthews & Lawrence & Bullen that I can bring my books together with little trouble when the time come[s]. I must ask you to make a like arrangement & to draw up such an agreement as to make the book return to me *unconditionally at the end of a term of years.*"[32]

Although Yeats thought, as he told Unwin, that he had made arrangements with his publishers that would enable him to bring the works together with little trouble when the time came, he was later to learn differently. He had trouble not only with Unwin, but also with Mathews and, in particular, with Lane. Having tossed aside Mathews' written agreement of 1894, Yeats failed subsequently to put anything in writing, not even the details of his and Mathews' arrangement with the notoriously wily Lane for the American rights. Consequently, when in February 1904 Yeats, traveling in America, decided to begin "discussing preliminaries" with Macmillan for the publication of a collected edition of his works in the States, the poet found himself at odds with Lane over the duration of the American rights. Since there was no legal document specifically stating the term of Lane's hold on the American copyright, Yeats, on the advice of his literary agent, A. P. Watt, found himself appealing to Mathews for a letter "stating your recollection of the arrangement we made with John Lane about my book."[33] Mathews, glad of an opportunity to "hit" Lane (Yeats's later suspicion), complied, submitting to Watt a letter which stated that American rights to *The Wind* held by Lane were of the same duration as his own, *that is*, seven years. But since Lane refused to acknowledge this, Yeats was forced to turn to the Society of Authors, which then advised him that since the arrangement with Lane from a legal standpoint had been made through Mathews, it was incumbent on the publisher to deal with Lane. Yeats, recognizing that all depended on Mathews, again had to appeal to him, rather histrionically writing, "You are my sheet anchor and I will be very much obliged if you would write to Lane for the accounts [of *The Wind*]. You will see that not only did A. Watt but the Society of Authors consider that you are the fitting person to do this, the agreement being with you. I will be very much obliged if you will do this at once, as I want to get my collected American edition out in the autumn."[34]

Mathews did contact Lane, who in September 1905 replied that he would write his New York office immediately and advise Mathews as soon as possible. But as late as July 1906 nothing seems to have been resolved when Lane again wrote Mathews to say that since the Bodley Head's offer to sell the plates of *The Wind* to Macmillan for its collected edition had been declined, "Mr. Yeats cannot remove the book without he makes some provisions for my interest in it. Consequently the matter is still in abeyance."[35] The matter was concluded when Mathews—again at Yeats's urging—appealed to the Society of Authors, which, on the basis of Mathews' testimony in his letter to Watt, got the book out of Lane's hands.[36]

In the autumn of 1905, as the term of his rights to the English edition of *The Wind* neared its end, Mathews was approached by Yeats with a request to allow Bullen to include *The Wind* along with the poet's more recent verse in a new volume. Mathews, no more disposed than Lane to let the book go, doubtless saw in Yeats's plans a means of extending his control over *The Wind*, and proposed to allow Bullen to include *The Wind* in the new volume if his rights to publish the book were extended and if Bullen were willing to share with him a certain percentage of the new volume's profits. Since this proposal if accepted would have raised the price of the book as well as extended Mathews' control over *The Wind* beyond the original term, Yeats concluded that it would be unwise to accept Mathews' proposal. "If we agree to make the book 8/6, and not less than 7/6 for five years after 1907," he wrote Bullen, we tie our hands very seriously when the time comes for you to have all my books. It would make any kind of a popular edition impossible. It would be better I think either to buy out Mathews, which I daresay you won't think worth while, or to publish the present book without the lyrics from the *Wind among the Reeds* volume at say 5/-. It would be practically a volume of new work. . . . And it will be a great matter to have an entirely free hand in 1907.[37]

But by February 1906 Yeats had changed his mind about excluding *The Wind*, observing to Bullen that "when I wrote to you about it I was inclined to think that *The Wind among the Reeds* poems were in a mood so different from these later poems that they would be no great help, but so many people have asked me will it contain those lyrics that I suppose I was wrong." Consequently, he inquired:

> Would it be worth while making another attempt to get *The Wind among the Reeds* out of Mathews? I don't think it is any use—[Frank] Sidgwick [Bullen's partner] going, for [Mathews] has a quarrel on with Sidgwick about some book of I think Bliss Carman's [*Ballads and Lyrics* published by Bullen in 1902]. I am so disinclined to go again, as the failure of my last negociation was [sic] rather spoils my chances, but we could try him with A. P. Watt. Some months have now passed since I saw Mathews with Sidgwick, and Mathews's term with the book is so much nearer its end. It occurs to me that we might offer him whatever sum he is accustomed to make in a year of it and something more. This sum to be calculated on the average of the last three years, like the Income Tax people. I suppose he would be content to estimate his own profits as the same amount I get out of the book. The sum isn't very considerable and we could let him go on selling the book. If you think well of it I will see A. P. Watt when I get to London. I think Mathews is striking at his own interest to some extent out of spite over the Bliss Carman book and because he is cross at my book passing out of his hands at all. A letter from A. P. Watt might persuade him to look at the matter from a business point of view alone.[38]

If Watt wrote Mathews conveying Yeats's ideas, it came to nothing, for in June 1906 (shortly before the publication of *Poems, 1899–1905*) Bullen replied to an inquiry from Mathews as to the status of the matter, informing Mathews that Yeats's "new volume has been on the stocks for an unconscionable time. There seems to have been a good deal of misunderstanding in regard to 'The Wind among the Reeds.' I should prefer this new volume to be issued without 'The Wind among the Reeds,' and I think that Yeats now takes this view."[39]

Despite the fact that *Poems, 1899–1905* appeared (as its title suggests) without *The Wind*, which fact supposedly left Yeats with "an entirely free hand" in 1907, Mathews got an extension of his rights to the volume out of Bullen, and this enabled him to publish another printing of *The Wind* in 1907. And Mathews, finding it convenient now to fall in with Yeats's contention that there was no agreement for *The Wind*, only his memory of the arrangements, continued to gain advantages from the easygoing Bullen, whom Yeats—always concerned about maneuverability—cautioned against making deals with Mathews and Unwin which might stand in the way of popular editions of his books "if they are found desirable." Accusing Mathews of "telling lies about that agreement [re *The Wind*]," Yeats continued: "I will tell you this not because I am likely to object or that Watt is likely to object to any arrangement you make, but because there is no reason why Elkin Mathews, drunk or sober, should bully you into giving him better terms than you want to give by pretending there is no agreement. You can write to A. P. Watt and tell him that I have no objection to two years' extension on the understanding that Mathews 'takes fifty sets of the collected edition at half price' if he [Watt] has no objection."[40] As a result of further arrangements with Mathews, Bullen was able to include *The Wind* in the collected edition of Yeats's poems of 1908 and in *Poems: Second Series*, published in 1910. Mathews issued a fifth printing of *The Wind* in 1907 and a sixth in 1911 as well as a further American printing in the same year. Although Yeats continued to be "a little anxious" about Bullen's arrangements with Mathews and Unwin, his fears that Bullen would give Mathews more than his rightful share of the profits from *The Wind* and continue to extend Mathews' rights to the book appear not to have been realized.[41]

Although Mathews and Yeats did not develop a long and fruitful relationship as publisher and poet, Mathews' publication of *The Wind among the Reeds* must be seen as one of his major achievements. Not only was the book distinctive in its format and design, but it was significant in its content. The culminating achievement of the Symbolist movement in England in the nineties, *The Wind*, in the opinion of Richard Ellmann, "set the method for the modern movement, as in 1798 Wordsworth's and Coleridge's *Lyrical Ballads* shaped the Romantic Movement."[42] Besides, it was the finest volume of poetry produced by the Celtic movement, exploiting as only Yeats could the special mix of symbols and Celtic lore which is characteristic of the literature at its best. Through the continued use of the symbolic Rose in poems such as "Aedh Tells of the Rose in His Heart," and Celtic legend in such poems as "The Hosting of the Sidhe," Yeats gave definitive expression to the theme of world-weariness so central to the literature of the movement, that yearning for a dim, green world of past innocence and loveliness where "your image that blossoms a rose in the deeps of my heart" was no longer wronged by "unshapely things." And in verse such as "The Song of the Wandering Aengus," the magical mix of imagery, tone, language, and lore produced the ultimate evocation of Celtic Twilight, that moment of white moths and mothlike stars in which Aengus "dropped the berry in a stream / And caught a little silver star."

Mathews' association with the Celtic movement and its most distinguished figure also resulted in the publication of one other of Yeats's books, *The Tables of the Law and The Adoration of the Magi.* "The Adoration of the Magi" had originally been scheduled to be one of the stories in Yeats's volume *The Secret Rose,* but it was excluded because the publisher, A. H. Bullen, was uncertain about the reception of a piece dealing rather unorthodoxly with a religious subject. Consequently, it was combined with "The Tables of the Law" and privately printed in June 1897.

After apparently having failed to rile the Victorian bourgeoisie, the book appeared some seven years later as number 17 in Mathews' Vigo Cabinet series. Work on the little book had begun in the autumn of 1903, when Mathews secured a copy of the privately printed edition from Bullen and left it at Yeats's rooms in Euston Road with instructions to make his "additions and corrections and let me have them back as soon as possible."[43] Shortly after, on 3 November, Yeats returned the book with corrections and a short preface written out in pencil on the back of Mathews' note stating that the two stories would not have been reprinted "had I not met a young man in Ireland the other day who liked them very much, and nothing else at all that I have written."[44] Although scholars have assumed that the "young man" was James Joyce—who, according to Ellmann, knew "The Tables of the Law" by heart—Robert O'Driscoll has produced evidence that the person to whom Yeats referred probably was P. S. O'Hegarty.[45]

As in the case of the *The Wind*, there appears to have been some doubt as to whether or not a contract for *The Tables of the Law* existed, for when Yeats returned proof sheets to Mathews in the spring of 1904, he confessed that he could not remember whether he and Mathews had a formal agreement. However that may be, he wrote, "I believe my edition with you was not to interfere with my right to incorporate these stories with other stories of mine at some later time."[46] *The Tables of the Law* was published in June 1904 in an ordinary printing bound in dark blue paper wrappers and selling for a shilling, as well as in a deluxe printing on slightly thicker paper and bound in blue-gray paper boards with buff linen spine, lettered in black. Mathews reprinted the book in brown paper wrappers in 1905. According to Wade, copies appeared later in green cloth with eight pages of advertisements containing Mathews' list for 1909 bound in at the back.[47]

Referred to by Yeats as "half prophecy of a very veiled kind,"[48] *The Tables of the Law and The Adoration of the Magi* is, according to Linda Dowling, like *The Secret Rose* itself, in the tradition of the so-called "fatal books" much in vogue in the late nineteenth century. Describing the volume as "another inverted Bible," Dowling goes on to characterize it as "a gospel of antinomianism, with one part devoted to a rewritten Decalogue and another to a geographically and morally relativistic survey of human laws."[49] Both stories, then, like "Rosa Alchemica," are apocalyptic annunciations of a new dispensation and therefore are part of Yeats's design to create, in the words of Ellmann, "a secret spiritual propaganda in Ireland," the purpose of which was to bring about the return of the gods and "the ancient things."[50]

LIONEL JOHNSON

Yeats, as we know, not only worked assiduously to propagandize and popularize the Celtic cause through his own work, but he also was tireless in his efforts to seek out and encourage other promising young writers of Irish descent—either real or imaginary. Ann Saddlemyer has observed that Yeats, "like all successful autocrats inclined to create, alter, or discard on the sincerity of the moment, . . . was willing to extend his interpretation of Anglo-Irish letters not only to embrace his good friends Lionel Johnson and Arthur Symons, but to sense an undefined Celtic sympathy even in such opposite forces as William Blake and Maurice Maeterlinck."[51] One of the promising and eager young aficionados of the Celtic cause whom Yeats recruited and assisted as well as learned from was, as Saddlemyer notes, Lionel Johnson, an Englishman who sought to divorce himself from the materialistic, bourgeois world of Victorian England by throwing himself zealously, in the fashion of the convert, into the cause both of Celticism and Catholicism. Although Johnson claimed in a letter to T. W. Rolleston that "my people lived in Ireland for about two centuries, and became as usual Hibernis Hiberniores: I have endless swarms of Irish relatives; and I am connected with Yeats, which ought to be enough of itself to make me Irish,"[52] his ties, in truth, with Ireland and the Celtic race were few: a great-grandfather, Sir Henry Johnson, who had once been governor of Ross Castle in Ireland and had commanded the British forces at New Ross in the Irish Rebellion of 1798, and a Welsh grandmother on his father's side. Johnson, nevertheless, while a student at Winchester School, had felt a spiritual kinship with the Celtic peoples as early as his reading of Matthew Arnold's seminal lectures collected as *On the Study of Celtic Literature.* His interest in things Celtic was further stimulated when in the summer of 1884 his family took up residence near Mold, Flintshire, Wales, where during his vacations from school he responded with enthusiasm to the wilder aspect of the Welsh landscape, associating it in his earliest poems with the spiritual melancholy so characteristic of the Celtic Twilight.

Johnson's active engagement in the Celtic movement, however, dates from 1889, when he first knew Yeats. Attempting, according to Ian Fletcher, "to strike a balance between a somewhat coarse popular opinion in Ireland and what he saw as an ideal for national literature," Yeats sensed in Johnson an ally who with his exalted concept of art and his high-minded zeal for the cause would be valuable "in [Yeats's] struggle with Sir Charles Gavan Duffy and those who wished to prolong the tradition of the Young Ireland movement of the 1840's, with its narrowly patriotic verse and its blunt rhythms."[53] Consequently, Yeats—soon after Johnson's arrival in London from Oxford in 1890—introduced his friend and admirer to the Irish Literary Society, in the work of which Johnson became a devoted participant, lecturing not only in London but in Dublin and Belfast on literature and its relationship to the Celtic movement. For example, in a speech first made before the Irish Literary Society entitled "Poetry and Patriotism," Johnson, like Yeats, eloquently argued for a wider conception of Irish literature than that espoused by the poets of Young Ireland, urging that "if we are to foster, encourage, and develop Irish literature, and not least of all, Irish poetry, it must be with a wise generosity; in a finely national, not in a pettily provincial, spirit."[54]

During the early nineties, Johnson was writing his best poetry, some of it in the service of the Celtic cause; and like other Celts in the Rhymers' Club, he included several pieces in its anthologies, the well-known "To Morfydd" appearing in *The Second Book of the Rhymers' Club*. Increasingly pained by the fact that while his friends Yeats and Symons had published a volume of verse, he had not, Johnson was anxious to see one of his own in print. Since Mathews and Lane were in the process of publishing his critical study *The Art of Thomas Hardy*, Johnson naturally turned to the Bodley Head when in early 1894 his manuscript of poems was ready for submission. "After rejecting more than a hundred poems," Johnson informed Lane in a letter accompanying the manuscript, "I have made an absolutely final selection of less than an hundred," which should, he imagined, "make a book of nearer two hundred pages than two hundred and fifty." Seeking to pin down the publisher to a definite date, Johnson inquired, "Can you give me a positive decision [on the manuscript] by the first of March?"[55] When he had heard nothing from Lane some two weeks after his March deadline, Johnson wrote again, clearly expressing impatience:

> Please let me have an answer about my poems, by the *first of May*: that is two weeks [i.e., months] later than I first asked. I want them to be accepted and published, this year, or, rejected by you at once, so that I may try my luck elsewhere. I can't let them go hanging on and hanging on, for an indefinite time. If you really can't give me an answer by *first* of

89

May, I must withdraw them, and go elsewhere: which I should be sorry to do. I see that Hardy is put off to May. That I don't mind: but I am keen [?] about the poems, and want a definite reply: I am entirely in earnest about this. I would rather be rejected at once, than published this time next year. Please let me know.[56]

Appeased by what he considered to be a "most gratifying and satisfactory letter" from the publishers,[57] Johnson set about waiting for some positive results. But once again after another long delay, he was constrained to write Lane, asking for news and reminding him of what he had said in his last letter (presumably the gratifying reply to his inquiry of mid-March): "Any news? In the firm's last letter you said, you hoped Hardy would be out 'long before May'. This is June, and your new list makes no mention of it. It will be too absurd, if it is put off til the autumn. And the poems? You wrote, that they should go to press on the appearance of it.: but if H. is to be indefinitely delayed, I shall have to send the poems elsewhere: I am determined to have them, at least, out this year. Please tell me how things stand."[58] Increasingly exasperated as the summer of 1894 wore on, Johnson in yet another letter to his publishers detailed his reasons for urging prompt publication of his poems: he believes more strongly in his verse than in his prose; Pater has praised them; he has other work ready for publication; a volume of his poems has been continuously announced for the last two years.[59] But nothing he could do seems to have moved the Bodley Head to action, prompting one to speculate, as no doubt Johnson did, about the long delays which bedeviled the publication of both *The Art of Thomas Hardy* and the poems.

One possible reason may lie in the fact that Johnson's poetry manuscript fell into the hands of Richard Le Gallienne, Johnson's fellow Rhymer and the Bodley Head's chief reader, who duly filed a report which damned the poems with faint praise even though it affirmed that the "devotion to learning, the scholastic passion—finely celebrated in the dedicatory poem to Winchester" pervading the whole volume are "a rare quality at present."[60] Since Le Gallienne was Lane's man, his lack of enthusiasm for Johnson's poems may have prompted Lane to stall their publication. A more plausible reason is that Lane, who had promised to provide a bibliography of Hardy's works for Johnson's critical study, kept delaying the book through his inability to complete the task, either for want of time or inclination.[61]

90

Since Lane had linked the publication of the poems to the appearance of the *Hardy*, they, too, were put off.

Then, of course, with the approach of late summer, Johnson became, as Fletcher surmises, the "victim of those difficulties in temperament and method which were to dissolve the partnership between Lane and Mathews."[62] There can be little doubt that the dissolution of the partnership at the close of September 1894, and the struggle between the partners for the firm's authors, had a good deal to do with the excessive length of time it took to produce Johnson's *Art of Thomas Hardy* and the poems. For instance, even after Lane apparently had completed his bibliography, he was urging Johnson to put off publication of *Hardy* until the autumn, a suggestion Johnson refused to entertain: "I shall be delighted to hear . . . that the bibliography is done, and in Constable's [the printer's] hands. I repeat that I cannot listen to any suggestion about publication in the autumn. Upon that I am absolutely decided and resolved. Mathews has no objection. So please let us get the book clean off our hands at once, and have no more bother: we must be all sick of it. I consider you bound to agree, in justice to myself."[63] That Lane continued to press for delay even after having completed his bibliography suggests that his purpose now was to postpone publication of *Hardy* until after the dissolution of the partnership, and this is substantially confirmed in a letter of 17 September in which Mathews informed Johnson of Lane's intentions.[64] And even though by this time an agreement had been worked out under which Johnson's critical study of Hardy and all future prose works would be published by Lane and his forthcoming volume of poetry and all future books of verse would be published by Mathews,[65] Lane continued to insist on the postponement. Ultimately Lane prevailed; *The Art of Thomas Hardy* did not appear in print until early October 1894, after the dissolution. But since in a letter of 19 September Johnson had told Mathews that he particularly desired his "book to appear under the name of the [old] firm, not of Lane alone,"[66] the Hardy study bore the imprint of both Elkin Mathews and John Lane. The fact that Lane had taken over the book was indicated in some copies by a pasted-in label (which Lane also inserted in other books) stating: "This book is now published by John Lane at the Bodley Head in Vigo St. London W."

With *Hardy* in print, the way was paved for the belated publication of Johnson's poems. Having often made clear to Mathews and Lane that he considered his poetry more important that his prose, Johnson not surprisingly sought, like Yeats, to provide his poems with a fitting format. On coming up to London in 1890, Johnson had lived at 20 Fitzroy Street in an Adam building dating from the late eighteenth century known as "the Fitzroy Settlement," home to the Century Guild, a Morris-inspired gathering of architects, artists, designers, and poets dedicated to the rehabilitation of the arts. Here Johnson had come to know one of the guild's founders, Herbert P. Horne, who had won celebrity as the editor of that beautifully designed and finely printed journal of the arts *The Century Guild Hobby Horse*. Horne had also distinguished himself in the early nineties as a designer of books, including Arthur Symons' *Silhouettes* (which the Bodley Head had published in 1892) and his own exquisite little volume of verse, *Diversi Colores*. Naturally enough, Johnson turned to Horne for the title-page decoration, colophon device, and typographical design of his book of poems. Informal discussions between designer, poet, and publisher concerning the volume's general design, type, and paper evidently were going on as early as September, when Johnson informed Mathews: "As to poems, whatever Horne says is right."[67] Among suggestions entertained was Mathews' desire to provide the book with a frontispiece of its author drawn by Will Rothenstein, whose remarkable series of drawings gathered under the title *Oxford Characters* recently had been published by the Bodley Head. Johnson, however, rejected the idea, conveying his views to Rothenstein in a charming note: "A portrait in my book would be too great a vanity, even for me. Wait till the Laureateship is mine, or—don't be insulted—the P.R.A. is yours. I am explaining to Mathews, that the very portrait itself would blush: which is undesirable for a lithograph by you. Only Academicians' portraits ought to blush. Seriously, in a first volume of verse, it would be a little absurd: greatly as I should appreciate the honour of immortality from your hands. You must give it me later."[68] Another focus of discussion was Horne's idea to use taller than usual capital letters at the beginning of poetic lines, an innovation which after some hesitation Johnson was willing to accept: "As to the caps.," he wrote Mathews, "I leave the question to you and Horne: at first, I did not altogether take to them: but by reading through the whole proofs, many times, I grew to like them, and hardly to notice anything odd or unusual in them. And the public will probably do the same."[69]

Despite these ongoing discussions, neither a date for publishing the poems had been set nor Mathews' final go-ahead to Horne had been given when in November Johnson wrote Mathews that "Horne is waiting, I believe, to hear from you, before going on in any way with his work upon my book." Reminding Mathews of Horne's penchant for taking a long time over his work, Johnson averred that if the book "is to be out this side of Christmas, [Horne] must be urged to go on at once." Willing to leave what he called "the printing question" in Mathews' hands for decision, Johnson nevertheless made it clear that he was in favor of Horne's "already used type." Concluding, Johnson asked: "Will you communicate with [Horne], suggesting a date for publication, that he may be obliged to set to work upon title-page, etc.? Otherwise," he warned, "there will be great delays."[70] As Johnson had feared, "great delays" inevitably developed in connection with Horne's work making it impossible to bring out the poems "this side of Christmas." In fact, it was not until the middle of February that Horne finally completed his work on the plate for the title page and dispatched it to the engraver, informing Mathews, with just a hint of hurt feelings in his tone, that "there need now be no further delays so far as I am concerned."[71]

Although its publication had been announced in a November issue of the *Academy* for "early in the new year,"[72] Johnson's *Poems* was not published in England until March 1895 and in America until April, the title page bearing the imprint of Elkin Mathews in London, and Copeland and Day in Boston. A printing of 25 numbered copies bound in reddish-brown polished linen boards and lettered in gold on the spine, in which the entire statement of limitation was written out and signed by the author, preceded the ordinary printing of 750 copies for England and America, which was bound in grayish-blue paper-covered boards and lettered in black on the spine. Printed at the Chiswick Press on laid paper and bound with edges uncut, *Poems* immediately took its rightful place among the truly distinctive books of the nineties. Horne's beautifully designed hand-lettered title page, featuring an old woodcut of a Winchester School emblem, caught quite remarkably the chaste, somewhat austere tone of Johnson's verse. Among other notable elements of Horne's design was the placement (as in Symons' *Silhouettes*) of the page numbers in the table of contents immediately after the titles and the use in the ordinary printing of tall capitals at the beginning of poetic lines.[73]

Poems includes all the verse by which Johnson is usually known today—"By the Statue of King Charles at Charing Cross," "Plato in London," "Mystic and Cavalier," "The Dark Angel," and "The Church of a Dream"—but it also contains numerous poems which evoke what Oscar Wilde called the "pathos of things" which he associated with "us who are Celts" and "comes from our quickened sense of the beauty of life".[74] These include "To Morfydd" (which has been called the "most celtic verses" Johnson ever wrote), "A Cornish Night," "Moel Fammau," and "Gwynedd," which in its Pan-Celtic sweep, evokes powerfully an ancient world of melancholy loveliness:

> Desolate Cornwall, desolate Brittany,
> Are up in vehement wind and vehement wave:
> Ancient delights are on their ancient sea,
> And nature's violent graces waken there;
> And there goes loveliness about the grave,
> And death means dreaming, not life's long despair.

Interestingly, *Poems* also include "Parnell" and "Ireland's Dead," verse markedly political in content and radical in tone which reminds one more of the poetry of Young Ireland than that of the Celtic Twilight. Johnson's practice was not always in accord with his precepts, especially those which he held in common with Yeats and which he had expressed so eloquently in his lecture "Poetry and Patriotism." As he became more zealous in the Irish cause from 1893 onward, Johnson was increasingly given to poetry written, according to Yeats, "in the manner of the 'popular schools,'" which "'mixed up' with poetry religious and political opinions"[75]—the very kind of verse to which Yeats as leader of the Celtic movement in literature was so strenuously opposed. Consequently, in his essays dealing with Johnson's poetry, Yeats always focused his attention on what he called Johnson's "pure" poetry and either ignored his rhetorical effusions (as he did in "Three Irish Poets") or relegated them to a lesser status, as in "Mr. Lionel Johnson's Poems."[76]

The same disjunction persists in Johnson's second book of poetry, *Ireland, with Other Poems*, a volume in which the political verse full of rhetoric and dogma has increased proportionately to that expressive of "soul." In his review of the volume for the *Bookman*, Yeats used as his touchstone Arthur Henry Hallam's "On Some of the Characteristics of Modern Poetry" (an essay which had become very popular among Yeats and his fellow Rhymers) because it "defines," Yeats wrote, "more perfectly than any other criticism in English the issues in that war of schools which is troubling all the arts, and gradually teaching us to rank such 'reflections' of the mind as rhetorical and didactic verse, painted anecdotes, pictures 'complicated with ideas' that are not pictorial ideas, below poetry and painting that mirror the 'multiplied' and 'minute' and 'diversified' 'sensation' of the body and the soul."[77]

As Yeats is aware, *Ireland*, like the earlier *Poems*, exhibits Johnson's predisposition to write both kinds of poetry and therefore to take both sides in the "war." On the one hand in poems like "To Morfydd Dead," "The Faith," "An Ideal," "Westward," and "Evening in Wales," Johnson, Yeats observes, "has made for himself a twilight world where all the colours are like the colours in the rainbow, that is cast by the moon, and all the people as far from modern tumults as the people upon fading and dropping tapestries." In these poems, Johnson "is the poet of those peaceful, unhappy souls who, in the symbolism of a living Irish visionary, are compelled to inhabit when they die a shadowy island paradise in the West, where the moon always shines, and a mist is always on the face of the moon, and a music of many sighs always in the air, because they renounced the joy of the world without accepting the joy of God."[78] But on the other hand there is the title poem, "Ireland," a longish rhetorical poem of 275 lines, along with numerous others such as "Ninety-Eight," "To the Dead of '98," and "Christmas in Ireland" which Yeats relegates to "those Irish papercovered books of more or less political poetry which are the only imaginative reading of so many young men in Ireland."[79]

Ireland, with Other Poems was printed at the Chiswick Press on laid paper and bound in light bluish-gray paper-covered boards, lettered in black on the spine. As had been the case with both *Hardy* and *Poems*, Johnson had this book "ready for the press a long time" before it finally reached publication. Anxious to hurry Mathews along, Johnson, in a January 1897 letter to the publisher wrote: "I have been, and am, so busy, that I can fix no date, by which my essays will be ready:

but, if you would publish the poems in the spring, I could promise the essays for the autumn."[80] But delays plagued the publication of *Ireland*, Johnson, at one point exclaiming in exasperation to Louise Imogen Guiney, "But that maddening miniature of a publisher, Elkin Mathews, delays all things."[81] It was not until the autumn that Johnson (perhaps with the help of Olivia Shakespear, to whom he was related) corrected the first proofs. Despite a delay ironically caused by his own absent-mindedness (Johnson having mailed the corrected proofs to a wrong address), *Ireland, with Other Poems* was published by Mathews in London in November 1897 and by Copeland and Day in Boston in April 1898 in an edition of 300 copies for England and America.[82]

Like *Poems* a potpourri of his various categories of verse, *Ireland* was the last book Johnson saw through the press. Although he had planned to publish through Mathews a volume of his miscellaneous critical essays, delays in bringing out *Ireland* and his increasingly ill health and early death in 1902 closed his career as poet and critic. However, Mathews, who counted himself among Johnson's closest friends and held his work in the highest esteem, was determined to keep Johnson's reputation alive and almost single-handedly promoted Johnson's work during the first two decades of this century.[83] Having purchased from Johnson's executors the remaining stock and copyrights of both *Poems* and *Ireland* shortly after the poet's death,[84] Mathews was contemplating the publication of a selection of verse from both volumes in his Vigo Cabinet series as early as 1904 when he was approached by Yeats, who proposed to issue a selection of Johnson's poems from his sister's Dun Emer Press.[85] Although Mathews considered issuing simultaneously the Dun Emer Press edition and a Vigo Cabinet series edition (being of the opinion, as he wrote Yeats, that such a course would not be "injurious to the former, that being intended primarily for the collector"), he decided to let Yeats proceed with the Dun Emer Press edition, which, he concluded, "would be an aid to the issue of a popular one [i.e., one in the Vigo Cabinet series] later."[86] As a result of Mathews' decision, *Twenty-One Poems by Lionel Johnson* was issued from the Dun Emer Press in 1904, followed by Mathews' own *Selection from the Poems of Lionel Johnson* (which included some previously uncollected poems and a prefatory memoir by Clement Shorter) in October 1908 and *Some Poems of*

Lionel Johnson (a new selection which included an obituary essay by Louise Imogen Guiney) in February 1912—both published as number 34 in the Vigo Cabinet series.

These, however, were merely incidental to Mathews' plans ultimately to publish the complete works of Johnson in several volumes, the first of which to be issued was a collection of prose.[87] Entitled *Post Liminium: Essays and Critical Papers*, the volume nominally was edited by an American academic, Thomas Whittemore, who in the nineties had been a friend of the poet Louise Imogen Guiney, a central figure (along with the young publisher Fred Holland Day) in a Boston coterie devoted to the English Pre-Raphaelites and the poets of the nineties.[88] A graduate student at Harvard University and an instructor in English at Tufts College, Whittemore in the later nineties shared Guiney's admiration for Johnson's work and gained an introduction to the poet through Guiney (who had met Johnson in 1895) in the summer of 1899 while on a visit to England. Johnson, who at the time was recovering from another siege of illness, wrote Whittemore apologizing for not having acknowledged his "most welcome card, and Miss Guiney's kind introduction," and going on to invite him to his rooms, at which time they could "fix a day when you can dine with me."[89] Despite the fact that Whittemore soon after deserted literature for a career as archaeologist and art historian, it was to him that Guiney turned when in 1910 Mathews, with her help, decided to publish Johnson's prose pieces. Whittemore, having agreed to edit the book and write a preface, promptly set off on an expedition to the upper Nile, where for many months he was practically incommunicado. Consequently, Guiney—perhaps not unwillingly—undertook to do most of the work on the volume.

An interesting series of letters from Guiney to Mathews in the Princeton University Library detail her behind-the-scenes editing as well as her painstaking and time-consuming efforts to make *Post Liminium* the kind of volume she thought Johnson would have wished it to be. Having just returned from Belgium to England bringing "all the half-sorted mass" of Johnson's manuscripts with her, Guiney was "ready to tackle them" in October 1910 in an effort to get the essays and critical papers ready for the press.[90] Incredibly, within a month she had provided Mathews with "the material for an estimate" of the length and proposed costs of the volume, "complete, save for the minor things, like the Table of Contents and Mr. Whittemore's Preface."[91] Once proofs arrived in late April 1911, Guiney not only carefully read and corrected them but in consultation with Mathews made most of the editorial decisions. With Whittemore—"our fly away friend"—in "farthest Egypt" in the spring, Guiney also had the added burden of keeping track of the peripatetic editor, funneling both ideas and material for the book to and from him.[92]

By the early autumn of 1911, all the elements for *Post Liminium* were assembled at last, Guiney having received the final efforts of Whittemore's toil, which she then reported on to Mathews: "I have 'sailed' vigorously into the Preface, as you will see, and the Dedication I have clean thrown out. It wasn't right; in fact, it was grammatically demented, through haste, perhaps. This one will say what was meant." Fittingly the dedicatee, Guiney went on to observe: "Isn't it humorous for me to revise thus a dedication to myself? Lucky for me that I am so old a friend of T.W.'s! for he is always amiable and reasonable."[93] The only visible link between Guiney and *Post Liminium*, the rewritten dedication read: "Ludovicae Imogen Guiney / huius libris scriptori / curatorique / carissimae / superstes / D.D.D. / T.W."

Published in December 1911, *Post Liminium* was bound in dark green cloth over boards with beveled edges, lettered in gilt on the spine, the book bearing (like *Poems*) Horne's Winchester School emblem on the title page. A second impression (uniform with the first) was published by Mathews in 1912. Among the forty-one separate prose pieces which made up its contents was the important lecture "Poetry and Patriotism in Ireland." Two others concerned Irish personalities: Johnson's review of R. Barry O'Brien's *Life of Charles Stewart Parnell* and his essay on the writer Clarence Mangan.

Mathews apparently intended the complete poems to follow shortly as the second volume of Johnson's works, but unfortunately, he relied on the assistance of one of Johnson's companions from his Oxford days, Arthur Galton, whose book *Two Essays upon Matthew Arnold* had been published by Mathews in 1897. Lacking the energy and sense of commitment which Guiney possessed, Galton appears to have been dilatory in carrying out his duties as Johnson's literary executor, moving Mathews to complain to Clement Shorter in a letter of 1913: "Johnson's complete poems should have been done long since, but next year *they will appear*—with or *without* Mr. Galton's assistance. Mr. G. does not seem to think procrastination matters!"[94] In the end, Mathews, having enlisted the help of Ezra Pound and Dorothy Shakespear to deal with the text and read proof, published the *Poetical Works of Lionel Johnson* in late October 1915, with Pound's preface.[95] The Chiswick Press printed 1,500 sets of sheets, of which 900 were used for the American issue. A "second thousand," bound in light gray paper-covered boards and lettered on the spine in black, was published in London by Mathews and in New York by Macmillan in 1917.[96]

Since serious objections very quickly arose to Pound's preface (in which he rejected the poets of the nineties, ironically using Johnson's unpublished critical notes to reinforce his own views), Macmillan refused to print the preface in the American issue of *Poetical Works*, and Mathews, according to Pound, withdrew it from as many copies of the first English issue as possible "in excited haste . . . due to pressure from the howly or howlink cawfliks. . . . They scared Mathews, threatening non sale of vol to all the pious who had boomed Lionel on acc/ his RRRRomanism so called. . . . I don't imagine any save the advance sales of the L. Jon have the preface. I believe Elkin even had bound copies unbound in order to efface it." As a consequence of Mathews' action, Ifan Kyrle Fletcher, the bookseller to whom Pound wrote his account, was of the opinion that "not more than a dozen" copies of *Poetical Works* with Pound's preface survived.[97]

In addition to these two volumes of Johnson's prose and poetic works, Mathews published a volume of poems selected by George F. Engelbach from *Poetical Works* entitled *The Religious Poems of Lionel Johnson*, with a preface by Wilfrid Meynell and title page dated 1916, and a supplementary volume of Johnson's prose, *Reviews and Critical Papers*, edited with an introduction by Robert Shafer in June 1921.[98]

JOHN MILLINGTON SYNGE

When Johnson died in 1902, Yeats already had entered what he later perceived to be a new phase in his efforts to bring about a change in Irish letters and culture. Later referring to his essays on the founding of the Irish dramatic movement in such magazines as *Beltaine, Samhain*, and the *Arrow*, Yeats observed that they "rang down the curtain so far as I was concerned on what was called 'The Celtic Movement'. An 'Irish Movement' took its place."[99] According to John P. Frayne and Colton Johnson, "what Yeats may have meant by this opposition was the change from the twilight prophecy to speaking in the clear cold light of the real world—the battles of J. M. Synge instead of the ephemeral dramatic projects of 'Fiona Macleod.'"[100] And just as Mathews had had his role in promoting the Celtic movement, so he had his part to play in the so-called Irish movement, centering as it so often did during the first decade of the twentieth century in the "battles of J. M. Synge." When Yeats met Synge in a Paris student's hotel on 21 December 1896 and advised him to go to the Aran Islands to study the common life, he was full of the notion that "it was only from the peasants that 'one could learn to write, their speech being living speech, flowing out of the habits of their lives, struck out of life itself.'"[101] Synge during his several sojourns among the peasants of Aran, beginning in the summer of 1898, realized firsthand the truth of Yeats's statement, utilizing not only his personal experiences among these simple, isolated people in his literary efforts but his expert knowledge of their language as well. Encouraged in his work by both Yeats and Augusta, Lady Gregory, Synge in the late nineties wrote *The Aran Islands*, a realistic account of his life among the peasants, and several dramatic pieces, among them the two one-act plays, *Riders to the Sea* and *The Shadow of the Glen*, which demonstrated the vitality and richness of the actual life and language of the Aran peasantry.

By the autumn of 1902, when he read and discussed these works with Yeats and Lady Gregory at her estate in Galway, Coole Park, Synge's genius and his potential value to their efforts on behalf of the generally more realistic Irish movement, were apparent. But for Synge to be really useful to the cause, it was imperative to get his writings into print. Yet repeated attempts to find a publisher for his manuscripts had come to nothing. Since Synge had begun circulating his Aran manuscript among London publishers in late November 1902, it had been rejected by numerous ones—including the enterprising young Grant Richards, who, like the others, believed that the book "would not secure the sale of seven or eight hundred copies,"

100

that is, enough to constitute what was considered a commercial suc-cess.[102] Persistent efforts, nevertheless, continued to be made on be-half of Synge's work not only by Yeats and Lady Gregory but by others. For example, the poet and critic Arthur Symons, having heard Synge read *Riders to the Sea* the night before, wrote Lady Gregory in February 1903, to ask if Synge "would like to publish his play in the *Fortnightly [Review]* before issuing it as a book?" Stating that he was "almost sure that [William Leonard] Courtney," the editor, "would take it," Symons went on in his typically generous way to volunteer his services in conveying the manuscript to Courtney along with his warm recommendation.[103] Unfortunately, Symons' efforts were in vain. Synge informed Lady Gregory in late March that "my play came back from the Fortnightly,—'as not suitable for their purposes.'" Moreover, he confided his pessimistic view that yet another pub-lisher, Reginald Brimley Johnson, did not intend "to bring out the Aran book." "I saw him on my way home," Synge continued, "but he seemed hopelessly undecided, saying at one minute that he liked it very much, and that it might be a great success, and that he wanted to be in touch with the Irish movement, and then going off in the other direction and fearing that it might fall perfectly flat! Finally he asked me to let him consider it a little longer."[104] And despite a letter from Yeats to Johnson commending Synge's work on the Aran islands—"a fine book, . . . indeed it has in some ways more of the country life in it than any book of the kind ever done in this country"—and offering to write a preface for it, Johnson, in the end, turned it down.[105]

Undaunted by the unadventurous commercial attitude and indif-ference of London publishers, Yeats and Lady Gregory toward the close of 1903 made another concerted effort to find a publisher who would recognize the worth of Synge's writings and risk their publi-cation. After A. H. Bullen a second time made his lack of interest in Synge's Aran manuscript apparent, Lady Gregory, constrained to write Synge that she and Yeats had "made a bad start with the M.S.S.," had some encouraging news to relate: that she had given the manuscript to the budding young poet John Masefield, who had read it and had spoken well of it to his publisher, Elkin Mathews.[106]

Masefield had met Synge the previous January at one of Yeats's "at homes," and had come to know and like him during the next several months of Synge's stay in London. Therefore, he was predisposed to help Synge, whose plays he had heard read. His response to the Aran book was positive; he referred to it as "excellent" in a letter of early December 1903 to Lady Gregory, and continued: "I have read some hundred and fifty books this year, and Synge's is certainly among the five best."[107] So impressed was he that he soon after called on Mathews—who had recently published his second book, *Ballads*, in the Vigo Cabinet series—and sang the book's praises to the publisher, adding that (as he reported the conversation to Lady Gregory) "Yeats would write an introduction and that we would all push the work in the press." Mathews, who had a reputation for being sympathetic to talented young writers, was "much impressed, and, much pleased." Although at the time he had not read the Aran manuscript, he told Masefield that "even without seeing it I should be glad to have it on such recommendations." Much to Masefield's surprise, no doubt, Mathews then and there expressed his desire to bring out the Aran book the following autumn, "if that would not be too late for Synge's debut."[108] Synge, on hearing the unexpected news from Lady Gregory, wrote his patroness to say that he was "delighted to find that there is a prospect of getting the book out at last, and equally grateful for the trouble you have taken with it. I am writing to Masefield today to thank him, and ask him by all means to get Mathews to do as he proposes."[109] It was not, however, until late January 1904 that Masefield wrote Mathews that he was "sending Mr. Synge's 'Aran' book of manuscript. He says that if you wish for photographs, as illustrations, he can give you some."[110] Meanwhile Masefield (hoping to take full advantage of the publisher's "excellent frame of mind") had approached Mathews about publishing Synge's one-act plays—*Riders to the Sea* and *The Shadow of the Glen*—and it soon became evident that Mathews was more interested in them than in the Aran book. In fact, when at Synge's suggestion Masefield also offered Mathews the two-act play *The Tinker's Wedding*—then in the process of completion—Mathews was willing that the volume include all three of what Synge called his "peasant plays."[111]

Initially of a mind to put the plays "on his spring list" and publish them in May 1904, "to act as a sort of John the Baptist to the Aran book appearing later in the year,"[112] Mathews met with Synge in the spring to discuss an agreement. But by June, having heard nothing further from the publisher, Synge was doubtless concerned as to what had happened, and Yeats, writing Mathews about another matter from Coole, began his letter to the effect that he had heard that the publisher was "hesitating about Synge's book." "I wish," he continued, "you would let me know what you propose to do. Synge is staying here now, and I think it very important for him and for our dramatic movement to have the plays published early in the autumn."[113] Mathews replied, more than a month later, that "with regard to Mr. Synge's work, I think I did hint to Mr. Dermot Freyer that I was a bit doubtful about issuing the Aran book this year." And although Mathews claimed to "find the Aran ms. very attractive," he was of the opinion that "it should come on later—the coming publishing season will probably be a bad one—and next year perhaps things may boom again!" He went on to emphasize that he did not include "the Plays in the doubt—anyhow in view of what you say I will certainly bring them on in the Autumn in the Vigo series. I understood from Masefield that either you or Lady Gregory will write a Preface."[114]

Whether Mathews' pessimism about "the coming publishing season" at length overwhelmed his intention to publish the plays in the autumn of 1904 or something else made him decide against it, it was not until late the following January that Synge heard from Mathews, who at last had taken up the plays with an eye to bringing them out in the spring of 1905. Replying to Mathews' query as to the whereabouts of "the 3rd play" (i.e., *The Tinker's Wedding*), Synge reminded him that at their meeting the previous spring he had taken it away with him in order to make corrections. Obviously no longer sanguine about including it in the proposed volume, the playwright observed: "Being in two acts, it is about as long as the other two plays together, so if they are long enough to fill your volume, I suppose you would hardly have room for 'the Tinkers' with them. As far as I am concerned I would rather have the two plays you have[,] brought out now together, and hold over the third[,] as a character in the Tinkers Wedding is likely to displease a good many of our Dublin friends and would perhaps hinder the sale of the book in Ireland."[115] Consequently, *The Tinker's Wedding* was eliminated from the book of plays, as was the preface, Synge, in a letter to Mathews, stating his preference not to have one, believing it to be irrelevant: Yeats, he explained, has "spoken favorabl[y] of my work in Samhain and also in a short

From

TELEGRAMS: "*Verbaliser, London.*"

Elkin Mathews

Publisher and Vendor of
Choice Books & Rare Editions
in *Belles Lettres*

LONDON, VIGO STREET, W.

Jany. 20 1905

To J. M. Synge Esq.
31 Crosthwaite Park
Kingstown Co. Dublin

Dear Mr Synge

Did you tell me you had three plays for publication or is the idea due to my imagination? For I find that besides your Aranmor Ms. I have only two plays, viz. "In the Shadow of the Glen" (typed) and "Riders to the Sea" (in Samhain). These two would I think be just sufficient to make up a volume for the Vigo Cabinet Series. As I want to put the latter in Printers' hands will you kindly let me hear from you? Yours sincerely

Elkin Mathews

Elkin Mathews to J. M. Synge, 20 January 1905, concerning the publication of *The Shadow of the Glen and Riders to the Sea* (1905). Trinity College Library, Dublin

preface he has done for the new play in three acts which Mr. Bullen is bringing out, so I fear if I get any more introductions people will cry out that we are log-rolling!"[116]

Synge sent his revised texts of the two one-act plays to Mathews in early February[117] and finalized the agreement with his publisher for the book on 22 March 1905. In their meeting a year earlier, Mathews—perhaps because Masefield had initially suggested a 15 percent royalty on Synge's behalf[118]—proposed paying the playwright a slightly higher royalty than he usually allowed a new, unpublished author: 12.5 percent after production costs had been recovered. Later, however, Synge sought to alter these terms, asking Mathews in a letter of January 1905: "Would you think it possible to give me a per-centage—even a lower one, say 10% [—] from the first—instead of 12½% when the book had paid its expenses as I think you suggested? If you wish to hold to this latter arrangement how many volumes do you count necessary to pay off the expenses? i.e., after the sale of how many volumes would my royalties begin?"[119] Presumably having had a reply from Mathews, Synge again in a letter of early February stated his preference for a "per-centage coming from the outset," adding that since "the trade price sometimes fluctuates I think it would be more satisfactory to have the royalty on the published price." "If," Synge concluded, "10% is too high I will consider any other that you care to offer."[120] As the agreement shows, author and publisher ultimately worked our a compromise of sorts which called for Synge to "receive a royalty of 10 per centum on the Trade price (10d) from the first copy counting 13 copies as 12 after expenses have been paid from proceeds of sales." This agreement (which Synge later thought was "not a very fair one") also included a clause which gave Mathews "for [a] term of seven years the exclusive rights of printing and publishing in Great Britain and Ireland the United States of American and all countries a volume containing two Plays, viz. 'The Shadow of the Glen' and 'The Riders to the Sea.'"[121]

The moment for which Synge and his supporters had waited was at last at hand—the publication of that crucial first book which would prepare the way for others. Notifying Synge in a letter of 3 May that he intended to publish his plays the following week, Mathews brought out *The Shadow of the Glen and Riders to the Sea* on Monday, 8 May 1905, as number 24 in the Vigo Cabinet series.[122] Unlike the

105

usual five-shilling hardcover book, which required a sale of some 700 to 800 copies to achieve a commercial success (as Richards had intimated), Synge's little book of plays, bound in pale gray-green wrappers with lettering and series design in black, cost comparatively little to produce. This, in addition to the plays' high literary quality, their appeal to Irish readers, and the favorable press (insured by the efforts of Synge's friends), accounts for the great success of the book. Within two years of its publication, the first edition of 1,000 copies had sold out, and further editions (bound in both paper wrappers selling at 1/– and hard covers selling at 1/6) were called for in 1907 and 1909. So successful was the book that a fourth thousand was issued in 1910 and a sixth thousand in 1911.[123]

In accordance with the plan to use the plays to herald the prose work, Synge, as late as September, looked to Mathews to bring out his Aran book.[124] Mathews, however, continued to show a reluctance to publish it, predisposing the playwright to look with favor on a proposal from George Roberts, managing director of the new Dublin firm of Maunsel & Company, to publish the Aran book in an ordinary edition in the autumn and in an expensive edition sometime later. In a letter of 7 November written from his sickbed, Synge discussed Roberts' proposal, addressing himself specifically to the subject of royalties and stating his willingness to close the deal if his terms were agreeable. Fully aware of the fact that breaking the news to Mathews would not be easy, he asked Roberts to write Mathews, observing, "I am hardly able to write to him now and you are in a hurry." Synge suggested that Roberts "put it to him as nicely as you can explaining how the idea [of publishing the Aran book in Dublin] arose, and telling him that I am not well enough to write myself."[125] Shortly afterwards, however, Synge, in improved health, wrote Mathews himself, giving his reasons for transferring the manuscript to Maunsel:

> One or two of my plays have made me very unpopular with a section of our Irish Catholic public and I feel it will be a great advantage to me to have this book printed and published in Dublin on Irish paper—small matters that are nevertheless thought a good deal of over here. Then I can get terms here very much more satisfactory than those that you were good enough to offer me. It is nearly two years now since you first spoke of publishing the book, so I dare say you do not feel very sure of

its fate, and I am sure you will be just as glad that we should take the risk over here.[126]

But Mathews, faced with the loss of a manuscript by a writer whose first book had proven highly successful, was not so amenable as Synge had hoped and refused to renounce his right to publish the Aran book. Ultimately, a compromise between the parties was worked out, and Synge's *The Aran Islands* was published jointly by Maunsel in Dublin and Mathews in London in late April 1907, over five years after its completion. Although M. J. MacManus's bibliography of Synge's work does not mention it, P. S. O'Hegarty's "Some Notes on the Bibliography of J. M. Synge, Supplemental to Bourgeois and MacManus" calls attention to the fact that there are some copies of the small-paper issue of *The Aran Islands* dated 1906; O'Hegarty suggests that they represent advance copies sent to Elkin Mathews "for Xmas, 1906, in expectation of the book being ready to publish by Xmas." However, the earliest known presentation copy from the author, to Miss Mary Allgood, is dated 28 April 1907.[127]

The small-paper issue, bound in slate-blue buckram and lettered in gilt on front and back, sold for five shillings and was embellished with twelve full-page drawings in black and white by Jack B. Yeats.[128] The large-paper issue, of 150 copies printed on handmade paper and numbered and signed by both Synge and Yeats, was bound in light brown buckram, lettered in gilt on front and back, and sold for a guinea, the illustrations hand-colored by the artist.

Synge's further relations with Mathews had to do with his efforts over the next several years to publish collected editions of his plays in America and Ireland. Since Mathews' rights to *The Shadow of the Glen* and *Riders to the Sea* extended to the spring of 1912, plans and financial arrangements for any collected edition necessarily involved him. Discussing a possible collected edition of the plays in America, Synge, in September 1907, wrote John Quinn, the American lawyer and patron of Irish authors, who was advising him, that he did not think Mathews' share in the rights should "give us much trouble" since his agreement "has only four more years to run from next spring."[129] And Synge's supposition appears to have been correct, for a year or so later Mathews accepted a 1 percent royalty on a proposed one-volume American edition of the plays which Synge wrote him about: "You have heard I think that we propose to issue my plays in America in one volume,—the plays you have published for me will of course make a very small portion of the volume so it [will] be fair I think if we allow you a royalty of one percent.—while your agreement with me is still in force. The terms offered by the American publisher do not admit I need hardly say, of our allowing you a larger royalty."[130]

Arrangements with Mathews for a collected edition of the plays at home, however, fared less well. Since the Vigo Cabinet edition of the plays was still selling strongly in 1909, three years before Mathews' rights were to run out, the publisher, having taken the initial risk, was obviously not anxious to share the plays with another publisher unless the terms were exceedingly generous. That Mathews' negotiating stance was a tough one is indicated in Synge's reply of January 1909 to a proposal put forward jointly by the London firm of Sidgwick and Jackson and Maunsel of Dublin to publish a collected edition of his works. Somewhat pessimistically, Synge, writing from Ireland, informed Frank Sidgwick that an edition of his plays in one volume already under consideration "has come to nothing for the present—in this country at least—chiefly owing to impossibility of coming to what we thought a satisfactory arrangement with Mr. Matthews [sic]."[131] And although no such arrangement between Mathews and another publisher seems to have been finalized by the time of Synge's death in March, there appears to have arisen some confusion as to who actually held the rights to the plays, Messrs. Maunsel, in the summer of 1909, informing James Joyce, who was seeking permission to have his Italian translation of *Riders to the Sea* produced in Italy, that they had the rights to the play and, as Joyce wrote Mathews, "were making new arrangements with regard to it." Mathews, however, in his reply to Joyce's query as to who held the rights to *The Shadow of the Glen* and *Riders to the Sea*, returned a terse but firm, "I do," presumably having made no deals with Maunsel or any other publisher.[132]

Although the Mathews-Synge relationship was not of long duration, ending for all intents and purposes with the publication of *The Aran Islands* in 1907, it launched Synge's career, producing two books of enduring quality—*The Shadow of the Glen and Riders to the Sea* and *The Aran Islands*. The first book demonstrated his brilliance as a playwright and the second his genius as a master of prose realism. The publication of these books enabled Synge within the scant two years remaining to him to establish himself firmly in the eyes of the public as a major force in the Irish literary movement. It is doubtful that he could have accomplished so much had it not been for Mathews.

Although Yeats was aware of an opposition between the Celtic movement and what he called the Irish movement, he nevertheless recognized a common thread running through the whole fabric: the "dream" in which he and others in the nineties had become entangled, and which, he later wrote, found expression in the work of A.E., in his own poetic plays and poems, and in Synge, who saw "all the world as a withered and witless place in comparison with the dazzle of that dream."[133] After Synge's death, Yeats saw it in the work of a young Irish aristocrat, Lord Dunsany, who, as he observed, "has seen it once more and as simply as if he were a child imagining adventures for the knights and ladies that rode out over the drawbridges in the piece of old tapestry in its mother's room." And although Dunsany's imagination was, Yeats admitted, more at home with "those magic lands of his with their vague Eastern air" than with those of "the old Irish legendary world," Yeats argued in his introduction to the Cuala Press *Selections from the Writings of Lord Dunsany*, that "it is all but one dream," attempting to persuade his readers of the relevance of Dunsany's work to the cause and of the importance of his role "in that change I have described" in Irish literature and culture. By enshrining Dunsany's "tender, pathetic, haughty fancies among books by Lady Gregory, by A.E., by Dr. Douglas Hyde, by John Synge, and by myself," Yeats sought to validate, so to speak, Dunsany's credentials as a spokesman for the Celtic movement.[134]

Just as Mathews had supported the movement in both its Celtic and Irish phases (to use again Yeats's oppositions), he, too, supported Dunsany, who had seen the dream and expressed it in his tales even during the horrific realities of World War I. Unusually susceptible to the kind of poetic, fantastical prose fiction which was Dunsany's hallmark, Mathews published the young writer's first book, *The Gods of Pegāna*, in 1905, replete with those romantically apt illustrations in photogravure by S. H. Sime which gave the book added charm. Over

Frontispiece of Lord Dunsany's *The Gods of Pegāna* (1905) by S. H. Sime

the next fifteen years or so, Mathews published four more of Dunsany's books, even though the author later confessed that he had aimed at having his "work published with bigger concerns" than Mathews'. As was the case in 1913, when Dunsany could not find a publisher for his *Fifty-One Tales*, he "came back again and again," as he later wrote the publisher's widow, "to Mr. Mathews and always found a welcome."[135] In addition to *Fifty-One Tales*, which he pub-

110

lished in 1915, Mathews also brought out Dunsany's *Tales of Wonder* (also illustrated by Sime), *Unhappy Far Off Things*, and a second edition of the earlier *The Book of Wonder* near the end of his career, once again demonstrating his readiness, as the reporter had written in 1906, "to assist the Celtic Movement."

CHAPTER FOUR

James Joyce's First Publisher:

Elkin Mathews and the Advent of *Chamber Music*

W HEN J AMES J OYCE completed his suite of poems *Chamber Music* about 1904[1] and began to look about for a publisher, there were (as we have seen) few publishing opportunities for young, unknown poets either in newspapers and journals or in book form. "One difficulty," Laurence Binyon wrote, was "that the big [publishing] firms, with wide organization, won't take trouble about poetry because at best the return is so small."[2] Although Joyce perhaps was, at the outset, unaware of this, he learned from experience before *Chamber Music* was accepted for publication by Elkin Mathews in January 1907.

Joyce's initiator into the realm of poetry publishing was the critic and poet Arthur Symons, who had first met and received Joyce at his apartment in Maida Vale, London, in early December 1902, on which occasion he saw some of his visitor's poems and offered to help get them published.[3] Symons, the author of several volumes of verse as well as of the influential critical study *The Symbolist Movement in Literature* (1899), had some talent in spotting genuine literary ability and a real interest in promoting new talent. Besides, he knew well the London literary scene, including some influential editors and publishers. Consequently, when Joyce (seemingly intent on placing his poems with a London publisher) later asked him for help, Symons, who saw Joyce as "a curious mixture of sinister genius and uncertain talent," was both willing and able.[4]

Unfortunately, Symons was in Italy when Joyce's letter of 14

November 1903 asking him for help in finding a publisher arrived in Maida Vale. As a result, it was not until the following April that Symons wrote a reply: "What have you done with the poems?" he asked. "If they are still unpublished, it would interest me to see them, and if I can advise you what to do with them, I will gladly."[5] Joyce, no doubt relieved to hear at last from Symons, dispatched his poems to him without delay. And by early May Symons, having read them, wrote: "Remarkably good. They certainly ought to be published." Fully aware of the difficulty in finding a publishing opportunity for poetry, Symons concluded: "I don't know whether I can do anything, but I will try."[6] Having almost immediately placed a poem from the suite in the *Saturday Review*, Symons set about finding a publisher for the book, cautioning Joyce from the outset against false optimism. During the two and a half years in which he worked to place Joyce's poems with a publisher, Symons never minimized the task ahead, often emphasizing to Joyce the unfavorable conditions of the times. "I am now going to show the book to a publisher," he informed Joyce just before he handed the manuscript over to Duckworth and Company in early May. "But it is very difficult to publish even the best verse."[7] The difficulty, as Symons wrote to Joyce in September, arose from the fact that "hardly any verse pays, as you may well imagine."[8]

This, indeed, seems to have been the sticking point so far as Joyce's poems were concerned. Traditional, well-established firms simply would not run the financial risk of publishing a book of poems by a virtual unknown. So when Symons sent Joyce's poems to Duckworth, the London firm which had recently brought out his *Plays, Acting and Music*, they were rejected almost certainly on the grounds that the volume would not pay, although the official word was that the poems were "too 'slight.'"[9] Symons next sent the manuscript to the more adventurous young publisher Grant Richards, whose avant-garde tastes would ordinarily have predisposed him to publish *Chamber Music*. Richards was forced to leave Joyce dangling for over two years because financial difficulties precluded any high-risk publishing venture, especially at a time when, he wrote Joyce, "the public seems to care increasingly little for verse by new writers."[10] Symons reported to Joyce in late September that Richards "fully admired the verses, but had very little hope of selling them"—a serious drawback to one on the brink of bankruptcy, as Richards was.[11]

By mid-November 1904, Symons, stymied, wrote Joyce in a mood of resignation and defeat: "If I could, I would gladly help you further, but I do not quite see what I could do." After advising Joyce to try placing some of the poems in journals and newspapers—he mentioned the *Westminster Gazette* and the *Speaker*, even the American *Smart Set*—he concluded: "I wish I could make more definite suggestions, but I am afraid I can not."[12]

Almost a year later, in October 1905, having recently published his *Spiritual Adventures* with Constable, Symons got that firm to agree to see Joyce's *Chamber Music* and his recently completed *Dubliners*. But neither he nor Joyce had much hope that the well-established, traditional publisher would agree to bring out the books. As Symons wrote to Joyce, Messrs. Constable and Company "have promised to give them attention, but of course it is most uncertain if they will think them likely to make a paying success: that is the difficulty."[13] As expected, Constable rejected both books, but by this time a way to skirt the difficulty was finally in the offing.

In the late summer of 1906, Symons once again heard from Joyce, who was upset with Grant Richards, who several months before had promised to publish *Dubliners*, only to renege later. In his reply, Symons, having advised Joyce to hold Richards to his contract, then turned to the poems with a statement that must have surprised and delighted Joyce, who surely had become inured to cautiously worded advice and the rejection slip. "I feel sure," he wrote, "that I could get Elkin Mathews to print them in his shilling 'Garland' series."[14] Symons, in fact, was referring to the Vigo Cabinet series, in which his own translation of Baudelaire's *Petits Poèmes en Prose* had recently been published as *Poems in Prose*. This renewal of his acquaintance with Mathews, who had published Symons' book of poems, *Silhouettes*, in 1892, doubtless had recalled to mind Mathews' uncanny ability among London publishers to publish poetry cheaply. Mathews, as I have shown, had established a tradition of publishing young, unknown poets in attractive limited editions in small and odd-shaped formats at less than the usual five shillings a volume. In thinking of Mathews, therefore, in the autumn of 1906, Symons probably hit upon the one publisher in the whole of Britain who was prepared to entertain seriously and realistically a proposal to publish *Chamber Music* at his own risk.

Despite the fact that Symons warned him that he "would get little money from" Mathews,[15] Joyce readily gave Symons permission to approach the publisher on his behalf. Accordingly, in October Symons wrote Mathews:

> Would you care to have, for your Vigo Cabinet [series], a book of verse which is of the most genuine lyric quality of any new work I have read for many years? It is called 'A Book of Thirty Songs for Lovers,' and the lyrics are almost Elizabethan in their freshness, but quite personal. They are by a young Irishman called J. A. Joyce. . . . I consider that in offering you this—at my own suggestion, not his—I am offering you a book which cannot fail to attract notice from everyone capable of knowing poetry when he sees it. I should make a point of reviewing it myself in the Athenaeum or Saturday [Review], and would tell others about it.[16]

Symons' strong recommendation must have impressed Mathews, for he replied almost immediately: "I am very much obliged to you for drawing my attention to Mr. Joyce's work and I feel, from what you tell me of its quality that it would be a great acquisition to my Vigo series. So will you please put me into communication with Mr. Joyce, or arrange with him for me to see his ms."[17] At once Symons forwarded Mathews' letter to Joyce with a request that he send the manuscript. Joyce, impressed with Mathews' reply, quoted it entire to his brother, Stanislaus, in a letter of 18 October, adding that he had written to the publisher to say that he "was re-arranging the verses but would send the ms. in a few days."[18] Toward the end of October Joyce sent off the manuscript (dated 24 October 1906), along with a note which briefly recounted the story of the poems' long bondage to Richards and which pressed the publisher for an early decision.[19] Mathews promptly penned a reply dated 30 October in which he promised, "As soon as I get some of my most pressing work out of the way I will turn to and examine it, and write you thereon."[20]

Of course, Joyce, rebuffed by publishers for almost three years, was more anxious than ever to have an answer from Mathews now that at last he sensed a real possibility of publication. But whether he was aware of it or not, he had submitted his manuscript to the publisher at the busiest season of the year—late October, when Mathews was struggling to bring out his new list of books for the fall season. As he went on to explain to Joyce: "I dare say you realise that you would not in any case get [Chamber Music] published this side of Christmas, as the season is too far advanced to get anything more through, and as this is the case you will no doubt see that there is no great hurry."[21]

Critics have been quick to fault Mathews for responding thus to Joyce's plea, seeing the incident as typical of the lordly treatment meted out by publishers to lowly authors. Herbert Gorman, for example, takes the occasion to expound on the provoking behavior of publishers in general, who, he declares, "are never to be hurried. While they will press and harry authors most unreasonably, they regard the author's natural impatience as an insolent form of *lèse-majesté*." Referring to Mathews as "the solid slow-stepping Britisher," Gorman leaves the impression that the publisher was needlessly callous and unresponsive to Joyce's plight.[22] Yet no one contemplating Mathews' autumn list for 1906—containing some fifteen new titles, not to mention eight more added to the Vigo Cabinet series—can doubt that Mathews (who could afford but little help) had his hands full.[23] True to his word, he promptly turned to the manuscript of *Chamber Music* as soon as the Christmas season had ended and on 11 January 1907 sent off an agreement for Joyce's approval along with a note in which he described the format: "Pott 8vo. is a very pretty size. If you know the Golden Treasury series you will be able to judge the size at once." Proposing to publish the book "sometime this Spring," Mathews closed with the assurance that Joyce "need not fear that *I* shall keep it in bond for years!"[24]

The terms of the agreement were, in the main, what Mathews usually offered his more promising new clients, that is, a percentage of the book's sales once he had recovered the production costs. Thus, the agreement that Joyce signed (having shown it to his lawyer, St. Lo Malet) allowed the author a royalty of 15 percent to be paid after the first 300 copies had been sold, counting 13 as 12. The publisher was granted the exclusive right to publish the book "during the legal term of copyright of printing in Great Britain and all countries." Provisions also were made for dividing equally between publisher and author any fees accruing from the granting of musical rights to the poems. Given the depressed poetry market and the reluctance of large firms to risk publishing new poets, Mathews' willingness to offer Joyce a royalty and to share equally any fees, was generous.[25]

As originally planned, *Chamber Music* was to have been included in the Vigo Cabinet series, but sometime between the decision to accept the book for publication in early January and the pulling of proofs in late February, Mathews changed his mind and proceeded to produce a book in hard covers with a decorated title page. I suspect, given Symons' high opinion of the book and his promise not only to review but to push it, Mathews thought he might have one of those rare hits in the offing, one worthy of a more attractive and substantial format. Moreover, the thirty-six lyrics represented more text than was usually found between the fragile paper wrappers of the series' numbers.

However that may be, a first set of proofs reached Joyce at Rome in late February 1907, eliciting from the author his well-known remark to his brother: "It is a slim book and on the frontispiece is an open pianner!"[26] On 1 March, Joyce wrote Mathews: "I send you back by this post the proofs of *Chamber Music* with corrections. If you will be kind enough to let me have a second proof I shall return it by the same post."[27] Accordingly Mathews dispatched a second set to Rome a few days later only to receive a card from Joyce saying he was going to Trieste. Mathews, a bit perturbed, dashed off a reply: "Your card to hand with thanks. What a pity you did not let me know [you] were going to Trieste as I have sent 2 copies of revise to Via Monte Brianzo 51, IV°, Rome on the 13th inst. I hope you left instructions to have letters readdressed."[28] Despite the confusion which accrued and some loss of time, Joyce was able to notify Mathews on 28 March that the proofs had reached him that evening and that he had "corrected and returned them." Moreover, he expressed his satisfaction "with the binding and printing" and made one request: that the year's date appear on the title page. "I have," he concluded, "also made one or two corrections of errors which escaped me on the first reading."[29]

Although he had never given Mathews any hint of it, Joyce had for some time been increasingly disenchanted with his suite of poems, due, to some extent, to his sense of having grown beyond it and, in the words of Stanislaus, in whom he confided, to a "thought that the sentiment of the poems was false."[30] In early March Joyce told his brother, "I don't like the book," but he was still willing to see it in print because he had come to think of it as forming "a record of my past."[31] Nevertheless, in early April, hardly a month before publication, Joyce told his brother that he was going to cable Mathews to halt publication. Stanislaus, concerned, accompanied him to the post office in Trieste, where the two spent the night debating the matter. The poet seemed adamant, but by dawn Stanislaus had prevailed, arguing that the publication of *Chamber Music* would facilitate the publication of other books.[32] One can only imagine the consternation of Mathews if, indeed, he had received such a message. Given the amount of money he had invested in the book, with no way of recovering his costs except through publication, it would have been difficult for Mathews to have complied with Joyce's request. Fortunately, Joyce put his doubts behind him and did not demur when Mathews wrote him proposing to publish *Chamber Music* "on Monday next 6 May." Moreover, he promptly responded to the publisher's request for suggestions "as to the furtherance of sales of the book" by recommending that review copies be sent "to the chief Dublin papers and, if you approve of it, copies also to the chief booksellers there," supplying names and addresses.[33]

Joyce surely was proud of his first book when copies reached him in Trieste shortly after publication—certainly proud enough to busy himself and Stanislaus with sending copies around to relatives and friends.[34] For so inexpensive a volume—it sold for only a shilling and a sixpence—*Chamber Music* was surprisingly handsome in its light green gilt-stamped cloth boards and its ornate, almost baroque, title page divided between a large harpsichord (Joyce's "pianner") centered in the top half and "Chamber / Music / by / James Joyce" centered in the lower. Columns draped in bunting decorated with simulated musical notations provided the border, topped off with the date "1907" (as Joyce had requested). Its format, size (16 x 11 cm, or, to use Mathews' measurements, 6½" x 4⅜"), and especially its title page were typical of the delightful books of poetry Mathews and Lane had produced in the early nineties, though less frequently by 1907. Printed by Gilbert and Rivington, the first edition, according to Gorman, numbered 509 copies.[35]

The advent of *Chamber Music* was heralded by Elkin Mathews' advertisement in the *Publishers' Circular* on the Saturday before publication, which listed Joyce's book among others, and by an advance notice in the *Book Monthly* which linked Joyce with W. B. Yeats. It was also announced among the new books listed in the *Athenaeum* on 11 May.[36] Among the early responses was that in the *Bookman* for June, which referred to *Chamber Music* as "a little book of poetry which charms, provokes criticism, and charms again." "Mr.

118

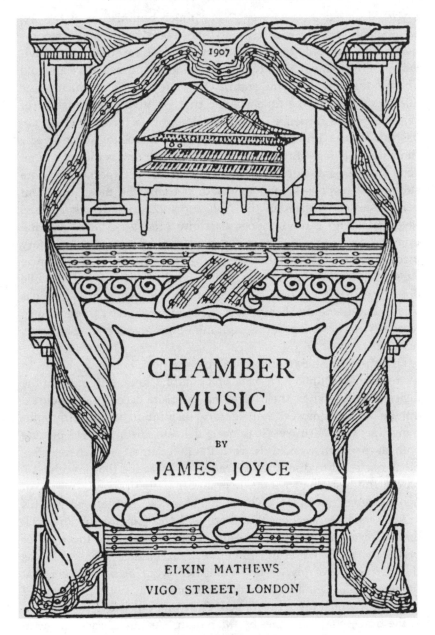

Title page of James Joyce's *Chamber Music* (1907)

Joyce," declared the reviewer, "has a touch reminiscent of the six-
teenth century poets, with here and there a break in his lines' smooth-
ness which can only be smoothed by an old-time stress on the syl-
lable, such as Vaughan and Herbert demand. At times there are bold
liberties taken with rhyme and rhythm; but there is so much music
and quaintness in the little volume that we give praise instead of
censure."[37] The response to *Chamber Music* in a June issue of *Publishers' Circular*, however, was quite negative, labeling Joyce's verse
"immature . . . regretful and rather weak. Much of it is the echo of an
echo, and the influence of Ernest Dowson is very marked."[38] More
substantial responses soon followed, perhaps the most important
being Symons' review in the *Nation* on 22 June, which advised
"everyone who cares for poetry to buy *Chamber Music*." Bearing
unmistakable signs of Symons' aesthetic orientation, the laudatory
piece drew the reader's attention to the fact that "there is almost no
substance at all in these songs, which hardly hint at a story," while
observing that the lyrics "are so slight, as a drawing of Whistler is
slight, that their entire beauty will not be discovered by those who go
to poetry for anything but its perfume" (Symons' favorite patchouli,
no doubt).[39]

Like the English Symons, Joyce's compatriot Thomas M. Kettle, in
his review for Dublin's *Freeman's Journal* of 1 June, duly noticed the
delicacy of the lyrics, their "rare and exquisite accent," and pointed
out the book's "almost entirely literary" inspiration, while deftly sum-
ming up Joyce's artistry: "It is clear, delicate, distinguished playing
with harps, with woodbirds, with Paul Verlaine." But whereas Symons hastened to disabuse his readers of any idea that Joyce was a
part of the Irish literary movement and to assure them that the poet
had nothing "obviously Celtic in his manner," Kettle reproved his
friend when he observed that there was "no trace of folklore, folk
dialect, or even the national feeling that have coloured the work of
practically every writer in contemporary Ireland."[40] Whether it was
this perception of Joyce's first published work or some other that
prejudiced the Dublin press, there certainly was not the all-out response for which Joyce had hoped. Only one other review appeared
at the time—that in *Hermes* by "Mananan." Arthur Clery's review in
the *Leader* under his pseudonym, "Chanel," appeared several years

later.[41] Nevertheless, various reviews of *Chamber Music* did continue to appear in English and Scottish newspapers and journals throughout the summer, leading Joyce, in early September in response to the notices Mathews had sent him, to write that he was "glad that they seem so favourable."[42]

Encouraged by the early reception of his poems, Joyce appears to have decided that the time was ripe to approach Mathews about publishing *Dubliners*, which had been the subject of a long and bitter controversy between Joyce and Grant Richards, with Richards finally refusing to publish it.[43] On 24 September 1907 he wrote Mathews that he had "a second book ready for publication. It is a book of fifteen stories entitled 'Dubliners', and as you have published my first book I think it is right that I should offer it to you in the first instance. At the same time I do not know whether you publish books of prose or not nor do I know whether the result of 'Chamber Music' from your point of view was such as to warrant you in considering any other book of mine with a view of publishing."[44]

As had been the case with the *Chamber Music* manuscript, Joyce broached the subject of *Dubliners* at a most unpropitious time, asking Mathews for a decision on the stories "at your earliest convenience as in any case I should like to have the matter definitely arranged this autumn either with you or with another publisher so that the book might appear next spring."[45] Mathews replied apologetically almost a month later: "My only excuse is that I am now up to my eyes in work—with the season's books. Whether I take up your new book or not it would give me pleasure to see the ms. if you still have it by you. If you send it I will consider it as soon as possible."[46] Joyce dispatched the manuscript without delay, hoping still, no doubt, for a quick decision. But to no avail. For Mathews, in acknowledging receipt of the manuscript, underlined the fact that he would "be very busy for some time," promising again that he would "turn to it as soon as possible."[47] As soon as possible turned out to be (as was the case with *Chamber Music*) after the new year, when Mathews set about developing his list of books for the spring season. But, unfortunately for Joyce, the decision this time was not favorable. On 6 February 1908, Mathews wrote Joyce that he had "carefully examined 'Dubliners' and also got a reader's opinion with the result that I have decided not to publish it, mainly because I think it could be handled better by a Dublin firm." Consequently, Mathews went on to say, "I mentioned it to Mr. Home (Maunsel & Co., Dublin) the other day, and he said 'Oh, send the ms. on to us, as it might suit us'—so if you have no objection this is what I will do."[48]

Mathews—whose reader, John Mavrogordato, had "somewhat equivocally endorsed" Dubliners[49]—doubtless had other and more weighty reasons for rejecting Joyce's stories, reasons that came to light some five years later when in March 1913 Mathews once again rejected Dubliners. Replying to Joyce's recent proposal that the publisher "take on immediately the publication of my famous book Dubliners," Mathews wrote: "The proof sheets came to hand and I have read them. I should think the book should appeal to the publisher of realistic full blooded fiction; it is full of go and colour but is quite out of harmony with the style of book I publish. I publish little fiction and when I do—it is more of the idealistic poetic kind."[50]

Here, then, is the precise reason why Mathews twice rejected one of the world's great collections of short stories. The book's unromantic, naturalistic treatment of Dublin life simply didn't appeal personally to a man who was a great friend of the Irish literary movement, especially in its Celtic Twilight phase. Whereas the Ireland of folk and fancy delighted him, the dismal Ireland of present realities left him cold. And although Mathews had published a fair amount of fiction—Ronald Firbank's first book, Odette D'Antrevernes, and Lord Dunsany's The Gods of Pegāna, for instance, and plays such as John Millington Synge's The Shadow of the Glen and Riders to the Sea, among others—his primary interest lay in producing books of poetry which, ideally, expressed in traditional terms and modes sentiments about nature, love, and life which soothed and reassured. Mathews had been willing to publish Chamber Music because its lyrics were, in the words of Symons, "full of ghostly old tunes, that were never young and will never be old, played on an old instrument,"[51] but the "realistic full blooded fiction" of Dubliners was quite another matter.

Mathews' rejection, expressed obliquely in his letter, led Joyce to write again on Easter Day to express his thanks for the publisher's prompt reply and to request clarification: "I do not understand from it . . . whether you definitely decline my proposal or not," and to sweeten, so to speak, his offer:

My proposal (based on my knowledge of the fact that, as you say, 'the book is not in harmony with your usual publications') was that the printing should be charged to me (if necessary, in advance), that 100 copies be taken by me at sale price and that my preface (which, of itself, should suffice as a striking advertisement) should be printed. I am willing to add to these another condition: to give you the refusal of the novel which I am engaged on and shall finish this year *A Portrait of the Artist as a Young Man*, a book about which you may have heard something from your Irish acquaintances. Let me hear from you on this point.[52]

In his effort to make his meaning plainer, Mathews in his reply added yet another reason for not taking up Joyce's offer: "so many irons in the fire that I could not possibly give your book proper attention."[53]

Although relations between Joyce and Mathews had gone well immediately after the publication of *Chamber Music*, Mathews' rejection of *Dubliners* and slow sales of the poems both disappointed and vexed Joyce, who, needless to say, had every right to feel frustrated given his professional and financial difficulties. Over the next few years, Joyce's difficulties worsened, disturbing his equanimity. Consequently, it is little wonder that on several occasions in his later dealings with the habitually serene and even-tempered Mathews over matters arising from the music rights and sales of *Chamber Music*, Joyce expressed a bit of temper. For instance, Joyce who had a fine tenor voice and enjoyed singing, had written the lyrics of *Chamber Music* with an eye to their being set to music. "The book," he later wrote, "is in fact a suite of songs and if I were a musician I suppose I should have set them to music myself."[54] And in March 1907 when Joyce had grave doubts about publishing his suite, his belief that the lyrics were "pretty enough to be put to music" may in the end have reinforced his decision to publish the book. Fortunately, soon after publication, his hope that someone would set the poems to music, "someone that knows old English music such as I like,"[55] was realized when he received a letter from Geoffrey Molyneux Palmer, an English organist and composer, proposing to set some of the lyrics. Ill at the time, Joyce, through Stanislaus, signalled his entire willingness to have Palmer proceed, and Palmer did, providing musical settings for eight of the poems over the next several years. Joyce, delighted, continued to encourage Palmer, expressing to him his hope that the composer might "set all of *Chamber Music* in time."[56]

So anxious was Joyce that nothing stand in the way of anyone's attempt to set the lyrics to music that when on a trip to Ireland in the autumn of 1909 he heard from a Belfast music critic, a Mr. W. B. Reynolds, that Mathews "had refused to give him permission to set" several of his poems, Joyce wrote Mathews, demanding to know why.[57] Mathews, who had heard not a word of complaint from Reynolds and was entirely innocent of the suspicions the music critic had maliciously raised in Joyce's mind, settled the misunderstanding by pointing out to Joyce that the sole musical rights to poem number xxxi, "0, it was out by Donnycarney," which Reynolds had sought permission to set, had been disposed of previously to a Mr. Adolph Mann for a fee of two guineas.[58] Although, as Joyce's letters show, there were several composers—O'Brien Butler among others—who provided musical settings for some of the lyrics, the only fees Mathews received for musical rights as of 24 May 1910 were the two guineas from Mann, one guinea from Reynolds to set number xxix, "Dear heart," and one guinea for printing Palmer's setting of number xxxi, "0, it was out by Donnycarney," in the Royal College Music Patrons' Fund program—a total of four guineas in all, of which Joyce received a check for half, that is, two guineas.[59]

A more vexed matter over which Joyce and Mathews clashed during the years after the publication of *Chamber Music* was its sales and the payment of royalties. Despite the favorable reviews his suite of poems received, sales of the book were slow from the outset. Barely six months after its publication, Mathews wrote Joyce that "'Chamber Music' is going very slowly." Nevertheless, he assured the author, "I shall not cease to push it."[60] Having heard nothing more from the publisher about the sales, Joyce in July 1908 wrote him for an accounting. In his reply, Mathews reported that the sales of *Chamber Music* had been "very poor," a statement which the accompanying account sheet clearly bore out. Although 205 copies had been disposed of—61 to reviewers, 12 to Joyce (as per agreement), 1 to the British Museum Copyright office, 4 to public libraries (as required by law), and 127 sold—more than a year after publication, 295 remained in stock.[61] And although Joyce in a letter of early 1909 expressed to Mathews a hope that the publisher "may have sold off some more of that large remainder," sales had, if anything, worsened. "'Chamber

Music' had been standing still—like most poetical books—since Xmas," Mathews replied, himself hoping that "sales will look up by and by."[62]

Unfortunately, there is nothing to suggest that the hopes of the two men for better sales were realized throughout 1909.[63] Increasingly puzzled, Joyce, citing both favorable press notices and considerable interest on the part of composers to set his lyrics to music, wrote Mathews the following year that he was "quite at a loss to understand how the book has brought me nothing so far."[64] And having subsequently received another account of sales, Joyce, a month later, expressed his surprise "at the fewness of the copies sold" and went on to accuse Mathews of not pushing the book more "in view of the good notices it got."[65]

Joyce's assumption that the slow sales of *Chamber Music* (and, in consequence, his failure to accrue royalties) were the fault of the publisher can readily be understood. When he signed the contract with Mathews to publish *Chamber Music* in early 1907, Joyce probably believed that the sale of the 300 copies needed for him to earn royalties would be merely a matter of a few months. The early reviews obviously reinforced this belief. Thus Joyce's increasing vexation, frustration, and disappointment as sales lagged and, over the next several years, fell far short of the requisite 300. Joyce's misapprehension, of course, was due to his lack of knowledge of the poetry market in Britain during the first decade of the twentieth century. Unlike the heyday of the so-called "minor" poets in the early nineties, when Mathews and Lane at the Bodley Head were winning acclaim for their successful promotion of such poets as Richard Le Gallienne, William Watson, Alice Meynell, "Michael Field," John Davidson, Francis Thompson, Oscar Wilde, and Arthur Symons, the first decade of the twentieth century was quite different. As Mathews observed in an interview in 1906,

> There will always be a certain market for really good poetry. Still, it would be inaccurate to say that there is now the demand that there was some twelve years ago. We publishers are waiting patiently for a new boom such as there was in 1893–4. In those days there were men like [William Ewart] Gladstone and [H.D.] Traill, who made a business of discovering promising poets. Their successors have yet to be found. You

125

can realise that encouragement from such high quarters went far towards influencing public taste. Poets are now, unfortunately, given little
encouragement.[66]

Consequently, when Joyce published *Chamber Music*, the minor
poet had fallen on evil days. As Mathews pointed out in his rejoinder
to Joyce's uncomprehending assertions:

> I don't know why you should be surprised at the sales of your book.
> Some poets I meet with whose sales have not exceeded a dozen copies
> seem to accept their small circulation with some degree of equanimity
> and composure, and I wish you to know that I have pushed it (the book)
> for all it is worth, and also that I have spent far more in advertising it
> than was profitable. The advt, subjoined [author, title, size, and price of
> *Chamber Music* with an excerpt from Symons' review] I have inserted
> again and again.[67]

But Joyce, who was not, he wrote Mathews, "of the philosophical
temper of the poets you allude to," still was unable to comprehend
the situation; though admitting that "possibly the book was well
pushed in England as you say, it certainly was not in Ireland. When I
was there last summer very many people complained to me that it
had never been in the windows at all."[68] Mathews, a bit exasperated
by Joyce's attitude, countered with both more energy and more bite
than usual: "Well, all I can say is with regard to pushing your book in
Dublin various booksellers were approached at the time but with no
success. I know I saw Mr. Roberts at Maunsell's [sic] too. I can't say
now whether he took copies or not—all was done that could be done
with an unknown volume of poetry by an unknown poet. You evidently don't know what it is to secure sales in such a case."[69]

Mathews would no doubt have done more to push *Chamber Music*
if he had had the means. Certainly there is no evidence to suggest that
he did less for Joyce's poems than he did for any other "unknown
volume of poetry by an unknown poet." In addition to continuing to
list the book with excerpts from reviews in his catalogues and advertisements, Mathews, at least early on, took pen in hand to acquaint
editors and other influential persons in the literary world with the
merits of Joyce's book—for example, his letter to Wilfrid Meynell, the
influential journalist, biographer, and poet: "I wish to draw your
special attention to the little volume entitled 'Chamber Music' by

126

James Joyce. Arthur Symons who introduced the poet to me considers the work has 'the most genuine lyric quality of any new work I have read for many years.'"[70]

After this exchange of letters about the disappointing sales of *Chamber Music*, Joyce now with a better understanding of the poetry market and of Mathews' efforts, bestirred himself in the hope that by his own efforts he might spur sales. Shortly before *Chamber Music* had been published, Mathews had invited Joyce to supply him with names of booksellers in Trieste who might stock copies of the book and to offer suggestions "as to the furtherance of sales of the book."[71] Now three years later, in 1910, Joyce had a leaflet printed at his own expense entitled "Press Notices of *Chamber Music*" containing excerpts from twelve reviews; he hoped that by placing this in copies of *Dubliners* which Maunsel now had in proof, he could "give the verses a further push."[72] Although his plan came to naught when Maunsel stopped publication of the stories, Joyce went ahead and distributed the leaflet to friends in cities where he lived over the next several years and then revived the plan for an insert when publication of *Dubliners* by Grant Richards appeared imminent in 1914. Perhaps because few copies of the leaflet remained, Joyce this time announced his intention to insert them only in review copies of the stories. Nevertheless, as he informed Mathews, "I think this ought to sell off a few more copies of *Chamber Music*."[73] Mathews, who had welcomed Joyce's efforts, assuring him that he was "equally keen with yourself in promoting the sales of the book," also distributed the leaflet at Joyce's suggestion, at one point asking for "a hundred or two,—indeed as many of the prospectuses as you can spare."[74] In addition to the leaflet, Joyce sought to put copies of *Chamber Music* in the hands of a Trieste bookseller who had agreed to take some copies of *Dubliners*. More important, he purchased copies of the poems from Mathews at a shilling each plus postage and sold them.[75]

By May 1912, Joyce, encouraged by the fact that he had placed "nearly 50 copies of the book . . . in the hands of friends of mine" in Trieste, asked the publisher "if any royalties stand to my credit," thinking that "the limit [of 300 copies] must have been passed after such a long lapse of time."[76] But Mathews' "a/c of sales to date" drawn up the following February shows that while a further 64 copies of *Chamber Music* had been disposed of since 7 September 1909 (largely through Joyce's efforts), for royalty purposes only a total of 177 copies out of 300 had been sold.[77] On 26 February, Joyce wrote Mathews thanking him "for note and a/c received," adding that he had sold 12 more copies. But since the main business of his letter was to ask Mathews to "take on immediately the publication of my famous book *Dubliners*," Joyce may well have felt it judicious to withhold any expression of disappointment.[78]

Although Joyce from time to time continued to ask Mathews for an account of sales,[79] his concern with *Chamber Music* shifted in 1915 to securing its publication in America. By this time the New York publisher B. W. Huebsch had come into Joyce's life, holding out the hope that his books might find an American outlet. Shortly after reaching Zurich in July 1915, Joyce wrote Mathews that he had just heard from Huebsch, who wanted to know if Joyce had "published anything else in book form except *Dubliners* as, if so, he would be glad to have an opportunity of considering it for American publication. I wrote telling him about my novel *A Portrait of the Artist as a Young Man* which has been appearing serially in *The Egoist* and also about *Chamber Music*. Perhaps you could send him a copy and to get into relations with him."[80]

Heubsch, who was anxious to provide Joyce's works a proper introduction in America, approached Mathews about publishing *Chamber Music*, but, receiving no response, sought the help of Joyce's English patron, Harriet Weaver, who in November 1916 forwarded him a copy of the poems along with Mathews' terms "on which he would be willing to dispose of the American copyright."[81] After having seen the English edition, Huebsch concluded that it was too slight a book of verse for the American audience. Publishing it, he wrote the New York lawyer and Joyce enthusiast John Quinn, "might partially defeat our desire to get general recognition for Joyce. People rebel against paying for a book and getting only a few printed pages no matter how high their quality."[82] Consequently, both Huebsch and Quinn urged Joyce to add more poems to *Chamber Music* so that Huebsch could publish a more substantial volume. Joyce, however, repeatedly refused to violate the integrity of his suite of poems.[83] Finally, Huebsch, unable to sway Joyce, published the first authorized American edition of *Chamber Music* on 30 September 1918, it having been preceded in the same year by an unauthorized printing that appeared in Boston.[84]

Meanwhile, in January 1918, Mathews himself had issued a second edition of the poems, perhaps with the idea that Joyce's work was beginning to catch on. Bound in gray laid paper wrappers printed in black, it sold for a shilling and three pence. Cloth-bound copies at two shillings were also advertised, although Slocum and Cahoon, having never seen a copy, conjectured that these might have been copies of the first edition.[85] The second edition, which concluded with an advertisement containing excerpts of press notices of *Chamber Music* from the *Oxford Magazine*, the *Scotsman*, and the *Nation*, attracted little critical attention. It was, however, noticed by Ezra Pound (who had been published by Elkin Mathews since 1908), who wrote at length about it, quoting several poems, in his essay on Joyce in *The Future*. "We have here," Pound observed, "the lyric in some of its best traditions, and one pardons certain trifling inversions, much against the taste of the moment, for the sake of the clean-cut ivory finish, and for the interest of the rhythms, the cross run of the beat and the word, as of a stiff wind cutting the ripple-tops of bright water."[86] Jabbing at H. G. Wells and others who criticized Joyce's prose, Pound saw *Chamber Music* as "an excellent antidote for those who find Mr. Joyce's prose 'disagreeable.'"[87] An unsigned review in Harriet Weaver's *Egoist* called the verse "good, very good," and went on to observe (perhaps with the reviews of the first edition in mind) that "it will be called 'fragile,' but is substantial, with a great deal of thought beneath fine workmanship."[88] With so little press notice, it is doubtful that Mathews had any better success with his second edition than he had had with his first. In March 1920, scarcely two years after its issuance, James B. Pinker, Joyce's literary agent, reported to Joyce that "owing to the cost of rent of type [Mathews] has given instructions to have [the *Chamber Music* type] moulded."[89]

The following year, Joyce authorized Harriet Weaver "to make any arrangements you wish with Mr. Mathews and Mr. Richards" to clear the way for the publication of *Chamber Music*, *Dubliners*, and *Exiles* by the Egoist Press, and shortly thereafter the arrangements were successfully concluded.[90] On hearing the news, Joyce (just four days before Mathews' death, on 10 November 1921) wrote Miss Weaver that he "was glad to hear that Messrs. Elkin Mathews and Grant Richards have ceased to be connected with me. I hope I shall hear no more of them in this world or the next. The name of the former will not appear in *Ulysses* as publisher of *Chamber Music*."[91] It is difficult to understand why Joyce in this his valedictory statement on his early publishers would lump Mathews with Richards. Unlike Richards, Mathews always had been straightforward, frank, and scrupulously honest in his dealings with Joyce. And although there had been times when Joyce, largely through misunderstandings, had seemed vexed with the publisher, relations between the two men over the fourteen years of their acquaintance were surprisingly good considering the fact that Joyce was known to be, in the words of Symons, "a difficult person to deal with."[92] Of course, given Joyce's miserable ordeal of getting his works before the public, one can easily imagine how difficult it was for him to look back upon those years with objectivity and forbearance.

As for Mathews' part, his publication of *Chamber Music* brought him little if any profit, and his relationship with Joyce, little if any pleasure.[93] Unable, like Symons, to recognize and relish great genius expressing itself in new and alien modes, Mathews had refused to publish *Dubliners* and *A Portrait of the Artist as a Young Man* when fate had laid them at his feet, but nevertheless had the desire and good sense to publish *Chamber Music* when no other publisher would touch it, thus achieving for himself the renown of being James Joyce's first publisher.

CHAPTER FIVE

Ezra Pound's First Publisher:

Elkin Mathews and the London Years, 1908–1921

IN SEPTEMBER 1908, during his twenty-third year, the unknown and impecunious Ezra Loomis Pound arrived in London, bringing with him from Italy copies of his first book of poetry, *A Lume Spento*, which (as he later wrote) he "DEEPosited with Elkin Mathews and 'Inigo' Lane, the two peaks of Parnassus."[1] As partners in the Bodley Head, Mathews and Lane had published the work of poets whose names became synonymous with the nineties—Oscar Wilde, William Butler Yeats, Lionel Johnson, Ernest Dowson, Arthur Symons, William Sharp ("Fiona Macleod"), and Richard Le Gallienne, among others.[2] Their reputation for patronizing writers and artists whose work was considered avant-garde (bearing, as much of it did, both aesthetic and decadent traits typical of the times) quickly spread to America, where their books, reflecting in their format and letterpress the aims of the revival of printing, were much admired, in particular by some energetic young men like Fred Holland Day, who in 1893 with Herbert Copeland established a publishing business in Boston along the lines of the Bodley Head. A devotee of D. G. Rossetti and his Pre-Raphaelite followers, Day eagerly sought to associate the new firm with aesthetic and decadent literature and art, and saw no better way to do so than to include in the firm's first list a number of books imported from the Bodley Head, among them Francis Thompson's *Poems*, Richard Le Gallienne's *English Poems*, John Davidson's *A Random Itinerary*, and Oscar Wilde's *Salomé*. Two other avant-garde publishing houses of the nineties brought out American editions of Bodley Head books: Stone and Kimball and Way and Williams, both of Chicago. And although Thomas B. Mosher of Portland, Maine, never published Bodley Head books under a joint imprint, he published attractive editions of some of their authors which in their subject matter, format, and letterpress reflected the influence of the London firm.

To Pound the books of the Bodley Head were no strangers: during his college years in America he had read Fiona Macleod, Dowson, and Symons, and had been guided in his reading by "Mr. Mosher," and he later described himself during this time as having been "drunk with 'Celticism', and with Dowson's 'Cynara', and with one or two poems of Symons.'"[3] Nor were the names of Elkin Mathews and John Lane. Given their fame as champions of the innovative poets of the nineties and their esteem among the elect as publishers of tasteful books, it is little wonder that the friendless Pound, soon after his arrival in London, made his pilgrimage to Vigo Street (like so many others before him), approaching the "two peaks of Parnassus" with an attitude akin to that of a religious devotee entering Mecca.

Mathews' shop in those days was very much as it had been in the early nineties. Small, the shop's walls were tight with bookshelves filled from floor to ceiling and overflowing with old volumes (reflecting Mathews' antiquarian interests) which mingled with new books just off the press, the fruit of his publishing ventures. As late as 1906, Mathews' premises, according to a reporter who visited them, still possessed a quiet, old-world charm reminiscent of the eighteenth-century bookshop. Compared to John Lane's office opposite, with its pseudo-Georgian façade, "Mr. Mathews' establishment is, for all practical purposes, the genuine thing," he observed; "and there is a distinct Georgian atmosphere about the crowded little shop, with its shelves of quaintly-bound volumes and its diminutive counter." "It only needed," the writer concluded, "that the genial proprietor should don a bob-wig and knee breeches to make the illusion complete."[4]

Neither the quaint little shop nor its genial proprietor had changed when Pound entered it for the first time some two years later. For Mathews was rather conservative and old-fashioned by nature and was unlikely to change his premises or his ways unless constrained by circumstances to do so. If the young American entered with any apprehension lest the other peak of Parnassus should strike him dead, he was soon put at his ease. The sanctum of the god was simply an old desk at the rear of the shop where the "monkish, medieval Mathews" (as *Punch* had dubbed him) sat enshrined in books over an old cellar—in reality a privy—in whose musty depths the rather shy publisher on occasion took refuge to avoid unpleasant confrontations. Quite at home in this unpretentious atmosphere, the man Pound met was an unassuming fellow of some fifty-seven years who, though sought out by those who admired him for his role as the poets' publisher, was not the object of lionization that his old partner, John Lane, had become.

Having used his copies of *A Lume Spento* as a pretext to meet Mathews and Lane, Pound evidently decided that Mathews, not Lane, was the man to cultivate. Although the Bodley Head under Lane's sole direction had burgeoned into a much larger, better-known publishing firm than Mathews' business, and although Lane himself had become something of a celebrity in the publishing world, with a reputation far exceeding that of Mathews, Pound concluded that Mathews was the more likely of the two to publish his poetry and the man more apt to spend time on his behalf introducing him to the London literati. Besides, Pound probably found Mathews more approachable, more tractable than Lane. The latter, aggressive and masterful, with something of a reputation for skullduggery, was unlikely to march to the tune of the brash Ezra, who had little to offer a publisher of one of the leading firms of the day. Consequently, Pound during the autumn and winter of 1908–9 established a relationship with Mathews which was to be an extraordinarily fortunate one for the young poet. Of the many men and women whom Pound would meet during his long sojourn in the British capital, few would prove more useful to him. At this crucial stage of Pound's early career, Mathews played an indispensable role as his publisher and as his entree to London literary society. Though of quite different temperaments, the young poet and the middle-aged publisher seem to have taken a liking to each other from the start, Pound seeing Mathews through the youthful eyes with a slight case of hero-worship, Mathews viewing the youth from a fatherly perspective.

Showing his liking for Pound, Mathews soon invited him to Chorleywood, Hertfordshire, for overnight stays at his home, "Russettings." Pound probably was referring to the first of these visits in a letter he wrote to Mathews from 48 Langham Street, his first London address, to say: "If it suits you to have me come into the country with you this Saturday, I shall be very glad to. If you want me, will you want me to meet you in Vigo St. & go out with you, or to come out later[?]" On these weekends, Pound would have met Mathews' wife and their daughter, Nest, who, eleven years old at the time, remembers how nice the surprisingly young-looking poet with "high, copper-coloured hair" was to her. Though struck by his pleasant and lively personality, she recalls how thin he appeared and how "spotty" and "pallid" his complexion was. Reinforcing her memory of the young Pound, Nest Elkin Mathews' diary entry for Saturday, 20 March 1909, reads: "Mr. E. Pound came to tea & supper . . . I think Mr. Pound is a very sickly young man."[5]

Once Mathews' sympathies were enlisted, Pound, given his deep interest in the Italian Renaissance and his penchant for promoting the work of others, set about what he later spoke of as his "first little job in London," that is, urging Mathews to bring out William Michael Rossetti's treatises, principally in prose, which elucidated and embodied three of Dante's canzoni.[6] Having successfully completed this first job—the work appeared in 1909 as *Dante and His Convito: A Study with Translations* by W. M. Rossetti—he then prevailed on Mathews to publish in late December 1908 a second printing of *A Quinzaine for This Yule*, a booklet of a few poems which Pound had gotten up for the Christmas season. Printed and published by W. J. Pollock and Company, the first printing of 100 copies had soon been exhausted.[7] Pound and Mathews used the second printing of *A Quinzaine*, consisting of another 100 copies, in their campaign to promote the poet's name among the London literati. Acknowledging with thanks the receipt of what was probably the agreement for *Personae*, Pound in a letter to Mathews continued: "I think you might send out 8 or 10 copies of the 'Quinzaine' where you think it will do the most good, Mr. Windham [*sic*] or whosoever."[8]

While Pound was busy with these enterprises during the autumn and early winter of 1908, he was also composing new poems which together with those in *A Lume Spento* were to make up the manuscript of his first important volume of poems, *Personae*. The brief account of how Pound proposed the publication of *Personae* to Mathews is one of the better-known stories in the annals of modern publishing history. Pound (who seems never to have tired of telling it), and others who repeated it, propagated it with a view to establishing and sustaining the myth of a brave young poetical genius who "came to London a complete stranger, without either literary patronage or financial means," and conquered. "Few poets," as T. S. Eliot was later to preface his account, "have undertaken the siege of London with so little backing."[9] So enamored was Pound of this image of himself as a kind of Dick Whittington of the London literary scene that he later rather harshly took the editor of the *Boston Evening Transcript* to task for ignoring the fact that he, not Robert Frost, was the first American poet of his generation who, "unheralded, unintroduced, untrumpeted," had "won acceptance of an English publisher on his own terms." To substantiate his point, Pound went on to acquaint the editor with what he referred to as "that touching little scene in Elkin Mathews' shop some years since," in which the poet had asked the publisher to bring out *Personae*:

> *Mathews:* "Ah, eh, ah, would you, now, be prepared to assist in the publication?"
> *E.P.:* "I've a shilling in my clothes, if that's any use to you."
> *Mathews:* "Oh well I want to publish 'em anyhow." And he did![10]

That the negotiations were concluded with so little ceremony may strike one as patently apochryphal; yet the brief dialogue rings true—the frank openness of Pound and the bashful demeanor of Mathews. Though it lacks the context of Pound's several months' acquaintance and business dealings with the publisher, the account nevertheless suggests the generosity of Mathews toward young poets, his offhand conduct when he found a volume of verse he personally liked, and what T. S. Eliot later referred to as his "acumen" in estimating the worth of a manuscript, which in the case of *Personae* was, indeed, "justified."[11] Given the publisher's taste for Pre-Raphaelite poetry, there can be little doubt that he responded with pleasure to the manuscript of *Personae*: it is largely the product of Pound's own sojourn in what Louis L. Martz has referred to as "Swinburne-land," which he describes as "a land of dreams and sorrows derived not simply from Swinburne, but also from Rossetti and the other Pre-Raphaelites with whom Swinburne began his career; and also from the heirs of Swinburne, the 'Decadent' poets of the 'Nineties, Dowson, Davidson, Lionel Johnson, and the rest, especially the early Yeats, with his Celtic variations on the Swinburnian dream."[12] One of the few things Mathews and Pound had in common—at least early on—was their mutual admiration for Rossetti, the poets of the nineties, and especially Swinburne, which is reflected years later in Pound's reference in Canto LXXXII to those first few months in London when he met lots of literary "big-shots":

> Swinburne my only miss
> and I didn't know he'd been to see Landor
>   and they told me this that an'tother
> and when old Mathews went he saw the three teacups
> two for Watts Dunton who liked to let his tea cool
> So old Elkin had only one glory
>   He did carry Algernon's suit case once
> When he, Elkin, first came to London.[13]

So impressed was Mathews with *Personae* that (as Pound's own account emphasizes) he offered to publish it at his own expense. Elated by this turn of events, Pound in early February 1909 wrote William Carlos Williams the good news, boasting that Mathews is "giving me the same terms he gives Maurice Hewlett," the popular novelist whose book of verse, *Artemisian: Idylls and Songs*, would be published by Mathews along with *Personae* in April.[14]

Having struck a bargain, Pound and Mathews were one in their determination to make *Personae* a success. Mathews sent the manuscript to the Chiswick Press, a firm with a distinguished reputation for high-quality work. Moreover, when the first proofs arrived in Vigo Street on 13 March 1909, Pound, according to an analysis made of them by C. G. Petter, "heavily revised" them, having "scrutinized" them "very carefully." The second proofs, which arrived a week later, on 19 March, "confirm the impression of self-conscious tinkering created by the first." In addition to Pound's painstaking efforts, "numerous markings on the second proofs" and holograph notes on the verso of an envelope addressed to Mathews and postmarked the exact date of the second proofs lead Petter to conclude that the publisher "personally supervised the marking of the second and possibly also the first proofs."[15] Furthermore, Pound's statement to Michael Reck "that he and Mathews measured out the poems with calipers so there would be no awkward breaks at the ends of lines and pages" is further evidence of the care and cooperation on the part of poet and publisher that went into the making of *Personae*.[16]

Heralded in Mathews' announcements and advertisements as early as 6 March 1909,[17] *Personae* was published on 16 April at 2/6 in drab paper-covered boards with gilt lettering on the front cover and spine. With its well-designed title page bearing the publisher's device in red, *Personae* was in the tradition of the tasteful, attractive books of poetry Mathews had been publishing since the early nineties. Although 1,000 copies were printed, only 500 were bound for sale. According to Chiswick Press records dated 31 March 1909, the cost of composition and printing, including the antique laid paper, was £13.10.0. Extra charges for small type, notes, and initials totaled £1.1.0 and for corrections and alterations in proofs were £1.19.6. Supplying a half ream of fine antique laid paper to the binder for endleaves at 7/– brought the total to £16.17.6. Cost of binding 500 copies came to £6.12.6, and advertising costs amounted to £6.3.0, bringing the total cost of producing *Personae* to £29.13.0.[18]

Given the fact that *Personae* was the work of a young, little-known American poet lately come to England, the book was received remarkably well. Besides the now famous review by the poet Edward Thomas—which, as Eric Homberger says, "'made' Pound's debut in London"[19]—in Ford Madox Hueffer's *English Review*, there were appreciative responses by the well-known editor and critic W. L. Courtney in the *Daily Telegraph*, by F. S. Flint in *New Age*, and by the very young Rupert Brooke in the *Cambridge Review*. And although there was the unsigned review in the *Nation* which accused Pound of poetic heresy, *Personae*, as Michael Reck points out, "soon became something of a sensation in London literary circles; Pound's suave irony and impeccable ear for verbal music gave him a modest fame."[20] Even *Punch* cast a satirical eye toward the red-haired young poet whom Yeats called "this queer creature Ezra Pound."[21] In a humorous parody of the humdrum publishers' announcements so common in the *Publishers' Circular* and other journals, *Punch* tweeked the nose of "Mr. Wilkin Mark's [Elkin Mathews'] New Poet."

Mr. Welkin Mark . . . begs to announce that he has secured for the English market the palpitating works of the new Montana (U.S.A) poet,

PERSONAE
OF
EZRA POUND

LONDON

ELKIN MATHEWS, VIGO STREET

MCMIX

Title page of Ezra Pound's second book, *Personae* (1909)

Mr. Ezekiel Ton, who is the most remarkable thing in poetry since Robert Browning. Mr. Ton, who has left America to reside for a while in London and impress his personality on English editors, publishers and readers, is by far the newest poet going, whatever other advertisements may say. He has succeeded, where all others have failed, in evolving a blend of the imagery of the unfettered West, the vocabulary of Wardour Street, and the sinister abandon of Borgiac Italy.[22]

The successful debut of *Personae* was, in part, a tribute to Mathews' considerable efforts during the winter of 1908–9 to make Pound known to the London literati. This was accomplished in several ways. First, Mathews introduced Pound to his authors and friends who frequented the shop in Vigo Street; these included Selwyn Image, one of the founders at the Century Guild and a designer of some of Mathews' books and title pages; Laurence Binyon, the young poet who had edited the Shilling Garland series for Mathews; Victor Plarr, the poet and friend of Ernest Dowson; and Ernest Rhys, the editor of the Everyman series, through whom Pound later met May Sinclair, and through her, Ford Madox Hueffer.[23] Second, Mathews put Pound in touch with men of letters not so readily accessible by taking him about to literary gatherings such as the meeting of the Poets' Club on the night of 23 February 1909, where he first met T. E. Hulme, through whom he later met F. S. Flint.[24]

The successful debut of *Personae* also was due to some extent to what seems to have been a bit of logrolling in which Pound and Mathews and, possibly, others were involved. For instance, there is a letter in which Pound tells Mathews, "I cannot change the dedication"—an apparent reply to a suggestion by Mathews that it would be politic to dedicate *Personae* to some notable and influential man of letters rather than to an unknown "Mary Moore of Trenton." "I have however at hand," Pound goes on to write, "letters from Leeds, Edinburgh, & Dublin universities from men whom Mr. Wilson Ring has enlisted in the propaganda (all of them holding chairs in literature) Mr. E. Dowden of Dublin is I presume the best known (at least to me). I hope this will compensate."[25]

Once the book was out, Mathews spent what was for him a considerable amount of money—some £6.3.0—on advertising. Planned and written with Pound's collaboration, the advertisements varied in form. A statement which appeared in the *Publishers' Cir-*

cular in June was carefully calculated in its wording to lure the avant-garde poetry-reading public: "This little book of musical and thoroughly artistic verse is permeated by the author's close familiarity with the impersonal note existing in Provencal poetry. The volume is one to be read in a thoughtful mood by those to whom the value of a poem consists greatly in its poetic beauty and construction."[26] Then there is the two-page leaflet of 2,000 copies printed at the Chiswick Press at a cost of 15/- which described *Personae* as "just out. —A new note in verse. The season's sensation in poetry," and contained excerpts from favorable press opinions.[27] In addition, the advertising campaign included the usual listings of *Personae* among Mathews' current books in advertisements appearing in such journals as the *Academy* and the *Publishers' Circular* and in Mathews' occasional catalogues.

Given the logrolling, the advertising, and the good press, Pound and his publisher doubtless had hopes that *Personae* would sell well. The fact that Mathews ordered a first printing of 1,000 copies strongly suggests he was persuaded that both *Personae* and its author had an unusually bright future. To anyone familiar with the meager sales of poetry during the first decade of the present century, Mathews' decision to print so many copies is a distinct surprise. In a roughly comparable situation two years before, Mathews—far more typically—had chosen to print only 500 copies of James Joyce's *Chamber Music*. One can only surmise that the impact of Pound's poetry and personality on Mathews was strong enough to persuade him to risk printing in the case of *Personae* far more copies than usual, hedging his bet by initially binding only 500 copies. Judged again in the light of Joyce's *Chamber Music*, sales of *Personae* during the first year were, indeed, good. Whereas *Chamber Music* had sold only 127 copies within a year of publication, *Personae* had sold 303 copies. In addition to these, 98 more copies had been disposed of: 5 (as required by law) to the libraries of deposit, 6 (as required by agreement) to the author, 14 to the author at half-price, and 73 to reviewers, bringing the total number of copies disposed of to 401, enough to require the binding of another 100 copies.[28]

Perhaps spurred on more by the recognition gained for him by *Personae* than by its sales, Pound sought to reinforce his newly won fame and increase the public perception of him as "the most remarkable thing in poetry since Robert Browning" by bringing out another volume of poetry as soon as practicable. Composing poetry with remarkable facility during the summer of 1909, Pound submitted the manuscript of his next volume, *Exultations*, to Mathews for consideration in early August. Although Mathews (exhibiting a sensitivity to material which might be objectionable to the reading public on religious grounds) voiced doubts about the propriety of publishing what turned out to be the book's most famous poem, "The Ballad of the Goodly Fere,"[29] he nevertheless accepted *Exultations* for publication.

An agreement dated 16 September 1909 shows that Mathews took upon himself "the entire risk of production with the exception of the charge for corrections and alterations" in the proofs which Pound was called upon to pay. Moreover, it stipulates that Mathews, "after the cost of production out of the sales of the book has been met" agreed "to pay the Author 10% up to 500 copies and 12½% afterwards counting 13 copies as 12 on all copies sold." As to the proceeds from the sale of rights of translation and advance rights to the United States, the agreement stipulated that Mathews would receive them although they were to be divided equally between publisher and author. Furthermore, "in the case of stereoplates, electroplates or shells sold to the United States of America the net proceeds of their sales after deducting the involved cost of their production shall be received and divided in the same way." In addition to this, the agreement gives Mathews "the exclusive right during the legal term of copyright of printing and publishing in Great Britain and all countries the work intended to be called 'Exultations of Ezra Pound.'"[30]

In a letter also dated 16 September which accompanied the signed agreement, Pound offered some friendly amendments. First, he objected to assigning the rights to Mathews for the duration of the copyright: "Considering that your business is practically dependent on your own personality & not upon a system or machine, I should prefer not to make a contract binding for so long a term of years. Therefore let us say for *10 years, or for so long as you personally are engaged in publishing*. This does not make me liable to be tangled up in business with some unknown third party in case you died or withdrew." Second, Pound suggested an alteration in the rate of royalty which actually favored Mathews: 10 percent on the first thousand copies, 12.5 percent on the second thousand, 15 percent on the third, and 20 percent on the fourth. "It is of course doubtful," he wrote, "that so many copies should be sold but if the book should meet with such success it seems to me this is equitable." Finally, he stipulated: "If I go to America & secure a publisher there *by my own effort*, I should feel entitled to 75% of the profit, leaving you the whole profit on sale of 'shells etc.' in any case. If on the contrary you secure the cooperation of a foreign publisher we would share alike."[31]

Probably sharing Pound's sense of urgency, Mathews as soon as the agreement was signed sent the manuscript of *Exultations* to the firm which had printed *Personae*, the Chiswick Press. That its format, paper, size, and type were the same as that of *Personae* facilitated the rapid production of the new book of poems. The first proofs having been corrected by the end of September, *Exultations* was published on 25 October at 2/6 and bound in dark red paper-covered boards with the lettering in gold on the front cover and spine.

Although 1,000 copies of *Exultations* were printed, as in the case of *Personae*, only 350 copies were bound for sale, perhaps reflecting initial sales of *Personae*. According to the Chiswick Press records of 22 October 1909, the cost of composing and printing 1,000 copies, including ten pages of advertisements, on antique laid paper was £13.10.0. Extra costs for small type, corrections and alterations, and end paper added another £2.6.6. Cost of binding 350 copies amounted to £4.12.9, and advertising came to £3.10.0, bringing the total cost of producing *Exultations* to £23.19.3.[32] In the hope that the critical acclaim accorded *Personae* would spur sales of *Exultations* and set the tone for reviewers, Mathews issued 2,000 copies of a leaflet listing excerpts from reviews of *Personae*. And although reviews such as that by F. S. Flint in *New Age*, were, on the whole, appreciative and quite encouraging, there were none that made the enthusiastic and persuasive case for *Exultations* that Edward Thomas had made for *Personae*. In fact, Thomas, who regretted having written his laudatory review, took the opportunity the new book afforded him to explain away his aberration. Having allowed what he called "the turbulent opacity" of Pound's "peculiarities to sink down," he now saw, as he explained in the pages of the *Daily Chronicle*, "very nearly nothing at all."[33] The first indication of how well *Exultations* was selling came in the form of Mathews' account of sales dated 3 March 1910, which showed that 203 copies had been sold and another 74 disposed of to the libraries of deposit, reviewers, and to the author.[34]

This account of sales which also included *Personae* was accompanied by a letter from Mathews which indicates how difficult it was for a publisher of belles lettres to recoup his costs. Referring to the old saw that "every little makes a mickle," Mathews observed that

> when the "mickle" is the sum of £55.10.9 [the total cost of publishing *Personae* and *Exultations*] it takes a multitude of 'littles' to make it. So, coming to close quarters with the accounts of 'Personae' and 'Exulta-tions'" I find there is still a deficit of £4.5.2 on the one and £6.4.8 on the other—or ten guineas in all. I hoped there would be a small dividend to declare, but it seems you must for the present rest upon your laurels and I must look forward to further sales before things balance themselves.

Throwing some light on the reception of these two early volumes in the United States, Mathews in a peevish tone of voice concluded: "I think some of your relations and American friends might have given you some support—but the help that came from that quarter was a negligible quantity."[35] Another accounting dated exactly one year later, 3 March 1911, revealed that only 89 more copies of *Personae* and 113 more of *Exultations* had sold. And although additional expenses of £10.5.3. for extra advertising had accrued, revenues from the further sales of the books had reduced the deficit on both volumes to £3.8.10.[36]

In the spring of 1910, Pound and Mathews were planning a new volume which ultimately was to become *Canzoni*. Initially it was to have contained the poet's prose-and-verse sequence "The Dawn," which Pound had read at the Shakespears' in February. Mathews agreed to publish "The Dawn" after J. M. Dent, the firm which later published Pound's *The Spirit of Romance*, declined to bring it out. In a letter of late April to Pound, who was sojourning in Italy, Mathews agreed to "take on 'The Dawn' together with the poems you have ready for a new autumn volume on the same terms as 'Exultations.'"[37] But Pound, after returning to the United States in the summer, arranged with the Boston firm of Small, Maynard to publish his new poems along with a selection of pieces from *Personae* and *Exultations* in a volume entitled *Provença* with the intention of bringing out the "new poems," as the blurb on the dust jacket stated, "in England separately under the title of *Canzoniere*."[38] Since *Provença* did not appear until November and Pound did not return to England until late February, and then only briefly, *Canzoni* actually was not published until the summer of 1911.

Meanwhile, the serious work of producing the new volume may be said to have gotten under way on 30 November 1910, when Pound dispatched the following letter to Mathews from New York: "I am sending you the Canzoni [manuscript] at last. You will find no Ballad of the Goodly Fere in it, but it is a much more interesting collection, to my mind, than either of the other books. It is longer, as you requested, and there'll probably be a few more poems, I can not be sure. I'd like it out as soon as possible ('as usual', you'll say). The contract can be the same as that for Exultations, except the American clause (which could hardly offer you the poems already published here)." "Disgusted with the botch" that Small, Maynard had made of *Provença*, and particularly with "the pale pewkish hue of a cover," Pound was at special pains to see that *Canzoni* was bound more suitably: "The colour to be that of 'Agape,'" he wrote, "that clear blue grey—with gilt lettering—([Anthony George] Sheil[l]'s 'Agape' I think it was)." "Doubly in hast" to get his canzoni "into respectable clothing," Pound sent Mathews a carefully typed manuscript which he hoped would preclude the necessity of more than one set of proofs.[39]

Although he had intended to return to England during the first month of the new year, Pound was ill at home in Philadelphia, too weak to travel, when he wrote Mathews on 23 January 1911, informing him that they "must proceed" with the business of the new book "as if I had not threatened invasion." Advising his publisher that "there are 4 lines to be added to 'A Prologue' and 10 to 15 pages of stuff to be added to the book," Pound conjectured: "You may have to sell the book at 3/–; in fact, I think it would be advisable to bind in cloth (same formate as P[ersonae] & Ex[ultations] in other respects) and sell at 3/6d. It won't be bad to have the new book cost more than the old ones & everyone who will pay 2/6 will pay 3/6, I think, by now." Still concerned about the binding, Pound told Mathews that if Mathews couldn't "match the Agape colour in cloth, use burlap or pongee coloured cloth. Preferably rough. (A very heavy pongee material would I presume be expensive & not durable???)."[40]

Pound's "threatened invasion" of England was finally at hand when he wrote Mathews in February in a somewhat jocular and peremptory mood to inform him that he would arrive aboard the *Mauretania*

> about 10 days after this epistle. I shall remain in London 20 minutes & perhaps longer. I shall bring you 18 pages of print. (I've counted it out pretty carefully) so your estimates can go on that basis. The volume will follow our classic & imperial precedent & call itself
>
> Canzoni
> *of*
> Ezra   Pound
> Given under our hand & ink this 13th day of Feb. *MCMXI*.

In light of his short stay in London, Pound, in a postscript, advised Mathews, "The more things you can have ready by Feb. 27 or 28, . . . the less we'll have to do by letter & profession of faith."[41]

Between 13 and 22 May 1911, Pound, in Paris, received the page proofs of *Canzoni*, which, according to Noel Stock, "he corrected and returned by the end of the month." These proofs, now in the Ransom Humanities Research Center at the University of Texas, reveal that Pound's changes in the text were of a minor nature, his deletion of a number of poems being the major alteration of the text.[42]

Canzoni was published in July at 3/6 and bound in streaky gray cloth boards lettered in gold. Pound was in Italy when word was received of its publication, and in a postcard to Mathews dated 15 July poured out his delight in a now-typical melange of languages:

> Right O: The book hasn't yet arrived *Ad E[lkin]*.
> *M[athews]. salutatio*
> "Hasn [*sic*] Sachs war ein Schyo. etc. Ezra *in ipsum opusculosque suos*.
> English? he wrote not, spoke not, But a sort of scholars jumbling poly-g[l]ot, & yet slewed out a bit the stiffest nuts, Until 'twas deemed his antic stuff had guts So some few praised it, but no man knew why. Touts droits de traduction reserves."[43]

As was the case with *Personae* and *Exultations*, the Chiswick Press printed 1,000 sets of sheets of *Canzoni*, but Mathews had the press bind only 250 copies for publication. According to the press's records, dated 20 June 1911, the cost of composing and printing 1,000 copies on antique paper supplied by Mathews was £9.14.0. Other charges, including £1.19.0 for corrections and alterations in proof and another

£1.19.6 for cancelled matter, came to £16.5.6. According to Mathews' records, total cost for producing *Canzoni*, including binding and advertising, amounted to £30.18.7.[44]

The critical reception of *Canzoni* was quite mixed. Several critics, exasperated by Pound's flagrant departures from the Victorian poetic mode, railed against his indifference to tradition and condemned his "eccentricities," his "affectation combined with pedantry." But at least one critic, J. C. Squire, writing in the pages of *New Age*, recognized the excellence of Pound's artistry and the "much hard thinking (though very little emotion)" that had gone into "the making of the poems."[45] By far the most important critique of *Canzoni*, however, came from outside the usual form of a review—that is, if Pound, himself, is to be believed. In August, shortly after *Canzoni* had been published, Pound joined his friend Ford Madox Hueffer, who was in a self-imposed exile in Giessen at the time. Years later in his obituary of Hueffer, Pound recalled his mentor's rather violent response to *Canzoni*, which the poet brought along hot off the press. So amused by what he considered to be the book's artificial diction and subject matter, Hueffer literally rolled on the floor holding his sides and laughing, and had the effect on the stunned poet of what Brita Lindberg-Seyersted refers to as "a brutal but salutary cleansing."[46] There can be little doubt that Hueffer's rather startling reaction to *Canzoni* profoundly altered Pound's own view of the book, enabling him finally to see its lack of shape. "This shaping up a book is very important," he later wrote Mathews:

> It is almost as important as the construction of a play or a novel. I neglected it in "Canzoni" and the book has never had the same measure of success as the others. It is *not* so good as the others. I was affected by hyper-aesthesia or over- squeamishness and cut out the rougher poems. I don't know that I regret it in that case for the poems weren't good enough, but even so the book would have been better if they had been left in, or if something like them had been put in their place.[47]

The declining enthusiasm in England for Pound's poetry which was registered in the reviews of *Canzoni* was reflected in the disappointing sales of the book. That out of 1,000 sheets, only 250 were bound, indicates Mathews' rather pessimistic assessment of the book's chances, an assessment borne out by the fact that only 134 copies had sold some year and a half later, when the publisher's account of sales showed that of the almost £31 he had invested in *Canzoni*, only £11.13.9 had been recouped.[48]

It was not long after the publication of *Canzoni* in the summer of 1911 that Pound left Mathews, lured away by the highly unusual offer made him by the firm of Stephen Swift and Company of £100 per year advance royalties for a period of ten years for the right to publish his future books. As Gallup has noted, "The first book to appear under this agreement was the English edition of the *Sonnets and Ballate of Guido Cavalcanti*," published in May 1912. The second was *Riposxtes*, which appeared the following October. Having been the recipient of such an extravagant offer, Pound should not have been surprised by the turn of events he described to his parents in November: "'Swift' is busted," he wrote, and the manager has absconded "with *some* of the goods" to Tangier.[49]

Shortly after, he was once again corresponding with Mathews, suggesting that "as a means of stirring up the trade" a two-volume edition of his poems be published. "i.e. Personae & Exultations bound together, cloth, at 3/6. Riposxtes & Canzoni bound together, cloth at 3/6. Riposxtes are same size as Canzoni so it will be easy enough to do this. It's only a matter of binding the sheets now on hand. Also for *adv*[ertisements] & reviews it will be stimulating to have the stuff altogether complete & handy. We can produce this as soon as the copies now bound separately are sold off. Let me hear if this inspires you & we can discuss the matter viva voce."[50]

Pound's proposal was probably prompted by his receipt of an account of sales for *Personae, Exultations*, and *Canzoni* which Mathews compiled on 18 November as perhaps a part of a general "stocktaking" preceding a resumption of relations between poet and publisher. Although sales receipts for *Personae* and *Exultations* now exceeded the production costs, receipts for *Canzoni* amounted to only £15.12.8, still some £11.13.9 in the red. And if Pound was hoping for royalties accruing from the sales of *Personae* and *Exultations*, Mathews disabused him of any such notion in a note he penned at the bottom of the accompanying letter which made quite clear that no royalties would be forthcoming until production costs for all three books were recouped and Pound had discharged another debt: "In addition to this sum of £11.13.9 which has to be made up by sales before I can pay you royalty—you have had copies of the various books to the tune of £5.14.3—this however is reduced to £4.9.3 by a payment you made some time ago of 25/-."[51]

Faced with overcoming a deficit of £16.3.0, Pound was now seeking a way of selling off more of the still-sizable lot of unbound copies of his poems and thereby settling his account with Mathews and possibly earning some royalties as well. Mathews, seeing sense in Pound's proposal, consequently proceeded to implement it by having half titles and title leaves for the two composite volumes printed. Chiswick Press records dated 26 April 1913 show that "500 copies of combined preliminary matter to *Canzoni & Ripostes of Ezra Pound*" were printed on paper supplied at a cost of £1.12.6. Similarly, records dated 3 May 1913 indicate that "500 copies of joint title, etc. *Personae and Exultations of Ezra Pound*" were printed on antique laid paper provided by the publisher at cost of 19s.6d.[52]

Although Mathews had printed enough preliminary pages to bind and issue 500 copies of each of the composite volumes, nowhere near that number were ever actually bound for sale. As Gallup observes in his entries for the two volumes in his Pound bibliography, "The rare occurrence of the composite volume in comparison with its separate components indicates that fewer than the intended number were actually issued."[53] An estimate of the number of copies actually bound can be gathered from the fact that according to Mathews, a total of 600 copies of *Personae* and 500 copies of *Exultations* ultimately were bound.[54] Since there were 260 unbound sets of sheets of *Personae* and 310 sets of *Exultations* still on hand at the binder, Matthew Bell and Company, as late as May 1916,[55] not more than 140 sets of sheets could possibly have been bound up in the composite volume. Similarly, the number of copies of *Canzoni & Ripostes* also can be estimated. Although the number of sets of sheets of *Ripostes* printed is unknown, 1,000 sets of sheets of *Canzoni* were printed, of which 250 were bound.[56] This and the fact that 610 sets of sheets remained unbound at Matthew Bell's in May 1916 indicate that about 140 copies of the second (as of the first) of the composite volumes were issued. Published in May 1913, *Personae & Exultations*, bound in drab

148

paper-covered boards lettered in gold and *Canzoni & Ripostes*, bound in brown paper boards lettered in gold, sold at 3/6 each.

In January 1913, Mathews, having been forced to vacate his premises at 6b Vigo Street, moved to 4a Cork Street, several blocks toward Bond Street. This move serves to mark the close of the first phase in his relations with Pound, a phase which had begun with mutual respect and affection and ended with a growing sense of estrangement. The common bond between Pound and Mathews had been from the outset their mutual admiration for the Pre-Raphaelite poets, Swinburne, and the poets of the nineties. Pound had seen Mathews as something of a hero for his role in publishing the poets of the nineties and thereby promoting their cause; Mathews had seen Pound as an attractive, spirited, and talented young poet destined to carry on that tradition and champion that cause in the twentieth century. The first tangible expression of this bond was *Personae*, a copy of which Pound inscribed "To my sacred Father in Books, to the ever blessed Aticus, C. Elkin Mathews."[57] That Mathews for some years continued to think of Pound as a poet after his own heart can be seen in his continuing enthusiasm for Pound and his early poetry. For instance, Harriet Monroe, who had been taken to Vigo Street in 1910 and introduced to Mathews by May Sinclair, later recalled that the publisher "was vividly enthusiastic about the work of a young American in London, Ezra Pound. 'That is real poetry!' he exclaimed, as he showed me the *Personae* and *Exultations*."[58] And a year later, when Marianne Moore and her mother happened into Mathews' shop, the publisher, like a proud father, showed her photographs of Pound.[59] Another mark of Mathews' continuing esteem for Pound was his sending to Sir Arthur Quiller-Couch a copy of *Canzoni* and in an accompanying letter urging the well-known and influential critic to select several poems for inclusion in *The Oxford Book of Victorian Verse*, which "Q" was compiling in the autumn of 1912. There can be little doubt but that the appearance of two poems from *Canzoni*— "Portrait" and "Ballad for Gloom"—in this important (but to some extent misnamed) anthology was due to Mathews' initiative.[60]

But by 1912 Mathews had begun to realize that Pound was a different poet from what he once was. Although after his move from Vigo Street he included Pound among his "Cork Street poets," he was increasingly unable to ignore the note of modernity—clear imagery, flexible language, free verse—sounded strongly and persistently for the first time in *Ripostes*. Even though Mathews took over *Ripostes* after the failure of Swift and Company, published it along with *Canzoni* in the second volume of Pound's poems, and brought out the fourth printing in April 1915, he could have taken little satisfaction in

Jean de Bosschère's cover for his *Twelve Occupations* (1916). Yale Collection of American Literature, Beinecke Rare Book and Manuscript Library, Yale University.

its contents. Pound's clear emergence as a modern poet in *Ripostes* noticeably weakened the bond which once welded the poet and publisher together. And although Mathews subsequently published *Cathay* in 1915, *Lustra* and Pound's anonymous translation of Jean de Bosschère's *Twelve Occupations*, with its superb cover design and twelve illustrations by the author, in 1916, and, the year before his death, *Umbra*, the relationship became increasingly strained and attenuated during the second and final phase of their association.

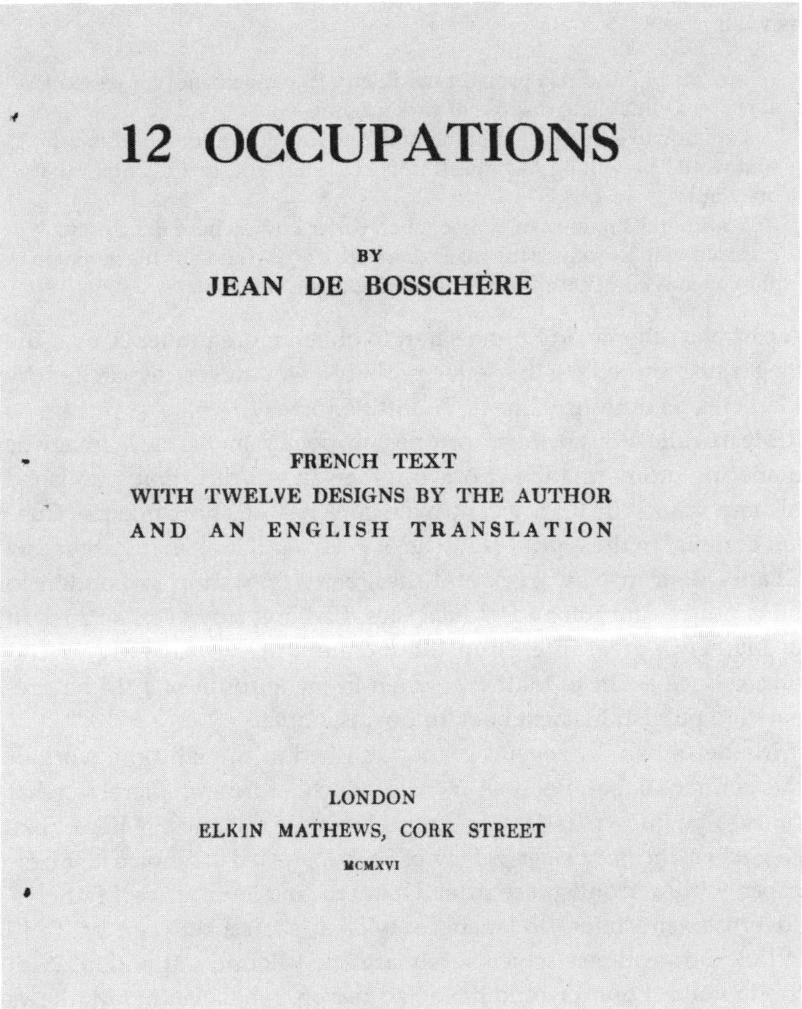

12 OCCUPATIONS

BY

JEAN DE BOSSCHÈRE

FRENCH TEXT

WITH TWELVE DESIGNS BY THE AUTHOR

AND AN ENGLISH TRANSLATION

LONDON

ELKIN MATHEWS, CORK STREET

MCMXVI

Jean de Bosschère's title page for his *Twelve Occupations*.

151

Despite the loosening bond, Pound continued to have considerable leverage with Mathews. For instance, he prevailed on him to bring out William Carlos Williams' first commercially published book of verse, *The Tempers*, in March 1913,[61] and the following year brought Mathews around to the point of approaching Harriet Monroe for the right to publish *Poetry: A Magazine of Verse* in England, or so it would seem, for there is a draft letter in Pound's handwriting presumably to have been written and signed by Mathews to Monroe which indicates not only the publisher's intentions but Pound's role in forming them as well:

> Mr. Ezra Pound has brought me Poetry [the magazine] for a second time. I was unable to dispose of earlier numbers.
>
> I am however interested in the numbers for May & June of this year, and would be willing to publish it in English if you can maintain that standard.
>
> Mr. Pound's name's of course much better known here than yours & it would help introduce the magazine here if we would use his name on the cover as contributing editor or something of that sort.[62]

A part of a scheme on Pound's part to obtain more influence over the magazine's direction, the letter probably was never dispatched by Mathews, as nothing came of Pound's efforts.

Meanwhile Pound, busy composing poetry in his new imagistic mode and promoting the efforts of others in this direction, published his important but highly controversial series of short poems "Contemporania" in the April 1913 issue of *Poetry* and looked to Albert and Charles Boni in New York and the Poetry Bookshop in London to bring out his anthology *Des Imagistes*. Perhaps, however, as a result of Mathews' great interest in the literature of the Far East, Pound turned once again to Mathews when in the autumn of 1914 he prepared to publish his next book of poems, *Cathay*.

Mathews had for several years published in England the work of the eminent Japanese poet Yoni Noguchi, forming thereby what came to be known as "a new Anglo-Japanese Alliance."[63] Books like Noguchi's *The Pilgrimage: A Book of Poems*, printed on choice Japanese paper with a frontispiece after Utamaro and bound, as Mathews' advertisement states, "in Japanese style," appeared between 1910 and 1915, exotic volumes which surely attracted Pound's attention. With this in mind, Pound would have had reason to believe that Mathews would look with favor on his new manuscript, the product of his momentous encounter with the notebooks and papers of the late Ernest Fenollosa, the distinguished philosopher and student of Chinese and Japanese art and poetry. Poring over these manuscripts in the winter of 1913–14 while sharing a cottage with Yeats in Sussex, Pound recognized in Fenollosa's transcriptions and translations of classical Chinese poetry a close relationship between its reliance on clear, concise, concrete images and the kind of poetry he himself had attempted in such poems as "In a Station of the Metro" and "Fan-Piece, for Her Imperial Lord." Fascinated with Fenollosa's "Essay on the Chinese Written Character" and its concept of the ideograph, Pound recreated in a highly original way Fenollosa's literal translations of Chinese poetry, producing one of his most influential and brilliant books.

Mathews apparently had agreed to publish *Cathay* when on 30 December 1914 Pound wrote the news to his parents, adding that its publication was expected in March.[64] Pound was reading proofs on 12 February, but *Cathay* did not actually appear until 6 April 1915, a booklet of 32 pages bound in heavy tan paper wrappers printed in black which sold for a shilling. According to Chiswick Press records, the cost of composing *Cathay* plus extra charges for small type, corrections, and the like was £4.5.6; the cost of printing 1,000 copies came to £1.2.0; this in addition to printing 1,000 copies of the wrapper on Majestic Crown paper and making the zinco-block for the Chinese design which appeared on the front cover of the wrapper, brought the total bill to £7.14.6.[65]

As he had done with Pound's earlier books, Mathews published an advertisement leaflet in 2,000 copies to publicize *Cathay* and prepare the way for its critical reception—which, as it turned out, was quite warm. The poems won praise from critics as diverse as Clutton Brock, Ford Madox Hueffer ("The poems in *Cathay* are things of a supreme beauty. What poetry should be, that they are"), A. R. Orage, and Carl Sandburg.[66]

Meanwhile Mathews, despite the evidence of Pound's modernism in *Ripostes*, attempted to use Pound to push a little book of verse by Evangeline Ryves, whose work he apparently liked, for he published no fewer than four volumes of her poetry between 1906 and 1917. In the spring of 1913, Mathews approached Pound about writing a preface for Ryves's *Erebus: A Book of Verse*. Pound, however, immersed in the excitement of creating a genuinely new poetic mode, had no stomach for praising a poet whose work exhibited none of the signs of modernity which Pound was looking for. Turning down Mathews' proposal, Pound (unable to resist the opportunity to indulge his creeping paranoia) began his letter with the excuse that a preface by him wouldn't "do the book any good" because "a number of people will attack anything I praise, which is all right so far as my own work is concerned but would be rather rough on 'Erebus.'" Then he voiced his real reason for declining the proposal. "Besides," he wrote, "I'm running a campaign for a certain new school of verse, or rather for certain conformities to the best tradition, and much as I enjoyed the poems I don't in the least know where they would come out, under the new standard of measurements. I don't want to be ungracious about it but I feel very uncertain of what I'd be able to say."[67]

Despite this, a year or so later Mathews asked Pound to edit and write a preface to his collected edition of Lionel Johnson's poems. This move to secure Pound's help may have been prompted in part by his friend Olivia Shakespear, Dorothy Shakespear's mother and a relation of Johnson's. She had helped prepare his *Ireland, with Other Poems* (1897) for the press. But more important, Mathews—who almost singlehandedly continued to keep Johnson's reputation alive in the twentieth century by periodically publishing his poetry and criticism—once again, as in the case of Ryves, thought Pound, whom he now recognized as the leader of "a certain new school of verse," would lend weight to his effort to assist the reputation of one of his favorite authors. As Pound later surmised, Mathews was looking for "some definite proof that Lionel Johnson was still respected by a generation, or, if you will, by a clique, of younger poets who scoff at most things of his time."[68] Surprisingly, Pound accepted the job of editing Johnson's poems, although his heart was not in it. There is little to suggest, for instance, that he spent much time over Johnson's text; indeed, he confessed some years later to Lord Alfred Douglas that he "certainly did not bother about Lionel's text other than to, I think, select from some inédits."[69] This was unfortunate, for although the text included Johnson's holograph corrections of some of the pieces in his *Poems* (1895), it also embodied a number of corruptions.[70] Pound did, however, read the proofs, returning some of them to Mathews on 16 October 1914 along with a letter in which he wrote:

"Enclosed proofs of 'Poems.' Can't do Ireland [*Ireland, with Other Poems*] till I have the text as well. Miss Shakespear and I have both been over this lot." After listing some corrections, he continues: "The reader for the press [i.e., the Chiswick Press] has put in a lot of queeries [*sic*] but Johnson spelled on a system and his idiosyncrasies of this sort should be left as he wished 'em."[71]

Although Pound's editorial efforts left a great deal to be desired, the text of Johnson's collected poems was not the disaster Pound's preface proved to be. Why Pound agreed to write the preface to the collected poems—or edit them, for that matter—is difficult to fathom. It may, of course, have been simply that he needed the money. It may also have been, as Mathews knew, that Johnson along with Dowson and other members of the Rhymers' Club once had been a significant influence on Pound's work. And although in a letter of 1911 to Floyd Dell, Pound had made clear that "they," meaning the Rhymers, "are not *us*," meaning the Imagists, nevertheless, he had then believed that "the whole set of 'The Rhymers' did valuable work in knocking bombast, and rhetoric and Victorian syrup out of our verse."[72] But if it had been any part of Pound's plan to write the preface as a tribute to the Rhymers, the opportunity the preface afforded him to make a statement about the difference between the poetry of the nineties and the new poetry proved too great. To Mathews' chagrin, the preface turned out to be a devastating blow not only to Johnson but to other poets of the nineties as well. Declaring that Johnson was not "in accord with our present doctrines and ambitions" and therefore passé, Pound went on to quote at length from Johnson's own "stark naked" judgments on some of his fellow poets like William Watson, John Davidson, Richard Le Gallienne, "Michael Field," and Arthur Symons—all of whom Mathews had published.[73]

Nevertheless, Mathews published *Poetical Works of Lionel Johnson* with Pound's preface in late October 1915, an act which he would soon regret. For example, as soon as she had heard that Pound's name had been linked to Johnson's through his job as editor of the poetical works, Louise Imogen Guiney, the American author and friend of Johnson's who had lavished so much of her time helping edit the poet's posthumous collection of essays and critical papers, *Post Liminium*, wrote Mathews from Wales in a tone of absolute disbelief: "Will you tell me if it be true that Mr. Ezra Pound (of all imaginable folk!) is

155

really editing Lionel? I know not, and cannot believe it, and some of my American correspondents are growling over that collocation of names!"[74] Furthermore, one can imagine the consternation of Guiney, who had written so reverently of Johnson in the obituary essay which Mathews had used as a preface to *Some Poems of Lionel Johnson* (1912), when she heard that Pound was writing the preface. The upshot of the protest by Guiney and other Johnson admirers in America was that Macmillan, the publisher of *Poetical Works* in the states, refused to print Pound's preface, a decision which Guiney wholeheartedly approved. Referring to a letter from Mathews which had informed her of Macmillan's decision, Guiney in her reply wrote:

> As to the Macmillan cable, I didn't know American objections [to Pound's preface] had gone so far as all that! but who can wonder at it? Surely the gentleman in question stands for everything in (and out of) art which Lionel most hated. It can't count for much, it seems to me, that he has become related to L. over L's head, as it were, a dozen years after L's emigration to a world of no books. However, that collocation of names is ended, at least in my perceiving native land.[75]

As a consequence of Macmillan's decision and the protests from English admirers of Johnson as well, Mathews never reprinted Pound's preface in further English editions. In fact, if we are to believe Pound, the publisher was so frightened by the protests that he actually tried to have the preface ripped out of the first edition. In a letter he wrote many years later to the book dealer Ifan Kyrle Fletcher, Pound asserted that "the preface of L.J. was withdrawn in excited haste by Elkin due to pressure from the howly or howlink cawfliks. . . . They scared Mathews; threatening non sale of vol to all the pious who had boomed Lionel on acc/ his RRRRomanism so called. . . . I don't imagine any save the advance sales of the L. Jon have the preface. I believe Elkin even had bound copies unbound in order to efface it."[76] This letter, which is the basis of Fletcher's opinion that 'not more than a dozen" copies were extant with Pound's preface, though revealing as to the source of the outcry over his preface, is in error about the unbinding of copies.[77] There is no evidence that Mathews tried to efface his first edition of *Poetical Works*; though scarce today, it is known to exist in many copies.

Pound's ability, as seen in his preface, to ruffle Mathews' feathers by voicing views of poetry the publisher did not share is but one of a number of signs that relations between the two were increasingly difficult. Another was Pound's *Catholic Anthology*, which Mathews brought out shortly after Johnson's *Poetical Works*. Like his anthology of 1914, *Des Imagistes*, Pound's *Catholic Anthology* was one of several collections during the teens inspired by the success of *Georgian Poetry* (1912), the first of the so-called "Georgian" anthologies. Containing Pound's "Contemporania" suite and the first published poems of T. S. Eliot, including "The Love Song of J. Alfred Prufrock," the anthology also contained poems by W. B. Yeats, Carl Sandburg, William Carlos Williams, Harriet Monroe, and Edgar Lee Masters, among others. Although the Poetry Bookshop had published *Des Imagistes* in London, Pound once again turned to Mathews to publish his new anthology. In a letter of March 1915 to Harriet Monroe, the poet wrote: "Now about the *Anthology*: I believe Mathews is to publish it though I haven't the matter in writing. He says, 'Yes.' (Admitted he hasn't seen the contents, still I think the thing is fairly sure.) I have now got about all the people I can use."[78] According to Stock, the manuscript was sent to the Chiswick Press on 12 September,[79] and the *Catholic Anthology, 1914–1915*, was published in November 1915, at 3/6. in an edition of 500 copies bound in Caledonian gray paper wrappers printed in black with a design by Dorothy Shakespear.

As is now well known, Mathews was immediately set upon by Francis Meynell, a member of the influential Meynell clan, which included the poet and critic Alice, who had descended in high dudgeon along with William Watson on Mathews and Lane at the Bodley Head in 1894 after Oscar Wilde's arrest, insisting that Aubrey Beardsley be fired as art editor of the *Yellow Book*. Although Mathews in his advertisements—no doubt at Pound's suggestion—attempted to alert the public to the precise nature of the anthology, describing it as "representing the more active tendencies in contemporary verse,"[80] Meynell objected vehemently to the book's title, and he and other prominent Catholics harassed Mathews, who was always sensitive to charges that his books in any way contained material offensive to religious readers. Writing to Douglas Goldring shortly after its publication, Pound remarked, "Elkin is now in such a funk over the title of the anthology that he'd probably let you have special rates if you stocked a lot of it."[81] Upset and chagrined, Mathews blamed Pound for the unfortunate title in a scene between the publisher and the poet which Pound later described: "Poor Elkin wailing, 'Why, why will you needlessly irritate people?' E.P.: 'Elkin, did you ever know Meynell to *buy* a book?' E.M.: 'n n n n n n-no, I ddddon't know that he ever did. He always wants me to be giving him books: He he he said, "You won't sell a copy, sir, you won't sell a COPY," banging the table with his fist.'"[82]

So troubled was Mathews by Meynell's threats that Pound, several months later, was afraid that that "mouse Mathews" might not have sent out any copies for review.[83] Or, as he put it in a letter of March 1916 to Kate Buss, "The Jesuits here have, I think, succeeded in preventing [the anthology's] being reviewed in press (at least I have seen no review during the past months)."[84] Despite this, a brief notice of the book appeared as early as 29 January 1916 in the *Publishers' Circular*, and a fairly lengthy review was published in the *Athenaeum* in February.[85] Pound seems, himself, to have had little enthusiasm for most of the poems in his anthology. Informing James Joyce in a letter of late november that "my small anthology is out" and that he intended to send him "a copy the next time I get down to Mathews," Pound went on to say that he had published the book "for the sake of a couple of poems by Eliot; I doubt if the rest of it will in any way entertain you."[86] Reviewers seem to have shown little enthusiasm for either the anthology or Eliot's poems. Merely noting the book's "Futurist" cover, the *Athenaeum* reviewer quickly passed on to the poems, which he found "exceedingly clever, and occasionally rather improper. . . . They give odd, surprising significances to trivial matters; they have a novel range in the way of imagery; they show a pretty ingenuity in the matter of sneering; and they appear at once daring and profound. But, on examination, they are found to be none of these things in quite so high a degree as it seemed on the first reading, and they prove nothing."[87] Since other reviews, including one by Alec Waugh, were equally negative, there is little wonder that but few copies sold. As late as April 1936, *Catholic Anthology*, according to Gallup, was "still in print in the original—and only—edition, at the published price."[88]

If Mathews' discomfiture over the anthology had been considerable, it was nothing compared to the anquish in store for him as a result of his decision to publish Pound's *Lustra*, a volume which the poet described as containing "*Cathay*, some new Chinese stuff and all my own work since *Ripostes*" (much of which had already appeared in such periodicals as *Poetry*, the *Smart Set*, and *Blast*).[89] The "long and comic" history (as Pound later referred to it)[90] of the controversy over *Lustra* apparently began shortly after the publication of *Catholic Anthology*, which suggests that Mathews was not so unhappy with Pound as to be unwilling to consider yet another of his manuscripts. Although Stock says that Pound delivered the typescript of *Lustra* to Mathews "early in 1916," there is in Mathews' diary an entry which suggests he was already reading it and puzzling over its title on a Saturday in December 1915: "'Lustros' a Greek shoe black. Lustroi (plu)."[91] However that may be, Mathews, in due course, sent the typescript to William Clowes and Sons, a long-established, highly reputable printing firm, where the entire text was set up in print and page proofs were run off. In early May, Mathews received Clowes's estimate for "Lustra of Ezra Pound," which listed the cost for composing and printing 500 copies at £20.10.0 and 1,000 copies at £23.5.0.[92] But toward the close of May, Pound, who had been expecting page proofs momentarily, received a letter from W. B. Yeats which, according to Stock, "said that both Mathews and Clowes, having read the poems in proof, were horrified."[93]

What apparently had happened was that at the last minute the page proofs had been brought to the attention of the senior director of the printing firm, the elderly W.C.K. Clowes, a man who had held a number of distinguished positions in his profession, such as the first chairman of the London Master Printers Alliance and Master of the Stationers' Company.[94] In light of the recent suppression of D. H. Lawrence's novel *The Rainbow*, he concluded that he did not want his firm's name associated with a book of poetry whose contents contained such irreverent parodies as "Winter is icummen in, / Lhude sing Goddamm," bore such titles as "Coitus," commanded the reader to "Dance the dance of the phallus," and referred to whores, among whom was the "scrawny but amorous" Phyllidula. He communicated his views to Mathews, who, alarmed, seized the occasion to liberally blue-pencil the proofs of *Lustra*, following the lead of his reader, whose report he had received in the form of a postcard with comments on the poems reduced to pithy phrases such as "An impudent piece," "Silly nonsense," "Smelly like its subject," "Delicious lasciviousness."[95] That Clowes was the source of the *rencontre* which followed between Mathews and Pound seems to be indicated by a note (evidently written for posterity) in Pound's hand on the half-title page of the first proofs of *Lustra*, now in the Humanities Research Center at the University of Texas: "First proofs. Deletions by E. Mathews instigated by Clowes, pres. master printers assn., pres. printers pension ass."

At the time Pound received the emasculated page proofs (which he likened to "the greek statues in the Vatican with tin fig leaves wired onto them"),[96] he was immersed in efforts to help James Joyce through his difficulties in finding an English publisher for *A Portrait of the Artist as a Young Man*. Instantly he saw himself, like Joyce, a victim of the "please the mediocre-at-all cost doctrine" of British publishing.[97] So long a warrior on behalf of others, Pound was primed to do battle now in his own behalf. In a wild burst of activity during the last few days of May, Pound consulted the Home Office; saw the literary agent, James B. Pinker; and heard the views of Yeats, who had been consulted by Mathews. From Pound's side of the correspondence which ensued, one gathers that Mathews' main reason for objecting to certain poems was his fear of prosecution. Consequently, Pound repeatedly sought to allay Mathews' fear, in one letter saying, "It is nonsense to imagine that there can be trouble over poems which have already appeared not only in England but in America," and reminding the publisher of his needless worry some years before over the publication of "The Goodly Fere" in *Exultations*.[98] In a follow-up postcard Pound urged: "Do get the prosecution mania out of your mind. I have gone into the whole thing with Mr. Pinker. I will write you details later this P.M. when I get a spare half hour. The details are comforting. More anon. Despond not O Elkini mihi."[99]

That the poet believed Mathews' fears to be sincere is reinforced by his repeated efforts during the last several days of May to put the publisher's "mind at rest on the subject of prosecutions." In a long rambling letter of the thirtieth Pound reported to Mathews that he had "gone into the matter with Mr. Pinker, as I said on my post card. No prosecution is of any effect unless the Home Office takes it up. And," he assured his publisher, "I am not the sort of person whom the Home Office attacks, and the Home Office will not make a fool of itself over my book, nor would any informed man stand against the defence I have made in my note." Observing that "the present panic among printers has been caused by the suppression of Lawrence's 'Rainbow'"—a fact that was hardly news to Mathews—Pound went on to assert that he was not

> for one instant going to compare my book with the Rainbow. There is no immoral tendency in my work. I don't know that there was in the Rainbow, but it was nearer the order of W. L. George and "Three Weeks" than to the order of Catullus and Heine. It was a novel sexually overloaded, a sort of post-Wellsian barrocco and it depended for its sale precisely on its sexual overloading.
>
> Now "Lustra" does not depend on any such thing. Where it is harsh it is clean cut satire, written in the speech of the best English classics and with the vocabulary of all the classics that ever were.[100]

Comparing *Lustra* with the classics was one of Pound's tactics to overcome Mathews' objections to certain poems on the grounds that they were immoral and, as the publisher complained to Yeats, not fit to be read by women—"not only men come into this shop, *but ladies,*" he is reported to have exclaimed. Assuring his publisher that *Lustra* was not "undertaken in a trivial spirit," Pound went on to assert that "it expresses . . . a 'philosophy of life', or what I would rather call a 'sense of life' which is common to all the classics." Opining that Mathews, given his "recluse life," had perhaps "got a little out of touch with the tone of contemporary London" and observing that "you are one man when you are reading the English classics [at home] in Chorley Wood, and another when you come into the day's round of occupation"—a not too precise way of telling him that he was a liberal-minded man in the country but a closed-minded Victorian in town—Pound sought to open his publisher's eyes to the enduring, classical qualities of language and theme in his poems.[101]

Meanwhile Mathews had received word from Yeats that Yeats agreed with him about the so-called "violent" poems in *Lustra* but not about the indecent ones. As Stock reports it, Yeats "thought that a man should be allowed to be as indecent as he liked."[102] Moreover, he had engaged in an exchange of letters with Augustine Birrell, whom Pound had enlisted in his cause. Expressing the view that "it is simply out of the question that any of the poems [in *Lustra*] are exposed to the risk of prosecution for indecency," Birrell—who had been consulted by the Home Office in connection with the *Rainbow* case and had been of the opinion that, as Pound reported, the book was too dull to bother about—then went on to write: "It is really a great pity that this kind of question between an author, his publisher and the printer should be unnecessarily raised. One hardly sees when it is to stop and who is to be the judge. In this instance as I have already said there seems to me no doubt that there is no case whatsoever for prosecution."[103]

Immediately replying to Birrell's letter, Mathews asked, "But are not there other considerations for a publisher besides the mere avoidance of prosecution?"—implying, I suppose, that a publisher must also consider his reputation among the public. "Also I am not at all sure that my objections were unnecessary," he continued, posing a question which must have bedeviled any reputable publisher of the day: "and how is a layman to determine the limits of safety in these matters?"[104]

Some days later, Birrell wrote again, saying: "I don't want you to mistake me. I think a publisher is well within his rights in refusing to *publish anything* he does not think worth while. Poets can print their own poems, at their own risk, if so minded. Were I a publisher, it never would have occurred to me to publish *Lustra*. But indecency is another matter."[105]

Having digested as best he could all of these opinions, Mathews wrote Pound a letter which, in marked contrast to the poet's own effusions of the last several days, was calm, concise, and to the point, stating his position visa-à-vis *Lustra*:

> I have again carefully gone through the printed proofs of 'Lustra' and have also carefully considered the objections and suggestions of your several discursive letters with the result that I have drawn up a list of the minimum number of emendations and omissions which must be made before I can consent to publish the work and a copy of which I enclose for your information. You will see I have made great allowances and concessions and further than this I am not prepared to go.
>
> Kindly let me know at once whether you accept my terms—which are, I must repeat—final.[106]

Mathews' enclosed list called for the omission of nine poems, including "Meditatio," "Phyllidula," "The Patterns," and "The Seeing Eye," all of which he judged "very nasty"; "Atthis," which he thought "anything but 'delicate'"; and "Ancient Music," which he referred to as "a damned parody."

Reflecting perhaps Mathews' recent encounter with Francis Meynell over *Catholic Anthology*, the list required the deletion of the word
"Christ" in the last line but two of "Further Instructions," since, Mathews observed, "it won't affect the sense—its retention would only
give needless offense"; and the substitution of "Jupiter" for "God" in
"The Lake Isle." In addition, it called for the deletion of sizable portions of the poems "Salutation the Second" and "Commission,"[107]
requirements to which Pound strongly objected. "I can not alter
'Salutation II', nor 'Commission' nor 'Further Instructions,'" he wrote
in reply to Mathews' ultimatum. "Nor will I utterly ruin the poem to
Atthis, nor will I substitute an utterly unspeakable 'Jupiter', a term
which is not living speech, for 'God.'" Informing Mathews that he
couldn't "fathom" his objection to "Meditatio," he continued: "It is
merely a reversal of 'Plus qu' je vois l'homme, plus j'aime le chien.' It
seems to me rather complimentary to mankind than otherwise. Again
'The Seeing Eye', I still don't see the objection. However the poem is
not of vital importance." Conceding that "your other points seem to
me negotiable" since they "would not form any fatal obstacle," Pound
left the way open for further discussions.[108] In the end, both poet and
publisher, willing to compromise, reached an accord reflected in Mathews' letter of 10 June, in which he informed Pound: "I now find
Messrs. Clowes are willing to print the ordinary published edition of
the above [*Lustra*] with all the emendations and corrections as in the
list agreed on by ourselves." And as a concession to Pound and his
friends, Mathews told the poet that Clowes had consented to do "a
privately printed edition of 200 copies unexpurgated, with the exception of the four following poems, viz. 'The Temperaments', 'Ancient
Music', 'The Lake Isle' & 'Pagani's, November 8th' which they decline
to print in any form whatever."[109]

Accepting the inevitable—largely because he had nowhere else to
turn[110]—Pound, nevertheless, was not pleased, having been "beguiled," as he termed it in a letter to Harriet Monroe, "into leaving out
[of *Lustra*] the more violent poems to the general loss of the book." He
continued: "The dam'd bloody insidious way one is edged into these
tacit hypocrisies *is* disgusting. I don't mean I have left out anything I
put into the ms. Certainly the 'Cabaret' is there in its entirety, etc., but
the pretty poems and the Chinese softness have crept up in number
and debilitated the tone."[111] Even though it had been Mathews who

163

had "beguiled" the poet into accepting a less than perfect text of *Lustra*, Pound sympathized with his publisher, who, having himself "been persuaded into doing 200 copies unabridged for the elect," was, according to Pound in a letter to Iris Barry, "allowed to have the rest of the edition almost as modest as he" liked. "God knows, the whole thing [the text of *Lustra*] is innocent enough, but the poor man has had an awful week of it.—I suppose he has some right to decide how he'll spend his money."[112]

In August Pound wrote Barry that he thought "that imbecile Mathews will never finish with *Lustra*,"[113] but the 200 privately printed copies finally appeared in September 1916, selling for 5s. each and bound in tan cloth boards lettered in dark blue. Although technically not published, this so-called unabridged edition (which nevertheless omitted the four poems Clowes refused to print) was, as Gallup points out, "in fact sold by Elkin Mathews to those who requested the unabridged text when ordering the book."[114] This "unabridged edition" was followed in October by the abridged version of *Lustra*, the 800 copies also selling for 5s. each. It, too, was bound in tan cloth boards, but the lettering was in a lighter shade of blue. In addition to the four poems omitted from the "unabridged edition," nine others were deleted from the abridged text: "Salutation the Second," "Commission," "The New Cake of Soap," "Epitaph," "Meditatio," "Phyllidula," "The Patterns," "The Seeing Eye," and the Atthis poem "Iueppw"—in other words, the additional poems marked for omission or emendation in Mathews' list of 31 May.

Critical opinion about *Lustra* was, as might be expected, quite varied. The reviewers for both the *Observer* and the *Daily Chronicle* praised it, but the critic for the *Times Literary Supplement* of 16 November noticed that although Pound's illusion of ordinary speech "gives an air of liveliness to his poems," it is a liveliness purchased "at too high a price. Certainly," he continued, "the original poems as well as the translations show that he has talent—one can read them all with some interest—but why should he use it to express so much indifference and impatience? Why should he so constantly be ironical about nothing in particular? . . . One suspects a hidden timidity in this air of indifference, as if Mr. Pound feared above all things to give himself away."[115]

Despite the additional strains in their relationship which had resulted from the struggle over *Lustra*, Pound and Mathews remained on friendly terms, Mathews continuing to be Pound's best hope of getting published in England. But a sign, perhaps, of the poet's waning influence with his publisher was Mathews' refusal in the spring of 1917 to publish T. S. Eliot's first book of poems, *Prufrock and Other Observations*. Since the appearance of several of Eliot's poems in *Catholic Anthology*, Pound had been urging Eliot to bring together a selection of his poems in book form. When with Pound's help he had put together a small collection, Pound offered it to Mathews, whom he hoped would publish it at his own expense. Mathews, however, unwilling to take a chance on a book of only twelve poems authored by an almost unknown poet, laid down conditions—including an advance on the cost of publication—which Pound could not accept.[116]

Although Mathews apparently was not eager to publish Eliot, he continued to show an interest in publishing Pound. In a letter of April 1918 in which he thanked the poet for a copy of Eliot's *Ezra Pound, His Metric and Poetry*, which he had read "with keen interest," Mathews expressed a desire to see *Pavannes and Divisions*; Knopf, however, published this book in the United States in June.[117] In the autumn Pound offered Mathews *Quia Pauper Amavi*, writing John Quinn on 2 December that "Mathews says he will bring it out here in March." But, the poet added, "he hadn't read the mss. when he said so. I warned him Propertius lived in a world uncontaminated by the Christian faith."[118] When Mathews suggested that he omit "Homage to Sextus Propertius" and "Moeurs contemporaines," Pound took the manuscript to the Egoist, under whose imprint it appeared in 1919.

Poet and publisher, unable to agree on the new, got together on the old, Mathews contracting with Pound to bring out a selection of early poems. With the long title *Umbra, the Early Poems of Ezra Pound, All that he now wishes to keep in circulation from "Personae, "Exultations," "Ripostes," etc.*, the volume—since it proved to be their last venture together—was appropriate, bringing the relationship, in a sense, full circle. *Umbra* appeared in June 1920, a little less than a year and a half before Mathews' death. Bound in gray paper boards with canvas back lettered in blue, it was issued in an edition of 1,000 copies, selling at 8/– each.

Embodying, as Edwin Muir observed in a review in *New Age*, "the author's judgment upon his earlier works," *Umbra*, Muir noted, "provides also the material which should enable us to discover what are the qualities which set him apart—so very far apart—from the mass of his contemporary poets." Although Mathews was unable to appreciate Pound's later and far more distinctly modernist poetic, he did recognize in Pound's early work what Muir identified as "a sort of fastidious vigour: a subtle form of strength" which marked his real difference from most of the poets of the early twentieth century.[119] This recognition led Mathews to publish Pound at his own expense and befriend him at a crucial time when his future as a poet was at stake. That Pound never forgot this is amply attested to in the letter he wrote to Mathews' widow, Edith Elkin Mathews, after the publisher's death on 10 November 1921. Observing that "the poets will be rather homeless now despite younger enterprises—and I see no one likely to take his place—certainly no one who will be interested in the content of his publications," Pound expressed regrets on hearing of the death of "my old friend—he was always much more friend than publisher." Admitting that Mathews had "disapproved more or less of my late works," he nevertheless assured Mrs. Mathews that "that was always balanced by memories of 1908 & '09 and the vigour with which he had brought out [?] Personae & Exultations." In a postscript, Pound concluded: "I certainly shall not forget" that it was "he who first accepted my works when I landed in London, *sans sous*. These beginnings," he declared, "account for more than the middle steps of the journey."[120]

Epilogue

HAVING HEARD about Mathews' death, Lily Yeats in a letter to her father, John Butler Yeats, wondered what would "become of all those piles and piles of books—and all his knowledge," which she hoped "is not wasted, but that he will be able to use it—and add to it—in the other world."[1] Although the fate of Mathews' knowledge must be left to conjecture, the disposition of "those piles and piles of books" must be a matter of concern to all those who are interested in his publishing activities simply because Mathews often used his personal copies of books as repositories of business documents pertaining to their publication.

At the time of his death, Mathews' books were divided between his private library in his home at Chorleywood and his business premises in Cork Street. His private library was sold at auction by Messrs. Hodgson and Company on 26–28 April 1922, and Hodgson's catalogue affirms that Mathews' own copies of books often contained important business documents loosely inserted. Although many of these books no doubt found their way at that time into university libraries and other public collections, a significant number of books sold at the auction apparently were bought by A. J. A. Symons and remained in his hands until his library was sold—interestingly enough—in 1931 to Elkin Mathews Limited (as the firm was styled after it was sold by Mathews' widow in April 1922 to A. W. Evans and his partners). Subsequently Symons' library was offered for sale in the firm's now famous catalogue 42, *Books of the 'Nineties*, with an introduction by Holbrook Jackson.[2] Numerous items in this catalogue were almost certainly from Mathew's private library: for example, a copy of Lionel Johnson's *Poems* (which Mathews had published in 1895) into which was loosely inserted two signed autograph letters (a.l.s.) from the author to Mathews about the book's publication and one a.l.s. from Herbert P. Horne, the book's designer, to Mathews about its title page; a copy of Ernest Dowson's *Dilemmas* (published by Mathews in 1895) into which was loosely inserted the manuscript draft of the original agreement for the publication of the book, two a.l.s. from Dowson to Mathews, and Richard Le Gallienne's original reader's report; and the original typescript, signed, with a few holograph additions, of Ezra Pound's preface to *The Poetical Works of Lionel Johnson* along with the typescript of a few of the poems collected for this edition.

As to the disposition of the books which were on the shelves of the premises in Cork Street, they were taken over by the new proprietors of the firm, who then listed most of them in their early catalogues, in particular, the first one issued: *A Catalogue of Rare Modern Books, First Editions and Finely Printed Books, Etc.* (1922). Although this catalogue was compiled by Evans and his staff, it was, as Evans acknowledged in his brief foreword, "nevertheless mainly the result of [Mathews'] activities." Speaking of Mathews' "*flair* as a collector of books," Evans went on to observe that "the volumes now offered for sale are some of those that he assembled during the many years he lived in close touch with several of the most distinguished men of letters of his time." As in the case of the earlier Hodgson catalogue and the later *Books of the 'Nineties*, this first catalogue issued by Elkin Mathews Limited contained books into which important documents had been loosely inserted. For example, one item was a copy of *A Question of Memory* by "Michael Field" (which Mathews and Lane had published in 1893) containing four a.l.s. from the authors to Mathews concerning its publication, the preface, a list of errata, a preliminary note in the handwriting of one of the authors, and three p.c.s. from the authors to Mathews. Another item was a copy of John Gray's celebrated *Silverpoints* (published by Mathews and Lane in 1893) including two a.l.s. from Gray to Mathews and a photograph of Gray inscribed by him to the publisher. Fortunately, a significant number of the items from these catalogues have since made their way into research libraries, mainly in the United States, and along with the material which makes up the Elkin Mathews Archive, sold by Miss Nest Elkin Mathews to Reading University in 1965, they constitute the bulk of documents available to scholars interested in the firm's history.

As to the disposition of the firm itself, it was sold for the estimated sum of £4,500 in 1922,[3] at which time the name became Elkin Mathews Limited. Under the direction of Evans, the firm continued to operate both as an antiquarian book business and as a publishing house, the publishing business becoming styled Elkin Mathews and Marrot Limited in 1926.[4] Percy Muir, who joined the firm as a partner in 1929 with the task of creating order out of the near chaos of the rapidly expanding business, tells the story of the firm after Mathews' death in his autobiography *Minding My Own Business*. Having kept the firm alive through the Great Depression and World War II largely on his own, Muir continued the antiquarian book business until his death in 1979; since that time it has been continued under the direction of his widow, the author Barbara Kaye, from her home, "Scriveners," at Blakeney in Norfolk and her son David in his bookshop at Coggeshall in Essex. Although the publishing business was sold to George Allen and Unwin in the 1930s, the Elkin Mathews imprint survives today, the latest addition to it being Kaye's *The Company We Kept*, published in the summer of 1986 as a sequel to *Minding My Own Business*.[5]

APPENDICES

NOTES

INDEX

Elkin Mathews and the Daniel Press

One of the outstanding private presses of Victorian England was that of Dr. C.H.O. Daniel, who, having begun printing in an amateurish sort of way at his father's vicarage at Frome, Somersetshire in 1845, resumed printing on a more serious scale at Oxford in 1874 and continued to issue books from time to time until his death in 1919.[1] In his book on the Daniel Press, Falconer Madan wrote that Dr. Daniel produced his books primarily "to please and interest his friends,"[2] a statement which has, perhaps, led some to believe that the books of the press received very little circulation beyond the environs of Oxford. For instance, in her essay "British Book Typography," P. M. Handover asserted that Daniel's books "were restricted to circulation in Oxford or among his [Daniel's] academic friends elsewhere."[3] There is, however, ample evidence to suggest that Daniel's books were more widely distributed. Because Daniel Press books were attractive to collectors and connoisseurs of limited and rare editions—a growing breed in the eighties—booksellers in both England and Scotland made efforts to secure copies from Dr. Daniel, who readily complied with their wishes. In fact, he had begun to price some of his books and issue prospectuses as early as 1883, when he offered for sale an Elizabethan translation of Theocritus, *Sixe Idillia*.[4] Soon after, the Oxford bookseller W. H. Gee (whose name, along with that of Messrs. Quaritch of London, appears among the subscribers for Robert Bridges' *Prometheus the Firegiver*, issued by Daniel in 1883) was listed in the prospectus for Canon R. W. Dixon's *Odes and Eclogues* as one from whom copies could be obtained.[5] Gee continued to be named on several occasions as a supplier of Daniel Press books. As late as 1888 he was mentioned in that capacity in the "Recent Verse" column of the *Academy*, which called its readers' attention to the latest production of the Daniel Press, Dixon's *Story of Eudocia and Her Brothers*. "The dainty little quarto," it observed, "is limited to an edition of fifty copies, of which twenty-five have been placed for sale with Mr. Gee, High Street, Oxford."[6] And although Gee continued to sell copies of Daniel Press books which remained after distribution to friends and subscribers, Daniel's books achieved their widest circulation through Elkin Mathews.

That Mathews largely supplanted Gee and formed a loose sort of business relationship with Daniel is in part revealed in a series of letters from Daniel to Mathews written in 1889–90. Replying in March 1889 to what one assumes to have been an offer from Mathews to serve as agent for his books, Daniel with characteristic modesty wrote: "My impressions are so limited, and I produce so little that I hardly aspire to the business dignity of a London 'agency.'"[7] Daniel, nevertheless, agreed to inform Mathews "of my productions from time to time and if you like, supply you with copies" at a discount of 10 percent. Moreover, he enclosed advertisements for books still on hand, such as Bridges' *Poems*.[7] Despite Daniel's reluctance to have a London agency for his books, the relationship established in this letter over the next few years in effect provided Mathews with that privilege. For example, Daniel in a letter of the following May informed Mathews of the availability of his latest production: "I have printed for Mrs. Woods, author of 'The Village Tragedy', and daughter of the Dean of Westminster a little book of 'Lyrics'—Sm. 4, Whatman paper—paper wrapper 59 pp—The number of the Impression 124. Of these her friends have had most; but she has let me sell some 10 copies—not through booksellers at 10/6 each. There remain 18 copies. Will you take these at the above price, less, of course, bookseller's allowance—15 per c."[8] When Bridges' play *The Feast of Bacchus* was issued by Daniel toward the close of 1889, it too found its way to the Bodley Head, Daniel's prospectus stating that copies could be obtained either from the printer or Elkin Mathews.[9] Furthermore, the Bodley Head sold copies of both of the Daniel Press productions of 1890: F. W. Bourdillon's *Ailes d'Alouette* and Bridges' *Growth of Love*. Not only did Mathews take copies of Daniel's current releases but he sought copies of Daniel Press books which were still on hand: this, one may infer from a Daniel letter to Mathews listing his "whole stock," which consisted of R. W. Dixon's *Lyrical Poems*, 9 copies; John Webster's *Love's Graduate*, 8 copies; *Sixe Idillia*, 8 copies; and possibly one copy of Dixon's *Eudocia* ("I think I can make up a perfect copy—but am not sure").[10]

Since in this same letter Daniel had written, "I can have no objection to your placing in your circular any of my books which you may have in stock, or with which I can supply you," Mathews began to include in his catalogues listings of Daniel Press books.[11] For example, under the heading of "Mr. Elkin Mathews' New and Forthcoming Books," Bourdillon's *Ailes d'Alouette* is advertised as being "choicely printed in Fell's type, on Alton Mills handmade paper, by the Rev. C. H. Daniel, at his Private Press; limited to 100 copies; very few remain." Bridges' *Growth of Love* and *The Feast of Bacchus* are similarly described. In fact, all the titles mentioned by Daniel (with the exception of Dixon's *Eudocia*, of which possibly one copy remained) appeared later in Bodley Head catalogues. Consequently, Mathews had effectually cornered the market, so to speak, on Daniel Press books. As a result, even Daniel found himself referring customers to Mathews for copies. By October 1890 Mathews had all the remaining copies of Bridges' *Feast of Bacchus*, so that Daniel was forced to direct Messrs. Deighton, the Cambridge booksellers, to the Bodley Head for copies.[12] Shortly thereafter, Daniel referred applicants for Bridges' *Growth of Love* to Mathews,[13] who, recognizing the profitability of such limited-edition books, had soon after its printing relieved Daniel of what remained beyond copies distributed to subscribers.

As one might expect of a publisher who during the days of the early Bodley Head dealt almost exclusively in limited editions, Mathews' interest as a bookseller in Daniel Press books was to a marked degree speculative. Once any limited edition had been exhausted, copies were almost bound to rise in price at a time when there was a growing clientele for rare books. Gambling on this, Mathews, having secured Daniel's remaining stock and his promise to supply future productions, was free to set whatever price on them he deemed the market would bear. That this was his design is borne out by the fact that the price of every title he secured from Daniel was listed in his catalogues for considerably more than Daniel himself had priced them.

Initially, it would seem, Mathews adhered to Daniel's advertised price—as, for example, in the case of Bridges' *Feast of Bacchus* (1889): a postcard advertisement provided Mathews by Daniel shows that although Mathews crossed out Daniel's name and address and supplied his own, the price of 10/- per copy remained unaltered. Yet Bourdillon's *Ailes d'Alouette* (1890), advertised by Daniel at 5/- per copy, was listed in Mathews' catalogue of 1890 at 7/6 per copy. Later (with the phrase "very few remain" appended) its price had risen to £1.10.0. Similarly, copies of Woods' *Lyrics* (1888), which Daniel had sold to Mathews in 1889 for 10/6 less a 15 percent discount per copy,[14] were selling for £2.0.0 in 1893. Even more spectacular is the rise in price of Bridges' *Growth of Love* (1890). According to Madan, Daniel's announced price was 12/6 per copy, and a letter from Daniel to Mathews confirms this: "I am in receipt of your second letter, asking for 50 copies of the Growth of Love instead of 24. I was out of Oxford yesterday, but in the course of the day will forward these by GWR [Great Western Railway]. After having numbered them I will send them to address at Stoke Newington [Mathews' London residence]. I enclose Receipt for cheque for £25 [i.e., 50 at 12/6 each less discount]: for which I am obliged. Specimen copy shall be thrown in in acknowledgement of such prompt payment."[15] Yet the Bodley Head catalogue entry for 1893, with the phrase "very few remain" attached, lists the book as selling for £2.12.6, a price which Bridges labeled "exceptionally astounding" on seeing the entry.[16] What must have been his reaction two years later when he saw the book listed in Mathews' catalogue at £3.3.0![17]

That Daniel initially had assumed that Mathews would sell his books at the prices set by him is suggested by the fact that he provided Mathews with a quite reasonable discount of 15 percent, designed to enable the London bookseller to make a decent profit at Daniel's prices.[18] This can also be inferred from Daniel's letter to Mathews of 1889, in which he seemed to assume that Mathews would sell his 18 copies of Woods' *Lyrics* at Daniel's price of 10/6. Revealing "that an Edition [of lyrics] is alas announced by Bentley which of course will be much cheaper than mine," he reassured Mathews by adding, "I fancy there will be a good many people prefer mine at my price."[19] By the autumn of 1890 Daniel appears to have known that Mathews was exceeding his own prices, remarking to a friend that he was "curious to know how" Mathews would price the few copies that remained of *The Growth of Love*.[20]

Despite Mathews' speculations in Daniel Press books, the liaison between the printer and the publisher seems to have been amicable with the exception of a small problem over the Bodley Head catalogue listings of Bridges' *Growth of Love*. Bridges was from the outset uneasy about Dr. Daniel's arrangement with the Bodley Head; in a letter of 1889 he told Daniel: "I hope that your London bkseller will turn out all right and send you the money for the copies [of *The Feast of Bacchus*] wh. he had."[21] Although transactions between Mathews and Daniel had been few at this time, there is no reason to believe that Bridges' worries were legitimate, since the evidence I have seen suggests Mathews sent checks to Daniel along with his orders of books.

Nevertheless, Bridges perhaps had more substantial concerns when he noticed that in the "List of Books in *Belles Lettres* Published by Elkin Mathews and John Lane" dated July 1893, *The Growth of Love* appeared among the regular entries, suggesting—at least to Bridges—that Lane, an active partner in the Bodley Head since January 1892, was perhaps up to something. In a postscript to a letter to Daniel of 1893, Bridges wrote: "By the way I see that Messrs Elkin Mathews and John Lane have taken to putting 'the Growth of Love' among their own *publications*. To which statement there is no qualification except that at the head of the list they say 'including some transfers of remainders from other publishers' or words to that effect. . . . I object very much to this and shall tell them so. Do not you think that you might object too? [T]he 'announcement' might cost me American copyright."[22] Having informed Lane of Bridges' objections, Daniel conveyed in turn to Bridges Lane's desire to know his wishes in the matter. Accordingly on 23 October, Bridges, conveying to Lane his sense of how "the thing may have come about" continued:

> The objection which I have is this—that the advertisement might be used as evidence that 'The Growth of Love' was *published*[,] in which case it might cost me the American copyright. It may seem needless to take such a precaution, but I think that you shd make up your list so as to avoid the statement (which you make) that the book is either published by you, or is a purchased '*remainder*'.
>
> You could either put the words 'not published' or 'privately printed' after the book in question; or you might set all Mr. Daniel's books under his name. But if you see my objection you will know best how to meet it.
>
> I hope to see Mr Daniel tomorrow, and will tell him that I have written to you

And in a postscript he concluded: "I think also that perhaps my publishers might have a sentimental if not a businesslike objection to my name appearing in a list of your clients. You will know whether this wd be so."[23]

Further disturbed by the fact that he had received no reply from Lane, Bridges on 2 December wrote again to Daniel, this time to ask that he get a disclaimer in writing from Lane to the effect that the Bodley Head was not the publisher of *The Growth of Love*. If Lane is unwilling to "write a formal disclaimer to you or to me I must," Bridges asserted, "put an advertisement in one of the London papers. Else I may find some day that he has an American editn of the Growth of Love. Do you mind sending him a note something to this effect. If you had rather not write again to him let me know. and I will."[24] Although Lane acceded to Bridges' wishes—both the entry for *The Growth of Love* and that for Bourdillon's *Ailes d'Alouette* in the January 1894 catalogue were accompanied by the statement "Not published"[25]—Bridges was still not satisfied. In a postcard of early 1894, he acknowledged the receipt of a copy of Laurence Binyon's *Lyric Poems* containing the new catalogue; nevertheless, he went on to tell Lane: "I shd like to send a note to Athenaeum, or put a note in one of my books to tell my readers that I do not publish with you—which would you prefer? I am still afraid that there may be a misunderstanding".[26] Bridges' apparent distrust of Lane probably lies behind the fact that Bridges' *Shorter Poems* (1894) was not listed in future Bodley Head catalogues.

Shortly before the dissolution of the partnership between Mathews and Lane, Mathews wrote Daniel to inform him of arrangements made in regard to Daniel's books. "You are no doubt aware," he wrote, "that in a few days Mr. Lane and I dissolve partnership." "I shall continue," Mathews went on to say,

> to carry on at the old premises in Vigo Street, the old book business together with the publishing on the lines we have hereto followed—Mr. Lane confines himself strictly to publishing.
>
> Consequently I have taken over all the books from your private press, and I hope you will kindly give me notice and the privilege of taking a certain number of copies as in the past of your private issues.
>
> I propose at the end of my catalogue of publications a list of such of your books I have in stock under the following heading[:] "Books printed at the Private Press of the Rev. C. Henry Daniel Fellow of Worcester Coll Oxford" provided you have no objection.[27]

Although Mathews got the Daniel Press books on hand at the Bodley Head at the time of the breakup of the partnership, both he and Lane continued to act as agents for Daniel's books during the years immediately following. For instance, Daniel's prospectus for 1896, listing Laurence Binyon's *Poems*, Keats's *Lyrics*, and Mrs. Woods's *Songs New and Old*, included the statement: "Of these a few copies remain—price 12/6—and may be obtained of the Printer, or of Mr. John Lane, Vigo Street W." Shortly after the breakup Mathews' catalogue for 1894–95 listed both Bridges' *Shorter Poems* and *The Growth of Love*, and his catalogues dated 1895 and 1895–96 included *Hymni Cura Henrici Daniel* (1882), *Blake His Songs of Innocence* (1893), and Milton's *Ode on the Morning of Christ's Nativity* (1894). Moreover, when Mathews published Binyon's *First Book of London Visions* in his Shilling Garland series in 1896, Binyon's Daniel Press volume entitled *Poems (1895)* was listed on the verso of the dedicatory page with the statement that it "may still be had from Mr. Daniel, Worcester House, Oxford, or from Mr. Elkin Mathews." Thus, with the exception of books printed by Daniel for strictly personal use or printed and sold for charities—such as *Herrick His Flowers* (1891), printed for sale on behalf of St. Thomas's orphanage, Oxford; *Christmas from the Noble Numbers of Robert Herrick* (1891), sent to friends of Daniel's daughter, Rachel and Ruth, as a Christmas gift; and Walter Pater's *An Imaginary Portrait* (1894), issued at a Venetian fete in aid of St. Thomas's parish—Mathews either as partner in the Bodley Head or as independent proprietor of his own firm after 1894 sold virtually all the Daniel Press titles produced during the eighties and early nineties.

Although the direct relationship between Mathews and the Daniel Press appears to have ended with these books, the tie was, in a sense, not entirely broken. Since Mathews had published F. W. Bourdillon's *A Lost God* in November 1891, there had been a connection between Daniel Press authors and those of the Bodley Head. An especially important figure in this respect was Binyon, who published books of poems with both Mathews and Daniel and who as editor of Mathews' Shilling Garland series gave it a distinctly Daniel Press aura. Not only did he lead off the series with his *First Book of London Visions*, but he also recruited other Daniel Press authors: Bridges, Mrs. Woods, Canon Dixon, and Mary Coleridge. Although Mathews' price of 1/– per booklet made it impossible for him in this series to vie with Daniel's finely printed books on high-grade paper, his preference for small, well-designed books of poetry tastefully produced, as well as his predilection for contemporary poets like Binyon and Bridges, link him to Dr. Daniel, who like Mathews did much to encourage and foster careers of struggling poets both young and old.

Elkin Mathews and Gordon Bottomley:

The Publication of the *Chambers of Imagery* Volumes

Among the most beautifully designed and illustrated books Elkin Mathews published was *The Gate of Smaragdus* which appeared in 1904. Described as "a collection of lyric, narrative, and elegiac poems, eclogues and idylls, with, generally, an underlying dramatic intention; ranging in subject from classical and Renaissance to fantastic and modern themes,"[1] *The Gate of Smaragdus* was the work of a young poet, Gordon Bottomley, who would later gain considerable fame as one of the so-called Georgian poets. How closely his beautiful book came to being destroyed before publication is a story worth recounting. As the poet later told it, the book

> was all ready for publication with the Unicorn Press, and the agreement signed, when at the very moment it should have been issued the Unicorn Press was annihilated; its stock was sold by auction (for anything it would fetch) . . . and I had a lively and exciting time rescuing the edition of my book. It had fortunately been removed before the sale, as it was my own property; and eventually I found the cases containing it in the cellar of a shipping warehouse in the City, among bales and cases ready to start for India and the Colonies. Then Mr. Elkin Mathews undertook the publication.[2]

Not only did Bottomley supply the poems for *The Gate of Smaragdus*, but he also designed the book and, despite being an invalid confined to bed much of the time because of tuberculosis, directed its production, even finding a printer. The printer—"certainly a craftsman," in the opinion of Claude Colleer Abbott[3]—William Holmes, who lived in the town of Ulverston, Lancashire, near Bottomley's home at Cartmel near the southern tip of Lake Windermere, engraved and printed the blocks, set the type, and bound the book in accordance with Bottomley's wishes. Bottomley also commissioned a friend, the young Liverpool artist Clinton Balmer, to supply the illustrations. Greatly influenced by the revival of printing and the splendid work during the nineties in book illustration and design, Bottomley was, in particular, a devotee of Charles Ricketts and his close associate Charles Hazelwood Shannon. *The Gate of Smaragdus*, in its disposition of the type on the page and the use of capitals throughout, clearly imitates the page of contents in Ricketts and Shannon's beautiful journal of the nineties, *The Dial*. Shannon's influence is also seen in Balmer's illustrations, which catch quite remarkably Shannon's dreamy Pre-Raphaelite style. Bottomley, like D. G. Rossetti, Walter Pater, Oscar Wilde, and others, was very much concerned with the physical appearance of his books, believing, as they did, that the text, the artwork, and all other aspects of the physical book must complement and enhance each other. Therefore, it is not surprising that in his relations with Mathews concerning the publication of his books, Bottomley exhibited considerable interest in their production, a fact borne out by a series of important letters which he wrote to Mathews concerning his two books of poems entitled *Chambers of Imagery*, the first published in 1907 and the second in 1912.

Bottomley probably approached Mathews about publishing the first volume of *Chambers of Imagery* in February 1907, seeing in his mind's eye a mere "bibelot," as he referred to it—a book designed on a much smaller scale than *The Gate of Smaragdus* and without illustrations. Dependent upon the generosity of his parents for the support of himself and his wife, Bottomley conceived of *Chambers of Imagery* as a simple, well-designed, but inexpensive book. Consequently, he found Mathews' estimate of fifteen guineas for producing it excessive, explaining to the publisher that he "had put together this little pamphlet in the hope that it might be done for ten guineas or so, as some years ago another publisher did me a book of 96 pages (of 24 lines) for sixteen guineas."[4] Bottomley then went on to say that he had "hoped by having half the number of pages you give in the Vigo Cabinet [series]"—that is about 64 pages per booklet—"and more lines on a page, to reduce the cost of production somewhat also." Afraid that a cost of fifteen guineas would require a published price of more than a shilling if he was to have "much chance of making much more than expenses even if a large proportion of the edition sold at once," Bottomley went on to inquire, since Mathews was to publish his book on commission, "what your percentage and the bookseller's would amount to on each copy sold." Before making a decision on whether or not to go ahead with his book, Bottomley also asked Mathews if he would require him "to pay the whole amount at once or if a portion of it could go to my account with you to be paid for by the first copies sold."[5] As subsequent correspondence shows, Mathews did agree to allow the poet to add some of the costs of production to his account, one which apparently was not settled until 1916, when, as Bottomley had hoped, it had settled itself, "the years," as he wrote Mathews, having "reversed the balance."[6] That Mathews thought highly of Bottomley's poems and Bottomley thought highly of Mathews' name as a publisher soon brought the two men to an agreement about the production costs. By mid-April Bottomley wrote to say that he had received what he termed "the counterpart agreement," in which, he declared, "everything is satisfactory and complete."[7]

Although Bottomley obviously was concerned about production costs, he was primarily interested in producing a book tasteful in both design and materials, one aesthetically attuned to its poetic content. To this end, he had conceived in his mind's eye what he called a "shape of page" for *Chambers of Imagery* similar to that Mathews had employed in his Shilling Garland series. "Of course," he wrote the publisher, "I do not ask you to imitate the Garland for my benefit; but in size and number of pages and amount of matter on a page it is very much the kind of thing I should value your doing for me in this instance. The bibelot I see in my mind has even a rather larger page and a cover of old gold coloured paper (or cinnamon); and I can get a piece of admirable lettering to be reproduced in a lineblock for the cover.[8] As it turned out, the "shape of page" for *Chambers of Imagery* is strikingly similar to that of the Shilling Garland series booklet, only smaller (not larger, as Bottomley initially had hoped), measuring approximately 170 by 115 mm, as opposed to 180 by 115 mm.

On receiving specimen pages from Mathews in April, Bottomley declared himself "gratified. . . . the appearance and all the details of production are charming, and I could not want anything different." In fact, he told Mathews, "all your arrangements are so satisfactory that no suggestions are left me to make, and I shall be glad to have the proofs at your convenience, and to leave farther arrangements in your hands."[9]

As to the binding, Bottomley had in mind something more substantial in the way of a paper wrapper and more plain in design than that for the Shilling Garland books. After viewing "the parcel of cover-papers" Mathews sent him, Bottomley quickly agreed with the publisher that "the Abbey [Mills] series of papers [are] greatly superior to the others," observing that of the sample papers "in this book[,] No. 93, Ecru is the shade I like most, and I shall be glad if you think it suitable to use." Bottomley noted that "the cover of Mr. Underwood's book [i.e., Wilbur Underwood's *A Book of Masks*, recently published by Mathews] is in the 'Board' quality paper. I don't know if the Ecru is obtainable in that quality; and perhaps the 'Board' quality is more in harmony with the thicker paper of Mr. Underwood's book—in any case it is much more durable and serviceable. Please make your own decision on this point; I shall be glad to leave it with you."[10] Mathews, given the final say in the matter, chose the No. 93 Abbey Mills cover-paper in ecru, which, though less heavy than the "board" quality paper Bottomley seems to have been

Binding monogram used on back cover of Wilber Underwood's *A Book of Masks* (1907) and numerous other books published by Mathews

181

leaning toward, was stiffer and in texture more interesting than the paper Mathews had employed as a wrapper for his Shilling Garland series. The publisher's decision appears to have been a happy one, for when the poet received proofs of the wrapper in May 1907, he wrote Mathews declaring that "the cover-paper is exactly what I wished for." Coming very close to the effect, as Bottomley had desired of "old gold coloured paper," the paper wrappers in which *Chambers of Imagery*—both the first and second volumes—was bound also drew Bottomley's praise for "the way the cover is put on." Unlike the Shilling Garland and Vigo Cabinet books, which were published without endpapers, *Chambers of Imagery* was supplied with endpapers around whose fore-edge the binding paper was wrapped in the manner of a dust jacket. "Wholly delighted with the book and the effect of the cover," Bottomley had only one reservation about the ecru-colored wrapper with lettering in blue sent him in proof: "With your permission," he wrote Mathews, "I greatly wish the cover may be printed in *black* (as in the revise enclosed herewith)—as the slight resultant rustiness will, I think, be compensated by a better harmony of tone than that obtained by the rather sharp contrast of the blue. The soft quality of this black I should exceedingly like to have."[11] Mathews acceded to Bottomley's request.

Chambers of Imagery was published in June 1907. The little book offered a striking example of Mathews' ability to publish at the cost of a mere shilling an attractive volume tastefully designed and printed on quality paper. Simplicity itself, the front cover bore the title and author's name separated by a leaf device in a block of black lettering placed near the top and slightly to the left of center. Mathews' name and address in a block of smaller-sized type appeared directly below it at the bottom. The title page, so different from the title pages of the typical book of the last century, echoed the front wrapper, the title and author's name appearing in a slightly larger-sized type but of the same design in a block centered at the top of the page, the publisher's name and address with the year of publication in smaller type directly below at the foot.

It was not until the summer of 1910 that Bottomley, "at last having a little peace with my lung," began "to plan another series of 'Chambers of Imagery,' about which," he wrote Mathews, "I hope to consult you later."[12] Since the agreement for the "second series"—as the second volume was termed—was, as Bottomley observed to Mathews in a letter of 29 February 1912, "on the lines of that for the first series," it required the author to pay production costs and a percentage of the price of each book sold to the publisher. As correspondence between Bottomley and Mathews shows, the author sent the publisher a money order in the amoung of £11.10.0 to cover, if not all, at least a substantial part, of the production costs of the second book.[13] Mathews' percentage, as a letter of 1916 reveals, was 33.5 percent.[14]

As to the format and design of the second series, Bottomley wrote Mathews that he was "anxious that the book should be in all respects uniform with the first series." Since his health remained "very poor indeed," he told the publisher that he would "be grateful if you can see to this for me."[15] Anxious to add Bottomley's new collection to his spring list, Mathews went forward with its production, publishing *Chambers of Imagery* (Second Series) in April 1912. When, however, Bottomley's free copies reached him, he found much to his discomfiture that the books were bound in flimsy paper wrappers which "all but dropped off" when he tried to handle them. Mathews, having decided to rebind the whole edition, wrote Bottomley asking him to return his copies, which as per agreement amounted to 26 (i.e., two dozen copies counting 13 as 12). Unfortunately, the poet, "anxious to get them off to quarters where the interest of the book urgently required them," had sent most of his copies off and informed Mathews on 17 April that he was "returning what I can."[16] Subsequently, all copies of the second volume were rebound with the exception of the copies Bottomley had posted, the poet acknowledging receipt of "the parcel of rebound 'Chambers of Imagery' Series II," on 1 May, expressing himself "very pleased with the alteration as the books look so much better, and I am especially gratified that the same paper is being used as was used for Series I."[17]

Although the two books of poems, each issued in an edition of 500 copies, sold slowly, sales increased considerably after Bottomley's poems "The End of the World" and "Babel: The Gate of God"—both from *Chambers of Imagery* (Second Series)—appeared in the first of Edward Marsh's highly successful anthologies, *Georgian Poetry, 1911–1912*, which Harold Monro published from the Poetry Bookshop in December 1912. Appearances of Bottomley's poems in subsequent Georgian anthologies seem to have added further impetus to the sale of his books. In a letter of 1916, Bottomley thanked Mathews for his "kind words" about his work in *Georgian Poetry, 1913–1915*, agreeing that the response he had received was "re-acting favourably on the sales" of his books. Anxious to make the most of Bottomley's success, Mathews urged the poet to allow him to reprint his "earlier volumes of poems";[18] in addition, Bottomley had a third volume of *Chambers of Imagery* in mind. Although Bottomley neither reprinted his early volumes of poetry during Mathews' lifetime nor brought out a third series, nevertheless, the relationship between Bottomley and Mathews over the years seems to have been a most amiable and profitable one for both men, resulting in the production of some of Mathews' most tasteful and appealing books.

APPENDIX C

Making Ends Meet:

The Economics of Small-Scale Publishing

Elkin Mathews' fame as a publisher is commensurate with that of some of the largest commercial publishing firms of his time. Yet compared with their capital, number of books published, and profits, his business was quite small. As Laurence Binyon once observed, Mathews "makes no large profits, has small capital, and quite inadequate means for distribution on a large scale."[1] Under these circumstances, how did he survive as a publisher? It must be remembered that Mathews was not only a publisher but a bookseller, catering to the rare book collector and to the second-hand and new book buyer. Consequently, he was not wholly dependent on his publishing business for a living. Moreover, Mathews—once described as "shrewd in business, careful in a bargain, methodical in detail"[2]—kept expenditures to a minimum, both as to his premises and his staff. It is true that the Cork Street shop was more commodious and better appointed than the one in Vigo Street, but both were habitually described as cramped and crowded, depending for their charm on the dishabille one associates with the old-fashioned bookshop. And despite his telegraph address, "Elegantia," Mathews made no pretensions to elegance insofar as his premises were concerned. Similarly, his staff was small, apparently consisting of several clerks, a "traveller" (travelling salesman) whom he probably shared with several other publishers, and various readers who served Mathews over the years on an ad hoc basis.

Even more important, Mathews kept the cost of book production low, relying on a number of strategies which were especially compatible with the publication of poetry, such as employing larger-than-usual type sizes (above 10 point) and using more leading than normal between lines.[3] Since the printer's bill depended largely on the amount of type set, this habitual use of relatively little text per book substantially reduced the cost. Furthermore, Mathews made the most of the privilege printers and binders extended to publishers to store rent-free their unbound sheets,[4] a courtesy which enabled him to take advantage of the fact that 1,000 sheets of a book could be produced for little more than the cost of producing 500—the cost of composing the type being the same. Thus, he often printed an edition of 1,000 copies, initially binding only half and storing the remainder either at the printer's or at the binder's, a practice which substantially reduced his risk of being left with large numbers of unsold bound copies on his hands. He also reduced this risk by printing a small edition of a book and either leaving the type standing (for which he paid a modest rent) or having stereotypes or "shells" made from which further printings could be made. (These practices largely account for the fact that successive issues of Mathews' books often

184

appeared in variant bindings). Another means by which Mathews reduced production costs was to buy up at considerable savings remainders of paper which were inadequate to the demands of the large publishers. Since he seldom had more than 1,000 copies of a book printed, these remainders were just right for Mathews' needs. In addition, Mathews often bound his books inexpensively in paper wrappers or paper-covered boards.

As a consequence of his strategies, Mathews' books over the years cost

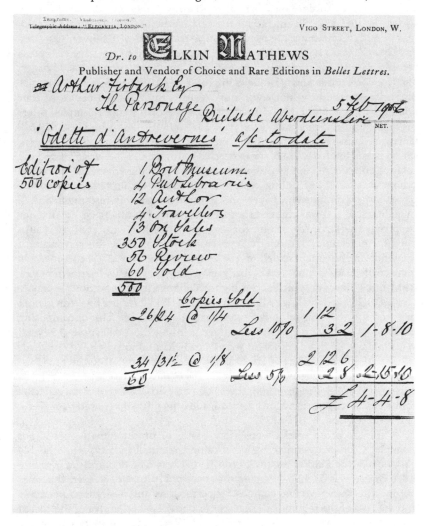

Mathews' account of sales for Ronald Firbank's first book, *Odette d'Antrevernes*, dated 5 February 1906. Berg Collection, New York Public Library.

surprisingly little. For example, the Sold Books (debit ledgers) of the Chiswick Press show that Percy Hemingway's *The Happy Wanderer and Other Verse* (1896) cost £19.14.0, including laid watermarked paper. Typsetting cost £8.16.0, plus £1.0.6 for the small type used in initial letters, etc., and £2.3.6 for corrections and alterations. The printing of the 500 copies of the book cost £6.19.6, plus 10/6 for six special advance copies and 4/- for "extra overlay of block title and printing same."[5] In 1908, the Chiswick Press's bill for printing 1,000 copies of Laurence Binyon's collected and augmented edition of *London Visions* totaled £17.13.1, including the cost of the antique laid paper (Add. mss. 50,922). Containing 104 pages, it can be compared with Binyon's *England and Other Poems* (1909), which cost £14.8.0, according to the Chiswick press records: £10.0.0 for composing the old-style small pica type for its 98 pages, 19/6 for corrections and alterations in proofs, £3.3.0 for printing 1,000 copies on paper supplied by Mathews, and 5/6 for printing 1,000 copies of four additional pages (Add. Mss. 50,923). Even a somewhat more complex printing job such as *Sonnets by Ferdinand Earle* (1910) cost a modest £19.6.0. Chiswick Press records show that composing the old style small pica type for the 88 pages totaled £7.14.0, the extra charge for small type was 5/-, and the cost for corrections and alterations in proofs including 25 special advanced proofs was £2.13.0. Printing costs for 500 copies on imitation handmade paper, 500 on antique laid paper, and 25 on Japanese vellum came to £6.0.0. In addition, £1.1.0 was charged for the "red printing in title page," £1.10.0 for supplying the Japanese vellum for 25 copies together with endleaves supplied to the binder, and 3/- for composing the lines for the certificate of limitation in the Japanese vellum copies (Add. Mss. 50,923). A considerably more costly book of poems was *Artemesian* (1909), by the well-known novelist Maurice Hewlett, which according to William Clowes and Sons' estimate cost £29.3.0, largely owing to the high cost of £15.15.0 for the fine Van Gelder paper on which it was printed. The estimate also included £10 for composing the type for the 104 pages and £3.8.0 for printing the 1,000 copies.[6] Several years later, the second edition of John Masefield's famous *Salt Water Ballads* (1913) cost a total of £20.14.0 (including paper wrappers). According to Chiswick Press records, composing the old-style Long Primer type for the 126 pages cost £11.18.0 and printing the 1,500 copies cost £4.16.0. Printing 1,500 copies of the "wrapper in blue ink into 1 side only with blue tinted paper" cost only £1.10.0 (Add. Mss. 50,925).

Of course, prose works were more costly to produce than poetry. For example, Clowes's estimate for composing the small pica type for the 144 pages of Victor Plarr's *Ernest Dowson* (1914) was £14.18.0 and for printing 1,000 copies was £4.12.0, bringing the total to £19.10.0. However, this does not include the inevitable charges for corrections and alterations in proofs and the cost of the required 4 1/2 reams of paper.[7] A better idea of the cost of producing a book of prose before World War I can be gotten from the Chiswick Press records pertaining to Masefield's book of stories *A Mainsail Haul* (1913), which cost £33.1.3, including the paper wrappers. Composing the old-style Long Primer type for the book's 200 pages cost £23.8.3, including the extra charge of £1.9.6 for composing the small-type mixture and £2.5.0 for corrections and alterations in proofs. Printing the 1,500 copies cost £7.14.6. Two shillings were charged for the overlay for Jack Yeats's frontispiece and 6/6 for making the photo-zinco block. Printing "1500 wrappers in blue ink into one side only with blue tinted paper" cost an additional £1.10.0 (Add. Mss. 50,925).

Although costs of book production rose considerably during World War I, records pertaining to books printed for Mathews at that time still reflect moderate costs. For example, composing the type for *The Poetical Works of Lionel Johnson*, which the Chiswick Press produced in 1915, amounted to £36.0.3, and printing 1,500 copies came to £14.0.6 (Add. Mss. 50,926). Clowes' estimate for composing and printing 1,000 copies of Ezra Pound's *Lustra* (1916) set in pica type—"22 ems. wide, 6 lead, 28 lines to a page," to quote the records—totaled only £23.5.0, excluding the cost of paper.[8] Hewlett's *Gai Saber: Tales and Songs*, also published in 1916, cost a total of £35.14.9, including among other charges £21.14.6 for composing the Long Primer type for the 176 pages of text and £6.1.0 for printing 1,000 copies on antique laid paper (Add Mss. 50,927). Production costs, however, appear to have risen sharply toward the close of Mathews' career, the cost of Martin Birnbaum's *Oscar Wilde, Fragments and Memories* (1920), a little book of some 36 pages (including two full-page illustrations) totaling £75.2.6. As Chiswick Press records show, this included £65.12.6 for composing the type, supplying the paper, and binding in paper-covered boards with printed label pasted on the front of the 750 copies, plus £ 6.5.0 for printing 50 copies on handmade paper and binding them in whole buckram, plus £1.17.6 for corrections in proofs, and £1.7.6 for making the drawing and supplying the line block for use on the cover of the 50 copies (Add. Mss. 50,928).

Mathews' most inexpensively produced books were his series books. Vigo Cabinet series booklets, usually containing 64 pages and bound in paper wrappers, cost between £9 and £15. For example, Arthur Symons' *Poems in Prose from Charles Baudelaire* (VC29) cost £14.14.0, and Chiswick Press records indicate that the 1,000 copies of *Six Lyrics from the Ruthenian of Taras Shevchénko* (VC86) cost £11.13.6 (Add. Mss. 50,924)—little more than the £11.11.6 charged to produce 750 copies on antique laid paper of Charles E. Moyse's *The Lure of Earth and Other Poems* (VC87) (Add. Mss. 50,924)—and the 500 copies of Maria Steuart's *At the World's Edge* (VC93) cost only £9.19.6 (Add. Mss. 50,924).

Another way Mathews made ends meet was by often negotiating agreements with his authors which paid them little if any royalties. If during the early nineties Mathews and his partner John Lane had made it their policy to assume "the entire risk" of publishing their books and to accept an author's manuscript "with the distinct understanding that the author receives a royalty,"[9] such had not been the case before 1892, nor was it after the dissolution of the partnership in 1894. Mathews on his own often published books on commission—that is, at the author's own expense—with Mathews receiving a percentage of the book's receipts for acting as publisher. This seems to have been the case with *Renascence, A Book of Verse* (1891); its author, the well-known artist Walter Crane, inquired of Mathews: "I presume if an author pays his own printing etc.: you undertake the publication of the book at the usual percentage?"[10] As Ian Fletcher has said, Mathews continued the practice "into the new century," thereby laying himself open to Harold Monro's jibe: "I see more and more every day that there is no market for booklets, and E. Mathews, Stockwell and others are doing their best to spoil what little market/remains."[11] In 1912 Gordon Bottomley in a letter to Paul Nash (who had been seeking an introduction to Mathews in hopes of finding a publisher for his book), cautioned: "But even if he likes your work he will want you to pay him from £10 to £15 before he will publish it. That is all right, of course, if you think the money will be of the most use to you spent in that way; but you cannot be certain, especially with a first book, that the sales will recoup you for the outlay."[12] Even as late as 1921 Nancy Cunard subsidized the publication of *Outlaws*, a practice which, according to her biographer, Anne Chisholm, "was more usual and acceptable then than it is now."[13]

Acting as publisher for largely young and/or unknown authors, Mathews was constrained by the economics of small-scale publishing throughout his career to ask clients who had as yet not made a name in the realm of literature to pay the costs of producing their books and in some instances (perhaps a later practice) to bear the cost of the reader's fee. A case in point was the young Herbert Read, who in January 1915 gladly paid both the reader's fee and the subsequent publication costs for his first book of poems, *Songs of Chaos*, which Mathews published later that same year.[14] Of course, many authors were not so amenable as Read when asked to pay to publish their own books and/or supply the fee for a reader's opinion. For example, the young John Drinkwater withdrew the manuscript of "Graven Images" along with a few shorter poems which he had submitted to Mathews after being asked to pay for the book, informing Mathews that "I should not in any case be prepared to bear cost of publication."[15] And Lord Dunsany, having been requested to pay the production costs of his *Fifty-One Tales*, objected: "I only meant the ordinary method of publication. I do not very much like the 'commission' method, and have never used it since the first edition of Pegāna [i.e., *The Gods of Pegāna*, which Mathews had published in 1905]."[16] Moreover, as one gathers from a remark Mathews made to one of his readers, John Mavrogordato, Compton Mackenzie felt insulted when asked to pay a reader's fee, Mathews opining: "But even if his stuff is as good as reported, I don't see why he should be irate at being asked to assist his bantling into the world by paying a fee for a reader's opinion."[17]

Although Mathews published books on commission, it was his policy whenever possible to assume the entire risk of publishing a book (that is, to undertake to pay for the paper, printing, binding, advertising, and distribution) and to offer his authors a modest royalty—usually between 10 and 20 percent. For example, the second section of an agreement in Mathews' hand ostensibly drawn up for John Corbin's *Elizabethan Hamlet* (1895) states that "the publisher agrees to print and publish such work at his own expense in such style as he deems best suited to the sale of the work and to pay the author _____per cent on the retail price of each copy of said by him sold."[18] Although this agreement form may be taken as typical of those Mathews used in the mid-nineties, there is evidence to suggest that he often altered it to suit a particular author and/or work. The draft of the contract for Ernest Dowson's book of stories, *Dilemmas* (1895), for instance, indicates that Mathews agreed to pay the author a royalty of 6d a copy, the selling price of which was 3/6. What makes this agreement somewhat unusual is the fact that it called for the publisher to pay the royalty on the first 300 copies (of an edition of 600) on the day of publication—something Mathews seldom found it possible to do.[19] Arthur Symons was referring to a more typical situation when in urging James Joyce to send his *Chamber Music* manuscript to Mathews, he wrote: "You would get little money from him, but I think it would be worth your while to take what he offered—probably a small royalty after expenses are covered."[20] Such—as the agreement shows—was the case: Mathews offered a royalty only after he had recouped expenses, clearly stipulating in the contract that 300 copies of *Chamber Music* "shall be sold before any royalty be computed it being understood that the author receives no royalty on these three hundred copies the proceeds of which are solely intended to go towards the initial expenses of the book after which the Author shall receive fifteen percent (15%) on the net proceeds sold beyond the above number counting 13 as 12."[21] Similarly, the agreement for Ezra Pound's *Exultations* (1909) calls not only for Mathews to assume "the entire risk of production with the exception of the charge for corrections and alterations" in the proofs, but to pay the author a royalty of 10 to 12.5 percent only "after the cost out of the sales of the book has been met."[22]

At least two of the books which Mathews published for the artist Jack Yeats were also published on similar terms. A "memorandum of an Agreement" made on 17 September 1902 between Yeats and Mathews called for the publisher to defray "all the costs of production, including paper[,] blocks, composition[,] advertisements and other needful outgoings," for which he would receive "one equal moiety or half share of and in all net proceeds accruing from the sale of a book entitled 'The Treasure of the Garden', the other half share to be paid to the Author as hereinafter provided." But, as Mathews' agreements typically read, "no profits shall be computed until these various charges have been repaid to the Publisher from the proceeds of the book."[23] The agreement for Yeats' *Little Fleet*, which was in all respects the same and was signed by Yeats on 13 September 1909, stipulated, as did that for *The Treasure of the Garden*, that "should an American Edition be arranged[,] the profits of such edition to be equally divided between Author and Publisher."[24] Some idea of Yeats' share in the profits of his books can be gathered by a check for £18.17.4 which Mathews sent the artist in 1921 "in final settlement of royalty on the six books remaining hitherto unsettled, viz: 'Scourge of the Gulph,' 'Treasure of the Garden,' 'Little Fleet,' 'The Bosun,' 'Jack B. Yeats,' 'The Fancy.' 'The Broadsheet' and 'James Flaunty' were settled up previously. Nothing now remains to be accounted for."[25]

A somewhat different arrangement concerning royalties was concluded between Mathews and J. M. Synge for the Irish playwright's *The Shadow of the Glen and Riders to the Sea* (VC24), perhaps because of Synge's strong backing by Yeats, Lady Gregory, and Masefield. The agreement stated "that the Author [shall] receive a royalty of 10 per centum on the trade price (10d.) from the first copy counting 13 copies as 12 after expenses have been paid from proceeds of sales,"[26] an arrangement which ultimately yielded Synge £3.11.3 on the first edition of 1,000 copies, which sold out within two years. Mathews' income from sales to the trade totaled £35.12.6 (i.e., 10d X 855 copies).[27] If Mathews' production, advertising, and distribution costs for Synge's little book were that of the average Vigo Cabinet series book—say £13.0.0—the publisher's profit—less Synge's royalty of £3.11.3—in this rather happy but unusual instance was about £19.1.3.[28]

That Mathews was from time to time constrained to strike a hard bargain even with established authors whose work, nevertheless, did not sell well is suggested by his agreement with the celebrated nineties authors Katherine Bradley and her niece, Edith Cooper, who jointly wrote under the pen name of Michael Field. Mathews who had published their "trialogue," *Stephania*, and a book of poems, *Sight and Song*, in 1892, and *A Question of Memory: A*

Publisher's device by Jack B. Yeats on back cover of the artist's *A Little Fleet*

Play in 1893, appears to have had doubts about accepting their latest play, *Attila, My Attila*, before he was spurred into action by a letter in the hand of Bradley, who wrote, "Please let me know your decision with regard to my play. I wish very much publishers could be 'taken up' for detaining the m.s.s. of unhappy authors. Then—what warrants should be issued."[29] While he was unable to pay the authors any royalty on their play, Mathews was willing to issue the work at his own risk provided that they conceded to him "the copyright of the play 'Attila my Attila' and all the profits that may arise from its sale" and leave "the whole management" in his hands.[30]

The economics of his business also from time to time constrained Mathews to allow an author a larger royalty than he had offered originally. A case in point is the poet W. H. Davies, whose *New Poems* Mathews had published in 1907. The fact that Davies recently had contributed poems to the highly popular anthology *Georgian Poetry, 1911–1912* made his new book of poems, *Foliage*, difficult for Mathews to refuse when it was offered to him in 1913. Not unpredictably, the publisher made Davies an offer which the self-styled "Super Tramp" in a letter promptly thanked him for only to refuse it. Davies then proceeded to deliver Mathews something of an ultimatum: if Davies could not "get fifteen percent on the published price" of his new volume, he must, he declared, publish it himself. "If you can offer those terms," he went on to write, "I shall be very pleased to let you have it." In addition, Davies listed two other desiderata: that Mathews secure publication of his book in America through Macmillan and that he advertise a short list of his other books of poetry at the beginning of the proposed volume. Having responded to an apparent suggestion by Mathews—"'Foliage' is a good title, and I like it very much"—Davies concluded, "Please let me know if you can agree to all this."[31]

Another case in point is Henry Newbolt, whose sudden rise to fame upon the publication of his *Admirals All and Other Verses* (SG8) in the autumn of 1897 prompted Mathews to immediately schedule the publication of a second book of Newbolt's poems entitled *The Island Race*. Mathews initially offered Newbolt "a royalty of 15% on the full published price on all copies sold (counting 13/12) should the price be 5/–; or 10% on a 3/6 volume reckoned in the same way, the royalties to begin with the first copies sold," but then, concerned lest he lose Newbolt, shortly after decided to raise the royalty on *The Island Race* to "15% on all copies sold up to 2000 and 20% afterwards— whatever the price be fixed at."[32] Even so, Mathews soon lost Newbolt to larger publishing firms which, unlike Mathews, were able to pay the large advances and high royalties necessary to maintain the loyalty of the most popular authors of the day. In at least one instance—and no doubt in others—Mathews himself is known to have paid an advance to an author; this was John Drinkwater, the draft agreement for whose book, *Prose Papers* (1917), called for an advance to be paid on the delivery of the manuscript.[33]

Mathews' dilemma as a publisher of small means during World War I is rather graphically illustrated in an exchange of letters during the summer of

1916 between Lord Dunsany and himself, Dunsany affirming in one letter that if he found enough material for another book of tales, he would have to have from Mathews a royalty commensurate with that obtainable from such American firms as Luce and Little, Brown and from the English firm of T. Fisher Unwin. In other words, he wrote, I shall have to have "a real 15% without deductions that one way and another whittle it down to about 10%. I mean an actual 15% on the published price. Two of those four [publishers listed earlier] give, & a third in England offers, an advance of £100; but though I can get this I do not demand it and should not dream of asking you to handicap your business by paying me anything before I had earned it and you received it."[34] Mathews in several drafts of a reply wrote: "I fear from your letter that you do not realize the difficulties and the deductions a Publisher has to put up with before he can make even the smallest profit on his venture. It is quite true that books are supplied to the trade 13 as 12 at trade price, but you apparently do not know that when after some months of patient waiting the account is paid they have the right to deduct a further sum of 10% from the unfortunate publisher." Referring to Dunsany's *Fifty-One Tales*, which he had published in 1915, Mathews then produced figures to show that Dunsany's book, instead of producing the sum he imagined, actually worked out as follows:

say 13 copies as *12*	@ 5/– net per copy =	3———
	less 2d in the 1/– discount	10
		2.10
	less 10% discount	5
		2.5
	less 13th copy free	5
		2.0

Continuing, Mathews wrote: "In addition to all these deductions there is my traveller to pay—an occasional bankruptcy and many other things more easily explainable by word of mouth than in a letter. Where did[?] the publisher's enormous profits come in. Indeed enormous sales are needed to make even a bare living in times like these when it is difficult enough to make both ends meet."[35]

On occasion Mathews helped make ends meets by acting as publisher (agent and distributor) for books actually produced by someone else. For example, he distributed and acted as publisher for Reginald Hallward's Woodlands Press books. The terms on which Mathews undertook to act as publisher are indicated in several letters which he wrote to Hallward in 1906–07 about Hallward's books of poems, *Wild Oats* and *Apotheosis*. Citing the

WILD OATS

❖THE WOODLANDS PRESS❖

Where was his dwelling-place?
What was his name?—you say.
Neither this hour to-morrow, or yesterday,
Own any more to a trace of locality.
Sprung from wherever night changes to-day,
        Voice of humanity.—

———

———

LONDON:
ELKIN MATHEWS, VIGO STREET, W.
1906.

Title page with design by Reginald Hallward of the Woodland Press for his *Wild Oats* (1906)

193

fact that he had to allow the trade "2d off the shilling, 5% and 13 copies as 12," Mathews offered to handle Hallward's books

on the same terms as [those of] the *Pear Tree Press* viz:

2/	= 1/8	20%	&	5%	13/12
2/6	= 2/1	do.		do.	do.[36]

Several days later, after more negotiating, Mathews agreed to act as publisher for Hallward's books for a year—

I accounting to you for all books sold on the following terms:
13 copies as 12, 2d. off 1/- on published price and a discount of 10% and 5%.
All advertising to be at your expense, copies for review to be supplied by you.[37]

Thus it was through a thorough knowledge and understanding of the economics of the publishing trade and a determination to carry on his business within the strict bounds of the laws governing that trade that Mathews successfully survived as a small publisher for over thirty years when many others failed.

APPENDIX D

Checklist of the

Elkin Mathews Imprint

The checklist which follows is, I believe, a reasonably full and accurate list of the nearly seven hundred books, periodicals, and other printed materials bearing the imprint of Elkin Mathews from the time when his partnership with John Lane was dissolved in the autumn of 1894 to his death in 1921 and the sale of the business by Mrs. Edith Elkin Mathews to A. W. Evans in April 1922, at which time the firm came to be known as Elkin Mathews Limited.

The checklist does not include those books—often referred to as "ghosts"—which were never anything more than titles in Mathews' advertisements and announcements, titles such as *The Letters and Papers of Adam Legendre*, which was listed in Mathews' *Catalogue of Publications, 1896–97* and was intended by its author, Herbert P. Horne, for the Diversi Colores series; both the series and the book itself were abandoned when Horne went off to Italy in 1895. Another "ghost" is *Some Account of the Old Church at Chelsea and of Its Monuments* by R. R. Davies, which appeared in Mathews' early catalogues, advertisements, and announcements only to reappear later under the title of *Chelsea Old Church*, published in 1904 by Duckworth. The checklist also excludes books transferred by other publishers to Mathews, who often listed them indiscriminately among books with his own imprint in his advertisements: for example, *Good King Wenceslas*, the famous carol written by Dr. Neale and pictured by Arthur Gaskin, was listed among "Elkin Mathews' New and Forthcoming Books" in the *Academy* for 9 November 1895 but appeared later in the *List of Books Published by Elkin Mathews, 1898*, properly identified with the phrase "transferred to the present publisher." Similarly, books sold by Mathews through an arrangement with their publishers—often the authors themselves—are not included: that is, publications such as Pamela Colman Smith's arty journal *The Green Sheaf*, published during 1903–4, and the books of the Pear Tree Press, for which Mathews acted for a time as London agent. Furthermore, the checklist does not include those books published by Mathews and John Lane at the Bodley Head which remained with Mathews after the dissolution of the partnership—e.g., Laurence Binyon's *Lyric Poems* (1894) and Dr. Conrad Abbott's *Travels in a Tree-Top* (1894). Later editions of these books which remained with Mathews, however, are listed: thus, while the checklist does not include the first and second printings of John Addington Symonds' *In the Key of Blue*, it does include the third printing of 1895 and the "unaltered reprint" of 1918, both of which were published after the dissolution of the partnership.

In other words, the checklist includes only those books, periodicals, and other printed documents published between 1894 and 1922 which bear Mathews' imprint either on the title page, cancel title page, colophon, or, occasionally, on a slip on the title page pasted over a previous imprint. (Those interested in the books Mathews published during his several years as a bookseller and publisher in Exeter and later during his Bodley Head years—that is, between 1887 and 1894—will find them listed in Appendix A in my *The Early Nineties: A View from the Bodley Head*.)

Each title included in the checklist is assigned a number consisting of its actual year of publication and its probable chronological position within that year. Information is presented in each entry in the following order (though not all of these details appear in every entry):

(1)   Author and title, and translator or editor where pertinent.
(2)   Title-page year, in brackets, if different from actual publication year.
(3)   Indication of genre, if known and not clear from title: F = fiction D = drama P = poetry Pr = prose
(4)   Series name and number.
(5)   Month (or month and day) of publication, as determined from such evidence as Mathews' letters, British Library deposit dates, *Publishers' Circular* entries, and contemporary advertisements and listings.
(6)   Number of copies printed.
(7)   Form of issue (i.e., large paper, wrappers, etc.) and prices.
(8)   Illustrations and/or cover designs.
(9)   Printer.
(10)   American or previous British publisher.
(11)   Later printings (often called "editions") with dates, numbers of copies, prices, and other available information.
(12)   References to author bibliographies, other pertinent bibliographies, and catalogues. (Page numbers are designated by "p[p]." or, where there is a volume number, by a colon between volume and page; all other numbers refer to items or entries.)
(13)   Location of copies examined, with indication of significant inscriptions or annotations.

Location symbols always refer to first printings except when otherwise specified.

The following abbreviations are used:

Series Designations

BUR	Burlington Series
DC	Diversi Colores Series
SG	Shilling Garland Series
SAT	Satchel Series

SAV	Savile Series
VC	Vigo Cabinet Series

Printer Designations

Brendon	William Brendon & Sons, Plymouth
B&T	Butler & Tanner, The Selwood Printing Works, Frome and London
Chiswick	Chiswick Press, Charles Whittingham & Co., London
Clowes	William Clowes & Sons, London
Dargan	W. H. Dargan, Ltd., London
Folkard	R. Folkard & Son, London
G&R	Gilbert & Rivington, Ltd., London
Mayflower	Mayflower Press (special imprint of William Brendon & Sons, Plymouth)
Riverside	Riverside Press, Edinburgh
UP	The University Press, Aberdeen

General References and Bibliographies

Ashley	The Ashley Library. *A Catalogue of Prints & Books, Manuscripts and Autograph Letters Collected by Thomas James Wise*. 11 vols. London: Printed for Private Circulation, 1927.
BAL	*Bibliography of American Literature*. Compiled by Jacob Blanck and Michael Winship. New Haven: Yale UP, 1955–.
BMA I	Henry Danielson. *Bibliographies of Modern Authors*. London: The Bookman's Journal, 1921.
BMA II	C. A. Stonehill and H. W. Stonehill. *Bibliographies of Modern Authors*. 2nd ser. London: John Castle, 1925.
BMA III	P. H. Muir, S. Nowell Smith, and Dr. A. Mitchell. *Bibliographies of Modern Authors*. 3rd ser. London: The Bookman's Journal, 1931.
Benkovitz	Miriam J. Benkovitz. *The Bibliography of Ronald Firbank*. 2nd ed. Oxford: Clarendon Press, 1982.
Colbeck	*A Bookman's Catalogue: The Norman Colbeck Collection of Nineteenth-Century and Edwardian Poetry and Belles Lettres in the Special Collections of the University of British Columbia*. 2 vols. Compiled with a Preface by Norman Colbeck and edited by Tirthankar Bose. Vancouver: U of British Columbia Press, 1987.

197

Danielson	H[enry] Danielson. "A Bibliography of Lionel Johnson." Bibliographies of Modern Authors, no. 16. *Bookman's Journal and Print Collector* n.s. 5, nos. 1–3 (Oct.–Dec. 1921).
FEC	*A Bibliographical Catalogue of the First Loan Exhibition of Books and Manuscripts Held by the First Edition Club, 1922.* London: First Edition Club, 1922.
Fredeman	William E. Fredeman. *Pre-Raphaelitism: A Bibliocritical Study.* Cambridge: Harvard UP, 1965.
Gallatin	A. E. Gallatin. *Aubrey Beardsley: Catalogue of Drawings and Bibliography.* New York: Grolier Club, 1945.
Gallup	Donald Gallup. *Ezra Pound: A Bibliography.* Charlottesville: U of Virginia Press, 1983.
Gaskin	*Arthur and Georgie Gaskin: Exhibition Catalogue.* Birmingham: City Museum and Art Gallery, 1982.
Gawsworth	John Gawsworth [Terence Armstrong]. *Ten Contemporaries: Notes towards Their Definitive Bibliography.* London: Ernest Benn, 1932.
Harvey	David Dow Harvey. *Ford Madox Ford, 1873–1933.* Princeton: Princeton UP, 1962.
Hayward	John Hayward. *English Poetry: A Catalogue of First and Early Editions of Works of the English Poets from Chaucer to the Present Day.* N.p.: Cambridge UP, 1947.
Hinton	Percival Hinton. *Eden Phillpotts: A Bibliography of First Editions.* Birmingham: Greville Worthington, 1931.
Hoffman	Frederick J. Hoffman et al. *The Little Magazine: A History and a Bibliography.* 2nd ed. Princeton: Princeton UP, 1947.
Janelle	Pierre Janelle. "Bibliography." In *Robert Southwell, the Writer.* London: Sheed & Ward, 1935.
Kable	William S. Kable. *The Ewelme Collection of Robert Bridges: A Catalogue.* Bibliographical Series, no. 2. U of South Carolina Dept. of English, Columbia: 1967.
Kershaw	Alistair Kershaw. *A Bibliography of the Works of Richard Aldington from 1915 to 1948.* London: Quadrant Press, 1952.
Kramer	Sidney Kramer. *A History of Stone & Kimball and Herbert S. Stone & Co. with a Bibliography of Their Publications, 1893–1905.* Chicago: U of Chicago Press, 1940.
Kraus, *C&D*	Joe W. Kraus. *Messrs. Copeland & Day.* Philadelphia: MacManus, 1979.
Kraus, *W&W*	Joe W. Kraus. *A History of Way & Williams with a Bibliography of Their Publications: 1895–1898.* Philadelphia: MacManus. 1984.

Krishnamurti   G. Krishnamurti. *The Eighteen-Nineties: A Literary Exhibition*. London: National Book League, 1973.

Krishnamurti, *Supp.*   G. Krishnamurti. *Supplement to the Eighteen-Nineties.* London: Francis Thompson Society and Enitharmon Press, 1974.

MBP III   *Minor British Poets, 1798–1918*, Part Three: *The Later Victorian Period, 1870–1899.* Davis: Library of the U of California, Davis, 1986.

MBP IV   *Minor British Poets, 1789–1918*, Part Four: The Edwardian Period, 1900–1918. Davis: Library of the U of California, Davis, 1984.

MacCarvill   [Eileen MacCarvill]. "Jack B. Yeats—His Books." Bibliographies of Irish Writers. *Dublin Magazine* n.s. 20 (July–Sept. 1945): 47–52.

McKay   George L. McKay. *A Bibliography of Robert Bridges.* New York: Columbia UP, 1933.

Murphy   [Gwendolyn Murphy]. "Bibliographies of Modern Authors No. III: W. H. Davies." *London Mercury* 17, nos. 97 and 99 (Nov. 1927 and Jan. 1928): 76–80, 301–2.

Nelson   James G. Nelson. Appendix A, "Check List of Bodley Head Books, 1889–1894." In *The Early Nineties: A View from the Bodley Head.* Cambridge: Harvard UP, 1971.

Pafford   J.H.P. Pafford. *Isaac Watts, Divine Songs: Facsimile Reproduction with Introduction and Bibliography.* London: Oxford UP, 1971.

Potter   Ambrose George Potter. *A Bibliography of the Rubaiyat of Omar Khayyam together with Kindred Matter in Prose and Verse Pertaining Thereto.* London: Ingpen and Grant, 1929.

Quaritch   *Four Centuries of English Books.* Cat. 1043. London: Bernard Quaritch, Ltd., n.d.

Quaritch Misc.   "Miscellany Five: English Books and Manuscripts." *New Series*, Bulletin 19 (1984). London: Bernard Quaritch Ltd.

Reade   Brian Reade. *Aubrey Beardsley.* New York: Viking, 1967.

Ridler   William Ridler. *British Modern Press Books: A Descriptive Check List.* New enlarged ed. Folkestone, Kent: Dawson, 1975.

Reilly   Catherine W. Reilly. *English Poetry of the First World War: A Bibliography.* New York: St. Martin's Press, 1978.

Roth   William M. Roth. *A Catalogue of English and American First Editions of William Butler Yeats.* New Haven: Yale UP, 1939.

Simmons   Charles H. Simmons. *A Bibliography of John Masefield.* New York: Columbia UP, 1930.

Slocum and Cahoon John J. Slocum and Herbert Cahoon. *A Bibliography of James Joyce.* New Haven: Yale UP, 1953.

Taylor   John Russell Taylor. *The Art Nouveau Book in Britain.* Cambridge: MIT Press, 1966.

Turn of a Century   *The Turn of a Century: 1885–1910.* Exhibition catalogue. Cambridge, Mass.: Houghton Library, Harvard U., 1970.

Wade   Allan Wade. *A Bibliography of the Writings of W. B. Yeats.* London: Rupert Hart-Davis, 1958.

Williams   I. A. Williams. *Bibliographies of Modern Authors, No. 2: John Masefield.* London: Leslie Chaundy, 1921.

Wilson   George F. Wilson. "A Bibliography of William Henry Davies." Bibliographies of Modern Authors, no. 17. *Bookman's Journal and Print Collector* 5, no. 6 (March 1922).

Location Symbols

Location symbols are based whenever applicable on the alphabetic symbols listed on the end sheets of the *National Union Catalog, Pre-1956 Imprints.*

BL	British Library
CSmH	Huntington Library
CtY	Yale U. Library
CU-A	Library, U. of California, Davis
GC	Library, Grolier Club, New York City
GK	Library of G. Krishnamurti
IaU	Library, U. of Iowa
ICN	Newberry Library
ICU	Library, U. of Chicago
IU	Library, U. of Illinois, Urbana
JGN	Library of the author
MB	Boston Public Library
MH	Harvard U. Library
MSL	Library of Mark Samuels Lasner
NEM	Library of Nest Elkin Mathews
NjP	Princeton U. Library
NN	New York Public Library
NNC	Columbia U. Library
OU	Ohio State University Library
PHC	Haverford College Library

PKC	Library of Dr. Philip Kent Cohen
PM	Library of Percy Muir (in the possession of Barbara Kaye [Mrs. Percy Muir])
PSC	Library, Swarthmore College
RUL	Library, Reading U.
TNJ	Library, Vanderbilt U.
TXU	Harry Ransom Research Center, U. of Texas, Austin
WM	Milwaukee Public Library
WU	Library, U. of Wisconsin, Madison

1894.1   FREDERICK WEDMORE. *English Episodes.* (Pr). Nov. 3/6. J. Miller & Son. USA: Charles Scribner's Sons. "Second edition," 1895. Colbeck, 2:906. BL, JGN, MSL.

1894.2   THE HOBBY HORSE, No. 3, ed. Herbert P. Horne. Nov. £1 per annum. Kraus, *C&D*, 3.

1894.3   PERCY HEMINGWAY [William Percy Addleshaw]. *Out of Egypt: Stories from the Threshold of the East.* [1895]. Nov. 3/6. Cover design by Gleeson White. Ballantyne Press. Second printing, Dec. 1896. Colbeck, 1:4. BL, GK (both pink and gray cloth-bound issues).

1894.4   CHARLES G. HARPER. *Revolted Woman: Past, Present and to Come.* Nov. 5/-. Illus., some by the author. Strangeways and Sons. BL.

1894.5   FREDERICK WEDMORE. *Pastorals of France.* [1895]. (Pr). 15 Dec. 3/6. J. Miller & Son. Fourth printing of a volume, a third printing of which Mathews and Lane had published (along with Wedmore's *Renunciations*) in Oct. 1893 and which remained with Mathews after the dissolution of his partnership. USA: Charles Scribner's Sons. Krishnamurti, 704; Nelson, 63. GK, NN.

1894.6   FREDERICK WEDMORE. *Renunciations.* [1895]. (Pr). 15 Dec. 3/6. J. Miller & Son. Third printing of a volume, a second printing of which Mathews and Lane had published in Jan. 1893 and reissued with Wedmore's *Pastorals of France* in Oct. 1893. Both books were retained by Mathews after the dissolution of his partnership. USA: Charles Scribner's Sons. Nelson, 43, 63. JGN, NN.

1894.7   ELIZABETH RACHEL CHAPMAN. *A Little Child's Wreath: A Sonnet Sequence.* Second issue of a book first published by Mathews and Lane in June 1894 and retained by Mathews after the dissolution of his partnership. Dec. 3/6. Title page and cover design by Selwyn Image. USA: Dodd, Mead. Nelson, 87.

1895.1   CHARLES CONRAD ABBOTT. *The Birds about Us.* (Pr). 2nd ed. Jan. 5/6. Seventy-three illustrations. USA: J. B. Lippincott. BL.

1895.2   BLISS CARMAN and RICHARD HOVEY. *Songs from Vagabondia.* "Second edition" of a book first published in England under the imprint of Elkin Mathews and John Lane in Nov. 1894, and retained by Mathews after the dissolution of the partnership. Jan. 750. 5/-. Decorations by Tom B. Meteyard. John Wilson and Son (Cambridge, Mass.). USA: Copeland and Day. "Third edition," Nov. 1895, 750. "Fourth edition," Mar. 1897, 750. *BAL*, 2622; Kraus, *C&D*, 12 and 12a. BL (vellum issue of 4th ed.), IU, PHC (4th ed.).

1895.3 [SELWYN IMAGE]. *Poems & Carols*. [1894]. DC2. Jan. 500. 5/-. Title page and typography by H[erbert] P. Horne. Chiswick. Colbeck, 1:422. BL, GK, JGN, PKC, MSL.

1895.4 LIONEL JOHNSON. *Poems*. March. 750. Special issue of 25 copies numbered and signed by the author, 15/-. After the special issue was printed, the first and last gatherings were revised and reset, and the 750 copies of the ordinary edition printed, 5/-. Title-page design by Herbert P. Horne. Chiswick. USA: Copeland and Day. Ashley, 10:138; Colbeck, 1:432; Danielson; *FEC*; Hayward, 304, 307; Kraus, *C&D*, 18, 18a; Krishnamurti, 369; *MBP III*, 1676; Quaritch, 263, 289, 290; Taylor, 70. MSL (copy of the special issue of 25), PKC (Johnson's own copy of the ordinary issue, a copy of the special issue of 25, and an ordinary copy in the American binding with "Copeland & Day" at foot of spine once belonging to Thomas Whittemore), RUL. In Pharos Books, Cat. Two, Summer 1986, item 189: is a copy inscribed: "L.J. to L[ouise] I[mogen] G[uiney]" containing Guiney's pencilled notes and textual corrections.

1895.5 MAY PROBYN. *Pansies: A Book of Poems*. March. 3/6. Cover design and title page by Minnie Mathews. Folkard. Colbeck, 2:658; Krishnamurti, *Supp.*, 28; *MBP III*, 2472. BL, CU-A, GK, MSL.

1895.6 JOHN CORBIN. *The Elizabethan Hamlet: A Study of the Sources, and of Shakspere's Environment*. Prefatory Note by F. York Powell. April. 3/6. USA: Charles Scribner's Sons. Colbeck, 2:656. BL, JGN. A four-page draft agreement drawn up for this book in Elkin Mathews' hand inserted in Colbeck copy.

1895.7 *Dublin Verses by Members of Trinity College*. Ed. H[enry] A. Hinkson. April. 5/-. Folkard. Ireland: Hodges, Figgis. BL, JGN, PKC.

1895.8 RICHARD DODDRIDGE BLACKMORE. *Fringilla; or, Some Tales in Verse*. June. 500. 10/-. Also a decorated, vellum-bound issue of 25 printed on hand-made paper. Illustrations, vignettes, and initials by Louis Fairfax-Muckley; three additional illustrations by James W. R. Linton. Folkard. Taylor, 60; *Turn of a Century*, 36. BL, CSMH, JGN.

1895.9 ERNEST DOWSON. *Dilemmas: Stories and Studies in Sentiment*. June. 600 for England and America. 3/6. J. Miller & Son. USA: Frederick A. Stokes. "New and cheaper edition," 1912, 2/6. "Third impression," 1915. *BMA II*, 47; Colbeck, 1:222. BL, JGN, MSL (Mathews' copy with his early bookplate), PKC (English binding both with and without "Elkin/Mathews" at foot of spine; American issue in dark blue-green cloth without the ads; reprint of 1912 in crimson cloth over bevelled boards).

1895.10   G[EORGE] E. MORRISON. *Alonzo Quixano, Otherwise Don Quixote*. 15 June. 1/–. B&T. Second Printing. BL.

1895.11   MAY BATEMAN. *Sonnets & Songs*. Nov. 3/6. Title-page design by John D. MacKenzie. Folkard. *MBP III*, 233. BL, CU-A, JGN.

1895.12   HAVERING BOWCHER [M. H. Bourchier]. *The C Major of Life*. [1896]. (F). 14 Nov. 3/6. Folkard. USA: Frederick A. Stokes. BL.

1895.13   MICHAEL FIELD. [Katherine Bradley and Edith Cooper]. *Attila, My Attila! A Play*. [1896]. 11 Nov. 5/–. Folkard. Colbeck 1:248. BL, JGN, NN, PKC, WU.

1895.14   MRS. ARTHUR [Georgie] GASKIN. *ABC: An Alphabet Written & Pictured by Mrs. A. Gaskin*. [1896]. Nov. 1,000. 3/6. Also a limited issue on Japanese vellum. Folkard. USA: A. C. McClurg. "Second thousand," 1895. *Gaskin*, B10. BL.

1895.15   PERCY HEMINGWAY [William Percy Addleshaw]. *The Happy Wanderer & Other Verse*. [1896]. 14 Nov. 500 for England and America. 5/– and $1.50. Special advance issue of 6 copies. Title-page design by Charles I. Ffoulkes. Chiswick. USA: Way & Williams. Colbeck, 1:4; Kraus, *W&W*, 22; *MBP III*, 1502. BL, CU-A, GK, JGN, PKC.

1895.16   A.E.W. MASON. *A Romance of Wastdale*. (F). Nov. 3/6. Folkard. USA: Frederick A. Stokes. BL, WU.

1895.17   WALT RUDING. *An Evil Motherhood: An Impressionist Novel*. [1896]. 11 Nov. 1,000. 3/6. The initial issue of 6 copies (or 12 according to Mathews) appeared with Aubrey Beardsley's famous "Black Coffee" frontispiece glued in. The second issue appeared with Beardsley's substitute frontispiece. The third issue—several years later—appeared with the substitute frontispiece still in place but with "Black Coffee" inserted or tipped in. USA: George H. Richmond, 1896. Colbeck, 1:41; *FEC*, 1; Krishnamurti, 572–73; Gallatin, 975, 976; Reade, 394–95. BL, CU-A, GK, JGN (2nd and 3rd issues), MSL, PKC ("second thousand" with "G. H. Richmond & Co." at foot of spine, and title page reading: "London: Elkin Mathews; New York: George H. Richmond & Co., MDCCCXCVI.").

1895.18   WILLIAM SHARP ["Fiona Macleod"]. *Ecce Puella and Other Prose Imaginings*. [1896]. 28 Oct. Issued in both green and red cloth. 3/6. Folkard. USA: Way & Williams. Colbeck, 2:741; Kraus, *W&W*, 19; Krishnamurti, 596. BL, GK, JGN, MSL, PKC.

1895.19   JOHN ADDINGTON SYMONDS. *In the Key of Blue and Other Prose Essays*. "Third edition" of the famous book first published by Mathews and Lane at the Bodley Head in Jan. 1893 and reprinted the following July. The book remained with Mathews after the dissolution of the partnership. Nov. 8/6. Cover design by Charles Ricketts. Ballantyne, Hanson. USA: Macmillan. "Unaltered reprint" of the "third edition" of 1895, Oct. 1918, 8/6. USA: Macmillan. Nelson, 55. NN, PM.

1895.20 [ROBERT] LAURENCE BINYON. *First Book of London Visions*. [1896]. SG1. Dec. 1/–. Cover design and lettering by Selwyn Image. Folkard. "Second edition, revised," Dec. 1896, 1/–. Colbeck, 1:56; Krishnamurti, 75. BL, GK, JGN (1st and 2nd eds.), MSL, PKC, WU.

1895.21 PHILIP HENRY WICKSTEED. *Dante: Six Sermons*. Dec. 2/–. "Fourth edition," an "unaltered reprint" of the "third edition," of this popular book, first published by Kegan-Paul in 1879, published in a "second edition" by Elkin Mathews in 1890 and a "third edition" by Mathews and Lane in 1892. The book remained with Mathews after the dissolution of the partnership. This "fourth edition" was followed by another with Mathews' imprint in 1905. "Sixth thousand," 1905. Nelson, 11.

1895.22 C[HARLES] T. JACOBI. *Some Notes on Books and Printing: A Guide for Authors and Others*. Dec. 5/–. This "revised reprint" of Jacobi's *On the Making and Issuing of Books*, published by Mathews in 1891 (see Nelson, 18), was printed at the Chiswick Press in 1892.

1896.1 NICHOLAS BRETON. *No Whipping, Nor Trippinge: but a Kinde Friendly Snippinge*. [1895]. Isham Reprint no. 3. Jan. 200. 3/6. Large paper issue, 50, 5/–. Chiswick (preliminary matter only). BL.

1896.2 EMILY HICKEY. *Poems*. Jan. 5/–. Frontispiece by Mary E. Swan. Folkard. Colbeck 1:376; *MBP III*, 1528. BL, GK, JGN, WU.

1896.3 RODEN NOEL. *My Sea & Other Poems*. Intro. by Stanley Addleshaw. Jan. 3/6. Vignette and cover design by Charles G. Harper. USA: Way & Williams. Colbeck, 2:615; Kraus, *W&W*, 20; Krishnamurti, 520. BL, GK, JGN.

1896.4 R[OBERT] S[OUTHWELL]. *A Foure-Fould Meditation, of the Foure Last Things*. [1895]. Isham Reprint no. 4. Jan. 150. 5/–. Large paper issue, 50, 7/6. Chiswick. Janelle, 318. BL, JGN.

1896.5 ROBERT BRIDGES. *Ode for the Bicentenary Commemoration of Henry Purcell, with Other Poems*. SG2. April. 1,000. 1/–. Cover design and lettering by Selwyn Image. Folkard. USA: Way & Williams. Second printing (called "second edition"), 1,000, 1/–. According to Kraus, *W&W*, 24, copies with the joint imprint are marked "Second Edition." Kable, however, lists a copy of the joint imprint without "Second Edition" (54) and a copy with the notice "Second Edition" on the verso of title (55). Colbeck, 1:86. Kable 53, 54, 55, 56; Kraus, *W&W*, 24; BL, JGN, MSL, WU.

1896.6 STEPHEN PHILLIPS. *Christ in Hades and Other Poems*. SG3. April. 1/–.

Cover design and lettering by Selwyn Image. Folkard. Five other printings, with the fourth (type reset) and sixth containing additional poems. Colbeck 2:650. BL (2nd ed.), GK (6th ed.), JGN, MSL, PKC, WU.

1896.7 E[DMUND] H[ENRY] LACON WATSON. *The Unconscious Humourist and Other Essays*. April. 4/6. Folkard. USA: G. H. Richmond. BL, JGN.

1896.8 W. D[ELAPLAINE] SCULL. *The Garden of the Matchboxes and Other Stories*. May. 3/6. Title-page design by Miriam Garden. Folkard. BL, JGN, MSL.

1896.9 BLISS CARMAN. *Behind the Arras: A Book of the Unseen*. [1895]. May. 5/–. Designs by Tom B. Meteyard. Everett Press (Boston), USA: Lamson, Wolffe. According to Merle Johnson, *American First Editions*, 4th ed. rev. and enl. by Jacob Blanck (New York: Bowker, 1942), p. 96, "later states [of *Behind the Arras*] add the imprint of Briggs (Toronto) and Mathews (London)." *BAL*, 2628, PA.

1896.10 MARGARET L. WOODS. *Aëromancy and Other Poems*. SG4. July. 1/–. Cover design and lettering by Selwyn Image. Folkard. "Second edition," 1896. Colbeck, 2:949. BL, GK, WU.

1896.11 R[ICHARD] W[ATSON] DIXON. *Songs and Odes*. SG5. Oct. 1/–. Cover design and lettering by Selwyn Image. Folkard. BL, JGN.

1896.12 LILIAN WINSER. *Lays and Legends of the Weald of Kent*. [1897]. Oct. 500. 5/–. Title page, frontispiece, and other illus. by Margaret Winser. Folkard. *MBP III*, 3342. BL, CU-A, JGN.

1896.13 WALTER BLACKBURN HARTE. *Meditations in Motley*. Oct. 3/6. USA: Arena.

1896.14 *A Letter Written on October 4, 1589, by Captain [Francisco De] Cuellar of the Spanish Armada to His Majesty King Philip II. . . .* Translated from the original Spanish by Henry Dwight Sedgwick, Jr. Spanish Armada Tract no. 1. Nov. 4/6. J. J. Little (New York). USA: Geo. H. Richmond. BL.

1896.15 KATHARINE TYNAN. *A Lover's Breast knot*. (T). Nov. 500. 3/6. Decorated title page. Folkard. Colbeck, 2:885. BL, JGN, WU.

1896.16 PAULINE KING. *Alida Craig*. (F). Nov. 3/6. Illus. by T. K. Hanna, Jr. USA: Geo. H. Richmond. BL.

1896.17 CHARLES L[ATIMER] MARSON. *Turnpike Tales*. [1897]. Nov. 3/6. Cover design by Edith Calvert. BL, JGN.

1896.18 LEW ROSEN [Lewis Rosenthal]. *Napoleon's Opera-glass: An Histrionic Study*. [1897]. Nov. 3/6. Folkard. BL, GK, JGN.

1896.19 ISAAC WATTS. *Divine and Moral Songs for Children*. Nov. Ordinary issue, 3/6. Also a special issue on Japanese paper. Fourteen color illustrations, together with the designs for the upper and lower covers, by Mrs. Arthur [Georgie] Gaskin. Edmund Evans at the Racquet Court Press. "Second thousand" by 1897. Pafford lists the last reissue as probably 1901, but the *English Catalogue of Books* lists a "new edition" for Dec. 1905, at 1/6, and Mathews' catalogue for 1910 lists a "fifth thousand." Gaskin, B14, Pafford, B140, BL, JGN (ordinary and special issues).

1896.20 [ROBERT] LAURENCE BINYON. *The Praise of Life.* (P). SG6. Dec. 1/-. Cover design and lettering by Selwyn Image. Folkard. "Second edition," 1898? BL, MSL, PKC, WU.

1896.21 BLISS CARMAN. *Low Tide on Grand Pré: A Book of Lyrics.* "Second edition." Dec. 3/6. Although David Nutt published the first English edition in December 1893 and continued to issue the book in 1894, Mathews took over Nutt's stock, pasting a slip bearing his imprint over Nutt's imprint on the title page. One such copy, described as the "first English edition," and published by Nutt in 1893, is in the possession of Eric and Joan Stevens, booksellers. A copy published by Nutt in 1894 is described by Charles Cox in his Catalogue 21 (Spring 1983), item 71, as the "first English edition, third issue, with three additional poems and a slip bearing the imprint of Elkin Mathews pasted over Nutt's imprint on the title-page." Mathews, in his *Catalogue of Publications, 1896–97*, p. 5, referred to the book as a "second edition." *BAL*, 2617; Kramer, 12.

1896.22 VINCENT O'SULLIVAN. *Poems.* Dec. 500. 5/-. Title-page design by Selwyn Image. Chiswick. Krishnamurti, 524. BL, MSL.

1896.23 ALICE SARGENT [sic]. *The Fairy Fowk's Rade.* Broadsheet Ballads no. 1. Dec. Single-sheet folio printed on Japanese vellum. 6d. Picture by C. M. Gere. Printed by the Birmingham Guild of Handicraft. BL.

1896.24 WILLIAM CAREW HAZLITT. *The Lambs: Their Lives, Their Friends, and Their Correspondence.* [1897]. Second Printing. Dec. 6/-. Folkard, USA: Charles Scribner's Sons. BL.

1896.25 HENRY VAN DYKE. *The Poetry of Tennyson.* "Fifth edition" of a book the first English edition of which appeared under Mathews' imprint in 1890 (see Nelson, 4). Dec. 5/6. Riverside Press (Cambridge, Mass.). USA: Charles Scribner's Sons. During his partnership with Lane, Mathews also published second, third, and fourth printings of this very popular critical study. A "seventh edition, enlarged" appeared in 1898. NNC (7th ed.).

1896.26 DANTE. *La Commedia di Dante.* [Ed. A[rthur] J[ohn] Butler.] 4/6. T. and A. Constable, Edinburgh.

1896.27 T[HOMAS] GORDON HAKE. *Madeline with Other Poems and Parables.* Dec. 5/-. Second issue bound up for Mathews bearing Mathews' imprint at the tail of the spine. First published by Chapman and Hall in 1871. JGN.

1897.1 ANODOS [Mary Elizabeth Coleridge]. *Fancy's Guerdon.* (P). SG7. Mar. 1/–. Cover design and lettering by Selwyn Image. Folkard. "Second edition," 1898? Colbeck, 1:142. BL, GK, JGN.

1897.2 BLISS CARMAN and RICHARD HOVEY. *More Songs from Vagabondia.* [1896]. Mar. 5/–. Designs by Tom B. Meteyard. John Wilson & Son (Cambridge, Mass.). USA: Copeland & Day. *BAL,* 2634; Kraus, *C&D,* 56. BL, JGN.

1897.3 DOLLIE RADFORD. *A Light Load: Poems.* Mar. 5/–. Cover design, title page, full-page drawings, and initial letters by Beatrice E. Parsons. Folkard. Krishnamurti, *Supp.,* 29; Nelson 20. BL, GK, JGN, MSL, PKC.

1897.4 MARGARET ARMOUR and W. B. MACDOUGALL. *Thames Sonnets and Semblances.* May. 5/–. Decorated title page, tail piece, and other illustrations by W. B. MacDougall. Folkard. BL.

1897.5 GEORGE DARLEY. *Nepenthe: A Poem in Two Cantos.* April. 2/6. Frontispiece woodcut designed and done by Laurence Binyon. Folkard. Colbeck, 1:179; *MBP III,* 877. BL, CU-A, JGN.

1897.6 W[ILLIAM] J[OSEPH] IBBETT ["Antaeus"]. *A West Sussex Garland.* May. 50. 2/6. Chiswick. I have not seen a copy with Mathews' imprint; however, its printing is charged to his account in the Chiswick Press Records, and he consistently advertised it among his published books. Colbeck, 1:419.

1897.7 ROWLAND THIRLMERE [John Walker]. *Idylls of Spain: Varnished Pictures of Travel in the Peninsula.* Sept. 4/6. Folkard. BL, JGN.

1897.8 CHAS. T. JACOBI. *Gesta Typographica; or, A Medley for Printers and Others.* Oct. 1,000. 3/6. Also a Japanese paper issue of 50. Chiswick. BL (Jap. paper issue), JGN, WU.

1897.9 HENRY NEWBOLT. *Admirals All and Other Verses.* SG8. Oct. 1,000. 1/–. Large paper issue of 20 (only 10 for sale). Cover design and lettering by Selwyn Image. Folkard. Of the thirty printings, the tenth appeared with additional poems, as did the twenty-first and twenty-fifth. 1,000 copies each printing. USA: John Lane, 1898. Colbeck, 2:599, 600. BL, JGN (Newbolt's proof copy of the twenty-first printing with instructions to the printer, etc.; large paper issue), PKC.

1897.10 RODEN NOEL. *Selected Poems.* With a Bibliographical and Critical Essay by Percy Addleshaw. Oct. 4/6. Two photographic portraits of the author. Colbeck, 2:615. BL, JGN, MSL, WU.

1897.11 E[DMUND] H[ENRY] LACON WATSON. *An Attic in Bohemia: A Diary without Dates.* Oct. 3/6. BL, JGN.

1897.12 [WILLIAM STIRLING]. *The Canon: An Exposition of the Pagan Mystery Perpetuated in the Cabala as the Rule of All the Arts.* Preface by R. B. Cunninghame Graham. Nov. 12/–. Numerous illustrations. Chiswick. "New edition," 1903, 10/–. BL.

1897.13 ARTHUR GALTON. *Two Essays upon Matthew Arnold.* Nov. 3/6. Large paper issue. Birmingham Guild of Handicraft. BL, JGN (both issues), MSL, PKC.

1897.14 LIONEL JOHNSON. *Ireland with Other Poems.* Nov. 300. 5/–. Chiswick. Colbeck. 1:432; Danielson; *FEC*; *MBP III*, 1675. BL, CU-A, JGN (Mathews' copy corrected for the press; See *FEC* 89), MSL.

1897.15 DONALD G[RANT] MITCHELL ["Ik Marvel"]. *English Lands, Letters and Kings: The Later Georges to Victoria.* Vol. 4 of the series "English Lands, Letters and Kings." Nov. 4/6. Trow Directory, Printing and Bookbinding Co. (New York). USA: Charles Scribner's Sons. BL, PKC.

1897.16 CLAUD NICHOLSON. *The Joy of Youth.* (F). Nov. 3/6. BL.

1897.17 A[DA] STOW and E[DITH] CALVERT. *Baby Lays.* Nov. 1/6. Decorated title page and fifteen pictures by Edith Calvert. See 1898.10. "Third thousand," 1910. BL, JGN, NEM.

1897.18 W. D[ELAPLAINE] SCULL. *Bad Lady Betty: A Drama in Three Acts.* Dec. 1/–. B&T. BL.

1897.19 *Elkin Mathews' Garland of New Poetry.* Vol. 1. [Some title pages dated 1898]. 6/–. Cover design by Selwyn Image. Folkard. *MBP III*, 1065. BL, CU-A, JGN.

1898.1 R. WARWICK BOND. *Another Sheaf.* Mar. 2/6. Frontispiece by J. Laurence Hart. B&T. *MBP III*, 393. BL, CU-A.

1898.2 [MABEL HOLLAND-GRAVE]. *Some Welsh Children by the Author of Fraternity.* (Pr). Mar. 3/6. Cover design and title page by the author. B&T. Reissue, Feb. 1920, 4/6. CTY, MH.

1898.3 M. H. BOURCHIER [Havering Bowcher]. *The Adventures of a Goldsmith.* (F). April. 6/–. B&T. BL, JGN.

1898.4 MANMOHAN GHOSE. *Love-Songs and Elegies.* SG9. April. 1/–. Cover design and lettering by Selwyn Image. Folkard. Krishnamurti, 255. BL, GK, JGN, PKC.

1898.5 ERNEST GILLIAT-SMITH. *Fantasies from Dreamland.* [1899]. Oct. 4/–. Cover design and illus. by Flori Van Acker. St. Austin's Press; printed by Desclee, De Brouwer (Bruges, Belgium). *MBP III*, 2827. BL, CU-A.

1898.6 H. DEVEY BROWNE. *Papers from "Punch" in Prose and Verse.* Nov. 3/6. Illus. by G. Du Maurier, Linley Sambourne, J. Bernard Partridge, and others. B&T. BL.

1898.7   H[ENRY] W[ADSWORTH] LONGFELLOW. *The Singers*. Oct. 2/6. Edition de luxe, 40 copies numbered and the principal etchings signed by the etcher, 10/6. Nine etchings by Arthur Robertson. Printed by F. Goulding. *BAL*, 12930. BL, JGN.

1898.8   HENRY NEWBOLT. *The Island Race*. (P). Oct. 1,000. 5/–. Large paper issue, 65 (only 50 for sale). Folkard. USA: John Lane (printed in New York by J. J. Little and containing only 25 of the 40 poems that were in the first English edition). "Fourth edition," Aug. 1901, 3/6. "New edition with additions" ("sixth thousand"), 1907. "Seventh thousand," 1909. "New edition," Dec. 1914, 2/6. Colbeck, 2:599; Krishnamurti, 511; *MBP III*, 2267. BL, CU-A, GK, JGN (ordinary and large paper), MSL (large paper).

1898.9   ALICE SARGANT. *A Book of Ballads*. Nov. 15/–. Five etchings by William Strang. B&T. BL.

1898.10   ADA STOW and EDITH CALVERT. *More Baby Lays*. Oct. 1/6. Title page and thirteen pictures by Edith Calvert. "Second thousand," 1899?, 1/–. BL, JGN, NEM.

1898.11   ADA STOW and EDITH CALVERT. *Baby Lays and More Baby Lays*. "Small edition on superior paper," 4/6. Issue hand-colored by the artist, "A few copies," price on application. Pictures by Edith Calvert.

1898.12   R[OBERT] LAURENCE BINYON. *Second Book of London Visions*. [1899]. (P). SG10. Dec. 1/–. Title- page design and lettering by Selwyn Image. Folkard. Colbeck 1:56. BL, GK, MSL, WU (copy inscribed by the author to Selwyn Image).

1898.13   JOHN A. BRIDGES. *In a Village*. (P). Oct. 500 (only 200 bound). 5/–. Chiswick. *MBP III*. 457. BL, CU-A, JGN, PC.

1898.14   *The Garland of New Poetry by Various Writers*. [1899]. 10 Dec. 3/6. Cover design by Laurence Binyon. Folkard. *MBP III*, 1066. BL, CU-A, WU.

1899.1   R. WARWICK BOND. *Zenobia: A Drama in Four Acts*. 3/6. B&T. *MBP III*, 396. BL, CU-A, GK (one of about 12 advance copies without the date on the title page and the printer's name).

1899.2   *Elkin Mathews' Garland of New Poetry*. Vol. 2. Feb. 6/–. Cover design by Selwyn Image. Folkard. Colbeck 1:56; *MBP III*, 1065. BL, CU-A, JGN.

1899.3   ALICE FURLONG. *Roses and Rue*. (P). Mar. 2/6. Folkard. MBP III, 1208. BL, CU-A.

1899.4   W. B. YEATS. *The Wind among the Reeds*. April. 500. 3/6. Deluxe vellum issue, 12. Cover design by Althea Gyles. The University Press of H. O. Houghton and Co. (Cambridge, Mass.). USA: John Lane. Second printing (issued simultaneously with the first), 500, 3/6. Further editions in 1900, 1903, 1907, and 1911. Ashley, 9:159;

Colbeck, 2:961, 962; *MBP IV*, 2300 (5th Ed.); Roth, no. 43; Wade, 27, 29. JGN, MH (Harold Wilmerding Bell's copy of the deluxe vellum issue with his note concerning number of vellum copies issued), MSL (presentation copy from the author to "Fiona Macleod"), PKC. A vellum-bound copy of the first edition, listed as no. 143 in the Parke-Burnet Catalogue of the C. Walter Buhler sale, 1 May 1941, contained a letter laid in from Yeats to Mathews dated 20 Sept. n.y., suggesting that Gyles' design be printed on vellum copies only. There was also a copy of the first edition, listed as no. 146, in the Buhler sale catalogue, accompanied by "correspondence, memorandums, etc., by Elkin Mathews, A. P. Watt, Charles Whittingham & Co. and letterpress copies of letters, all relating to the publication of the book." John Quinn's vellum-bound copy of the fourth ed. of 1903 in possession of Prof. John L. Brown, Jr.

1899.5 CHARLOTTE MANSFIELD. *Flowers of the Wind.* (P). June. 2/6. Decorated title page by H. P. Horne. Folkard. Krishnamurti, 437; *MBP III*, 2032. BL, CU-A, GK.

1899.6 EGAN MEW. *A London Comedy and Other Vanities.* "Second edition." (P). Oct. 4/–. Six reproductions of pictures by Maurice Greiffenhagen. Clowes. *MBP III*, 2094. BL, CU-A, JGN.

1899.7 ROSA MULHOLLAND [Lady Gilbert]. *Vagrant Verses.* Reissue, with a new title page, of the first edition. Oct. 3/6. Title-page design by E. Miriam Garden. Kegan Paul. Colbeck, 1:289–90. BL.

1899.8 W. D. CRAUFURD. *The Realm of Fairyland.* [1900]. Nov. 1/6. Illus. by Edith Calvert. Folkard. BL.

1899.9 WILLIAM CAREW HAZLITT. *Lamb and Hazlitt: Further Unpublished Letters and Records.* [1900]. Oct. 4/6. Folkard. BL, JGN.

1899.10 ALICE M. HORTON. *An Alphabet with Rhymes and Pictures.* Nov. 1/6. Folkard. "Second edition," 1900; "third thousand," 1901? BL.

1900.1 JOHN HUNTLEY SKRINE. *The Queen's Highway and Other Lyrics of the War, 1899–1900.* VC1. May. 1/–. Folkard. Second ed., 1900? Colbeck, 2:761. BL, JGN (2nd ed.); MB (2nd ed.).

1900.2 SYDNEY DOBELL. *Home in War Time: Poems.* VC2. Selected and ed. by William G. Hutchison. May. 1/–. Folkard. BL, JGN.

1900.3 HAMILTON ADRIAN PIFFARD. *Marforio and Other Poems.* Sept. 3/–. Folkard. BL.

1900.4 W[ILLIAM] MONK. *Hampstead Etchings: A Series of Seven Original Copper Plates.* Oct. 100 sets of signed artist's proofs on Japanese vellum in portfolio. £5.5.0.

1900.5 *A Horn-Book.* Oct. 5/–. Described in Mathews' advertisements as "oak, on Morris paper, under thin horn, within copper rimming, 7 X 3 inches. . . . made up after an Elizabethan example."

1900.6   ARTHUR SHEARLY CRIPPS. *Titania and Other Poems.* Oct. 2/6. Title-page design by Bertram Priestman. Folkard. BL, GK.

1900.7   ARTHUR HOPKINS. *Sketches and Skits.* [1901]. Nov. 5/–. Twenty large cartoons. Southwood, Smith. BL.

1900.8   JESSIE MACGREGOR. *Christmas Eve at Romney Hall.* Nov. 2/6. Illus. with pencil drawings by the author. Folkard. BL.

1900.9   CHARLES PETTAFOR. *The Rabbit Book.* Oct. 1/6. Fifteen drawings by the author. Folkard. BL.

1900.10 F. ERNLEY WALROND. *Silence Absolute and Other Poems.* VC3. Nov. 1/–. Folkard. BL, CSMH.

1901.1   CHRISTOPHER SMART. *A Song to David.* Ed. with an intro by R. A. Streatfeild. Jan. 1/–. Folkard. BL, JGN.

1901.2   GUY J. BRIDGES. *Sea Verse.* VC4. May. 1/–. Folkard. *MBP IV,* 229. BL, CU-A.

1901.3   C.J.W. FARWELL. *Poems.* May. 3/6. Folkard. BL, JGN.

1901.4   CATHERINE MARY PHILLIMORE. *In Memoriam—"Chere Reine": Two Odes.* May. 1/6. Folkard. BL.

1901.5   [GRACE E. TOLLEMACHE]. *Songs of Lucilla.* May. 3/6. Folkard. BL, JGN.

1901.6   LILY THICKNESSE. *Poems.* Oct. 2/6. Folkard. *MBP IV,* 2048. BL, CU-A.

1901.7   A[LICE M.] BUCKTON. *Through Human Eyes: Poems.* With an introductory poem by Robert Bridges. Reprint of the Daniel Press edition with seven pieces added. Nov. 3/6. Folkard. *MBP IV,* 255. BL, CU-A, JGN.

1901.8   ESTELLE M. HURLL. *Child-Life in Art.* Nov. 5/–. Thirty-one photogravure and other illus. after Velasquez. J. Reynolds, Gainsborough, et al. Colonial Press (Boston). USA: L. C. Page. "New edition," 1902. BL.

1901.9   E[DMUND] H[ENRY] LACON WATSON. *Christopher Deane: A Character Study at School and College.* [1902]. Nov. 6/–. Folkard. BL, JGN.

1901.10 JACK B. YEATS. *James Flaunty; or, The Terror of the Western Seas,* (D), Nov. 1/–. Issue hand-colored by the author, Nov., 5/–. Farncombe and Son. See 1911.43. MacCarvill, 1; Colbeck, 2:955. BL.

1901.11 WILLIAM MONK. *London, Cité Lugubre: A Portfolio of Etchings.* Nov. £5.5.0.

1901.12 TINSLEY PRATT. *Harold the Saxon and Other Verses.* [1902]. VC5. Dec. 1/–. BL, MB.

1902.1   *A Broad Sheet.* Jan. 1902–Dec. 1903. 24 monthly numbers, 150 copies each number. "Specimen copies," 13d. post free; yearly subscription, 12/– post free (USA, $3.00). Portfolios to hold 24 copies, 2/– each or 2/6 post free. Edited during 1902 by Jack B. Yeats and Pamela Colman Smith; during 1903 by Jack B. Yeats. 1902: pictures hand-colored by Pamela Colman Smith and Jack Yeats. 1903: pictures hand-colored by Jack Yeats and others. Farncombe & Son. Hoffman, 376; MacCarvill, 2. NN.

1902.2   WILFRID WILSON GIBSON. *Urlyn the Harper and Other Song*. VC7. March. Wrappers, 1/–. Cloth, 1/6. Folkard. "Second edition," 1903. Colbeck, 1:286; Gawsworth, 74; Hayward, 317; *MBP IV*, 798. BL, CU-A, MB (2nd ed.), private collection (2nd ed.).

1902.3   HENRIK IBSEN. *Lyrical Poems*. Selected and trans. by R. A. Streatfeild. VC8. March. 1/–. Folkard. BL, JGN.

1902.4   *The Cynic's Breviary: Maxims and Anecdotes from Nicholas de Chamfort*. Selected and trans. by William G. Hutchison. VC6. April. 1/–. Folkard. BL.

1902.5   COUNT CHARLES DE SOISSONS [Charles Emmanuel de Savoie-Carignan]. *Fancies*. (P). April. BL.

1902.6   JONATHAN NIELD. *A Guide to the Best Historical Novels and Tales*. 12 May. 5/–. Folkard. Second edition with complete indexes to authors and titles, Oct. 1902, 5/–. "Third and cheaper edition, revised and enlarged," Feb. 1904, 4/–. Folkard. Fourth edition ("sixth thousand") revised with large supplement, April 1911, 8/–. BL, JGN.

1902.7   [ALFRED EDWARD THISELTON]. *Far Between: Sonnets and Rimes*. May. 1/–. Folkard. NNC (copy inscribed by the author to Elkin Mathews).

1902.8   DOUGLAS JAMES. *Ode for the Coronation of King Edward VII*. June. 1/–.

1902.9   [MRS. ALICE KIPLING and her daughter MRS. A. M. FLEMING (Rudyard Kipling's mother and sister)]. *Hand in Hand: Verses by a Mother and Daughter*. 25 Sept. 3/6. Frontispiece in photogravure by J. Lockwood Kipling. Folkard. USA: Doubleday Page. "New edition," April 1903. BL.

1902.10   *Journal of Edward Ellerker Williams, Companion of Shelley and Byron in 1821 and 1822*. With an intro. by Richard Garnett. 25 Sept. 3/6. Collotype portraits. Folkard. BL, JGN (copy inscribed by the publisher to A. Hugh Fisher).

1902.11   WILFRID WILSON GIBSON. *The Queen's Vigil and Other Song*. VC9. Nov. Wrappers, 1/–. Cloth, 1/6. Folkard. "Second edition," 1903. Colbeck, 1:286; Gawsworth, 76; *MBP IV*, 796. BL, CU-A, JGN, MB (2nd ed.).

1902.12   WILFRID WILSON GIBSON. *Urlyn the Harper [and] The Queen's Vigil and Other Song*. First editions of the two volumes bound as one, with original title pages and a new half title. 12? Folkard. Colbeck, 1:286; Gawsworth, 74. Private collection.

1902.13   ELIZABETH GIBSON [later CHEYNE]. *The Burden of Love*. VC10. Nov. 1/–. Folkard. Colbeck, 289; *MBP IV*, 785. BL, CSmH, CU-A, IU.

1902.14   JOHN SHUCKBURGH RISLEY. *Notes and Echoes*. (P). Oct. 5/–. Folkard. *MBP IV*, 1734. BL, CU-A.

1902.15 JACK B. YEATS. *The Treasure of the Garden: A Play*. Nov. 200 (165 for sale). 5/–. Eight drawings by Yeats, seven of which are hand-colored. Farncombe & Son. Colbeck, 2:955, MacCarvill, 4. BL.

1902.16 JOHN A. BRIDGES. *The Lost Parson and Other Poems*. Nov. 156. 3/6. Chiswick. *MBP IV*, 230. BL, CU-A.

1902.17 A[LBERT] E[UGENE] GALLATIN. *Aubrey Beardsley as a Designer of Book-Plates*. Dec. Ordinary issue, 85. Also an issue on Japanese vellum of 3. De Vinne Press. USA: Charles E. Peabody. Gallatin, 76–77. BL, GC.

1902.18 W. G. HOLE. *Poems Lyrical and Dramatic*. Nov. 3/6. Folkard. BL.

1902.19 ELIZABETH GIBSON. *A Christmas Garland*. (P). Dec. 1/–. Drawings by Edith Calvert. BL.

1902.20 HENRY VAUGHAN. *Heaven's Way: Quaint Cords, Coyles, and Love-Twists*. Selections from the works of Henry Vaughan by Adelaide L. J. Gosset. [1903]. Dec. 1/–. Folkard. BL.

1902.21 EVELYN F. MOORE. *The Company of Heaven*. [1903]. (P). VC11. Dec. 1/–. Folkard. *MBP IV*, 1433. BL, CU-A.

1902.22 ROSA [HARRIET] NEWMARCH. *Horae Amoris: Songs and Sonnets*. [1903]. Dec. 3/6. *MBP IV*, 1501. BL, CU-A, GK.

1902.23 W. G. BURN MURDOCH. *A Procession of Scottish History, from Duncan and Macbeth to George II and Prince Charles Stewart*. Aug.

1902.24 MARY E[LIZABETH] RICHMOND. *Poems*. [1903]. Dec. Folkard. BL, JGN.

1903.1 PAMELA COLMAN SMITH. *The Golden Vanity and the Green Bed: Words and Music of Two Old English Ballads with Pictures in Color*. Jan. 7/6. BL.

1903.2 F. H. DE QUINCEY. *Song-Tide Murmurs*. (P). April. 2/6. Folkard. *MBP IV*, 547. BL, CU-A.

1903.3 ARTHUR LEWIS. *Ginevra: A Drama*. April. 1/–. Folkard. BL.

1903.4 JOHN ROGERS. *With Elia and His Friends in Books and Dreams*. April. 2/6. Folkard. BL.

1903.5 ARTHUR F. WALLIS. *Stars of the Morning: A Play*. April. 3/6. Folkard. BL.

1903.6 E[DMUND] H[ENRY] LACON WATSON. *Verse Occasionally Humorous*. VC12. April. 1/–. Folkard. *MBP IV*, 2194. BL, CU-A.

1903.7 HARRIET L. CHILDE-PEMBERTON. *Carmela: A Poetic Drama*. May. 3/6. Riverside. BL.

1903.8 A[LBERT] E[UGENE] GALLATIN. *Aubrey Beardsley's Drawings: A Catalogue and a List of Criticisms*. May. 250 numbered copies. 20/–. Thirty copies hand-numbered and bound in full white parchment, 30/–. Six reproductions and a pastel portrait of Beardsley by Will Rothenstein. J. J. Little (New York). USA: Godfrey A. S. Wieners (at the Sign of the Lark). Gallatin, p. 77. GC, NJP.

1903.9 INDICUS [Charles Rathbone Low]. *The Olympiad: Classic Tales in Verse.* June. 5/–. Riverside. *MBP IV*, 1062. BL, CU-A, JGN.

1903.10 M. Y. HALIDOM. *The Gipsy Queen: A Romantic Play.* Aug. 3/6. Folkard. BL.

1903.11 ALFRED EDWARD THISELTON. *Some Textual Notes on "A Midsommer Nights Dreame."* Aug. 3/6. Folkard. BL.

1903.12 JOHN MASEFIELD. *Ballads.* VC13. 26 Oct. 762. Wrappers, 1/–. Cloth, 1/6. Folkard. "Second edition, revised and enlarged," April 1910. See 1910.24; 1911.6. Ashley, 3:121; *BMA I*, 160; Colbeck, 2:528, 529; *FEC*, 95; *MBP IV*, 1364; Simmons, 2. BL, JGN, CU-A (2nd ed.), MH (1st and 2nd eds.).

1903.13 ALICE EDWARDES. *Lyrics and Unfinished Romances.* VC14. Oct. 1/–. Folkard. *MBP IV*, 628. BL, CU-a.

1903.14 WILFRID WILSON GIBSON. *The Golden Helm and Other Verse.* Oct. 2/6. Folkard. Colbeck, 1:286; Gawsworth, p. 76; *MBP IV*, 793. CU-A, JGN (author's inscribed presentation copy to Elkin Mathews).

1903.15 G[EORGE] A. GREENE. *Dantesques: A Sonnet Companion to the "Inferno."* VC15. Oct. Wrappers, 1/–. Cloth, 1/6. Folkard. BL.

1903.16 GLADYS SCHUMACHER. *Fires That Sleep.* (P). Oct. 3/6. Folkard. BL.

1903.17 A.L.H. A[NDERSON]. *Notes from a Lincolnshire Garden.* (Pr). Oct. 2/6. Folkard. BL.

1903.18 WILLIAM AKERMAN. *Hereward: A Tragedy.* Nov. 5/–. Folkard. BL.

1903.19 ALIX EGERTON. *The Lady of the Scarlet Shoes and Other Verses.* VC16. Nov. 1/–. Folkard. *MBP IV*, 632. BL, CU-A.

1903.20 *Calendarium Londinense; or, The London Almanack for the Year 1903.* Issued annually, 1903–18. 2/6. William Monk. Each with a fine etched plate done by William Monk of a famous London landmark. NEM.

1903.21 MORLEY ROBERTS. *The Wingless Psyche.* [1904]. (Pr). Nov. 2/6. Folkard. Colbeck, 2:682. BL, JGN.

1903.22 JACK B. YEATS. *The Scourge of the Gulph.* (D). Dec. 1/–. Issue hand-colored by the author, 5/–. Farncombe & Son. See 1911.43. Colbeck, 2:955, MacCarvill, 3. BL, WU.

1903.23 HENRY TREFFRY DUNN. *Recollections of Dante Gabriel Rossetti and His Circle.* Ed. and annotated by Gale Pedrick with a Prefatory Note by William Michael Rossetti. [1904]. Dec. 3/6. Folkard. USA: James Pott. Fredeman, 33.5. BL, PKC (U.S. issue).

1903.24 ST. JOHN LUCAS. *The Vintage of Dreams.* [1904]. (F). Dec. 3/6. BL.

1903.25 *The Seasons with the Poets: An Anthology.* Ed. and arranged by Ida Woodward. [1904]. Dec. 5/–. Riverside. BL.

1904.1 E[DMUND] S[IDNEY] P[OLLOCK] HAYNES. *Standards of Taste in Art.* VC18. April. 1/–. Colbeck 1:355. NN, NNC, JGN.

1904.2   *A Painter's Philosophy*. A translation of Alfred Stevens' *Impressions sur la Peinture* by Ina Mary White. April. 2/6. Decorated title page. Riverside. BL.

1904.3   G[ODFREY] F[OX] BRADBY. *Broadland and Other Poems*. May. 2/6. Folkard. *MBP IV*, 219. BL, CU-A, JGN.

1904.4   ELIZABETH GIBSON [later CHEYNE]. *From a Cloister*. VC19. May. 1/−. Folkard. CSMH, MB, NN.

1904.5   EVA DOBELL. *Songs and Sonnets*. VC20. May/June. 1/−. Folkard. *MBP IV*, 563. BL, CU-A.

1904.6   THEOPHILA NORTH [Dorothea Hollins]. *The Herbs of Medea*. (F). June. 2/6. Colored frontispiece mounted. Tudor Press. BL.

1904.7   *The Views of Christopher*. Preface by Coulson Kernahan. SAT. June. Wrappers, 1/−. Cloth, 2/−. "Second edition." "Third thousand" by 1910. BL.

1904.8   W. B. YEATS. *The Tables of the Law and The Adoration of the Magi*. (F). VC17. June. Wrappers, 1/−. Cloth, 1/6. Edition de luxe, 2/6. Some copies in paper-covered boards. Folkard. According to Wade, "copies of this edition were issued later in green cloth" and "a reissue in 1905, in brown paper covers." Colbeck, 2:962; Roth, no. 90; Wade, 25. BL (edition de luxe), JGN (wrappers and paper-covered boards), WU.

1904.9   EVELYN F. MOORE. *The Fortune-Seeker*. VC21. June/July. 1/−. Folkard. *MBP IV*, 1434. BL, CU-A.

1904.10   GORDON BOTTOMLEY. *The Gate of Smaragdus*. (P). Oct. 400. 10/−. A small number of large paper copies bound in full vellum. Decorated by Clinton Balmer. William Holmes (Ulverston, Lancs.). Colbeck, 1:77, Ridler, p. 291; Taylor, 145. BL, JGN.

1904.11   ELIZABETH GIBSON [later CHEYNE]. *A Flock of Dreams*. (P). VC22. Sept./ Oct. 1/−. Folkard. BL, CSMH.

1904.12   H[ENRY] D[AWSON] LOWRY. *The Hundred Windows*. (P). Oct. 3/6. Folkard. Colbeck, 1:498; *MBP IV*, 1225. BL, CU-A, GK, JGN.

1904.13   A. ST. JOHN ADCOCK. *London Etchings*. (Pr). SAT. Nov. Wrappers, 1/−. Cloth, 1/6. Arden Press. BL, JGN.

1904.14   MRS. ALFRED BALDWIN. *A Chaplet of Verse for Children*. Nov. 3/6. Twenty-one illus. by John D. Batten. Folkard. *MBP IV*, 94. BL, CU-A.

1904.15   DOROTHEA GORE BROWNE. *Sweetbriar: A Pastoral with Songs*. [1905]. Nov. 2/6. Cover design and illus. by Edith Calvert. Reissue? 1915. BL, IU.

1904.16   JACK B. YEATS. *The Bosun and the Bob-tailed Comet*. (F). Nov. 1/−. Issue hand-colored by the author, 2/−. Issue hand-colored with an original sketch in color by the author, 5/−. Farncombe & Son. Colbeck, 2:955; MacCarvill, 5. BL.

1904.17 CICELY FOX-SMITH. *Wings of the Morning.* (P). Dec. 3/6. BL.

1904.18 JOHN TODHUNTER. *Sounds and Sweet Airs.* [1905]. (P). VC23. Nov./ Dec. Wrappers, 1/–. Cloth, 1/6. Folkard. Colbeck, 2:870; Krishnamurti, 670; *MBP IV*, 2096. BL, GK, JGN, MB, WU.

1904.19 HENRY CULLIMORE. *The Garden of Francesca.* [1905]. Dec. 3/6. Folkard. *MBP IV*, 476. BL, CU-A.

1904.20 A[LBERT] E[UGENE] G[ALLATIN]. *Whistler's Art Dicta and Other Essays.* 175. Illustrations and facsimiles in line and photogravure. D. B. Updike, the Merrymount Press (Boston). USA: Charles E. Goodspeed. Gallatin. NJP, NN, NNC, private collection (copy signed "1905 Graham S. Steel[?] specimen of infringement"—i.e., a copy used at Gallatin's trial for infringement of rights), WM.

1904.21 ARTHUR LEWIS. *Days of Old Rome.* [1905]. Dec. 3/6. Illus. by Edith Calvert. Folkard. BL

1905.1 HENRY A. WISE WOOD. *Fancies.* [1904]. (P). Feb. 3/6. Plimpton Press (Boston). USA: W. J. Ritchie. BL.

1905.2 ELIZABETH GIBSON [later CHEYNE]. *Love's Fugitives.* (P). VC25. March/ April. 1/–. BL, CSMH.

1905.3 ARTHUR DILLON. *The Greek Kalends.* (D). April. 3/6. Folkard. Krishnamurti, 196. BL, GK.

1905.4 ALICE MADDOCK. *An Autumn Romance and Other Poems.* VC26. April. 1/–. Folkard. BL, CSMH, NJP.

1905.5 MARGARET SACKVILLE. *A Hymn to Dionysus and Other Poems.* April. 3/6. Folkard. Colbeck, 2:716; *MBP IV*, 1797. BL, CU-A, JGN.

1905.6 J[OHN] M[ILLINGTON] SYNGE. *The Shadow of the Glen and Riders to the Sea.* VC24. May. Wrappers, 1/–. Cloth, 1/6. Folkard. Second edition, Dec. 1907, G&R. Third edition, 1909. "Fourth thousand," 1910, Clowes. "Sixth thousand," 1911, Clowes. Colbeck, 2:827. BL, JGN, NN (copy containing the following note in pencil on the verso of the title page: "I hereby certify that the first edition was published by me on the 8th May 1905. Elkin Mathews Vigo Street W. 3").

1905.7 ARTHUR [ANNESLEY RONALD] FIRBANK. *Odette D'Antrevernes and a Study in Temperament.* (F). June. 500. 2/–. Copies were bound up in both rose-colored wrappers lettered in blue and gilt-printed wrappers. Special large-paper issue for presentation by the author, 10, none priced for sale. Folkard. Benkovitz, A1a, A1b; *BMA III*, p. 3, item 1. BL, JGN (gilt-printed wrappers), NN.

1905.8 [RICHARD GARNETT]. *De Flagello Myrteo: Thoughts and Fancies on Love.* 1 June. 2/6. Folkard. Second edition, revised and enlarged, March 1906, 2/6, G&R. Third edition "as revised by the author," May 1906, 2/6, G&R. Another issue of the third edition preceded by "A Preface to *De Flagello Myrteo* with 42 omitted 'thoughts' and some Quotations from the Author's letters" by "Neva" [Violet E. Neale], Nov. 1906, 2/6, G&R. Colbeck, 1:283. BL, JGN (1st, 2nd, 3rd eds. and uncorrected proof copy with author's revisions and instructions to printer for second edition); WU (3rd ed.).

1905.9   WILFRID WILSON GIBSON. *The Nets of Love*. VC28. June. 1/–. Folkard. Colbeck, 1:286; Gawsworth, p. 77; *MBP IV*, 795. BL, CU-A, GK, JGN, MB.

1905.10   JOHN MASEFIELD. *A Mainsail Haul*. (F). SAT. 1 June. 1,000. Wrappers, 1/–. Cloth, 1/6. Frontispiece by Jack B. Yeats. Chiswick. "Second edition, revised and much enlarged," 17 July 1913, 1,500, 3/6, Chiswick. *BMA I*, 161; Colbeck, 2:528, 531; Simmons, 3, 3a. BL, JGN (1st and 2nd eds.), NN.

1905.11   VICTOR PLARR. *The Tragedy of Asgard*. VC27. May. Wrappers, 1/–. Cloth, 1/6. Folkard. Colbeck, 2:654. BL, JGN, NN.

1905.12   POST WHEELER. *Poems*. Sept. 5/–. BL.

1905.13   LORD DUNSANY [EDWARD JOHN MORETON DRAX PLUNKETT]. *The Gods of Pagāna*. (F). Oct. 1,000. 5/–. Cover design, frontispiece, and seven illus. in photogravure by S[idney] H. Sime. Riverside. Second printing, 1911. Third printing, 1919. *BMA I*, 83; Colbeck, 1:236; Taylor, 145. BL, JGN.

1905.14   CHARLES F. GRINDROD. *Studies in Rhyme and Rhythm*. Sept. 3/6. Folkard. BL, MH.

1905.15   LILIAN STREET. *Shadow and Gleam*. Oct. 2/6. Hazell, Watson & Viney. *MBP IV*, 1999. BL, CU-A.

1905.16   A[LICE] M. BUCKTON. *The Pastor of Wydon Fell: A Ballad of the North Country*. Nov. 1/–. Cover design by the author. BL.

1905.17   ARTHUR DILLON. *King William I: The Conqueror*. Nov. 4/6. Hazell, Watson & Viney. *MBP IV*, 550. BL, CU-A, GK.

1905.18   ELIZABETH GIBSON [later CHEYNE]. *Shadows*. VC31. Nov. 1/–. Ballantyne. CMMH.

1905.19   FREDERICK GURNEY. *Leaves of Holly for Christmas*. (P). Nov.? 1/–. BL.

1905.20   ALEXANDRA VON HERDER [Mrs. Frederick Grantham]. *The Little Mermaid: A Play*. [1906]. Nov. 3/6. Vignettes by Edith Calvert. G&R. BL.

1905.21   R. G. KEATINGE. *Sea Danger and Other Poems*. VC30. Nov. 1/–. Ballantyne. CSMH.

1905.22   *Poems in Prose from Charles Baudelaire*. Trans. Arthur Symons. VC29. Nov. Wrappers, 1/–. Cloth, 1/6. Ballantyne. Colbeck, 2:281. BL, GK (cloth), JGN, WU.

1905.23   F[RANK] P[EARCE] STURM. *An Hour of Reverie*. (P). VC32. Nov. 1/–. Ballantyne. BL, CSMH, NUC.

1905.24   A. ST. JOHN ADCOCK. *Admissions & Asides about Life and Literature*. SAT. Dec. Wrappers, 1/–. Cloth, 1/6. BL, JGN.

1905.25　JOHN HAMILTON REYNOLDS. *The Fancy*. (P). Prefatory memoir and notes by John Masefield. SAT. Dec. Wrappers, 1/-. Cloth, 1/-6. Thirteen illus. by Jack B. Yeats. Colbeck, 2:528; Simmons, p. 129. BL, JGN, WU.

1905.26　ALBERT F. CALVERT. *Summer in San Sebastian: Being an Account of a Yachting Cruise in the Bay of Biscay*. Dec. 5/-. Over 200 illustrations.

1906.1　*Poems by Aurelian*. VC33. March. 1/-. G&R. *MBP IV*, 76. CSMH, CU-A.

1906.2　JOHN GURDON. *Dramatic Lyrics*. March. 3/6. G&R. *MBP IV*, 894. BL, CU-A.

1906.3　C[HARLES] F. A. VOYSEY. *Reason as a Basis of Art*. March. 1/-. BL.

1906.4　L[ANCELOT ALFRED] CRANMER-BYNG. *An English Rose*. April. Wrappers, 1/-. Cloth, 1/6. BL.

1906.5　ARTHUR DILLON. *The Maid of Artemis*. (D). March. 2/6. G&R. *MBP IV*, 551. BL, CU-A, JGN.

1906.6　CHARLES F. GRINDROD. *Songs from the Classics*. May. 3/6. G&R. BL.

1906.7　HESTER BANCROFT. *Poems*. May. 1/-. BL.

1906.8　FRED G. BOWLES. *The Tent by the Lake*. VC36. July. 1/-. BL, MB.

1906.9　HAROLD MONRO. *Poems*. VC37. July. 1/-. G&R. Colbeck, 2:562. NNC, WU.

1906.10　[REGINALD HALLWARD]. *Apotheosis: A Poem*. Sept./Oct. 2/-. The Woodlands Press. JGN.

1906.11　[REGINALD HALLWARD]. *Wild Oats: A Poem*. Sept./Oct. 2/6. The Woodlands Press. JGN.

1906.12　ARTHUR DILLON. *King Arthur Pendragon*. (D). Sept. 4/6. G&R. *MBP IV*, 549. BL, CU-A.

1906.13　J[AMES] G[RIFFYTH] FAIRFAX. *The Gates of Sleep and Other Poems*. VC38. Oct. 1/-. G&R. *MBP IV*, 662; Potter, 1005. BL, CU-A, WU.

1906.14　HENRIETTA HOME. *The Child Mind: A Study in Elementary Ethology*. Oct. Wrappers, 1/-. Cloth, 1/6. G&R. BL.

1906.15　VIOLET TEAGUE. *Night Fall in the Ti-Tree*. Oct. 5/-. Woodcuts by Geraldine Rede, Violet Teague, and others. "Imprinted now by hand at the Sign of the Rabbit, Melbourne." BL.

1906.16　FRANCIS ERNLEY WALROND. *The Lady Beautiful and Other Poems*. VC39. Oct. 1/-. G&R. *MBP IV*, 2176. CSMH, CU-A.

1906.17　ISABEL CLARKE. *A Window in Whitechapel and Other Verses*. VC40. Oct. 1/-. G&R. BL, CSMH, MB.

1906.18　ARUNDELL ESDAILE. *Poems and Translations*. VC41. Oct. 1/-. G&R. *MBP IV*, 650. BL, CU-A, WU.

1906.19　GRAHAM HILL. *Guinevere: A Tragedy*. Oct. 2/6. E. Goodman and Son. BL.

1906.20　BEATRICE KELSTON. *The Garden of My Heart*. (P). Nov. 2/6. G&R. BL.

1906.21   JESSIE POPE. *Paper Pellets: Humorous Verse.* [1907]. SAT. Nov. Wrappers, 1/–. Cloth, 1/6. G&R. *MBP IV*, 1657. BL, CU-A, JGN.

1906.22   WILLIAM T. SAWARD. *William Shakespeare: A Play.* [1907]. Nov. 2/6. G&R. IAU.

1906.23   *The Songs of Sidi Hammo.* Trans. R.L.N. Johnston; verse renderings by L. Cranmer-Byng; ed. with a preface by S. L. Bensusan. [1907]. Nov. 2/6. Facsimile frontispiece and cover design. G&R. BL.

1906.24   WILBUR UNDERWOOD. *A Book of Masks.* [1907]. (P). Nov. 1/6. G&R. BL, JGN.

1906.25   RATHMELL WILSON. *An Exile from Fairyland with Other Writings.* Nov. 1/6. G&R. BL.

1906.26   WILLIAM H. DAVIES. *New Poems.* [1907]. 3 Dec. 1,000. 1/6. G&R. Second printing, Oct. 1913, 1,000, 1/6, Clowes. Colbeck, 1:184; *MBP IV*, 515; Murphy, pp. 77–78; Wilson, p. 202. BL, CU-A, JGN (publisher's copy with his bookplate; 2nd printing).

1906.27   EDITH ESCOMBE. *Phases of Marriage.* [1907]. Dec. 3/6. G&R. BL.

1906.28   R.G.T. COVENTRY. *Poems.* [1907]. Dec. 5/–. G&R. *MBP IV*, 437. BL, CU-A, JGN (copy with reader's report inserted).

1906.29   LOUIS DAVIS. (Songs by Dollie Radford). *The Goose Girl at the Well: A Fairy Play.* Dec. 250. 3/6. Cover design and frontispiece by Davis. Chiswick. Second printing (bound in plain paper-covered boards with cloth spine), 250, 3/6, Chiswick. Colbeck, 2:662. BL, GK (both issues), JGN.

1906.30   DOROTHEA HOLLINS ["Theophila North"]. *The Seven Wayfarers: A Tale for Children, Old and Young.* [1907]. Dec. 2/6. G&R. BL.

1906.31   [EVANGELINE RYVES]. *Lyrics by the Author of "Erebus."* Dec. 2/6. G&R. NNC (copy inscribed by author to Elkin Mathews).

1906.32   WILL H. OGILVIE. *Rainbows and Witches.* [1907]. VC42. Dec. Wrappers, 1/–. Cloth, 1/6. G&R. "Second edition." "Third edition," 1907. "Fourth edition," 1910. *MBP IV*, 1544. BL, private collection: (3rd ed.), CU-A (4th ed.), JGN.

1906.33   RATHMELL WILSON. *Hinemoa and Tutanekai: A Maori Legend with Other Stories.* 2nd ed. [1907]. (F). Dec. 1/6. United Press Assoc., London. BL.

1906.34   WILLIAM T. SAWARD. *Orestes: A Drama.* Dec. 2/6. "Second edition" of a book first published by Grant Richards in 1903.

1906.35   STANHOPE BAYLEY. *The Sacred Grove and Other Impressions of Italy.* [1907]. Dec. 4/6. G&R. BL.

1907.1   ARNOLD HARRIS MATHEW and ANNETTE CALTHROP. *The Life of Sir Tobie Matthew, Bacon's Alter Ego.* March. 12/–. "With numerous illustrations from scarce prints." G&R. BL.

1907.2   LILIAN STREET. *Stray Sonnets*. VC43. March. Wrappers, 1/–. cloth, 1/5. G&R. BL, CSMH.

1907.3   FRED BERESFORD. *The Wayfarer's Garland: Songs and Pastoral Pieces*. April. 1/6. G&R. *MBP IV*, 165. BL, CU-A.

1907.4   J[OHN] M[ILLINGTON] SYNGE. *The Aran Islands*. [Some copies dated 1906 on the title page]. (Pr.). April. 5/–. Large paper issue with illustrations colored by hand, 150, £1.1.–. T. and A. Constable. Twelve full-page drawings by Jack B. Yeats. Dublin: Maunsel. Colbeck, 2:827; MacManus. CSMH.

1907.5   A. E. G[ALLATIN]. *Whistler: Notes and Footnotes and Other Memoranda*. April. 250. Issue on Italian handmade paper numbered and signed, 75. Issue on Imperial Japanese vellum numbered and signed ("Edition de luxe"?). 10, £1.1.0. Eight full-page illus. USA: The Collector and Art Critic Co. BL.

1907.6   EDWARD HENRY BLAKENEY. *The Angel of the Hours & Other Poems*. May? Frontispiece by Maurice Page; colophon with Blakeney's bookplate printed in red designed by James Guthrie. William L. Prewer for the Pear Tree Press, Harting, West Sussex. Ridler, p. 204. ICN, JGN.

1907.7   ARTHUR DILLON. *Orpheus*. (P). May. 2/6. G&R. BL.

1907.8   JAMES JOYCE. *Chamber Music*. (P). 6 May. 509. 1/6. According to Quaritch. Misc., only "fifty or a hundred copies" of the "true first issue" bound in "light green cloth, with thick laid-paper endleaves, and sheet C correctly folded, having the poems properly centered on each page," were bound up. Quaritch also points out that "there are two other 'variants'— issues, really—characterized by a misfolded sheet C (the poems are improperly centered), slightly darker green cloth, and thick or thin wove paper endleaves" (Quaritch Misc., item 47). G&R. Second edition, Jan. 1918. Wrappers, 1/3. Cloth, 2/–. Clowes. Colbeck, 1:434; Slocum and Cahoon, A3, A4. BL, CSMH (1st and 2nd eds.), CTY (Mathews' personal copy), NN, WU (2nd ed.).

1907.9   RUTH YOUNG. *The Heart of the Wind*. VC44. May/June. 1/–. CSMH.

1907.10 G[EORGE] L. ASHLEY-DODD. *The Days of a Year*. June. 2/6.

1907.11 GORDON BOTTOMLEY. *Chambers of Imagery*. (P). June. 500. 1/–. G&R. Ashley, 9:18; Colbeck, 1:77. BL, JGN.

1907.12 GEORGE C. COPE. *Poems*. June. 4/6. G&R. *MBP IV*, 417. BL, CU-A.

1907.13 ARTHUR SCOTT CRAVEN. *Joe Skinner; or, The Man with the Sneer*. (P). June. 1/6. G&R. BL.

1907.14 S. KENRICK BEVAN. *The Vine of Life: A Sonnet Sequence*. July. 2/6. Cover design by the author. G&R. BL, JGN.

1907.15 A[LICE] M[ARY] BUCKTON. *The Garden of Many Waters: A Masque.* July. 1/–. BL.

1907.16 A[LICE] M[ARY] BUCKTON. *A Masque of Beauty and the Beast.* July. 1/–. Remainder of the first edition of the book, first published for the author in 1904 by C. F. Hodgson & Son, London, as the first book of *Masques and Dances,* of which *The Garden of Many Waters* (1907.15) was the second.

1907.17 JAMES [ELROY] FLECKER. *The Bridge of Fire: Poems.* VC45. Sept. 1/–. G&R. Ashley, 9:75; BMA I, (99); Colbeck, 1:257. BL, CSMH, JGN.

1907.18 A. ST. JOHN ADCOCK. *The Shadow Show.* (P). SAT. Oct. Wrappers, 1/–. Cloth, 1/6. Frontispiece by Starr Wood. Clowes. Colbeck, 1:3; *MBP IV*, 18. BL, CU-A, JGN.

1907.19 [ROBERT] LAURENCE BINYON. *Porphyrion and Other Poems.* Second edition of a book first published by Grant Richards. Oct. 5/–. Cover decoration by William Strang. Chiswick. GK, JGN.

1907.20 ST. JOHN LUCAS. *The Marble Sphinx: A Short Story.* Oct. 1/6. BL, IU, NjP.

1907.21 ARTHUR E. SHAW. *Forty Years in the Argentine Republic.* Oct. 2/6. Buenos Aires: Mitchell's Book Store. BL.

1907.22 MABEL TRUSTRAM. *Verses to a Child.* Nov. 2/–. G&R. Illus. by Edith Calvert. BL, NEM.

1907.23 VERONICA MASON. *I Heard a Child Singing.* (P). Nov. 1/–. Cover design and other decorations by Arthur Burgess. Clowes. "Second edition," 1909, 1/–. BL.

1907.24 ROSALIND TRAVERS. *Thyrsis and Fausta: A Pastoral with Other Plays and Poems.* Dec. 3/6. BL.

1907.25 MARY E[LIZABETH] COLERIDGE. *Poems.* Ed. Henry Newbolt. [1908]. Dec. 4/6. "Special limited edition," "price on application." Clowes. "Second, "third," and "fourth" editions, 1908. "Fifth edition," 1909. "Seventh edition," 1918. Colbeck, 1:143; *MBP IV*, 394. BL, CU-A, GK, JGN.

1907.26 T[RUDA] H. CROSFIELD. *A Love in Ancient Days* [1908] (F) Dec. 6/– Eight illus. by W. B. Wollen. Clowes. BL.

1908.1 *Memories and Music: Letters to a Fair Unknown.* Jan. 3/6. Clowes. BL.

1908.2 ARTHUR DILLON. *The Heir's Comedy.* [1907]. (D). Jan. 3/6. Clowes. BL.

1908.3 ARTHUR LEWIS. *Enamels.* (P). Jan. Seven woodcuts by the author. Wincot Press, Chorleywood, Herts. PSC.

1908.4 GILBERT HUDSON. *Sylvia's Rose and The May Moon.* (D). VC46. April. 1/–. Clowes. BL.

1908.5 *The Efficacy of Prayer.* April. 100. Also, 3 special copies of pp. 53–81. Chiswick.

1908.6 L[EONARD] C. BROMLEY. *Poems.* June. 1/6. Clowes. BL.

1908.7 GEORGE KNOTT. *A Hidden World*. (P). June. 1/–. BL.

1908.8 ROSA MULHOLLAND [Lady Gilbert]. *Spirit and Dust: Poems*. June. 2/6. Clowes. Colbeck, 1:290. BL.

1908.9 ANTHONY GEORGE SHIELL. *Phases and Fancies: Verses*. June. 3/6. Clowes. *MBP IV*, 1876; Potter, 1136. BL, CU-A.

1908.10 LEONARD ALLEN COMPTON-RICKETT. *Philomela: A Lyrical Drama ... and Poems*. July. 3/6. Billing & Sons. *MBP IV*, 404. CU-A, NN.

1908.11 R.G.T. COVENTRY. *New Poems*. July. 5/–. Clowes. BL.

1908.12 ALICE MADDOCK. *The Knocking at the Door and Other Poems*. VC47. July. 1/–. Clowes. *MBP IV*, 1334. CSMH, CU-A.

1908.13 KATHARINE ALICE MURDOCH. *Caedmon's Angel and Other Poems*. VC48. July. 1/–. Clowes. CSMH.

1908.14 E. W. SUTTON PICKHARDT. *Ariadne Diainomene, a Tragedy, and Other Poems*. July. 3/6. Clowes. *MBP IV*, 1638. BL, CU-A, JGN.

1908.15 ERNEST RHYS. *The Masque of the Grail*. July. 1,000. 1/–. Chiswick. BL.

1908.16 ARTHUR DILLON. *The Tragedy of Saint Elizabeth of Hungary*. (D). Sept. 4/6. Clowes. BL, GK.

1908.17 LILIAN STREET. *Friendship*. VC49. Sept. 1/–. Clowes. CSMH.

1908.18 FRANCES WYNNE. *Whisper!* (P). Memoir by Katharine Tynan. VC35. Sept. 1/–. Clowes. Reprint of a book first published in London in 1890 by Kegan Paul, Trench, Trubner and later transferred to Mathews, appearing in 1893 with his cancel title page. Nelson, 77. CSMH.

1908.19 [ROBERT] LAURENCE BINYON. *London Visions: Collected and Augmented*. (P). Oct. 1,000. 2/6. Chiswick. "Second edition," 1909. Colbeck, 1:57; *MBP IV*, 180. BL, CU-A, GK, JGN (both eds.), WU (both eds.).

1908.20 N. W. BYNG. *In a Street—In a Lane*. (P). Oct. 1/6. Clowes. *MBP IV*, 288. BL, CU-A.

1908.21 VERA CANUTE. *Powder and Patches*. (P). Oct. Wrappers, 1/–. Cloth, 1/6. Dargan. BL.

1908.22 E[DMUND] S[IDNEY P[OLLOCK] HAYNES. *Early Victorian and Other Papers*. SAT. Oct. Wrappers, 1/–. Cloth, 1/6. Clowes. Colbeck, 1:355. BL, JGN.

1908.23 LIONEL JOHNSON. *Selections from the Poems of Lionel Johnson*. Prefatory memoir by Clement Shorter. VC34. Oct. Wrappers, 1/–. Cloth, 1/6. Colbeck, 1:432; Danielson. BL, GK, JGN.

1908.24 J. T. PRIOR. *My Garden*. (P). Oct. 5/–. Decorated title page and twelve collotype illustrations. Clowes. BL.

1908.25 EUGENE R[ICHARD] WHITE. *Songs of Good Fighting*. Prefatory memoir by Harry Persons Taber. SAT. Oct. Wrappers, 1/–. Cloth, 1/6. Arden Press. *MBP IV*, 2238. BL, CU-A.

1908.26   *Quatrains of Omar Khayyam.* From a literal prose translation by Edward Heron-Allen and done into verse by Arthur B. Talbot. VC53. Oct. Wrappers, 1/–. Cloth, 1/6. Clowes. "Second thousand corrected and revised," 1909. Potter, 377. BL.

1908.27   AGNES H. BEGBIE. *Christmas Songs and Carols.* VC50. Dec. Wrappers, 1/–. Cloth, 1/6. Illus. by Edith Calvert. BL.

1908.28   LADY ALICE EYRE. *Love as Pedlar and Other Verses.* Dec. Wrappers, 1/–. Cloth, 1/6. Dargan. BL.

1908.29   ELEANOR FARJEON. *Pan-Worship and Other Poems.* Dec. 2/6. Colbeck, 1:244. BL, JGN.

1908.30   ARTHUR GRAY. *Man and Maid.* (Pr). Dec. Wrappers, 1/–. Cloth, 1/6. Clowes. BL.

1908.31   EDITH LYTTELTON. *A Christmas Morality Play.* VC51. Dec. 1/–. Dargan. BL.

1908.32   EZRA POUND. *A Quinzaine for This Yule.* Dec. 100. 1/6. Pollock. Second issue of a book published by Pollock & Co. in early December 1908. Gallup, A2b. NN (John Quinn's copy with his bookplate).

1908.33   CHARLES WHARTON STORK. *Day Dreams of Greece.* VC52. Dec. 1/–. Dargan. *MBP IV,* 1988. BL, CU-A, MB.

1908.34   DAVID PLINLIMMON. *Vox Otiosi.* (P). VC54. Dec. 1/–. Dargan. BL, MB.

1908.35   ROBERT TURNBULL. *Musical Genius and Religion.* Dec.? 2/6. S. Wellwood.

1909.1   FLORENCE FARR. *The Music of Speech.* March. 2/6. Farncombe & Son. BL.

1909.2   JOSEPH THORP. *A Knight's Heart & Other Verses.* March. 2/6. Arden Press, Letchworth. IU.

1909.3   MAURICE HEWLETT. *Artemisian: Idylls and Songs.* April. 1,000? 3/6. Large paper issue, June 1909, 250, 7/6. Clowes. USA: Charles Scribner's Sons (LP issue only). *BMA III,* p. 21, item 21; Colbeck, 1:372; *MBP IV,* 983. BL, CU-A, GK, JGN (small and large-paper issues).

1909.4   W. R. TITTERTON. *River Music & Other Poems.* VC55. April. Wrappers, 1/–. Cloth, 1/6. *MBP IV,* 2089. BL, CU-A.

1909.5   GILBERT HUDSON. *Vanderdecken and Other Pieces.* VC56. April. 1/–. *MBP IV,* 1047. BL, CU-A.

1909.6   EZRA POUND. *Personae of Ezra Pound.* 16 April. 600. 2/6. Although 1,000 sets of sheets were printed, the first issue consisted of only 500 bound copies. Another 100 copies (which also sold for 2/6) were bound up and issued sometime before Nov. 1912. Not more than 144 sets of the remaining sheets were bound up with sheets of *Exultations* and published in a composite volume in May 1913 (see 1913.12). The remaining 256 sets of sheets may have been destroyed in the fire which occurred on 29 June 1915 at the printer

Matthew Bell, where Mathews stored much of his unbound stock. Chiswick. Gallup, A3a. BL, JGN, TXU (Pound's signed presentation copy to Elkin Mathews).

1909.7   LAURENCE ALMA TADEMA. *A Few Lyrics*. April. 2/6. Clowes. Colbeck, 1:13. BL, JGN.

1909.8   LAURENCE ALMA TADEMA. *The Meaning of Happiness: A Discourse*. April. 2/6. Clowes. Colbeck, 1:13. BL.

1909.9   RUTH YOUNG. *The Philanthropists and Other Poems*. VC57. April. 1/-. CSMH.

1909.10   DAISY BROICHER. *German Lyrists of To-day: A Selection of Lyrics from Contemporary German Poetry, Done into English Verse*. VC58. May. Wrappers, 1/-. Cloth, 1/6. CSMH, MB.

1909.11   GERTRUDE H. WITHERBY. *Phantasies*. VC59. May. Wrappers, 1/-. Cloth, 1/6. CSMH, BL.

1909.12   CHARLES F. GRINDROD. *Three Poems*. VC60. May. 1/-. CSMH, BL.

1909.13   ANNETTE FURNESS. *A Summer Garden*. (Pr). June. 3/6. Clowes. BL.

1909.14   WILBUR UNDERWOOD. *Damien of Molokai: Poems*. June. 2/6. Clowes. BL.

1909.15   THOMAS HERBERT LEE. *The Marriage of Iseult and Other Plays*. June. 2/6. Dargan. BL.

1909.16   ELLA ERSKINE. *Shadow-Shapes*. (F). Sept. 3/6. Clowes. BL.

1909.17   VISCOUNT DE ALMEIDA GARRETT. *The "Brother Luiz de Sousa."* (D). English trans. and intro. by Edgar Prestage. Sept. 3/-. Frontispiece portrait of the author. Clowes. MH, TNJ.

1909.18   E. HERRICK [Joan Thompson]. *Verse Pictures*. VC61. Sept. 1/-. Dargan. "Second edition," 1910. *MBP IV*, 980. CSMH, CU-A, IU, JGN, NJP.

1909.19   B. G. BALFOUR. *Rhymes in a Garden and Others*. VC62. Oct. 1/-. Dargan. IU, MB, MH.

1909.20   ARTHUR DILLON. *Leto Suppliant*. (D). Oct. 2/6. Clowes. BL.

1909.21   C[HARLES] F. GRINDROD. *The Shadow of the Raggedstone*. (F). Oct. 6/-. Cover design by Austin O. Spare. BL.

1909.22   ARTHUR LEWIS. *Wind O' the West*. Oct. Wrapper, 1/-. Cloth, 1/6. Clowes. *MBP IV*, 1200. BL, CU-A, JGN.

1909.23   JESSIE POPE. *Airy Nothings: Humorous Verse*. SAT. Oct. Wrappers, 1/-. Cloth, 1/6. Clowes. *MBP IV*, 1656. BL, CU-A, JGN.

1909.24   EZRA POUND. *Exultations of Ezra Pound*. 25 Oct. 2/6. Chiswick. Although 1,000 copies were printed, only 350 copies were bound up initially, constituting the first issue. Later, 150 copies were bound up, constituting the second issue. Since bound copies of the first printing exist with the front cover reading either "Exultations/of/ Ezra Pound" or "Exultations/Ezra Pound," I suspect the former is the first binding; the latter, the second binding. See 1913.12. Gallup, A4a. BL.

1909.25 HENRY NEMO [Henry Newbolt]. *Goodchild's Garland*. (P). Oct. Wrappers, 1/–. Cloth, 1/6. Chiswick. *Colbeck*, 2:600; *MBP IV*, 1487. BL, CU-A.

1909.26 RACHEL ANNAND TAYLOR. *Rose and Vine*. (P). Oct. 5/–. "Second edition," 1910, 5/–. UP. *Colbeck*, 2:835; *MBP IV*, 2040. BL, CU-A, JGN.

1909.27 G[EORGE] TYRRELL. *Versions and Perversions of Heine & Others*. Oct. 2/6. Arden Press. *Colbeck*, 2:888; *MBP IV*, 2142. BL, CU-A; JGN.

1909.28 JACK B. YEATS. *A Little Fleet*. Verses supplied by the Fleet Poet [John Masefield]. Oct. 100. 1/–. Issue hand-colored by the author, fewer than 50 copies, 5/–. Twelve illus. by the author. *Colbeck*, 2:955; MacCarvill, 7; Simmons, p. 132. BL, JGN (hand-colored issue).

1909.29 MARGARET ARNDT. *The Meadows of Play*. Intro. by G. K. Chesterton. (P). Oct. 2/6. Eight full-page black-and-white illus. by Edith Calvert. Dargan. BL.

1909.30 [ROBERT] LAURENCE BINYON. *England and Other Poems*. Nov. 1,000. 3/6. Chiswick. *Colbeck*, 1:57. BL, JGN.

1909.31 CHARLES BAUDELAIRE. *The Flowers of Evil*. Trans. into English verse by Cyril Scott. VC66. Nov. Wrappers, 1/–. Cloth, 1/6. Dargan. BL.

1909.32 F[RANK] S[TEWART] FLINT. *In the Net of the Stars*. (P). Nov. 2/6. Clowes. *Colbeck*, 1:259; *MBP IV*, 711. BL, CU-A, GK, JGN.

1909.33 LILIAN STREET. *Rupert and Other Dreams*. VC63. Nov. Wrappers, 1/–. Cloth, 1/6. Dargan. *MBP IV*, 1998. CSmH, CU-A.

1909.34 LILY THICKNESSE. *Poems Old and New*. Nov. Decorated title page. BL.

1909.35 GERTRUDE H. WITHERBY. *The Fairy Ring: A Children's Play*. VC68. Nov. Wrappers, 1/–. Cloth, 1/6. Clowes. *MBP IV*, 2274. BL, CSmH, CU-A.

1909.36 MRS. GEORGE CRAN. *The Song of a Woman*. (P). SAV1. Dec. 1/–. Clowes. *MBP IV*, 444. BL, CU-A.

1909.37 FRANCIS MACNAMARA. *Marionettes*. (P). Nov. 5/–. Dargan. BL.

1909.38 YONE NOGUCHI. *The Pilgrimage*. Second edition. (P). 2 vols. Dec. 8/–. Frontispiece after Utamaro. Valley Press, Kamakura, Japan. USA: Mitchell Kennerley, 1912. Another issue (one-vol. ed?), Jan. 1914, 4/–. BL, JGN.

1909.39 *The Poems of Sappho*. Translations and adaptations by Percy Osborn. VC65. Dec. Wrappers, 1/–. Cloth, 1/6. Dargan. *MBP IV*, 1556. BL, CU-A, JGN.

1909.40 LOGAN PEARSALL SMITH. *Songs and Sonnets*. VC64. Dec. Wrappers, 1/–. Cloth, 1/6. Dargan. BL, GK, JGN (wrappers and cloth).

1909.41 MRS. HAMILTON SYNGE. *The Vision*. (Pr). SAT. Nov. Wrappers, 1/–. Cloth, 1/6. Clowes. BL.

1909.42 F. A. WOLFE. *Vanities*. (P). VC67. Dec. Wrappers, 1/–. Cloth, 1/6. Dargan. BL.

1909.43 T[HOMAS] WESTWOOD. *Gathered in the Gloaming: Poems of Early and Later Years*. 7/6. Remainder of a first edition of a book printed at the Chiswick Press in 1885.

1909.44 HARTLEY COLERIDGE. *Poems*. Dec. 1/–. Probably the remainder of the selection of poems published in 1907 by S. Wellwood, London.

1910.1 CATHARINE BOUDINOT ATTERBURY. *Bubbles*. (P). Feb. 1/–. BL, CSMH, CTY, MH.

1910.2 ARTHUR SCOTT CRAVEN. *The Last of the English: A Play*. Feb. 2/6. Clowes. *MBP IV*, 446. BL, CU-A, JGN.

1910.3 CLAUDE FOSTER. *Poems*. Feb. 3/6. Clowes. *MBP IV*, 726. BL, CU-A, JGN.

1910.4 FORD MADOX HUEFFER [later FORD]. *Songs from London*. Feb. 1/–. Clowes. Harvey, A29. JGN, NN.

1910.5 MRS. DE COURCY LAFFAN. *Dreams Made Verity: Stories, Essays, and Memories*. Feb. 3/6. Clowes. BL.

1910.6 ALEISTER CROWLEY. *Ambergris: A Selection from the Poems of Aleister Crowley*. March. 3/6. Strangeways. NN, private collection, WU.

1910.7 E[DWARD] H. VISIAK [E. H. Physick]. *Buccaneer Ballads*. Intro. by John Masefield. SAT. March. Wrappers, 1/–. Cloth, 1/6. Frontispiece by Violet Helm. Clowes. Colbeck, 2:530; *MBP IV*, 2160; Simmons, p. 132. BL, CU-A, GK, JGN.

1910.8 [SAIF AL-TIJAN]. *Sword-of-the-Crowns*. Trans. Countess of Cromartie [Sibell Lilian Blunt Mackenzie]. April. 3/6. Clowes. BL, JGN.

1910.9 WILFRID WILSON GIBSON. *Daily Bread, Book I: The House of Candles and Other Dramatic Poems*. April. 500. Wrappers, 1/–. Cloth, 1/6. Clowes. "Second edition," 1911, 1,000. See 1910.10, 1910.20, and 1913.20. Gawsworth, p. 79. BL.

1910.10 WILFRID WILSON GIBSON. *Daily Bread, Book II: The Garret and Other Dramatic Poems*. April. 500. Wrappers, 1/–. Cloth, 1/6. Clowes. "Second edition," 1911, 1,000. See 1910.9, 1910.20, and 1913.20. Gawsworth, p. 79. BL, JGN (1st and 2nd ed.), MH (2nd ed.).

1910.11 GEORGE BENSON HEWETSON. *Poems of Empire*. VC69. April. Wrappers, 1/–. Cloth, 1/6. Clowes. BL.

1910.12 YONE NOGUCHI. *From the Eastern Sea*. Second English edition. (P). April. 4/–. Vignettes, cover design, and endpapers after Utamaro. Valley Press, Kamakura, Japan. JGN.

1910.13 EARL OF MARCH. *Records of the Old Charlton Hunt*. 12/6. Sixteen illustrations.

1910.14 J.F.G. [John F. Gore]. *The Silly Season*. (F). May. 2/6. Clowes. BL.

1910.15 *Stefan George: Selections from His Works*. Trans. Cyril Scott. VC71. May. Wrappers, 1/–. Cloth, 1/6. Dargan. BL.

1910.16 CHARLES KINROSS. *The Ballad of John Dunn and Other Poems.* VC70. Wrappers, 1/–. Cloth, 1/6. Clowes. GK, private collection.

1910.17 WILLIAM MICHAEL ROSSETTI. *Dante and His Convito: A Study with Translations.* May. 4/6. Clowes. BL.

1910.18 WINIFRED ROSE CAREY. *Songs of Awakening.* VC72. Sept. Wrappers, 1/–. Cloth, 1/6. Dargan. CSMH.

1910.19 HENRY E. CLAY. *Poems.* Sept. 3/6. Dargan. BL.

1910.20 WILFRID WILSON GIBSON. *Daily Bread, Book III: Mates and Other Dramatic Poems.* Sept. 500. Wrappers, 1/–. Cloth, 1/6. Clowes. "Second edition," 1911, 1,000. See 1910.9, 1910.10, and 1913.20. Colbeck, 1:287; Gawsworth, p. 80. BL.

1910.21 WILFRID WILSON GIBSON. *Akra the Slave.* (P). Sept. Wrappers, 1/–. Cloth, 1/6. Clowes. Colbeck, 1:287; Gawsworth, p. 80; *MBP IV*, 787. BL, CU-A, JGN.

1910.22 ARTHUR SCOTT CRAVEN. *Alarums and Excursions.* (P). Sept. 2/6. Clowes. *MBP IV*, 445. BL, CU-A.

1910.23 ALICE L. HEAD. *Lotus Leaves.* (P). Sept. 2/6. Clowes. BL.

1910.24 JOHN MASEFIELD. *Ballads and Poems.* 15 Sept. [2nd ed. enlarged of Ballads (1903)]. 2008. First issue on laid paper with watermark "Abbey Mills Greenfield." Wrappers, 1/–. Cloth, 1/6. Second issue on laid paper without watermark, 2/6. Clowes. "New and enlarged edition," Sept. 1913, 3/6. "Seventh thousand," Feb. 1916, 4/6, Clowes. "Eleventh thousand," 1919, Clowes. See 1911.6. Colbeck, 2:529, *BMA I*, 169; Simmons, 2, 12. BL. JGN ("seventh thousand" and "eleventh thousand"), MH (1st and 2nd issues).

1910.25 ELEANOUR NORTON. *Poems.* VC73. Aug. Wrappers, 1/–. Cloth, 1/6. Dargan. BL, MB.

1910.26 RACHEL ANNAND TAYLOR. *The Hours of Fiammetta: A Sonnet Sequence.* Sept. 2/6. Clowes. *MBP IV*, 2038. BL, CU-A, GK, JGN.

1910.27 E[DWARD] H. VISIAK [E. H. Physick]. *The Haunted Island: A Pirate Romance.* Sept. 2/6. Frontispiece by N. W. Physick. Clowes. BL.

1910.28 R.G.T. COVENTRY. *Sanctuary and Other Poems.* Oct. 5/–. Clowes. BL.

1910.29 LOUISE M. GLAZIER. *Animals' Tags and Tails.* Oct. 1/6. Pictured by the author. BL.

1910.30 E. HERRICK [Joan Thompson]. *Portraits and Sketches.* VC74. Oct.? Wrappers, 1/–. Cloth, 1/6. Dargan. *MBP IV*, 978. CSMH, CU-A, JGN.

1910.31 E. HAMILTON MOORE. *The Flame and Other Poems.* VC76. Oct. Wrappers, 1/–. Cloth, 1/6. Dargan. NNC (inscribed by the author to Elkin Mathews), CSMH, IU, NJP.

1910.32 YONE NOGUCHI. *Lafcadio Hearn in Japan.* (Pr). Oct. 6/–. Frontispiece in woodcut by Shoshu Saito. Illus. with many sketches by Genjiro Kataoka and Hearn. Valley Press, Kamakura, Japan. Yokohama:

Kelly & Walsh. Second edition, 1911. USA: Mitchell Kennerley. BL, GK, JGN.

1910.33 VICTORIA F. C. PERCY. *"There Is Nothing New": Poems*. Oct. Wrappers, 1/–. Cloth, 1/6. Clowes. *MBP IV*, 1607. BL, CU-A.

1910.34 DOLLIE RADFORD. *Poems*. Oct. 4/6. Clowes. Colbeck, 2:662. BL.

1910.35 LEWIS SPENCE. *Le Roi d'Ys and Other Poems*. VC77. Oct. Wrappers, 1/–. Cloth, 1/6. CSMH.

1910.36 CHARLES WHARTON STORK. *The Queen of Orplede*. (P). Oct. 2/6. Clowes. BL, JGN.

1910.37 THE COUNTESS OF CROMARTIE [Sibell Lilian Blunt MacKenzie]. *Out of the Dark*. (F). Nov. 3/6. Frontispiece by Henry J. Ford. Clowes. BL.

1910.38 EDITH KING-HALL. *Ports and Fair Havens*. (Pr). Nov. 2/6. Eight illus. by H. C. Seppings Wright. Clowes. BL.

1910.39 FRANK FRANKFORT MOORE. *The Discoverer and In the Queen's Room: Dramas in Metre*. Nov. 4/6. Clowes. BL.

1910.40 *Our Beloved King Edward*. (Poems by various authors). Ed. Elizabeth Woodruff. Nov. 500. 1/6. Special issue bound up in a gold-printed cover of heliotrope-tinted paper, 50. Chiswick. Second printing, Dec. 1910, 1,000 on laid paper. BL.

1910.41 CHARLES E. MOYSE. *Ella Lee: Glimpses of Child Life*. (P). Dec. Twelve illus. by W. H. Dyer. Clowes. *MBP IV*, 1462. BL, CU-A.

1910.42 FERDINAND EARLE. *Sonnets*. Dec. Issue on handmade paper, 500, 3/6. Another issue on antique laid paper, 500. A special issue on Japanese vellum numbered and signed by the author, 25. (Chiswick Press records indicate that 200 copies of the issue on handmade paper and 50 copies of the antique laid paper issue were bound up for the American market). Chiswick. BL.

1910.43 W. W. MARSH. *In the Net of Night*. VC75. Dec. 1/–. Dargan. *MBP IV*, 1359. BL, CU-A.

1911.1 ISABEL CLARKE. *Nomad Songs and Other Verses*. VC78. Jan. Wrappers, 1/–. Cloth, 1/6. Dargan. CSMH.

1911.2 JOHN HOGBEN. *Ground Flowers: Ventures in Verse*. Jan. 2/6. Clowes. JGN.

1911.3 CONSTANCE MORGAN. *The Song of a Tramp and Other Poems*. VC82. Feb. Wrappers, 1/–. Cloth, 1/6. Dargan. *MBP IV*, 1444. BL, CU-A.

1911.4 EVERARD WYRALL. *The Master's Advent: A Prologue*. March. 500. Chiswick. BL.

1911.5 E[DWARD] H. VISIAK [E. H. Physick]. *Flints and Flashes*. (P). SAT. March. Wrappers, 1/–. Cloth, 1/6. *MBP IV*, 2161. BL, CU-A, JGN.

1911.6 JOHN MASEFIELD. *Ballads*. April. 1/–. Third edition, revised and enlarged, containing selections from *Ballads* (1903) and *Ballads and Poems* (1910). Clowes. Simmons, 2, 12. MH, NNC.

1911.7 [GRANT DUFF] DOUGLAS AINSLIE. *Mirage: Poems.* May. 3/6. Turnbull & Spears, Edinburgh. Colbeck, 1:5. BL, JGN.

1911.8 *The Diary of Dr. John William Polidori, 1816.* Edited and elucidated by William Michael Rossetti. May. 4/6. Richard Clay & Sons. BL.

1911.9 THOMAS HOWITT MASON. *Sylva.* (P). May. 1/6. Clowes. BL.

1911.10 *Mrs. Alfred Trench.* By the author of "The Views of Christopher." May. 1,000. 2/6. Chiswick. BL.

1911.11 WILFRID THORLEY. *Confessional and Other Poems.* Preface by Maurice Hewlett. VC79. May. Wrappers, 1/–. Cloth, 1/6. Dargan. Colbeck, 1:373; *MBP IV*, 2073. BL, JGN, private collection (copy inscribed by author with author's holograph corrections of the text).

1911.12 A[LBERTA] V[ICTORIA] MONTGOMERY. *Angels and Symbols.* (P). VC80. May. Wrappers, 1/–. Cloth, 1/6. Dargan. MBP IV, 1429. CSmH, CU- A.

1911.13 IDA NORMAN. *Songs of the Birds.* VC81. May. Wrappers, 1/–. Cloth, 1/6. Dargan. BL.

1911.14 *The Salvation of Teddie: A Sketch in Two Scenes.* May. 100. Special issue, 2. Chiswick.

1911.15 BLANCHE EDWARDS. *The Dream-Merchant and Other Poems.* VC83. May. Wrappers, 1/–. Cloth, 1/6. Dargan. *MBP IV* 629. BL, CU-A, MB, JGN.

1911.16 KENNETH HARE. *The Green Fields.* (P). VC84. May. Wrappers, 1/–. Cloth, 1/6. Dargan. *MBP IV*, 925. BL, CU-A.

1911.17 LUCILLA [Grace E. Tollemache]. *Sonnets by "Lucilla."* [First series]. BUR1. May. 500. 2/6. Chiswick. BL.

1911.18 K.H.D. CECIL. *Coronation Poem and Love-Songs.* VC85. June. Wrappers, 1/–. Cloth, 1/6. Dargan. *MBP IV*, 342. BL, CU-A.

1911.19 T. C. MACNAGHTEN. *An Old Maid's Birthday.* July. 2/6. Dargan. BL.

1911.20 EZRA POUND. *Canzoni of Ezra Pound.* July. 250. Chiswick. Although 1,000 sets of sheets were printed, only 250 copies were bound initially. Later, not more than 140 sheets were bound along with *Ri-postes* in a composite volume published in May 1913 (see 1913.13). The remaining 610 sets of sheets may have been destroyed in a fire on 29 June 1915 at the printer Matthew Bell, where Mathews stored much of his unbound stock. Gallup, A7a. BL, TXU.

1911.21 WILLIAM GERARD. *Prospero and Other Poems.* Oct. 3/6. Dargan. BL.

1911.22 R. CHARLES MOIR. *Survivals.* (P). Oct. 2/6. Clowes. *MBP IV*, 1424. BL, CU-A.

1911.23 LOUISE M. GLAZIER. *A Book of Babes in Woodcut and Verse.* Sept. 1/6. BL.

1911.24 *Under Swedish Colours: A Short Anthology of Modern Swedish Poets.* Translated into English verse by Francis Arthur Judd; preface by

Edmund Gosse. VC87. Oct. Wrappers, 1/–. Cloth, 1/6. Sepiatone photogravure frontispiece. Dargan. BL, JGN (cloth), MB.

1911.25 HENRIETTA HOME. *The Fledglings*. (Pr [sketches of child life]). [1912]. Oct. 2/–. Clowes. BL.

1911.26 CHARLES E. MOYSE. *The Lure of Earth and Other Poems*. VC89. Sept. 250. 1/–. Chiswick. Second issue, 1912, 500, 1/–. Chiswick. *MBP IV*, 1463. BL, CU- A.

1911.27 JOHN RODBOROUGH. *Puck's Flight and Other Poems*. VC91. Oct. Wrappers, 1/–. Cloth, 1/6. Dargan. BL, MB.

1911.28 MARIA STEUART. *At the World's Edge: A Little Book of Verse*. VC93. Oct. 500. 1/–. Chiswick. *MBP IV*, 1971. BL, CU-A.

1911.29 *Miles Standish by H. W. Longfellow*. Dramatized for performance by Edith Ashby. VC88. Oct. 1/–. Clowes. BL.

1911.30 LUCILLA [Grace E. Tollemache]. *Sonnets by "Lucilla."* [Second series]. BUR2. Nov. 500. 2/6. Chiswick. *MBP IV*, 1235. CU-A.

1911.31 DENYS LEFEBURE. *The Lone Trek*. (P). Nov. 2/6. Frontispiece by G. S. Smithard. Clowes. BL.

1911.32 MARNA PEASE. *Poems*. Nov. 2/6. Clowes. MBP IV, 1599. BL.

1911.33 V. TAUBMAN-GOLDIE. *Escapades*. (P). VC90. Nov. Wrappers, 1/–. Cloth, 1/6. Dargan. BL.

1911.34 MURIEL ELSIE GRAHAM. *A Mere Song*. (P). VC94. Nov. 1/–. Dargan. *MBP IV*, 848. BL, CU-A.

1911.35 STANHOPE BAYLEY. *A Singer of Dreams: Voices of Moods and Places*. (P). VC95. Nov. Wrappers, 1/–. Cloth, 1/6. Dargan. BL.

1911.36 F[RANCIS] P. B. OSMASTON. *Art and Nature Sonnets*. Nov. 5/6. Numerous full-page and other illustrations in photogravure and woodcut by James Guthrie. Ballantyne Press. Although this book does not have the imprint of the Pear Tree Press, it was, according to Ridler, p. 205, obviously conceived and designed by James Guthrie, and on that basis it is included in Ridler's Pear Tree Press list. BL, NNC, WU.

1911.37 E[DITH] NESBIT [Mrs. Bland]. *Ballads and Verses of Spiritual Life*. Dec. 4/6. Clowes. BL.

1911.38 *Six Lyrics from the Ruthenian of Taraś Shevchénko*. Translated into English verse by E[thel] L[ilian] Voynich. VC86. Dec. 1,000. Wrappers, 1/–. Cloth, 1/6. Chiswick. Second printing, 1913, 500, 1/–. Chiswick. BL.

1911.39 RUTH YOUNG. *The Water Carrier of Venice*. (P). VC92. Dec. 1/–. Dargan. CSMH.

1911.40 C[ELIA] A[NNA] NICHOLSON. *The Comfort-Lady and Other Verses*. VC96. Dec. 1/–. Dargan. *MBP IV*, 1507. BL, CU-A, MB.

1911.41 LIONEL JOHNSON. *Post Liminium: Essays and Critical Papers*. Ed. Thomas Whittemore. Dec. 6/–. Clowes. USA: Mitchell Kennerley,

1912. "Second impression," 1912. Clowes. Colbeck, 1:433; Potter, 662. BL, GK, JGN (both impressions).

1911.42   ERNEST MARRIOTT. *Jack B. Yeats: Being a True Impartial View of His Pictorial & Dramatic Art.* Dec. 1/–. Issue hand-colored by Jack Yeats, 5/–. Colbeck, 2:956. JGN, WU.

1911.43   *Jack B. Yeats's Plays in the Old Manner.* Dec.? 2/–. Reissue of *James Flaunty* and *The Scourge of the Gulph* in one volume. MacCarvill, 3.

1912.1   W[ILLIAM] B. COTTON. *Verses.* [1911]. Jan. 500. 2/6. Chiswick. BL.

1912.2   WILFRID WILSON GIBSON. *Fires, Book I: The Stone and Other Tales.* Jan. 1,000. Wrappers, 1/–. Cloth, 1/6. Clowes. See 1912.27 and 28 and 1915.9. Colbeck, 1:287; Gawsworth, p. 81. BL, JGN (wrappers and cloth).

1912.3   HARRY B. HERMAN-HODGE. *The Search for Semperswig and Other Poems Old and New.* Jan. 2/6. Holywell Press, Oxford. BL.

1912.4   STANHOPE BAYLEY. *Anima Fanciulla.* (Pr). VC97. Feb. Wrappers, 1/–. Cloth, 1/6. Dargan. BL.

1912.5   STANHOPE BAYLEY. *The Campagna of Rome: A Symphony and In the Sleep of the Sun.* (Pr). VC99. Feb. 1/–. Dargan. BL, MB.

1912.6   LIONEL JOHNSON. *Some Poems of Lionel Johnson Newly Selected.* Intro. by Imogen Guiney. VC34. Feb. Wrappers, 1/–. Cloth, 1/6. Dargan. Colbeck, 1:433; *MBP IV*, 1084. BL, CU-A, GK, JGN (wrappers and cloth).

1912.7   F[RANCIS] P. B. OSMASTON. *The Future of Poetry: An Essay.* Feb. 500. 2/6. Chiswick. BL, IU, MH.

1912.8   PALLISTER BARKAS. *Storm Song and Other Poems.* March. 2/–. Clowes. BL.

1912.9   AGNES FOX. *Verses.* Feb. 2/6. Dargan. *MBP IV*, 734. BL.

1912.10   REGINALD L. HINE. *Anima Celtica.* (Pr). March. 2/6. Dargan. Colbeck, 1:379. BL, JGN.

1912.11   W[ILLIAM] E. LUTYENS. *Poems.* March. 500. 2/6. Chiswick. BL.

1912.12   *Strangers and Foreigners: Being Translations from the French, Italian, German and Middle High German.* English verse translations by Lois Saunders. VC98. March. 500. Wrappers, 1/–. Cloth, 1/6. Chiswick. BL, MB.

1912.13   CLINTON SCOLLARD. *Songs of a Syrian Lover.* BUR3. March. 500. 2/6. Chiswick. *MBP IV*, 1825. BL, CU-A.

1912.14   GORDON BOTTOMLEY. *Chambers of Imagery.* Second series. April. 500. 1/–. Clowes. Ashley, 9:18; Colbeck, 1:78. BL, JGN.

1912.15   F. GWYNNE EVANS. *In Mantle Blue.* (P)/ April. 500. 3/6. Chiswick. *MBP IV*, 652. BL, CU-A.

1912.16   GEORGE A. GREENE. *Songs of the Open Air.* April. 3/6. Clowes. *MBP IV*, 870. BL, CU-A, JGN.

1912.17 ALICE LAW. *Imaginary Sonnets of Tasso to Leonora and Other Poems.* VC100. April. 1/–. Dargan. Colbeck, 1:476; *MBP IV*, 1160. BL, CU-A.

1912.18 MARGARET J. BORTHWICK. *The Book of the White Butterflies.* (P and Pr). May. 100. 1/6. Second issue, Nov. 1918, 150, 1/6. Chiswick. BL.

1912.19 M. H. BOURCHIER [Havering Bowcher]. *Verses by the Way.* SAV2. May. 1/–. Clowes. BL.

1912.20 AUGUSTA KLEIN. *The Hidden Door: A Monologue.* May. 1/6. Dargan. BL.

1912.21 R[ICHARD] DIMSDALE STOCKER. *Illusions and Ideals: Poems.* VC2 (italicized nos. indicate VC 2nd ser.). May. Wrappers, 1/–. Cloth, 1/6. Dargan. BL.

1912.22 E[DWARD] H. VISIAK [E. H. Physick]. *The Phantom Ship and Other Poems.* SAT. May. Wrappers, 1/–. Cloth, 1/6. Frontispiece after a drawing by Violet Helm. Clowes. *MBP IV*, 2162. BL, CU-A, JGN.

1912.23 *German Lyrics and Ballads.* Translated into English verse by Daisy Broicher. VC3. June. Wrappers, 1/–. Cloth, 1/6. Dargan. BL, CSMH.

1912.24 FRANCES A[NNE] BARDSWELL. *Twelve Moons.* (Pr). Sept. 2/6. Frontispiece in color by Isabella Forrest. Clowes. BL.

1912.25 T[HOMAS] CHAMBERLIN CHAMBERLIN. *Songs from the Forest of Tane.* BUR4. Sept. 500. 2/6. Chiswick. BL.

1912.26 ARTHUR DILLON. *Pelops: A Tetralogy.* (D). Sept. Wrappers, 1/6. Cloth, 3/6. Clowes. BL.

1912.27 WILFRID WILSON GIBSON. *Fires, Book II: The Ovens and Other Tales.* Sept. 1,000. Wrappers, 1/–. Cloth, 1/6. Clowes. See 1912.2, 1912.28, and 1915.9. Gawsworth, p. 82. BL, JGN (wrappers and cloth).

1912.28 WILFRID WILSON GIBSON. *Fires, Book III: The Hare and Other Tales.* Sept. 1,000. Wrappers, 1/–. Cloth, 1/6. Clowes. See 1912.2, 1912.27 and 1915.9. Gawsworth, p. 82. BL, JGN (wrappers and cloth).

1912.29 W. LYON. *Huperourania.* (P). Sept. 1/–. Dargan. BL.

1912.30 YONE NOGUCHI. *The American Diary of a Japanese Girl.* Sept. 7/6. Frontispiece in color printed from twenty-five wood blocks by Yeiho Hiresaki. Valley Press, Kamakura, Japan. BL.

1912.31 *The Vigo Verse Anthology.* Preface by Elkin Mathews. VC1. Sept. Wrappers, 1/–. Cloth, 1/6. Dargan. BL.

1912.32 GEORGE FORESTER. [Sir Granville George Greenwood]. *Poems.* Oct. 1/6. Dargan. BL.

1912.33 LOUISE M. GLAZIER. *The Field-Flowers' Lore: A Collection of Legends.* Oct. 1,000. 2/6. Woodcuts by the author. Chiswick. BL.

1912.34 MADAME MURIEL RICHARD. *Essays in Song.* VC6. Oct. 1/–. Dargan. BL, ICU, MB.

1912.35 TREVOR BLAKEMORE. *Poems and Ballads.* Oct. 750. 3/6. Chiswick. BL.

1912.36 E[DWARD] H. VISIAK [E. H. Physick] and C. V. HAWKINS. *The War of the Schools.* Nov. 2/6. Clowes. BL.

1912.37 E. A. HENTY [Mrs. Edward Starkey]. *Australian Idylls and Other Poems.* VC4. Dec. Wrappers, 1/–. Cloth, 1/6. Blackfriars Press. BL, MB.

1912.38 MORROGH SHANNON. *The Howling Ships of Tarshish and Other Poems.* Dec. 750. 2/6. Chiswick. *MBP IV,* 1854. BL, CU-A.

1913.1 K. W. LUNDIE. *English Echoes from the Quartier Latin.* [1912]. (P). VC5. Jan. Wrappers, 1/–. Cloth, 1/6. Clowes. *MBP IV,* 1243. BL, CU-A, WU.

1913.2 FRANCIS ERNLEY WALROND. *The Gods of Africa and Other Poems.* [1912]. Jan. 1/6. Blackfriars Press. BL.

1913.3 FREDERICK WEDMORE. *Pages Assembled: Selections from His Writings.* SAT. Feb. Wrappers, 1/–. Cloth, 1/6. Clowes. Colbeck, 2:908. BL, GK.

1913.4 M[AUD] BARTLEET. *The Raised Rood and Other Poems.* VC7. Feb. Wrappers, 1/–. Cloth, 1/6. Clowes. BL.

1913.5 A. HUGH FISHER. *Poems.* VC8. April. Wrappers, 1/–. Cloth, 1/6. Clowes. *MBP IV,* 702. BL, CU-A, JGN.

1913.6 WILLIAM GERARD. *Piers Gaveston.* (D). April. 3/6. Clowes. BL.

1913.7 A. R. AMBLER. *The Little Inn [and] The Dream.* (F). May. 2/6. Clowes. BL.

1913.8 FRANCIS WILLIAM BOURDILLON. *Moth-Wings (Ailes d'Alouette).* (P). May. 500. 3/6. Chiswick. BL.

1913.9 RICHARD MONCKTON MILNES. *Good Night and Good Morning: A Ballad.* April. 2/6. Drawings by M. M. Gell. Another edition of this oft-published book. BL.

1913.10 ROBERT BOWMAN PECK. *Perceptions.* (P). April. 500. 2/6. Chiswick. Chiswick Press records for 12 March 1913 list the printing of 500 copies of the book. On 10 April 1913, the records list the printing of 500 copies of a cancel title page for the book. *MBP IV,* 1600. BL, CU-A.

1913.11 LOUISE JOPLING ROWE. *Poems.* May. 500. 2/6. Frontispiece portrait of author. Chiswick. *MBP IV,* 1772. BL, CU-A.

1913.12 EZRA POUND. *Personae & Exultations of Ezra Pound.* May. Not more than 140. 3/6. Chiswick. See 1909.6 and 1909.24. Gallup, A3b. ICN, MH, NN, WU.

1913.13 EZRA POUND. *Canzoni & Ripostes of Ezra Pound whereto are Appended the Complete Poetical Works of T. E. Hulme.* May. Not more than 140. 3/6. Chiswick. See 1911.20. Gallup, A7b. CTY, MH.

1913.14 EVANGELINE RYVES. *The Red Horizon, a Dialogue, and Other Verses.* VC9. May. 500. Wrappers, 1/–. Cloth, 1/6. Chiswick. BL.

1913.15 EVANGELINE RYVES. *Erebus: A Book of Verse.* May. reissue of the Unicorn Press edition with new preliminary matter including a preface by Elkin Mathews and press opinions. 440. Wrappers, 1/–. Cloth, 1/6. Unwin Bros., The Gresham Press; Chiswick (preliminary materials). *MBP IV*, 1789. BL, CU-A.

1913.16 SANDYS WASON. *Simon Dean and Other Poems*. SAV3. May. 1/–. Clowes. BL.

1913.17 W. ROBERT HALL. *Glimpses of the Unseen*. (P). VC10. July. Wrappers, 1/–. Cloth, 1/6. Clowes. BL.

1913.18 G[EORGE] RESTON MALLOCH. *Lyrics and Other Verses*. SAV4. July. 1/–. Clowes. BL.

1913.19 JOHN MASEFIELD. *Salt-Water Ballads*. Second edition of the famous book first published by Grant Richards in November 1902. July. 1,500. 3/6. Chiswick. "Third edition," Nov. 1913, 3/6. "Fourth edition," Feb. 1915. "Fifth edition" ["fifth thousand"], Feb. 1916 (not listed in Simmons). Colbeck, 2:530; *MBP IV*, 1370; Williams, 1. Of the 500 copies comprising the first edition of 1902, a portion appeared with a later cancel title leaf with the imprint of Elkin Mathews. See William Reese Co. Catalogue 43, Oct. 1986, item 63. BL, JGN.

1913.20 WILFRID WILSON GIBSON. *Daily Bread*. Third edition in one volume with an additional tale. July. 1,000. 3/6. Clowes. USA: Macmillan. Fourth edition, 1914, 1,000, 3/6, Clowes. BL.

1913.21 ETHEL ROLT-WHEELER. *Ireland's Veils and Other Poems*. VC11. Aug. Wrappers, 1/–. Cloth, 1/6. Clowes. *MBP IV*, 1759. BL, CU-A (signed presentation copy from the author with Ms. poem on lower free endpaper), MB.

1913.22 G. L. ASHLEY DODD. *Fishing Rhymes*. Sept. Wrappers, 1/–. Cloth, 2/–. Strangeways & Sons. BL.

1913.23 [ROBERT] LAURENCE BINYON. *Odes*. New edition revised and rearranged of the edition published earlier by the Unicorn Press. Sept. 1,000. 2/6. Chiswick. Colbeck, 1:57; Krishnamurti, 76; *MBP IV*, 181. BL, CU-A, JGN, MB.

1913.24 R[OBERT] SHELBY DARBISHIRE. *A Holiday in Verse*. Sept. 1/6. Clowes. BL.

1913.25 WILLIAM H. DAVIES. *Foliage: Various Poems*. Sept. 1/6. Clowes. Colbeck, 1:185; *MBP IV*, 512; Murphy, p. 301; Wilson, p. 29. BL, CU-A (publisher's presentation copy with stamp on half title), JGN.

1913.26 ISAAC GREGORY SMITH. *Reullera*. (P). SAV5. Aug. 1/–.

1913.27 MICHAEL HESELTINE. *Poems*. SAV6. Sept. 1/–. Clowes. BL.

1913.28 NORREYS JEPHSON O'CONOR. *Celtic Memories and Other Poems*. VC12. Sept. Wrappers, 1/–. Cloth, 1/6. Clowes. *MBP IV*, 1535. BL, CU-A.

1913.29 JOHN C. TAYLOR. *The Northern Sea: A Legend of the Norwegian Fiords and the North Cape*. VC13. Sept. Wrappers, 1/–. Cloth, 1/6. With sixteen illus. by the author. Clowes. BL.

1913.30 WILLIAM CARLOS WILLIAMS. *The Tempers*. (P). SAV7. 13 Sept. 1,000. 1/–. Clowes. Wallace, A2. BL, MH, TXU.

1913.31 MAX EASTMAN. *Enjoyment of Poetry*. Oct. 4/6. BL, JGN.

1913.32 WILLOUGHBY WEAVING. *Poems*. Oct. 2/6. Clowes. *MBP IV*, 2216. BL, CU-A.

1913.33 ELIZABETH WESTERMAIN. *Helen's Mirror and Other Verses*. SAV8. Oct. 1/–. Clowes. BL.

1913.34 ALFRED PERCEVAL GRAVES. *Irish Literary and Musical Studies*. Nov. 6/–. Clowes. Colbeck, 1:311. BL, JGN.

1913.35 PROF. [WILLIAM ANGUS] KNIGHT. *Coleridge and Wordsworth in the West Country*. Nov. 7/6. Eighteen illus. by Edmund H. New. Brendon. "Second edition, corrected and enlarged," 1914, 7/6.

1913.36 MARGARET SACKVILLE. *Songs of Aphrodite and Other Poems*. Nov. 500. 4/6. Special copies, 3. Chiswick. Colbeck, 2:716; *MBP IV*, 1799. BL.

1913.37 LEWIS SPENCE. *Songs Satanic and Celestial*. VC15. Nov. Wrappers, 1/–. Cloth, 1/6. Clowes. BL.

1913.38 A.L.H. ANDERSON. *Echoes: A Book of Verse*. Nov. 2/6. Clowes. BL.

1913.39 HARRIET MASON KILBURN. *The Sign of the Tree*. (P). Nov. 3/6. Vail-Ballou Press (Binghampton, N.Y.). BL.

1913.40 MARGARET ARNDT. *From across the German Ocean*. Dec. 2/6. Clowes. BL.

1913.41 M. A. [Dorothy Violet Wellesley, Lady Gerald Wellesley]. *Early Poems*. Dec. 500. 3/6. Chiswick. BL, JGN.

1913.42 RATHMELL WILSON. *Another Book of the Sirens*. (Pr, F, P). Dec. 2/6. Riverside. BL, JGN.

1914.1 YONE NOGUCHI. *Through the Torii*. (Pr). Jan. 5/–. Diadosha Press, Tokyo, Japan. BL.

1914.2 C[ICELY] FOX-SMITH. *Songs in Sail and Other Chantys*. VC14. Jan. 1,000. Wrappers, 1/–. Cloth, 1/6. Clowes. "Second thousand," March 1914, "Third edition": Oct. 1914. BL, JGN: 1st and 3rd eds.

1914.3 STANHOPE BAYLEY. *In the Fall of the Leaf*. (Pr). VC16. Jan. Wrappers, 1/–. Cloth, 1/6. Clowes. BL.

1914.4 F. GERALD MILLER. *The New Circe: Poems*. VC17. Feb. Wrappers, 1/–. Cloth, 1/6. Clowes. BL, JGN.

1914.5 LEO C. ROBERTSON. *Glimmer of Dawn: Poems*. VC18. Feb. Wrappers, 1/–. Cloth, 1/6. Clowes. *MBP IV*, 1744. BL, CU-A, JGN, MG.

1914.6 MARGARET CROPPER. *Poems*. VC19. April. Wrappers, 1/–. Cloth, 1/6. Clowes. *MBP IV*, 456. BL, CU-A.

1914.7 MAX WEBER. *Cubist Poems*. VC24. April. 1,000. Wrappers, 1/–. Cloth, 1/6. Edition de Luxe on handmade paper with a certificate, 100, 5/–. Chiswick. BL, JGN, WU.

1914.8   EDMUND VALE. *Elfin Chaunts and Railway Rhythms.* VC20. May. Wrappers, 1/–. Cloth, 1/6. Clowes. *MBP IV,* 2147. BL, CU-A.

1914.9   W. H. ABBOTT. *Vision: A Book of Lyrics.* May. 500. 2/6. Chiswick. *MBP IV,* 2. BL, CU-A.

1914.10   MAURICE HEWLETT. *The Wreath, 1894–1914.* [Printed for the author]. May. 25. Chiswick.

1914.11   *Florentine Vignettes: Being Some Metrical Letters of the Late Vernon Arnold Slade.* Ed. Wilfrid Thorley. May. 2/6. Decorated title page and end decoration by Wilfrid Thorley. Clowes. *MBP IV,* 2074. BL, CU-A, JGN.

1914.12   CECIL GARTH [Grace Carlton]. *The Song of the Five and Other Poems.* SAV9. May. 1/–. Clowes. BL.

1914.13   T. B. HENNELL. *The Lords of the Restless Sea and Songs of Scotland.* VC21. May. Wrappers, 1/–. Cloth, 1/6. Clowes. *MBP IV,* 971. BL, CU-A.

1914.14   R. H. LAW. *Moorland Sanctuary and Other Poems.* VC22. May. Wrappers, 1/–. Cloth, 1/6. Clowes. *MBP IV,* 1162. BL, CU-A.

1914.15   RITA FRANCIS [*sic*] MOSSCOCKLE. *Poems.* May. 5/–. Westminster Press. *MBP IV,* 1459. BL, CU-A.

1914.16   LLOYD ROBERTS. *England Over Seas.* (P). May. 2/6. Clowes. BL.

1914.17   MARY G. CHERRY. *Lyrics of the Open.* June. 2/6. Clowes. BL.

1914.18   TINSLEY PRATT. *Wayfaring: Ballads and Songs.* VC23. June. Wrappers, 1/–. Cloth, 1/6. Clowes. *MBP IV,* 1664. BL, CU-A.

1914.19   ETHEL CASTILLA. *The Australian Girl and Other Verses.* Second edition of a book first published in 1900. June. 2/6. Clowes. BL.

1914.20   JOAN TAMWORTH. *In the Time of Apple-Blossom and Other Poems.* Aug. 2/6. Frontispiece by Collier Ripley. Ferrestone Press. BL.

1914.21   MARGARET CHANLER [*sic*] ALDRICH. *The Horns of Chance and Other Poems.* Sept. 500. 2/6. Chiswick. BL.

1914.22   T[HOMAS] W[ILLIAM] H[ODGSON] CROSLAND. *The Absent-minded Mule and Other Occasional Verses.* Sept. Reissue of a book originally published by the Unicorn Press in 1899. 6d.

1914.23   WILFRID WILSON GIBSON. *Borderlands.* (D). Sept. 2/6. Clowes. Colbeck, 1:287; Gawsworth, p. 83; *MBP IV,* 789. BL, CU-A, JGN.

1914.24   WILFRID WILSON GIBSON. *Thoroughfares.* (P). Sept. 2/6. Clowes. Colbeck, 1:287; Gawsworth, p. 83; Reilly, p. 139. BL, JGN.

1914.25   MAUDE GOLDRING. *Lonely England.* Sept. Reissue of a book first published by Swift & Co. in 1911. 2/6. Illus. in color by Agnes Pike.

1914.26   HARRIOT WOLFF. *Italiana.* (P). Sept. 500. 2/6. Chiswick. BL.

1914.27 E. H. THOMSON [Mrs. Wilfrid Thomson]. *The Tragedy of a Trouba- dour: An Interpretation of Browning's Sordello.* (Pr). Sept. 2/6. Clowes. BL.

1914.28 MARION DURST. *A Prelude in Verse.* Oct. 2/6. Clowes. *MBP IV*, 614. BL, CU-A.

1914.29 *Some Slings and Arrows from John Galsworthy.* (Pr). Selected by Elsie E. Morton. VC27. Oct. 1/–. Clowes. BL, JGN.

1914.30 E. SCOTTON HUELIN. *Poems.* Oct. 1/–. Clowes. BL, JGN.

1914.31 C[ICELY] FOX-SMITH. *Sailor Town: Sea Songs and Ballads.* VC25. Oct. Wrappers, 1/–. Cloth, 1/6. Clowes. BL.

1914.32 GRACE E. TOLLEMACHE. *Lyrics and Short Poems.* Oct. 300. 1/–. Chis- wick. Krishnamurti, 672; Reilly, p. 316. BL, JGN.

1914.33 E[DMUND] H[ENRY] LACON WATSON. *A Conversational Tour in America.* Oct. 2/6. Brendon. BL.

1914.34 MAUDE GOLDRING. *The Country of the Young.* Preface by Katharine Tynan. (P). Nov. 2/6. Brendon. *MBP IV*, 822; Reilly, p. 142; BL, CU-A.

1914.35 ARTHUR LYNCH. *Sonnets of the Banner and the Star.* Nov. 4/6. Clowes. BL.

1914.36 [ROBERT] LAURENCE BINYON. *The Winnowing-Fan: Poems on the Great War.* Dec. Wrappers, 1/–. Cloth, 1/6. Cloth-bound issue on "finer paper," 2/6. Brendon. "Reprinted (500 copies), June 1915." "Second thousand," March 1916, 1/–. Colbeck, 1:57; *MBP IV*, 183; Reilly, p. 56. BL, CU-A, GK, JGN.

1914.37 MARY MORGAN [Gowan Lea]. *Glimpses into the Letters of a Wanderer.* (P). Dec. 1/6. Clowes. BL.

1914.38 VICTOR PLARR. *Ernest Dowson, 1887–1897: Reminiscences, Unpub- lished Letters and Marginalia.* With a bibliography by H. Guy Harri- son. Dec. 3/6. Riverside. USA: Laurence J. Gomme. Colbeck, 2:654; Krishnamurti, 215. BL, GK, JGN.

1914.39 T. EARLE WELBY. *Swinburne: A Critical Study.* Dec. 4/6. Clowes. BL.

1914.40 ELIZABETH BARRETT BROWNING. *Sonnets from the Portuguese.* Dec. Pro- bably the remainder of an edition published in London in 1906 by the Carodoc Press. Wrappers, 1/6. Cloth, 2/–.

1914.41 ROBERT BROWNING. *Browning's Essay on Shelley: Being His Introduc- tion to the Spurious Shelley Letters.* Ed. with an intro. by Richard Garnett. Probably the remainder of the "cheap edition" published in London about 1905 by the De la More Press. "Cheaper edition." Wrappers, 1/6. Cloth, 2/–.

1915.1 LAWRENCE ATKINSON. *Aura.* (P). March. 500. 3/6. Chiswick. BL.

1915.2 ARTHUR LEWIS. *Vineleaves.* [1914]. (P). VC26. March. 1/–. Clowes. BL.

1915.3   CUTHBERT WRIGHT. *One Way of Love.* (P). March. 2/6. Brendon. BL.

1915.4   EZRA POUND. *Cathay: Translations by Ezra Pound.* 6 April. 1,000. 1/–. Chiswick. Gallup, A9. BL, CSmH, MH, TXU.

1915.5   EZRA POUND. *Ripostes of Ezra Pound, whereto are appended The Complete Poetical Works of T. E. Hulme.* April. Fourth issue of a book first published in 1912 by Swift & Co. 400. 1/–. Cover design by Dorothy Shakespear. Neill and Co., Ltd. (Edinburgh); wrappers, cancel title leaf, and advertisement leaf printed by Chiswick. Gallup, A8d. MH, Cty.

1915.6   THEODORE BOTREL. *Songs of Brittany.* Translations into English by George Ebenezer Morrison. VC28. April. 1/–. Brendon. BL.

1915.7   STANHOPE BAYLEY. *Broken Rays.* (Pr). VC29. April. Wrappers, 1/–. Cloth, 1/6. Clowes. BL.

1915.8   LORD DUNSANY [Edward John Moreton Drax Plunkett]. *Fifty-One Tales.* April. 751. 3/6. Portrait of author in photogravure. Riverside. "Second thousand," 1917, 3/6, with new portrait of author in photogravure. *BMA I*, 90. BL, JGN.

1915.9   WILFRID WILSON GIBSON. *Fires.* Second printing of Books I–III (see 1912.2, 1912.27, and 1912.28) in one volume. April. 1,000. 3/6. Clowes. "Second thousand," 3/6, 1916. IU, JGN, TXU.

1915.10   [THOMAS] STURGE MOORE. *Hark to These Three: Talk about Style.* April. 1/6. Woodcut design by the author. Brendon. Colbeck, 2:573. BL, JGN, WU.

1915.11   HAROLD FEHRSEN SAMPSON. *Sounds from Another Valley.* (P). May. 1/–. Brendon. Reilly. BL.

1915.12   *A New Decalogue with the Eleventh Commandment.* VC30. June. 1/–. Clowes. ICU.

1915.13   HERBERT READ. *Songs of Chaos.* June. 1/–. Brendon. BL.

1915.14   GEORGE A. B. DEWAR. *Dreams.* (F). July. 2/6. Brendon. BL.

1915.15   LADY [HARRIET JULIA] JEPHSON. *A War-Time Journal, Germany, 1914, and German Travel Notes.* July. Wrappers, 1/6. Cloth, 2/6. Clowes. "New and cheaper edition," late 1915. BL, CtY, NN.

1915.16   ARTHUR GREEN. *The Sluice-Gate: Fugitive Verses.* Aug. 2/6. Brendon. *MBP IV*, 869. BL, CU-A, JGN.

1915.17   HAROLD BELL. *Poems and Sonnets.* Aug. 2/–. Brendon. *MBP IV*, 141. BL, CU-A.

1915.18   A[NNE] D. MUNCASTER. *On Quartermasters.* Sept. 1,000. 1/–. Chiswick. Second printing, April 1916, 500.

1915.19   WILFRID WILSON GIBSON. *Battle.* (P). Sept. Wrappers, 1/–. Cloth, 2/6. Clowes. "Third thousand," 1916, 1/–. "Fourth thousand," 1918, 1/3. Colbeck, 1:288; Gawsworth, p. 84; *MBP IV*, 788; Reilly, p. 139. BL,

CU-A, JGN (1st ed., third thousand, and variant binding in green wrappers).

1915.20   TOM STAVELEY. *Empty Day: Verses.* Sept. 1/–. Brendon. Reilly, p. 303. BL, JGN.

1915.21   CHARLES S. JERRAM. *War.* (P). Oct. 2/6. Clowes. Reilly, p. 181. BL.

1915.22   LIONEL JOHNSON. *Poetical Works of Lionel Johnson.* Preface by Ezra Pound (first English issue only). Oct. 1,500 sets of sheets printed, of which 600 were used for the English issue and 900 were used for the American issue. 7/6. Three collotype illustrations. Chiswick. USA: Macmillan. "Second thousand," 1917. (The 1926 reprint bears only Mathews' name on the title page, but the dust jacket lists the publisher as Elkin Mathews & Marrot. Colbeck, 1:433; Gallup, B9. BL, GK, (variant binding of first English issue with top edge tinted red), JGN ('second thousand').

1915.23   FREDERICK ARTHUR [Frederick Arthur Heygate Lambert]. *Unseen Horizons.* (P). Oct. 3/6. Clowes. BL, JGN.

1915.24   C[ICELY] FOX SMITH. *The Naval Crown: Ballads and Songs of the War.* VC31. Oct. Wrappers, 1/–. Cloth, 1/6. Clowes. *MBP IV,* 1920; Reilly, p. 296. BL, CU-A.

1915.25   *Catholic Anthology, 1914–1915.* Ed. Ezra Pound. Nov. 500. 3/6. Cover design by D[orothy] S[hakespear]. Chiswick. Gallup, B10. CtY, NjP, NN, TxU.

1915.26   ALVIN LANGDON COBURN. *Moor Park, Rickmansworth: A Series of Photographs.* Intro. by Lady Ebury. Nov. 2,000. 5/–. Chiswick. BL.

1915.27   MAUDE GOLDRING. *Charlotte Bronte the Woman: A Study.* Dec. 2/6. Clowes. BL.

1915.28   ROBERT [MALISE BOWYER] NICHOLS. *Invocation: War Poems & Others.* Dec. Wrappers, 1/–. Cloth, 2/6. Brendon. Colbeck, 2:611; Gawsworth, p. 118; Reilly, p. 236. BL, JGN.

1915.29   ROSALINE REEVE. *Armageddon.* [1914]. (P). Dec. 1/6. Clowes.

1916.1   GEORGETTE AGNEW. *Sonnets.* SAV10. Jan. 1/–. Clowes. Reilly, p. 37. BL, MH.

1916.2   E[DWARD] H. VISIAK [E. H. Physick]. *The Battle Fiends.* (P). SAT. Jan. 1/–. Brendon. BL, JGN.

1916.3   [ROBERT] LAURENCE BINYON. *The Anvil.* (P). Feb. Wrappers, 1/–. "Fine paper edition" in cloth, 2/6. Brendon. "Second thousand," 1917, 1/–. Colbeck, 1:57. BL, GK, JGN.

1916.4   PEGGY WEBLING. *A Sketch of John Ruskin.* Feb. 1/–. Silverpoint drawing of Ruskin by Ethel Webling.

1916.5   WILFRID WILSON GIBSON. *Stonefolds.* (D). Feb. "Second edition" of *The Stonefolds* and *On the Threshold,* which were first published in June and July 1907 by the Samurai Press. 1,000. 2/6. Clowes. *MBP IV*, 797. BL, CU-A. JGN.

1916.6 WILFRID WILSON GIBSON. *Friends*. (P). April. Wrappers, 1/–. Cloth, 1/6. Clowes. "Third thousand," 1917, 1/–. Colbeck, 1:288; Gawsworth, p. 84; *MBP IV*, 792; Reilly, p. 139. BL, CU-A. JGN.

1916.7 MAURICE HEWLETT. *Gai Saber: Tales and Songs*. May. 1,000. 4/6. Chiswick. USA: G. P. Putnam's Sons, 250. *BMA III*, p. 29, item 41; Colbeck, 1:374; *MBP IV*, 984; Reilly, p. 168. BL, CU-A. JGN.

1916.8 HELEN KEY. *Broken Music*. (P). VC32. April. 1/–. Brendon. Reilly, p. 187. BL, JGN.

1916.9 WALTER HULL. *Poems of Fantasy*. VC33. May. 1/–. Clowes. BL, JGN.

1916.10 F[RANCIS] HOPKINSON SMITH. *Outdoor Sketching*. [1915]. (Pr). May. 4/6. Colored illustrations by the author. Scribner Press (New York). BL.

1916.11 J. H[OWARD] STABLES. *The Sorrow That Whistled*. [1915]. (P). June. 1/–. Brendon. BL.

1916.12 TAURUS. *The Dawn of Sacrifice*. (D). June. 2/6. Clowes. BL.

1916.13 STANHOPE BAYLEY. *Modulations and A Spray of Olive*. VC34. July. Wrappers, 1/–. Cloth, 1/6. Clowes. BL.

1916.14 JEAN DE BOSSCHERE. *Twelve Occupations*. French text with twelve designs by the author and an English translation by Ezra Pound. Sept. 1/6. Special copies colored by the author, signed and numbered, 50, 21/–. Brendon. Gallup, B12a and b. BL, Cty.

1916.15 DRUSILLA MARY CHILD. *Every Day Poems*. VC35. Sept. 1/–. Clowes. *MBP IV*, 366. BL, CU-A.

1916.16 EZRA POUND. *Lustra of Ezra Pound*. Sept. First impression. 200 numbered copies. 5/–. Second impression (abridged), Oct., 800, 5/–. Frontispiece portrait of the author in photogravure. Clowes. Remaindered copies of first trade ed. bound up ca. 1935 with lettering on back in blind rather than in blue as in first trade ed. binding. Gallup, A11a, A11b. BL, JGN: remaindered issue.

1916.17 ROWLAND THIRLMERE [John Walker]. *Polyclitus and Other Poems*. Sept. 1/–. W. Holmes, Ulverston, Lancs. *MBP IV*, 2052; Reilly, p. 324. BL, CU- A.

1916.18 J. C. CHURT [J. C. Cohen]. *Rhythmic Waves*. (P). Oct. Wrappers, 1/–. Cloth, 2/6. Clowes. *MBP IV*, 376.BL, CU-A, JGN.

1916.19 THE ROMANY RAWNY [Betty Gillington]. *Gypsies of the Heath*. Oct. 5/–. Illustrated with photographs by Fred Shaw and John L. Gillington. Clowes. BL, JGN (late binding with Mathews & Marrot device on spine).

1916.20 ALEXANDER ROBERTSON. *Comrades*. (P). VC36. Oct. 1,000. Wrappers, 1/3. Cloth, 2/–. Clowes. "Second edition," Dec. 1916, 1,000, 1/3.

Frontispiece photograph of the author. Clowes. "Third edition," 5 Oct. 1918, 1,000, 1/3. *MBP IV*, 1740; Reilly, p. 276. BL, CU-A.

1916.21 C[ICELY] FOX SMITH. *Fighting Men*. VC37. Oct. Wrappers, 1/-. Cloth, 1/6. Clowes. *MBP IV*, 1918. BL, CU-A.

1916.22 LORD DUNSANY [Edward John Moreton Drax Plunkett]. *Tales of Wonder*. Oct. 5/-. Illus. by S. H. Sime. Brendon. "Second thousand," 1917. *BMA I*, 91; Colbeck, 1:237. BL.

1916.23 EDGAR M. BIRNSTINGL. *Destur Mobed and Other Stories*. Dec. 1,000. 5/-. Chiswick. BL.

1916.24 LIONEL JOHNSON. *The Religious Poems of Lionel Johnson*. Ed. George F. Engelbach; preface by Wilfrid Meynell. Dec. 750 for England; 500 for USA. 2/6. Large paper issue, 310, 7/6. Also a unique publisher's copy of large paper issue printed partly on thick paper and partly on thin. See *FEC*, p. 90. Chiswick. Jointly published in England with Burns & Oates. USA: Macmillan. Colbeck, 1:433; Danielson. BL, GK, JGN.

1917.1 A. YUSEF ALI. *Mestrovic and Serbian Sculpture*. [1916]. VC38. Jan. 1/-. BL.

1917.2 CLAUDE HOUGHTON [Claude H. Oldfield]. *The Phantom Host and Other Verses*. VC39. March. 1/-. Clowes. BL, GK, JGN.

1917.3 FRANCIS MAITLAND. *Poems*. VC40. April. 1/-. Clowes. BL.

1917.4 F[REDERICK] C[HARLES] OWLETT. *Kultur and Anarchy*. (P). Intro. by A. St. John Adcock. April. 2/6. Frontispiece by Edmund J. Sullivan. Clowes. BL.

1917.5 EVANGELINE RYVES. *Running Fires: Plays and Poems*. May. 2/6. Clowes. BL.

1917.6 RONALD LEWIS CARTON. *Steel and Flowers*. (P). VC41. June. 1/-. Clowes. *MBP IV*, 333. BL, CU-A.

1917.7 *Nelson's Last Diary*. Intro. and notes by Gilbert Hudson. June. 2/6. Clowes. "Star leaf" containing the missing portion of Nelson's diary printed and distributed gratis for 1d. stamp, Sep. 1917. "Cheaper edition," March 1918, 2/-. BL.

1917.8 F[RANCIS] P. B. O[SMASTON]. *The Call of Roll: A Poem*. June. 2/6.

1917.9 JOAN THOMPSON ['E. Herrick']. *Waifs*. VC42. June. 1/-. Clowes. *MBP IV*, 2067. BL, CU-A.

1917.10 H[UGH] G. LANG. *Simple Lyrics*. SAV11. July. 1/-. Clowes. "Second thousand," 1917. BL.

1917.11 E[RNEST] ARMINE WODEHOUSE. *On Leave: Poems and Sonnets*. Foreword by Sir Arthur Quiller-Couch. VC43. Clowes. "Second edition," Oct. 1917, *MBP IV*, 2276, BL, CU-A.

1917.12 THOMAS GORDON HAKE. *Parables and Tales*. Preface by the author's son, Thomas Hake. Aug. 5/-. Nine illus. by Thomas Hughes. Dalziel Bros., Camden Press (original 1st ed. material only). A reissue of the first edition published by Chapman and Hall in 1872, consisting of a new half title, title page, and son's preface followed by the half title, title page, and text and illustrations of the first edition. Colbeck, 1:335; Fredeman, 48.6. BL.

1917.13 C[ICELY] FOX SMITH. *Small Craft*. (P). Oct. 3/–. Clowes. *MBP IV*, 1921. BL, CU-A, JGN.

1917.14 ALYMER STRONG. *A Human Voice: Poems*. Oct. 5/–. Clowes. BL.

1917.15 LIONEL JOHNSON. "By the Statue of King Charles I. at Charing Cross." A Broadside. Oct.? 1/–. Le Soeur's equestrian statue in brass, cast in 1633, reproduced from an old print. OU.

1917.16 JOHN DRINKWATER. *Prose Papers*. Nov. 6/–. Brendon. "Second edition," 1919, 7/6. Ashley, 2:61; *BMA I*, 74; Colbeck, 1:227. BL, JGN.

1917.17 DOROTHY GRENSIDE. *Open Eyes*. (P). Nov. 500. 2/6. Illus. by Bessie Fyfe. Chiswick. *MBP IV*, 882. BL, CU-A.

1917.18 HELEN TAYLOR. *Fancy Free: First Book of Lyrics*. [1918]. VC44. Dec. 1/3. Clowes. BL.

1918.1 [ROBERT] LAURENCE BINYON. *The Cause: Poems of the War*. Feb. 5/–. H. O. Houghton at the Riverside Press (Cambridge, Mass.). USA: Houghton, Mifflin. Colbeck, 1:57. IU.

1918.2 DONALD H. LEA. *Stand-Down!* [1917]. (P). Mar. 2/–. Clowes. "Cheaper edition." BL.

1918.3 F. W. FREEMAN [Victor Chard]. *The Age of Gold*. (P). April. 1/3. De La More Press. BL.

1918.4 C[HARLES] NEVILLE BRAND. *The House of Time and Other Poems*. SAT. June. 1/3. Brendon. BL.

1918.5 HERBERT E[DWARD] PALMER. *Two Fishers and Other Poems*. July. 500. 1/3. Riverside. Gawsworthy, p. 141; Reilly, p. 248. BL, JGN.

1918.6 LEONARD [CHARLES] VAN NOPPEN. *The Challenge: War Chants of the Allies*. Aug. 2/–. Riverside. "Second edition," June 1919. Wrappers, 3/6. Cloth, 5/–. BL, JGN.

1918.7 FREDERICK MILLS. *Labour and Economics*. Sept. 1/–. De La More Press. BL, IN, NN.

1918.8 ALEXANDER ROBERTSON. *Last Poems*. VC45. Sept. 500. 1/3. Chiswick. *MBP IV*, 1741; Reilly, p. 276. BL, CU-A, MB.

1918.9 [ROBERT] LAURENCE BINYON. *The New World: Poems*. Oct. Wrappers, 2/–. Cloth, 3/–. Brendon. "Second edition," 1919. Colbeck, 1:57. BL, JGN, WU.

1918.10 F[REDERIC] W. MOORMAN. *Songs of the Ridings*. Oct. 1,000. Wrappers, 2/–. Cloth, 3/–. Riverside. "Second edition," Dec. 1918, 1,000. "Third edition," June 1919, 1,000. Wrappers, 2/–, Cloth, 3/–. *MBP IV*, 1441. BL, CU-A.

1918.11 F[REDERIC] W. D. BENDALL. *Front Line Lyrics*. Nov. Wrappers, 2/–. Cloth, 2/6. Riverside. *MBP IV*, 147. BL, CU-A.

1918.12 H[UGH] G. LANG. *Simple Nature Songs*. Nov. 1/6. Lewes Press. BL.

1918.13 ALICIA SHERIDAN. *The Pedlar's Way*. (P). Dec. 1/6. Brendon. *MBP IV*, 1872. BL, CU-A.

1918.14 ERNEST E. WILD. *The Lamp of Destiny and Other Poems: Being Some Indiscretions of the Long Vacation*. [1919]. Dec. Wrappers, 2/6. Cloth, 3/6. Brendon. BL, JGN.

1919.1 "FIREFLY." *Sunshine & Shadow: A Little Book of Fancies*. [1918]. Jan. 1/3. Riverside. BL.

1919.2 AGNES GROZIER HERBERTSON. *The Quiet Heart and Other Poems*. Jan. 2/6. Riverside. BL.

1919.3 WILLIAM GERARD. *Dramatic Vistas*. (P). March. 3/6. Riverside. *MBP IV*, 780. BL, CU-A, JGN.

1919.4 R[ODOLPHE] L. MÉGROZ. *Personal Poems*. March. 3/6. Pelican Press. Reilly, p. 22. BL, JGN.

1919.5 CECIL BARBER. *Sandbag Ballads and Snow-Water Songs*. April. 2/6. Riverside. BL.

1919.6 E[DWARD] H. VIZIAK [E. H. Physick]. *Brief Poems*. April. 1/6. BL.

1919.7 DOROTHY GRENSIDE. *Green Ways*. (P). May. 3/6. Riverside. BL.

1919.8 RAYMOND HEYWOOD. *The Greater Love: Poems of Remembrance*. May. Wrappers, 1/6. Boards, 2/6. Riverside. BL.

1919.9 RICHARD ALDINGTON. *Images of Desire*. (P). May. 2/6. Also a special issue signed and numbered. Riverside. Kershaw, 7 and 8; Reilly, p. 39. BL, JGN.

1919.10 C[ICELY] FOX SMITH. *Songs & Chanties, 1914–1916*. June. 6/–. Title vignette and frontispiece by Phil W. Smith. Clowes. Reilly, p. 296. BL, JGN.

1919.11 [ROBERT] LAURENCE BINYON. *The Four Years: War Poems Collected and Newly Augmented*. June. 7/6. Frontispiece portrait of the author from an engraving by William Strang. Brendon. "Second thousand," late 1919, 7/6. With gilt top, 8/6. Colbeck, 1:57. BL, JGN, MB, WU.

1919.12 CLOUDESLEY BRERETON. *Mystica et Lyrica*. (P). Oct. 6/–. Cover design by T. Sturge Moore. Riverside. "Second edition," 1919. Reilly, p. 66. BL, JGN.

1919.13 F. NOEL BYRON. *Athenian Days*. (P). Oct. Wrappers, 1/6. Cloth, 2/6. Riverside. BL, JGN.

1919.14 W. ROBERT HALL. *The Heart of a Mystic: Poems*. Oct. Wrappers, 2/6. Cloth, 3/6. Riverside. BL.

1919.15 LORD DUNSANY [Edward John Moreton Drax Plunkett]. *Unhappy Far-Off Things*. (F). Nov. 5/–. Brendon. *BMA I*, 96; Colbeck, 1:237. BL, JGN.

1919.16 M. C. URCH. *The City of Dreams*. (F). Nov. 5/–. Frontispiece and illus. by M. M. Gell. Riverside. BL, JGN.

1919.17 [JAMES] GRIFFYTH FAIRFAX. *Carmina Rapta: Being Verse Translations*. Nov. Wrappers, 2/6. Cloth, 3/6. Riverside. BL.

1919.18 LORD DUNSANY [Edward John Moreton Drax Plunkett]. *The Book of Wonder: A Chronicle of Little Adventures at the Edge of the World*. Nov. Second edition of a book first published by Heinemann in 1912. 1,000. 7/6. Illus. by S. H. Sime. Brendon. "Third thousand," Sept. 1920. Colbeck, 1:237. JGN.

1919.19 ALICE LAW. *Cupid and Psyche and Other Poems*. Dec. 1/6. Brendon. Colbeck, 1:476. BL.

1919.20 F[REDERIC] W. MOORMAN. *Plays of the Ridings*. Dec. 1,000. Wrappers, 2/6. Cloth, 3/6. Riverside. Second printing, Sept. 1920, 1,000. Wrappers, 2/6. Cloth, 3/6. BL.

1919.21 "RED BAND." *A Prisoner of Pentonville*. (P). Dec. Wrappers, 2/6. Cloth, 3/6. USA: G. P. Putnam's Sons. JGN.

1920.1 STANLEY CASSON. *Hellenic Studies*. (Pr). Jan. 6/–. Riverside. BL, NUC.

1920.2 GEORGINA DE B[ELLASIS] BOWEN COLTHURST. *It Is for Man to Choose*. (P). Jan. 1/6. Grey & Co., Ltd., Cork. BL.

1920.3 PERCY ADDLESHAW. *Last Verses*. With a Memoir by Arundel Osborne and Portrait. April. 2/6. Dunedin Press, Edinburgh. Colbeck, 1:4. BL.

1920.4 DAN MCKENZIE. *Pride o'Raploch and Other Poems*. April. Wrappers, 3/6. Cloth, 4/–. Dunedin Press, Edinburgh. BL.

1920.5 VERNON [OLDFIELD] BARTLETT. *Songs of the Winds and Seas*. May. 3/6. Riverside. Reilly, p. 50. BL.

1920.6 DAVID BOARDMAN JONES. *Amethysts: A Series of Social and Ethical Essays*. May. 7/6. Mayflower. BL.

1920.7 EDEN PHILLPOTTS. *As the Wind Blows*. (P). May. 1,000. 5/–. Riverside. USA: Macmillan. Hinton, p. 94; Reilly, p. 253. BL, JGN.

1920.8 CLAUDINE CURREY. *Love o'London*. (P). May. 1/3. Riverside. BL.

1920.9 EZRA POUND. *Umbra: The Early Poems of Ezra Pound*. (Includes poems by T. E. Hulme.) May. 1,000. 8/–. Edition de luxe numbered and signed by the author, 100, 25/–. Presentation copies, at least 4 extra copies of the deluxe issue lettered A through D; one of these 4 copies is in the Lilly Library, Indiana University. Riverside. Gallup, A20a, A20b. BL (edition de luxe no. 95), JGN.

1920.10 J[OHN] H[ELLAS] F[INNIE] McEWEN. *Poems*. June. 3/6. Mayflower. Reilly, p. 210. BL.

1920.11 R[OBERT] GORDON-CANNING. *Flashlights from Afar*. (P and Pr). Aug. 5/–. Riverside. BL.

1920.12 JOHN VAUGHAN. *The Music of Wild Flowers*. (Pr). Aug. 8/6. Riverside. BL.

1920.13 WILLOUGHBY WEAVING. *Algazel: A Tragedy*. Aug. 5/–. Riverside. BL.

1920.14 F[REDERIC] W. MOORMAN. *Tales of the Ridings*. With Memoir and Portrait. Sept. Wrappers, 2/6. Cloth, 3/6. Riverside. "Third thousand," 1921. BL, JGN.

1920.15 HERBERT EDWARD PALMER. *Two Foemen and Other Poems*. Sept. 550. 2/6. Mayflower. Gawsworth, p. 141; Reilly, p. 248. BL.

1920.16 M[AUD] BARTLEET. *Miniatures in French Frames*. (P). Oct. Wrappers, 2/–. Cloth, 3/–. Mayflower. BL.

1920.17 CHARLES WHITBY. *The Rising Tide and Other Poems*. Oct. 5/–. Riverside. Reilly, p. 335. BL, GK.

1920.18 E[RIC] STUART MONRO. *Gems of the Poor and Other Poems*. Oct. Wrappers, 2/–. Cloth, 3/–. Mayflower. BL.

1920.19 EVAN MORGAN. *A Sequence of Seven Sonnets*. Oct. 2/6. Mayflower. BL.

1920.20 MARTIN BIRNBAUM. *Oscar Wilde: Fragments and Memories*. Nov. 750. 7/6. Edition de luxe, 50. Frontispiece portrait of Wilde from life by James Edward Kelly. Chiswick. BL, JGN.

1920.21 F[REDERIC] W. MOORMAN. *More Tales of the Ridings*. Nov. 1,000. Wrappers, 2/6. Cloth, 3/6. Riverside. BL.

1920.22 C[ICELY] FOX SMITH. *Ships and Folks*. (P). Nov. 6/–. Riverside. BL.

1920.23 JOHN WESTROPPE. *Poems*. Nov. 3/6. Mayflower. BL.

1920.24 [ROBERT] LAURENCE BINYON. *The Secret: Sixty Poems*. Dec. 6/–. Riverside. Colbeck, 1:57; Reilly, p. 56. BL, GK, JGN, MB, WU.

1920.25 ARTHUR SYMONS. *Charles Baudelaire: A Study*. Dec. 15/–. Edition de luxe printed on handmade paper, numbered and signed by the author, 100. Mayflower. *BMA I*, 258, 259, BL, GK.

1920.26 JOHN TODHUNTER. *Essays by the Late John Todhunter*. Foreword by Standish O'Grady. Dec. 8/6. Riverside. BL, JGN.

1920.27 L[EONARD] C. BROMLEY. *The Picture and Other Poems*. Dec. 5/–. Riverside. BL. JGN.

1921.1 NANCY CUNARD. *Outlaws*. (P). Jan. 5/–. Mayflower. Reilly, p. 101. BL. JGN.

1921.2 DOROTHY ROBERTS. *The Child Dancer and Other Poems*. Feb. 2/6. Mayflower. BL. JGN.

1921.3 HERBERT EDWARD PALMER. *Two Minstrels*. (P). March. 500. Wrappers, 2/–. Cloth, 3/–. Mayflower. Gawsworth, p. 142. BL. JGN.

1921.4 H[ALBERT] J. BOYD. *Verses & Ballads of North and South*. April. 3/6. Riverside. BL.

1921.5 STANLEY CASSON. *Rupert Brooke and Skyros*. May. 6/–. Special issue, 21/–. Six woodcut illus. by Phyllis Gardner. Riverside. BL.

1921.6 LIONEL JOHNSON. *Reviews & Critical Papers*. Ed. with an intro. by Robert Shafer. June. 6/–. Riverside. USA: E. P. Dutton. Colbeck, 1:433. BL. GK, WU.

1921.7 MARY DEANE. *A Book of Verse*. June. 3/6. Riverside. BL.

1921.8 PETRONELLA O'DONNELL. *The Summer Book of Love and Rose Poems*. June. 100. 3/6. Mayflower. BL.

1921.9 WALTER RAY [Bolton King]. *Poems of Yesterday and Today*. July. 3/6. Riverside. BL.

1921.10 DANFORD BARNEY. *In the Comet's Hair*. (P). July. 5/–. Riverside. BL.

1921.11 F[REDERIC] W. MOORMAN. *Tales, Songs & Plays of the Ridings*. Moorman's collected dialect works. In addition to a memoir which is herein published for the first time, the book contains sheets (including title pages) of the four volumes previously published separately, viz., *Tales; More Tales of the Ridings; Songs* ("third thousand"); and *Plays* ("second thousand"). NNC, WU.

1921.12 HALBERT [J.]. BOYD. *Men and Marvels*. (F). Oct. 7/–. Riverside. BL.

1921.13 YONE NOGUCHI. *Selected Poems of Yone Noguchi*. Oct. 12/6. Special issue autographed by the author, 50, 15/–. USA: The Four Seas Co., Boston. BL.

1921.14 MILLICENT WEDMORE. *In Many Keys*. (P). Oct. 3/6. Mayflower. Reilly, p. 333. BL.

1921.15 ALICE E. MASSEY-BERESFORD. *An Invasion of Fairyland*. (P). Oct. 7/6. Illus. in color by Jennie McConnell. De La More Press. BL.

1921.16 DANIEL CORKERY. *I Bhreasail: A Book of Lyrics*. Oct. 5/–. Talbot Press (Dublin). BL, WU.

1921.17 WILLIAM GERARD. *The King of Thule: A Phantasy*. (D). Oct. 5/–. Mayflower. BL, JGN.

1921.18 C[ICELY] FOX SMITH. *Rovings: Sea Songs and Ballads*. Oct. 6/–. Illus. by Phil W. Smith. Riverside. BL, JGN.

1922.1 CYNTHIA DAVRIL. *Poems*. March. Wrappers, 2/6. Cloth, 3/6. Mayflower. BL.

APPENDIX E

Listing of Mathews' Series with Checklist Numbers

Shilling Garland Series

Series no.	Cklist no.
1	1895.20
2	1896.5
3	1896.6
4	1896.10
5	1896.11
6	1896.20
7	1897.1
8	1897.9
9	1898.4
10	1898.12

Vigo Cabinet Series

Series no.	Cklist no.
1	1900.1
2	1900.2
3	1900.10
4	1901.2
5	1901.12
6	1902.4
7	1902.2
8	1902.3
9	1902.11
10	1902.13
11	1902.21
12	1903.6
13	1903.12
14	1903.13
15	1903.15
16	1903.19
17	1904.8
18	1904.1
19	1904.4
20	1904.5
21	1904.9
22	1904.11
23	1904.18
24	1905.6
25	1905.2
26	1905.4
27	1905.11
28	1905.9
29	1905.22
30	1905.21
31	1905.18
32	1905.23
33	1906.1
34	1908.23 1912.6
35	1908.18
36	1906.8
37	1906.9
38	1906.13
39	1906.16
40	1906.17
41	1906.18
42	1906.32
43	1907.2
44	1907.9
45	1907.17
46	1908.4
47	1908.12
48	1908.13
49	1908.17
50	1908.27
51	1908.31
52	1908.33
53	1908.26
54	1908.34
55	1909.4
56	1909.5
57	1909.9
58	1909.10
59	1909.11
60	1909.12
61	1909.18
62	1909.19
63	1909.33
64	1909.40
65	1909.39
66	1909.31
67	1909.42
68	1909.35
69	1910.11
70	1910.16
71	1910.15
72	1910.18
73	1910.25
74	1910.30
75	1910.43
76	1910.31
77	1910.35
78	1911.1
79	1911.11
80	1911.12
81	1911.13
82	1911.3
83	1911.15
84	1911.16
85	1911.18
86	1911.38
87	1911.24
88	1911.29
89	1911.26
90	1911.33
91	1911.27
92	1911.39
93	1911.28
94	1911.34

Vigo Cabinet Series

Series no.	Cklist no.
95	1911.35
96	1911.40
97	1912.4
98	1912.12
99	1912.5
100	1912.17
1(n.s.)	1912.31
2	1912.21
3	1912.23
4	1912.37
5	1913.1
6	1912.34
7	1913.4
8	1913.5
9	1913.14
10	1913.17
11	1913.21
12	1913.28
13	1913.29
14	1914.2
15	1913.37
16	1914.3
17	1914.4
18	1914.5
19	1914.6
20	1914.8
21	1914.13
22	1914.14
23	1914.18
24	1914.7
25	1914.31
26	1915.2
27	1914.29
28	1915.6
29	1915.7
30	1915.12
31	1915.24
32	1916.8
33	1916.9
34	1916.13
35	1916.15
36	1916.20
37	1916.21
38	1917.1
39	1917.2
40	1917.3
41	1917.6
42	1917.9
43	1917.11
44	1917.18
45	1918.8

Satchel Series

Title	Cklist no.
Views of Christopher	1904.7
London Etchings	1904.13
Mainsail Haul	1905.10
Admissions & Asides	1905.24
The Fancy	1905.25
Paper Pellets	1906.21
Shadow Show	1907.18
Vict. & Other Papers	1908.22
Songs of . . . Fighting	1908.25
Airy Nothings	1909.23
Vision	1909.41
Buccaneer Ballads	1910.7
Flints & Flashes	1911.5
Phantom Ship	1912.22
Pages Assembled	1913.3
Battle Fiends	1916.2
House of Time	1918.4

Savile Series

Series no.	Cklist no.
1	1909.36
2	1912.19
3	1913.16
4	1913.19
5	1913.26
6	1913.27
7	1913.30
8	1913.33
9	1914.12
10	1916.1

Burlington Series

Series no.	Cklist no.
1	1911.17
2	1911.30
3	1912.13
4	1912.25

NOTES

The following abbreviations are used for manuscript sources:

Miss Nest Elkin Mathews	Hayes, nr. Bromley, Kent, England
Peter Newbolt	Cley, nr. Holt, Norfolk, England
Eric and Joan Stevens	London, England
Michael Yeats	Michael B. Yeats, Dalkey, Co. Dublin, Ireland

CHAPTER ONE. ELKIN MATHEWS, HIS LIFE AND CAREER

1. "A Chat with Mr. Elkin Mathews," *Publisher and Bookseller* 2 (24 Feb. 1906): 417. Details of Elkin Mathews' life have been derived from various legal records and from conversations with his daughter, Miss Nest Elkin Mathews; his grandniece, Miss Rosamond Griffin; and letters from his nephew, Cuthbert Mathews.

2. "A Chat," 418.

3. "About Mr. Elkin Mathews," *St. James's Budget* (Literary Supplement) 29 (1894): 26. In one of two corrected drafts of his reminiscences (c. 1909). EMA, Mathews wrote: "I had settled down in the native city of Sir Thomas Bodley but it was no good for ambition's ladder. I had already formed the fixed idea of joining the publishing ranks and my aim was to become the Edward Moxon of my time."

4. "Books and the Man. No. 5—Mr. Elkin Mathews," *Bookman's Journal and Print Collector* 1 (1920): 245.

5. P. H. Muir, *Minding My Own Business: An Autobiography* (London: Chatto and Windus, 1956), 1–2. Although Muir states that Mathews abandoned the use of "C. Elkin Mathews" when he returned to London, this imprint appears on the first Bodley Head book, Le Gallienne's *Volumes in Folio*, which was published in London in March 1889.

6. "A Chat," 418.

7. Ernest Rhys, *Wales England Wed* (London: J. M. Dent, 1940), 152. For a detailed account of the formation of the partnership and the establishment of the Bodley Head, see chapter 1 in my *Early Nineties: A View from the Bodley Head* (Cambridge: Harvard UP, 1971).

8. See Appendix A, "Elkin Mathews and the Daniel Press."

9. Mathews' reminiscences, EMA.

10. Ibid.

11. See "Belles-Lettres to Sell," ch. 3 in Nelson, *Early Nineties*; R. D. Brown, "The Bodley Head Press: Some Bibliographical Extrapolations," *PBSA* 61 (1967): 39–50.

12. Nikolaus Pevsner, *The Buildings of England*, 3 vols. (Harmondsworth: Penguin, 1951), 3:25; W. B. Yeats, *Autobiographies* (London: Macmillan, 1961), 113.

13. Pevsner, *Buildings*, 25.

14. Ian Fletcher, "Bedford Park: Aesthete's Elysium?" in *Romantic Mythologies*, ed. Ian Fletcher (London: Routledge and Kegan Paul, 1967), 170.

15. Mathews' reminiscences, EMA. Another important literary adviser to Mathews was his brother Thomas George, who in 1907 moved to Great Missenden, Bucks., on the same commuter railway line as Chorleywood, Mathews' home after 1903. Consequently, the brothers often traveled together on the same train on their daily trips to the city. According to Thomas George's son, Cuthbert, "the two brothers were very close and consulted one another on literary matters. I think Uncle Charlie placed considerable value on my father's opinions." Cuthbert Mathews to the author, 14 Nov. 1980.

16. "In Hoc Signo: Publishers' Devices, No. 12—Mr. Elkin Mathews," *Bookman's Journal and Print Collector* 2 (1920): 53.

17. T. and D. C. Sturge Moore, *Works and Days: From the Journal of Michael Field* (London: John Murray, 1933), 184. In 1892 Mathews had published a book of poems, *Sight and Song*, and a play, *Stephania*, by "Michael Field," the pen name for Katherine Harris Bradley and Edith Emma Cooper, and in November 1893 published another play, *A Question of Memory*.

18. Fletcher, "Bedford Park," 191.

19. In my possession. No fisherman, Mathews collected Walton's books and other relics which, as an antiquarian, he highly prized.

20. *Publishers' Circular* no. 1415 (1893): 164; *Fishing Gazette* n.s. 17 (1893): 147.

21. J. Lewis May, *The Path through the Wood* (New York: Dial Press, 1931), 142.

22. *My World as in My Time: Memoirs of Sir Henry Newbolt, 1862-1932* (London: Faber and Faber, 1932), 211.

23. See also Beardsley's caricature of Mathews as a round-faced, wizened, and bespectacled pierrot in his famous design for the prospectus for the *Yellow Book*, in Brian Read, *Aubrey Beardsley* (New York: Viking, 1967), pl. 343.

24. Later, Mathews characterized Yeats's light, bantering style of letter-writing as "charming persiflage." Mathews to John Butler Yeats, 29 Aug. 1918, quoted in William M. Murphy, *Prodigal Father: The Life of John Butler Yeats (1839-1922)* (Ithaca: Cornell UP, 1978), 482.

25. See, for example, du Maurier's "Aesthetic Love in a Cottage," *Punch* 76 (1879): 78. Being aesthetic types, perhaps, with something of the pre-Raphaelite "stunner" about them, and conveniently at hand, Minnie and Alice Mathews were especially useful to John Butler Yeats during this time when the painter had concluded that "using of models is a great discovery." See Letter XIII, 7 Dec. 1895. *Letters from Bedford Park: A Selection from the Correspondence (1890-1901) of John Butler Yeats*, ed. with introduction and notes by William M. Murphy (Dublin: Cuala Press, 1972), 17. Yeats's letters often mention the sisters as serving such a purpose while purveying the latest neighborhood gossip. For instance, on one occasion Alice sat for a sketch and, the elder Yeats wrote Lily, told all about the feud between Henry Hinkson,

Katharine Tynan's husband, and W. B. Yeats. See Murphy, *Prodigal Father*, 191. On another occasion, the painter wrote, "In the morning Minnie Mathews came in and sat for me—but a threatened faint interrupted matters for a time." Letter xv, 29 Dec. 1895, *Letters from Bedford Park*, 20.

26. Letter xix, 26 Jan. 1896, *Letters from Bedford Park*, 24.

27. Letter xxi, [early March, 1896], *Letters from Bedford Park*, 26-27.

28. Letter xxii, 20 Mar. 1896, *Letters from Bedford Park*, 27-28. L. Fairfax Muckley had done the illustrations for R. D. Blackmore's *Fringilla; or, Some Tales in Verse*, published by Mathews in 1895. Glimpses of the Mathewses are also provided by Lily Yeats's diary, which, for example, mentions them as having been present at 3 Blenheim Road on the evening of 3 August 1895 when "Willy [William Butler Yeats] read out his new story. They all sat with their eyes fixed on him and never blinked the whole time." Diary of Lily Yeats, 1 Aug. 1895–26 June 1896, in the possession of Michael Yeats, entry for 4 Aug. 1895. In addition to references to the Mathews sisters Minnie and Alice, several to another sister, Edith, suggest that she was in a constant "state of astonishment" (entry for 1 Sept. 1894). For instance, the entry for 7 August 1895 notes, "Edith Mathews came in and was so amazingly thick-headed and showed such astonishment at every word I said, that I could stand it no longer and knocked for Minnie and Alice, who had the effect of slightly diluting Edith." I thank Michael Yeats for permission to quote from Lily's diary and Professor William M. Murphy for transcribing the diary for me.

29. That Edward Shelley, the young clerk who had gone to work for Mathews at the age of sixteen, was spying for Lane is revealed in a letter from Shelley to Lane, 10 Sept. 1890, in the Lane Papers, Texas. According to Ian Fletcher, who has examined the correspondence, a series of letters from Shelley to Lane reveal that every week the clerk "sent Lane an account of the shop takings, reported comings and goings to the shop and dwelt on Mathew's [*sic*] descents into the cellar to stock take." "Introduction" to the Chadwyck-Healey microfilm of the Elkin Mathews Archive, Reading University. Shelley, who because of his relations with Wilde had become a figure of amusement to his fellow clerks, was dismissed by Mathews in the summer of 1893. The agreement for publishing *Mr. W.H.* was signed on 3 August 1893. Ironically, when the dissolution of the partnership was imminent, Wilde wrote Lane, "Let Mr. Mathews have 'Mr. W.H,'" proposing that Lane publish the less offensive plays. Horst Schroeder, *Oscar Wilde, "The Portrait of Mr. W.H.": Its Composition, Publication, and Reception* (Braunschweig: Technische Universität Carolo-Wilhelmina zu Braunschweig, 1984).

30. Wilde in *The Importance of Being Earnest* originally planned to call Merriman (Jack's country butler) "Mathews" to show his displeasure with his publisher—as he had also done by calling Algy's butler "Lane." That he changed "Mathews" to "Merriman" but allowed "Lane" to stand suggests that Wilde's animosity toward Mathews had subsided.

30. Mathews to Dr. Brushfield, 7 Feb. 1895, EMA. Even after the dissolution

of the partnership Lane continued to bedevil Mathews. For instance, Lane, having fired Aubrey Beardsley as art editor of the *Yellow Book* owing to the public's erroneous view that the artist was a close associate of the recently imprisoned Wilde, refused to allow anything of Beardsley's—including his drawing entitled "Black Coffee"—to appear in volume 5 of the *Yellow Book*, (April 1895). Consequently, Beardsley offered the drawing to Mathews for use in Walt Ruding's novel *An Evil Motherhood*. Lane, however, objected. Referring to the row, Beardsley in a letter to the publisher Leonard Smithers wrote: "The dreadful thing was a blaze up with Lane-cum-Mathews, and a drawing to be produced at the sword's point"—a reference to the fact that the artist, given Lane's action, had to produce a new frontispiece for Mathews' publication. Beardsley to Smithers, c. 10 Nov. 1895, in *The Letters of Aubrey Beardsley*, ed. Henry Maas et al. (London: Cassell, 1971).

31. "Literary Gossip," *Athenaeum* no. 3486 (1894): 225. For details of the dissolution of the partnership, see Nelson, *Early Nineties*, ch. 8, "The Breakup."

32. Mathews to Brushfield, 7 Feb. 1895. EMA; "About Mr. Elkin Mathews," *St. James's Budget* (Literary Supplement) 29 (1894): 26. Although novels were a minor part of what Mathews called belles lettres, he did publish a number of them, including Walt Ruding's *An Evil Motherhood: An Impressionist Novel* (with the famous Beardsley frontispieces) and A.E.W. Mason's *A Romance of Wastdale*.

33. Mathews probably met his wife-to-be through her close friend Lydia Bacon King, who had married Mathews' brother Thomas George in 1890.

34. Murphy, *Prodigal Father*, 589, n. 66.

35. Lily Yeats' remark occurred in a letter she wrote to her father after hearing of Mathews' death in 1921. Referring to a statement in a London newspaper to the effect that Mathews would be missed in the publishing world, Lily wrote: "We know he will—I am sorry—I liked the cross little man—I always went in to his shop and saw him when in London. He was happy and his marriage a success." Lily Yeats to John Butler Yeats, 5 Dec. 1921, NLI. That Mathews cultivated unusually good relations with his authors is attested to by Lord Dunsany, who in a letter to Edith Elkin Mathews wrote that relations between him and Mathews were "always such that I used to forget with him the natural antagonism that the business of publishing necessitates except in rare cases, between author and publisher." Letter dated 21 Jan. 1922, EMA. Another of Mathews' authors, Alfred Perceval Graves, also spoke of Mathews as one "who won the greatest personal esteem for . . . his honourable not to say handsome treatment of all who did business with him quite apart from his charming social qualities." Graves to Edith Elkin Mathews, 10 Dec. 1921. EMA.

36. Cuthbert Mathews to the author, 14 Nov. 1980. Mathews also owned a seaside cottage, "Green Shutters," at Cley, Norfolk, where he often spent portions of the summer.

37. See an account of the Izaac Walton cabinet in Mathews' obituary in *Publishers' Circular* 115 (1921): 503, 505.

38. *Literary World* 32 (1896): 12. The spokesman for the journal was responding to the annual compilation of publications for 1895 in *Publishers' Circular*.

39. Newbolt, *My World*, 279. That the market for poetry continued to be poor is attested to by Gordon Bottomley, who wrote that his work has found praise from "the best poets and painters now working in England; but on all hands there are signs that England at large does not much want anybody's poetry in this age." Bottomley to Thomas Bird Mosher, 18 Oct. 1909, Houghton.

40. "A Chat," 418.

41. Rhys, *Wales England Wed*, 152. According to one commentator, Mathews had "gained an honoured niche for himself by his introduction of poets of the quieter, less flaring sort who might not otherwise have gained a hearing." *Bookman* 26, no. 154 (July 1904): 147.

42. Sylvia Beach, *Shakespeare and Company* (New York: Harcourt and Brace, 1959), 19.

43. May, *Path*, 175; brochure notifying customers of Mathews' move, EMA. An announcement of the shop's move also appeared in "Trade Notes and News," *Publishers' Circular* 98 (4 Jan. 1913): 2. In the same issue, there is an advertisement with a map indicating the locations of both the old and the new shop. Mathews himself drew up a draft of an essay entitled "From Vigo Street to Cork Street" (EMA), in which he (displaying his antiquarian interests) discussed the history of Vigo Street and Cork Street. In conclusion, he wrote: "Today [Cork Street] with its hotels, two ladies clubs, one of which . . . is built on the site of The Blue Posts Tavern famous in its day for a homely well-cooked English dinner and the other—the Imperial Rifle Club adjoining Mr. Elkin Mathews' new place, give an air of dignity and quiet which the writer and booklover will appreciate after the noise and traffic of some of the adjoining thoroughfares." Also see the article on Mathews' move in the *Bookman* 43, no. 255 (Dec. 1912): 140.

44. Herbert Read, *The Contrary Experience: Autobiographies* (London: Faber and Faber, 1963), 163.

45. Elkin Mathews to Lord Dunsany, 5 July 1916, Berg.

46. Laurence Binyon to Ferris Greenslet, 23 Nov. 1916, Houghton. Binyon in an earlier letter to Greenslet (19 Oct. 1916) wrote that there is no use trying to get books published in a hurry in England, "as the shortage of labour among printers and binders makes delays inevitable."

47. See Return of Fire Calls, Tuesday, 29 June 1915, in London Fire Brigade Records, Greater London Records Office.

48. Mathews to Newbolt, 9 Aug. 1917, in possession of Peter Newbolt.

49. Catherine W. Reilly's *English Poetry of the First World War: A Bibliog-*

raphy (New York: St. Martin's Press, 1978) lists some forty-one separate titles published by Mathews.

50. Bernard Bergonzi, *Heroes' Twilight: A Study of the Literature of the Great War* (London: Constable, 1965), 62.

51. Ibid., 61.

52. Robert Scholes, "Grant Richards to James Joyce," *Studies in Bibliography* 16 (1963): 139.

53. "The Spring Lists," *Bookman's Journal and Print Collector* 3 (1921): 336. Nevertheless, in 1921 Mathews published Charles Whitby's *Rising Tide and Other Poems*, the title poem a study of the travail of childbirth written in unrhymed, irregular lines in the manner of Walt Whitman.

54. Mathews was buried on Tuesday, 15 November 1921, in Chorleywood churchyard. An obituary essay appearing in *Publishers' Circular* 115 (1921): 531, emphasized Mathews' modest demeanor: "He was a man who had known great men in the past and to whom great men still came. Yet he spoke not ever in vain-glory, nor set himself beyond the man he was." The obituary compared Mathews with Charles Lamb, who "might have made such another bookseller had his lot fallen upon shopkeeping."

55. *Bookman* 61, no. 363 (Dec. 1921): 1.

56. Alfred Perceval Graves to Edith Elkin Mathews, 10 Dec. 1921, EMA; Ezra Pound to Edith Elkin Mathews, 23 Dec. 1921, EMA.

57. Edward Thomas to Gordon Bottomley, 1 July 1904, in *Letters from Edward Thomas to Gordon Bottomley*, ed. and introduced by R. George Thomas (London: Oxford UP, 1968), 58.

CHAPTER 2. PUBLISHING POETRY CHEAPLY

1. "A Chat with Mr. Elkin Mathews," *Publisher and Bookseller* 2 (24 Feb. 1906): 418.

2. Laurence Binyon to an unidentified correspondent, 22 Feb. 1916, in my possession.

3. "Mr. Murray's New Shilling Library," *Publishers' Circular* 92 (29 Jan. 1910): 122.

4. Robert Bridges to Mathews, 13 Feb. 1896, EMA.

5. Binyon to Mathews, 26 July [1895], Texas.

6. Binyon to Mathews, 31 Aug. 1895, Texas.

7. William Butler Yeats, Introduction, *Oxford Book of Modern Verse, 1892–1935* (New York: Oxford UP, 1937), xvii; also see "The Poetry of Mr. Robert Bridges," *Academy* 53 (5 Feb. 1898): 156, in which the critic speaks of Bridges' influence on "the versification of such younger writers as Mr. Stephen Phillips and Mr. Laurence Binyon." Also, in his chapter on Robert Bridges in *English Poetry in the Later Nineteenth Century*, 2nd ed., rev. (London:

Methuen, 1966), B. Ifor Evans discusses Bridges' association with R. W. Dixon and Mary Coleridge.

8. For example, J. W. Mackail in his "Poetry of Oxford," in *Lectures on Poetry* (London: Longmans, Green, 1911), 249, writes: "About fifteen years ago, a series of tiny volumes of poetry came out, in paper covers, under the name of the Shilling Garland. . . . The greater number of the authors were Oxford poets."

9. *Bookman* 13, no. 78 (March 1898): 170. The Century Guild, founded in 1882 by the architect Arthur Mackmurdo, Selwyn Image, and Herbert P. Horne, was an arts and crafts guild dedicated to the rehabilitation of the arts. To this end the Guild published the *Century Guild Hobby Horse* (1886–92) and its successor, the *Hobby Horse* (1893–94), one of the most beautiful of the late-nineteenth-century periodicals.

10. "Literary Gossip," *Athenaeum* no. 3541 (1895): 322.

11. Mathews' reminiscences, EMA.

12. *Academy* 48 (14 Sept. 1895): 203. The attribution is incorrect. The verses from "The Splendid Shilling" (1701)—a parody of Milton's poetic idiom—actually were the work of another John Philips (1676–1709), whose last name was spelled with only one *l*.

13. Binyon to Mathews, 16 Sept. [1895], Texas.

14. Mathews' reminiscences, EMA.

15. *Academy* 48 (9 Nov. 1895): 394; *Bookselling* 2 (March 1896): 144.

16. See Joe W. Kraus, *A History of Way and Williams with a Bibliography of Their Publications: 1895–1898* (Philadelphia: MacManus, 1984), 11–12.

17. Binyon to Mathews, 19 Dec. [1895], Texas.

18. *Publishers' Circular* 64 (18 Jan. 1896): 83.

19. *Sketch* 13 (5 Feb. 1896): 53.

20. *Bookselling* 2 (March 1896): 144.

21. *Review of Reviews* 13 (Jan.–June 1896): 184.

22. See Gale's review of Stephen Phillips' *Christ in Hades,* in *Academy* 49 (23 May 1896): 424–25.

23. *Saturday Review* 81 (20 June 1896): 630.

24. *Bookman* 9 (March 1896): 189. Norman Gale in an unfavorable review saw Binyon's poetical excursions into the low life of Whitechapel as in danger of deteriorating "from the genuine bard to the philanthropist with a camera." *Academy* 49 (29 Feb. 1896): 175.

25. *Publishers' Circular* 64 (18 Jan. 1896): 83.

26. Probably Edward Fairbrother Strange, an authority on Japanese prints, who was an assistant at South Kensington Museum in the 1890s and later became keeper of woodwork at the Victoria and Albert Museum. In 1892 his *Palissy in Prison and Other Verses* was privately printed in London.

27. Binyon to Mathews, 17 Jan. 1896, EMA.

28. Binyon to Mathews, 23 Jan. 1896, EMA.

29. Binyon to Mathews, 8 Nov. 1895, Texas.

30. Binyon to Mathews, 11 Jan. [1896], Texas.

31. Although George L. McKay in *A Bibliography of Robert Bridges* (New York: Columbia UP; London: Oxford UP, 1933), does not list the joint imprint, William S. Kable in *The Ewelme Collection of Robert Bridges: A Catalogue*, Bibliographical Series, no. 2 (Columbia: U of South Carolina Dept. of English, 1967), items A54–56, lists it, as does Kraus, *History of Way and Williams*, items 24 and 24a, p. 71.

32. Binyon to Mathews, 27 Feb. 1896, EMA.

33. *Academy* 49 (29 Feb. 1896): 175.

34. *Publishers' Circular* 64 (11 April 1896): 397, and ibid (18 April 1896); 421.

35. *Academy* 52 (20 Nov. 1897): 425.

36. See Bridges' "Preface" to the *Ode*, which seems to convey this.

37. *Bookman* 10 (June 1896): 84. For other representative reviews, see *Academy* 49 (6 June 1896): 467; *Athenaeum* no. 3596 (26 Sept. 1896): 411–12.

38. *Academy* 49 (29 Feb. 1896): 175.

39. Binyon to Mathews, 23 Jan. 1896. EMA.

40. Binyon to Mathews, 27 Feb. 1896, EMA.

41. See two letters from Phillips to Colvin, [1896], Berg.

42. *Sketch* 14 (29 April 1896): 37; *Spectator* 76 (2 May 1896): 635–36; *Bookman* 10 (Sept. 1896): 161; *Saturday Review* 81 (20 June 1896): 629. In a letter to Colvin [1896] in the Berg Collection, Phillips is probably referring to this review when he wrote: "You will have seen Binyon's capital notice in the Saturday [Review]."

43. *Academy* 49 (23 May 1896): 424–25.

44. *Bookman* 11 (Nov. 1896): 31; *Academy* 50 (26 Sept. 1896): 223. "Edition" here means printing.

45. *Academy* 53 (15 Jan. 1898): 45.

46. *Academy* 52 (4 Dec. 1897): 484.

47. Binyon to Mathews, 27 Feb. 1896, EMA.

48. *Academy* 50 (12 Sept. 1896): 178–79.

49. *Saturday Review* 84 (17 July 1897): 68–69. Also see *Sketch* 14 (15 July 1896): 486; *Spectator* 77 (25 July 1896): 114–16; *Bookman* 11 (Oct. 1896): 23.

50. Bridges to Mathews, 8 April 1895, EMA; *Academy* 49 (23 May 1896): 426.

51. Bridges to Mathews, 8 April 1896, EMA.

52. "Memoir of Richard Watson Dixon," in *Three Friends* (Oxford and London: Oxford UP and Humphrey Milford, 1932), 111.

53. See Mathews' note on the verso of the title page of *Songs and Odes*. James Sambrook, *A Poet Hidden: The Life of Richard Watson Dixon, 1833–1900* (London: Athlone Press, 1962), 98, says that the only unpublished poem added to the volume was the brief lyric "Terror."

54. Bridges to Mathews, 8 April 1896, EMA.

55. Dixon to Mathews, 18 June and 3 Aug. 1896, EMA.

56. *Bookman* 11 (Oct. 1896): 4.

57. *Sketch* 16 (28 Oct. 1896): 16.

58. *Saturday Review* 82 (19 Dec. 1896): 656.

59. Ibid. 83 (13 Feb. 1897): 178. Cf. *Sketch* 16 (16 Dec. 1896): 320.

60. "The Wanderer" (literally, "upon no road"), the name of George MacDonald's hero in *Phantastes*, a favorite romance of Miss Coleridge's.

61. See Theresa [Furse] Whistler's introduction to *The Collected Poems of Mary Coleridge* (London: Rupert Hart-Davis, 1954), 61–67. Also see *My World as in My Time: Memoirs of Sir Henry Newbolt, 1862–1932* (London: Faber and Faber, 1932), 184.

62. *Books and Bookselling* 3 (April 1897): 72.

63. *Bookman* 13 (March 1898): 171.

64. Newbolt, *My World*, 196.

65. Ibid., 187.

66. Ibid., 196.

67. *Literature* 1 (1 Jan. 1898): 324. The reviewer—probably H. D. Traill—saw this resurgence of patriotic poetry as "a brisk and virile reaction" to the aesthetic and decadent content of much poetry of the nineties. Cf. *Academy* 55 (3 Dec. 1898): 371.

68. Newbolt, *My World*, 196.

69. Newbolt to Mathews, 26 Nov. 1897, in my possession.

70. Mathews to Newbolt, 15 Dec. 1897, in the possession of Peter Newbolt.

71. Mathews to Newbolt, 22 Dec. 1897, in the possession of Peter Newbolt.

72. "Book Reviews Reviewed," *Academy* 52 (11 Dec. 1897): 534.

73. Newbolt, *My World*, 196.

74. Newbolt to Mathews, 26 Nov. 1897, in my possession.

75. *Spectator* 79 (4 Dec. 1897): 823.

76. *Literature* 1 (1 Jan. 1898): 325; see also *Bookman* 13 (March 1898): 173.

77. "Literature," *Illustrated London News* 111 (20 Nov. 1897): 728.

78. *Academy* 52 (30 Oct. 1897): 349.

79. *Bookman* 13 (March 1898): 170.

80. *Academy* 53 (19 March 1898): 320; *Bookman* 13 (march 1898): 170.

81. *Bookman* 13 (March 1898): 171.

82. Donald Davidson, *British Poetry of the Eighteen-Nineties* (Garden City, N.Y.: Doubleday, Doran, 1937), 190.

83. See "List of Books Published by Elkin Mathews, 1898–9," bound at the back of Henry Newbolt's *The Island Race* (London: Elkin Mathews, 1898). The listing went on to state that "after the issue of No. 10 of the 'Shilling Garland,' Volume 2 of 'The Garland' will be published uniform with and same price as above."

84. Image's wreath design had previously appeared on the cover and title page of Elizabeth Rachel Chapman's *A Little Child's Wreath* (London: Elkin Mathews and John Lane; New York: Dodd Mead, 1894). Image's title page in both lettering and design anticipates his covers for the Shilling Garland series.

85. See Elkin Mathews' "List of Books" bound at the back of Newbolt's *The Island Race* (1898), 24.

86. Binyon to Mathews, [before 7 Sept. 1898], Texas.

87. Binyon to Mathews, 7 Sept. 1898, Texas.

88. Mathews, check to Binyon, 2 Nov. 1898, Texas. To be fair to Mathews, one must remember that Binyon got three books of poetry published out of the Shilling Garland venture for which he was paid royalties: £1.2.10 on 22 February 1897 (see Mathews' note on Binyon's letter to Mathews, 7 Sept. 1898, Texas) and £3.15.3 in royalties paid to Binyon "on Lond. Visions and Praise of Life to date" (Mathews' check to Binyon, Texas).

89. *Illustrated London News* 111 (20 Nov. 1897): 728.

90. See review of Ghose's *Love-Songs and Elegies* which appeared in *India*, quoted in listings of the series on the inside of Binyon's *Second Book of London Visions*.

91. *Academy* 51 (2 Jan. 1897): 6.

92. Binyon to unidentified correspondent, 22 Feb. 1916, in my possession.

93. As to judging the size of a printing, there is little to go on. Bridges, responding in February 1897 to Mathews' account of the sales of the *Purcell Ode*, revealed that the two printings of the *Ode* totaled 2,000 copies (of which fewer than 1,000 had sold). See Bridges to Mathews, 27 Feb, 1897, EMA. But since Bridges was an established poet, it seems unlikely that printings of relatively unknown authors such as Binyon and Coleridge would have been as large. Newbolt, however, initially had as little celebrity, yet printings of *Admirals All*, according to Patric Dickinson, a recent student of Newbolt's life and work, totaled "a thousand copies each." See Dickinson's introduction to *Selected Poems of Henry Newbolt* (London: Hodder and Stoughton, 1981), 18.

94. Binyon to unidentified correspondent, 22 Feb. 1916, in my possession.

95. See advertisement listing the titles in the Vigo and Satchel series bound in the back of Ezra Pounds' *Exultations* (1909).

96. Masefield to Synge, 18 Dec. 1903, quoted in the introduction by Ann Saddlemyer, ed., to *Plays, Book I*, vol. 3 of *J. M. Synge: Collected Works* (London: Oxford UP, 1968), xxvi. Since the tinted paper wrappers of the Vigo Cabinet series were subject to fading, the wrapper colors of extant copies may not always match that of the original. Moreover, when further printings of a number were required, if the original color-tinted paper was no longer available, another was substituted. For example, *Some Poems by Lionel Johnson* (no. 34) was issued in both pale gray wrappers and brown wrappers. See Henry Danielson, "A Bibliography of Lionel Johnson," *Bookman's Journal and Print Collector* n.s. 5 (Dec. 1921): 104.

97. Vigo Cabinet "Second Century" numbers are indicated in italics.

98. See Chiswick Press Records, Add. Mss. 50,926, vol. 17, p. 297, 3 April 1914, BL. Some copies were bound in blue- cloth-covered boards with a design of a tree and the title and author's name hand-drawn in gold on the front cover.

99. "Literary Week," *Academy* 58 (12 May 1900): 399.

100. *Bookman* 25 (Dec. 1903): 159–60.

101. Mathews also published Symons' *Charles Baudelaire: A Study* (1920).

102. *Publishers' Circular* 90 (June 1909): 899.

103. *Bookman's Journal and Print Collector* 1 (1920): 245. Although the war drove up the price of producing books, the price of Vigo Cabinet series books in wrappers remained 1/–, the price of the cloth-bound volumes rising to 2/– only toward the close of the war.

104. "A Chat," 418.

105. In "A Chat," Mathews referred to *The Fancy*—published in late 1905—as "the initial volume" of the series, which suggests that *The Views of Christopher*, published in June 1904 and listed as number 1 in the series in advertisements after 1909, was adopted into the series after the fact, so to speak. The fact that its format was that adopted by Mathews in 1905 as the format for the new series made this possible. Since the numbers Mathews assigned to the series volumes in his advertisements varied—for example, Mrs. Hamilton Synge's *The Vision* was listed as number 1 in an advertisement bound in back of Pound's *Exultations* (1909), and *The Views of Christopher* was listed as number 1 in the series advertisement on the back wrapper of Claude Houghton's *Phantom Host and Other Verses* (1917)—reference to individual volumes in the series by numbers is confusing and unreliable.

106. Both the *British Library Catalogue* and the *National Union Catalogue* attribute the anonymous work to Mathews along with several other books "by the author of 'The Views of Christopher,'" i.e., *The Showman* and *Mrs. Alfred Trench*.

107. *New Freewoman* 1 (1913): 227. Among the few critical comments on *The Tempers* in the contemporary press was that in the *Athenaeum* no. 4485 (11 Oct. 1913): 378, which declared: "These verses are not successful, and we find the writer straining grammar and meaning to produce his effects."

109. Gordom Bottomley to Mathews, 8 March 1907, in my possession. On the *Chambers of Imagery* volumes, see Appendix B.

108. Ficke's quote in Joy Grant, *Harold Munro and the Poetry Bookshop* (London: Routledge & Kegan Paul, 1967), 16.

CHAPTER 3. ELKIN MATHEWS, W. B. YEATS, AND THE CELTIC MOVEMENT IN LITERATURE

1. "A Chat with Mr. Elkin Mathews," *Publisher and Bookseller* 2 (24 Feb. 1906): 418.

2. David Perkins, *A History of Modern Poetry* (Cambridge: Harvard UP, 1976), 24.

3. For a discussion of Le Gallienne's role in the Bodley Head, see my *Early*

Nineties: A View from the Bodley Head (Cambridge: Harvard UP, 1971), ch. 1, "The Beginnings of the Bodley Head."

4. W. B. Yeats to Katharine Tynan, [10 Oct. 1889], in *The Collected Letters of W. B. Yeats*, ed. John Kelly and Eric Domville (Oxford: Clarendon Press, 1986) 1:190–91. Further on in this letter, Yeats wrote that Le Galleons [*sic*] publishers reader seems confident that publisher will sell *Oisin*." According to Kelly and Domville (*ibid.*, 1:191, n. 5), Mathews appears to have disappointed Yeats' hopes "that he would take over from Kegan Paul the unsold stock of *Oisin*," although Mathews did assume some of the financially troubled publishing firm's stock in 1890.

5. Ernest Radford to Mathews, 13 Jan. 1891, EMA. Mathews, who had published several books by Rhymers' Club members before he was formally introduced to the group—e.g., Richard Le Gallienne's *Volumes in Folio* (1889), John Todhunter's *A Sicilian Idyll* (1890), and Radford's *Chamber's Twain* (1890)—continued to attend Rhymers' Club meetings as late as 1895. See Karl Beckson, "Yeats and the Rhymers' Club," *Yeats Studies* 1 (1971): 40.

6. *The Autobiography of William Butler Yeats* (New York: Macmillan, 1953), 101. Despite its lack of any particular creed, the Rhymers' Club in the minds of many was associated with the Celts. For example, according to Desmond Flower and Henry Maas, the club began, "as a gathering of Irishmen living in London" and was later "reorganized on a broader basis." *The Letters of Ernest Dowson*, ed. Desmond Flower and Henry Maas (Rutherford, NJ: Fairleigh Dickinson UP, 1967), 181, n. 2. Edgar Jepson, who on occasion attended its meetings, states that the members "were all very Celtic too, for it was the days of the Celtic Fringe." *Memories of a Victorian* (London: Gollancz, 1933), 237. Also see Beckson, "Yeats and the Rhymers' Club," 24–26.

7. Yeats wrote Mathews on Thursday, 12 November 1891: "Lionel Johnson, George Greene and myself, three members of the Rhymers' Club, wish to see you about the publishing of 'The Book of the Rhymers' Club' (a volume of poems by the members) and propose to call on you next Monday [16 November] about 3 o'clock." Dowson, *Letters*, 125.

8. Although plans for a third Rhymers' Club book did not materialize (see Beckson, "Yeats and the Rhymers' Club," 40), Mathews published one other anthology which contained poems exemplary of the Celtic Movement: *Dublin Verses by Members of Trinity College* (1895), edited by Henry A. Hinkson. Mingling with verses such as "The Corn-Crake" by the West Briton Edward Dowden were poems very much in the Celtic mode, such as Douglas Hyde's "My Grief on the Sea," "Ringleted Youth of My Love," and "Star of My Sight"; Todhunter's "The Lament of Aideen for Oscar" and "Eileen's Farewell"; Alfred Perceval Graves's "The Rejected Lover"; Standish O'Grady's "Lough Bray"; and T. W. Rolleston's "The Spell-Struck."

9. See Ian Fletcher, "Bedford Park: Aesthete's Elysium?" in *Romantic Mythologies*, ed. Ian Fletcher (London: Routledge & Kegan Paul, 1967), 170.

10. Yeats to T. Fisher Unwin, 19 Oct. [1894], in Yeats, *Collected Letters*, 1:402–3.

11. That Yeats was affected by both the appearance and content of Mathews' books is revealed in several of his letters. In one to his sister, Lily, of 26 December [1894], *Collected Letters*, 1:420, he mentioned that Mathews had sent him proofs of Johnson's book of verse, going on to write that "it is exceedingly stately & impressive & will make a stir." In the same letter he said, "He has sent me also proofs of a charming little book by Selwen Image." In a letter to Mathews of 30 December 1894 (ibid.), he expressed his liking for the design of the books and his willingness to review them for the *Bookman*. In yet another letter to Mathews of 7 April 1895 (ibid., 458), Yeats thanked the publisher for a copy of Probyn's *Pansies*, which contained a highly decorative title page by Mathews' sister Minnie. "It is a delightful book in every way," Yeats exclaimed. "The poems are delightful & your sisters designs on title page & cover are worthy of the poems. They have just that quiet richness which the book requires."

12. Yeats to John O'Leary [late July ? 1894], in Yeats, *Collected Letters*, 1:395.

13. Indicated on stub of Mathews' checkbook, 3 June 1896, Columbia.

14. Yeats to Mathews, 10 Dec. [n.y.], Brotherton. In this extremely important letter, Yeats referred to the agreement which Mathews had sent him as "not . . . important & I cannot for some days go through the great heap I have made of the papers I brought from Ireland" (presumably) to look for it.

15. Mathews to Yeats, [n.d.], Brotherton.

16. Yeats to Mathews, [n.d.], Brotherton.

17. Lane brought out printings of *The Wind* in April 1899, in 1902, and in 1905. Another American printing came out with Elkin Mathews' imprint in 1911. See Allan Wade, *A Bibliography of the Writings of W. B. Yeats*, 2nd ed. (London: Rupert Hart-Davis, 1958), no. 28; hereafter, *Yeats Bibliography*.

18. W. B. Yeats, "A Symbolic Artist and the Coming of Symbolic Art," *Dome*, n.s. 1 (December 1898): 233, reprinted in *Uncollected Prose by W. B. Yeats*, ed. John P. Frayne and Colton Johnson, 2 vols. (New York: Columbia UP, 1976): 2:132–37. In his "Poet and Designer: W. B. Yeats and Althea Gyles," Ian Fletcher refers to Gyles's cover design for *The Wind* as her "most accomplished." *Yeats Studies* 1 (1971): 57. For references to Gyles' design and its relation to the content of *The Wind*, see Allen R. Grossman, *Poetic Knowledge in the Early Yeats* (Charlottesville: U of Virginia Press, 1969), 46, 48, 50–51.

19. Yeats to Mathews, [26 April 1897], Brotherton.

20. Fletcher, "Poet and Designer," 58. The article includes a reproduction of the frontispiece. Although Yeats later apparently sought to have this frontispiece retouched and used in a subsequent edition of *The Wind*, it never appeared in any of Mathews' editions. See Yeats to Mathews, 21 Aug. [1905] and [?] 1905, Brotherton.

21. Yeats to Mathews, 25 Oct. [1898], Brotherton.

22. Yeats to Mathews, 17 Nov. [1898], Brotherton.

23. Ibid.

24. Yeats to Mathews, 2 Dec. [1898], Brotherton.

25. See the note in pencil by the owner, Harold Wilmerding Bell, on the verso of the end paper of a vellum-bound first edition of *The Wind*, Harvard, which reads: "1st ed/one of the very few copies bound in vellum[,] Ricketts told me that 12 were bound in vellum and that he had suggested the idea to Yeats. The designer of the binding was Althea Giles [*sic*]."

26. Yeats to Mathews, Galway, 20 Sept. [n.y.], laid in a copy of a vellum-bound first printing of *The Wind* sold in the C. Walter Buhler sale, item no. 143, Parke-Burnet catalogue for Thursday, 1 May 1941. Quoted in *Yeats Bibliography*, 47.

27. Yeats to Mathews, 20 Sept. [1902], in *The Letters of W. B. Yeats*, ed. Allan Wade (London: Rupert Hart-Davis, 1954), 378.

28. For example, Yeats, having discussed a proposal by Archie Russell for twenty-five vellum-bound copies of *The Wind* in a letter to the publisher, continued: "Go ahead with the new edition, binding the ordinary copies in plain grey boards with a label possibly. You can bind the vellum copies as they are wanted, beginning with Archie Russell's edition of twenty five if you done [*sic*] want to risk more." Yeats to Mathews, 29 Sept. [n.y.], Texas.

29. *Yeats Bibliography*, no. 29.

30. The Parke-Burnet catalogue of the C. Walter Buhler sale, 1 May 1941, indicates a first edition of 500 copies (see item nos. 143–46). William M. Roth, however, in *A Catalogue of English and American First Editions of William Butler Yeats* (New Haven: n.p., 1939), indicates a first edition of 1,000 copies (see no. 43). Roth, I suspect, may have been confused by the fact that Mathews produced the first and second printings (each of 500 copies?) together, and then, according to Yeats, "sent out some copies of the 'second edition' first." Yeats's note in John Quinn's copy of *The Wind*, quoted in *Yeats Bibliography*, 46.

31. In the Note in the Houghton Library copy of *The Wind*, Ricketts is reported as having said that twelve copies were so bound.

32. Yeats to Unwin, 19 Oct. [1894], in Yeats, *Collected Letters*, 1:403.

33. Yeats to Mathews, 19 Feb. 1904, Brotherton.

34. Yeats to Mathews, 3 Aug. [1905], Brotherton.

35. Lane to Mathews, 13 Sept. 1905 and 10 July 1906, Brotherton.

36. Yeats to Mathews, 2 and 10 Sept. [1905], Brotherton; Yeats to Bullen, 4 July [1907?], in Yeats, *Letters*, 484.

37. Yeats to Bullen, 2 Nov. 1905 in Yeats, *Letters*, 464–65.

38. Yeats to Bullen, 13 Feb. [1906?], in Yeats, *Letters*, 470.

39. Bullen to Mathews, 20 June 1905, UD.

40. Yeats to Bullen, 4 July [1907?] in Yeats, *Letters*, 483–84.

41. Yeats to Bullen, 4 Oct. 1907, in Yeats, *Letters*, 498.

42. Richard Ellmann, "Discovering Symbolism," in *Golden Codgers* (London: Oxford UP, 1973), 111.

43. Mathews to Yeats, 28 Oct. 1903, Brotherton.

44. Yeats to Mathews, 3 Nov. 1903, Brotherton.

45. In his "Critical Introduction" to "*The Tables of the Law*: A Critical Text," *Yeats Studies* 1 (1971): 99, n. 9, O'Driscoll points out that in the copy of *The Tables of the Law* published by Mathews and housed in Yeats's library, there is a note by Mrs. Yeats which identifies the young man as "P.S.O'H."—that is, P. S. O'Hegarty.

46. Yeats to Mathews, 25 Apr. [1904], Brotherton.

47. *Yeats Bibliography*, no. 25.

48. Yeats to Fiona Macleod, [?—early Jan. 1897], in Yeats, *Letters*, 280.

49. Linda Dowling, *Language and Decadence in the Victorian Fin de Siècle* (Princeton: Princeton UP, 1986), 265.

50. Richard Ellmann, *Yeats: The Man and the Masks* (New York: E. P. Dutton, 1948), 118. An excellent discussion of these stories may be found in O'Driscoll's "Critical Introduction."

51. Ann Saddlemyer, "'The Noble and the Beggar-Man': Yeats and Literary Nationalism," in *The World of W. B. Yeats*, ed. Robin Skelton and Ann Saddlemyer, rev. ed. (Seattle: U of Washington Press, 1967), 10.

52. Lionel Johnson to T. W. Rolleston, 29 April 1892, Berg.

53. Ian Fletcher, "Introduction," *The Collected Poems of Lionel Johnson*, 2nd and rev. ed. (New York and London: Garland, 1982), xlvi.

54. Lionel Johnson, "Poetry and Patriotism in Ireland," in *Post Liminium: Essays and Critical Papers by Lionel Johnson*, ed. Thomas Whittemore (London: Elkin Mathews, 1911), 177.

55. Johnson to Lane, [early] 1894, Princeton.

56. Johnson to Lane, 15 March 1894, Berg.

57. Johnson to Mathews and Lane, 19 March 1894, Berg.

58. Johnson to Lane, 6 June 1894, Berg.

59. Quoted in *Books of the "Nineties,"* Catalogue 42 (London: Elkin Mathews, n.d.), no. 378.

60. Ibid.

61. In the preface to his "Thomas Hardy, a Bibliography," Lane denied that the long delay in publishing the *Hardy* "was owing to the incomplete state of my bibliography," suggesting it had been due, instead, to difficulties in arranging for an American publisher.

62. Fletcher, "Introduction," l.

63. Johnson to Lane, [ca. June 1894], Berg.

64. Mathews to Johnson, 17 Sept. 1894, quoted in Rev. Raymond Roseliep, "Some Letters of Lionel Johnson" (Ph.D. diss., U of Notre Dame, 1953), 152n.

65. Percy Muir, *Minding My Own Business* (London: Chatto & Windus, 1956), 10.

66. Johnson to Mathews, 19 Sept. 1894, Princeton.

67. Ibid.

68. Johnson to Will Rothenstein, 24 Oct. 1894, quoted in William Rothen-

stein, *Men and Memories*, 2 vols. (New York: Coward-McCann, 1935) 1:157. See also Johnson's letter to Mathews, 24 Oct. 1894, Texas.

69. Johnson to Mathews, 24 Oct. 1894, Texas.

70. Johnson to Mathews, 13 Nov. 1894, Princeton.

71. Herbert P. Horne to Mathews, 14 Feb. 1894, Texas.

72. *Academy*, no. 1177 (24 Nov. 1894): 422.

73. The 25 signed copies constitute the true first printing, often cited as the "first edition, first issue," the so-called "second issue" (i.e., the ordinary printing of 750 copies) being in effect the second printing. After the 25 copies of the true first printing were made, the first and last gatherings were revised, reset, and the second printing of 750 copies run off. See *Four Centuries of English Books*, Catalogue 1043 (London: Bernard Quaritch, n.d.), item 263. See also Henry Danielson in "A Bibliography of Lionel Johnson," *Bookman's Journal and Print Collector* n.s. 5 (Oct. 1921): 30, and *English Poetry: A Catalogue of First and Early Editions of Works of the English Poets from Chaucer to the Present Day*, comp. John Hayward (London: National Book League, 1947), no. 304. Mathews' own copy of the special limited edition of 25 was bound in terra-cotta buckram, one of apparently a few advance copies thus bound. See *A Bibliographical Catalogue of the First Loan Exhibition of Books and Manuscripts Held by the First Edition Club* (London: First Edition Club, 1922), 89. American copies of Johnson's *Poems* (1895) are distinguished by the presence of "Copeland / & Day" at the foot of the spine.

74. Oscar Wilde to Katharine Tynan, [n.d.], UK. Wilde went on to contrast the "pathos of things" with "the pathos of the English" which comes "from their sense of Life's ugliness."

75. W. B. Yeats, "Mr. Lionel Johnson's Poems," in Yeats, *Uncollected Prose*, 2:89.

76. Yeats, "Johnson's Poems" and "Three Irish Poets," ibid., 88–91 and 70–73.

77. Yeats, "Johnson's Poems," 89.

78. Ibid., 90. O'Driscoll in his "Critical Introduction to Yeats' *Tables of the Law*, 96, suggests Johnson was the prototype for Owen Aherne.

79. Yeats, "Johnson's Poems," 90–91.

80. Johnson to Mathews, 10 Jan. 1897, UK. The essays Johnson refers to were never published during his lifetime. They were eventually published by Mathews as *Post Liminium* in 1911.

81. Quoted in *Books of the "Nineties,"* no. 366.

82. Johnson to Mathews, [autumn 1897[, Princeton. Also see Roseliep, "Some Letters of Lionel Johnson," 178n. Danielson, "A Bibliography of Lionel Johnson," 30, says *Ireland* was limited to an edition of 500 copies, and he is followed in this by Joe W. Kraus, *Messrs. Copeland & Day* (Philadelphia: MacManus, 1979), no. 84. But there is a note to a customer on Elkin Mathews' letterhead and in his hand which states that it was published in an edition of

300 copies for England and America. Note in the collection of Mark Lasner, whom I thank for calling it to my attention.

83. Mathews in a draft copy of his reminiscences (EMA), recalled that he saw a "good deal" of the poet during the nineties, frequently visiting him "at his snug chambers in Grays Inn and elsewhere."

84. Mathews to Yeats, 19 July 1904, TCD.

85. Yeats, finding that Mathews owned the copyright, wrote the publisher asking for his approval, adding that he did not think the Dun Emer book would injure sales of *Poems* and *Ireland*, and might actually help. Yeats to Mathews, 17 June [1904], Brotherton.

86. Mathews to Yeats, 19 July 1904, TCD.

87. According to an advertisement on the inside front cover of *Some Poems*, the works of Lionel Johnson were to include—in addition to a volume of his prose essays, published as *Post Liminium*—a volume of his poems (published by Mathews in 1915), and a volume of his correspondence, with a memoir.

88. See Stephen Maxfield Parrish, "Currents of the Nineties in Boston and London: Fred Holland Day, Louise Imogen Guiney, and Their Circle" (Ph.D. diss., Harvard, 1954). Whittemore later gained considerable recognition as an art historian and is best known as the founder of the Byzantine Institute, which he organized in 1930 and for his work to uncover the grand mosaics in Santa Sophia at Istanbul.

89. Johnson to Thomas Whittemore, 25 July [1899], in the collection of Philip Cohen whom I thank for calling my attention to it.

90. Louise Imogen Guiney to Mathews, 12 Oct. [1910?], Princeton.

91. Guiney to Mathews, 5 Nov. [1910?], Princeton.

92. Guiney to Mathews, 7 Apr. 1911, Princeton. Whittemore had left in January on a British archaeological expedition to Egypt under the auspices of the Egypt Exploration Society.

93. Guiney to Mathews, 5 Oct. 1911, Princeton.

94. Mathews to Clement Shorter, 6 Dec. 1913, Brotherton.

95. In a letter to Lord Alfred Douglas, 18 May 1935, Pound wrote that he "certainly did not bother about Lionel's text other than to, I think, select from some inédits." Quoted in Donald Gallup, *Ezra Pound: A Bibliography* (Charlottesville: U of Virginia Press, 1983), 89. In a presentation inscription in a copy of *Poetical Works*, Mathews thanked Campbell Dodgson, Johnson's old school chum and friend, "for helping in the production of this volume." Quoted in *Victorian and Modern First Editions*, a catalogue issued by Sevin Seydi (London, 1987), item 88. Dodgson is also thanked in a printed note at the end of the preface.

96. Gallup, *Pound: A Bibliography*, B9.

97. See letter from Fletcher, 8 April 1930, inside front cover of a first edition of *Poetical Works of Lionel Johnson*, and a typescript of a portion of Pound's letter to Fletcher, Harvard. While it is not a common item, *Poetical Works* with Pound's preface is not so rare as Pound led Fletcher to believe.

98. *The Religious Poems* was actually published in January 1917. The ordinary issue of the volume—500 copies for America and 750 for England—appeared in three forms: (A) bound in gray-paper-covered boards with a tan cloth spine, lettered in black on front cover and spine, with the imprint of Elkin Mathews and Burns & Oates; (B) bound in blue-paper-covered boards but otherwise identical with (A); (C) identical with (A) except that the title page is printed in black and brown and bound in brown-paper-covered boards. (B) and (C) may have been trial copies. A large-paper issue of 300 (plus 10) copies on handmade paper bound in light gray paper-covered boards, lettered in black on the spine, was published by Mathews. According to *A Bibliographical Catalogue of the First Loan Exhibition*, 90, the large-paper copies "consisted of two issues, one on thick, the other on thin, paper." Mathews' copy was "printed partly on thick paper, partly on thin" and bears his written note certifying it to be the only one so printed. See also Henry Danielson, "A Bibliography of Lionel Johnson (III)," *Bookman's Journal and Print Collector* n.s. 5 (Dec. 1921): 103. The American printing with the imprint of Macmillan in New York and Elkin Mathews in London was bound in dark blue cloth-covered boards with lettering on front cover and spine in gilt.

Reviews and Critical Papers was bound in light green cloth-covered boards with beveled edges, lettered in gilt on the spine. It was uniform in size with *Post Liminium* and *Poetical Works*.

99. Yeats, *Explorations* (New York: Macmillan, 1962), 72.

100. Yeats, *Uncollected Prose*, 2:26.

101. Quoted in Ellmann, *Yeats: The Man and the Masks*, 147– 48.

102. Quoted in *The Collected Letters of John Millington Synge*, ed. Ann Saddlemyer, 2 vols (Oxford: Clarendon Press, 1983–84) 1:52, n. 2. In a letter of 22 February [1902] to Lady Gregory, Synge wrote to tell her of what he called "the evil fate of my Aran book" and ask her advice. "It has been to two publishers, to Grant Richards who was sympathetic, though he refused it as he said it could not be a commercial success, and to Fisher Unwin who was inclined to be scornful." Synge, *Letters*, 1:53. In addition to Richards and Unwin, during the course of 1902 Synge's book was rejected by Alfred Nutt and A. H. Bullen.

103. Arthur Symons to Lady Gregory, [11 Feb. 1903], in *Theatre Business*, ed. Ann Saddlemyer (University Park: Pennsylvania State UP, 1982), 39–40.

104. J. M. Synge to Lady Gregory, [26 March 1903], in Synge, *Letters*, 1:68– 69.

105. Yeats to R. B. Johnson, 28 March [1903], in Saddlemyer, *Theatre Business*, 44.

106. Lady Gregory to Synge, 13 Dec. [1903], ibid., 45–46. Lady Gregory enclosed Masefield's letters of 2 and 11 December 1903.

107. John Masefield to Lady Gregory, 2 Dec. 1903, ibid., 46.

108. Masefield to Lady Gregory, 11 Dec. 1903, ibid., 47–48. Mathews' reason for not publishing *The Aran Islands* in the spring of 1904, as Masefield

had hoped, was "that he had a good deal of prose on hand for the spring & that new books went best in the autumn." This gave Masefield the idea of suggesting that Mathews bring out Synge's plays in the spring instead.

109. Synge to Lady Gregory, 16 Dec. 1903, ibid., 48.

110. Masefield to Mathews, 26 Jan. 1904, quoted in item 457 in Christie's sale catalogue, *Modern Literature from the Library of James Gilvarry* (New York, 7 Feb. 1986).

111. In a letter to Synge of 18 December 1903, Masefield wrote that he had "seen Mathews about the plays, and he seems eager, on the strength of the Samhain tragedy [i.e., *Riders to the Sea* first published in *Samhain* in October 1903], to publish all three in one of his Vigo editions." Quoted in Ann Saddlemyer, ed., *Plays, Book I*, vol. 3 of *J. M. Synge: Collected Works* (London: Oxford UP, 1968), xxvi. Synge wrote Masefield on 17 December 1903, thanking him for his "good offices in speaking well of my Aran ms. to Elkin Mathews," and asking his advice about adding "the Tinker-play . . . so as to have three peasant plays?" Synge, *Letters*, 1:71-72.

112. Masefield to Synge, 18 Dec. 1903, quoted in Saddlemyer, *Plays, Book I*, xxvi.

113. Yeats to Mathews, 17 June [1904], Brotherton.

114. Mathews to Yeats, 19 July 1904, TCD. Quoted in part in Synge, *Letters*, 1:73, n. 4.

115. Draft fragment of a letter from Synge to Mathews [c. 29 Jan. 1905], in Synge, *Letters*, 1:105.

116. Draft fragment of a letter from Synge to Mathews, [?5 Feb. 1905], ibid., 107.

117. Ibid.

118. In his letter to Lady Gregory, 11 Dec. 1903, Masefield wrote: "I think I could get Mathews to grant 15%. Would that suit?" Saddlemyer, *Theatre Business*, 48.

119. Synge to Mathews, [c. 29 Jan. 1905], in Synge, *Letters*, 1:105.

120. Synge to Mathews, [?5 Feb. 1905], ibid., 107.

121. See the agreement signed by Synge, TCD, also transcribed in *John Millington Synge: Some Unpublished Letters and Documents* (Montreal: Red Path Press, 1959), 7-8. Synge's later opinion of the agreement was expressed in a letter to John Quinn, 5 Sept. 1907, *Letters*, 2:47.

122. Mathews' letter quoted in Saddlemyer, *Plays, Books I*, 233. A copy of the first edition in the Berg Collection has the following note in pencil on the verso of the title page: "I hereby certify that this the first edition was published by me on the 8th May 1905. Elkin Mathews Vigo Street W.3."

123. These issues represent further printings of the third (1909) edition. According to Mathews' account of sales of the first edition, dated 21 June 1907, TCD, total receipts amounted to £35.12.6, out of which Synge received royalties of £3.11.3. Synge's share of the receipts from the second edition of 1907 were £1.8.0. See *Synge: Some Unpublished Letters and Documents*, 17.

124. In a letter to Dr. Max Meyerfield, 1 September 1905, Synge wrote: "I have the MS of a book giving an account of my life on the Aran Islands which Mr. Elkin Mathews has promised to publish shortly." Synge, *Letters*, 1:127.

125. Synge to George Roberts, 7 Nov. 1905, ibid., 135.

126. Synge to Mathews, 11 Nov. 1905, ibid., 136. In his letter to Roberts, 7 Nov. 1905, Synge had asked for a royalty of "15% on published price from outset," leaving the royalties on the expensive edition to be arranged by Stephen Gwynn of Maunsel's later.

127. "Some Notes on the Bibliography of J. M. Synge, Supplemental to Bourgeois and MacManus," *Dublin Magazine* n.s. 17 (1942): 56–57. Mathews' copy (with his bookplate) in a variant binding with the publisher's imprint at the bottom of the spine was listed as item 450 in Christie's sale catalogue, *Modern Literature from the Library of James Gilvarry* (New York, 7 Feb. 1986).

128. Yeats apparently set to work on the illustrations for Synge's book in late 1905, writing the author early in 1906 to say that he "ought to have acknowledged the MS long ago" and to thank him for sending it. Referring to the illustrations, Yeats told Synge that he had "done several particularly bully ones!" and thanked him for the photographs of Aran peasants in picturesque settings which he pronounced "fine!" Yeats to Synge, 4 Feb. 1906. TCD.

129. Synge to John Quinn, 5 Sept. 1907, *Letters*, 2:47.

130. Synge to Mathews, 8 Jan. 1909. ibid., 247. Mathews in a letter to Synge, 13 Jan. 1909, TCD, wrote his acceptance of the 1% royalty.

131. Synge to Frank R. Sidgwick, 8 Jan. 1909, in Synge, *Letters*, 2:248.

132. James Joyce to Mathews, 12 July 1909, in *Letters of James Joyce*, ed. Stuart Gilbert (London: Faber & Faber, 1957), 66–67; Mathews to Joyce, 9 July 1909. Cornell.

133. W. B. Yeats, Introduction to *Selections from the Writings of Lord Dunsany* (Churchtown, Dundrum: Cuala Press, 1912).

134. Ibid.

135. Lord Dunsany to Mrs. Edith Elkin Mathews, 21 Jan. 1922, EMA, in which he went on to say: "I should like particularly to tell you that about the end of 1913, having had my stuff refused by publisher after publisher finishing up with the firm of Macmillan who had done it for the second time, & feeling very despondent, I came once more to Mr. Mathews & found him ready as ever to take my books."

CHAPTER 4. JAMES JOYCE'S FIRST PUBLISHER

1. A. Walton Litz in his preface to *Chamber Music, Pomes Penyeach, and Occasional Verse* (New York and London: Garland, 1978), xxxi, says *Chamber Music* was mainly written between 1901 and 1904.

2. Laurence Binyon to an unidentified correspondent, 22 Feb. 1916, in my possession.

3. Richard Ellmann, *James Joyce* (New York: Oxford UP, 1982), 111–12.

4. See Roger Lhombreaud's account of Symons' relations with his fellow authors in *Arthur Symons: A Critical Biography* (London: Unicorn Press, 1963), 221–22. Symons mentioned his early impression of Joyce in his epilogue to *The Joyce Book* (London: Sylvan Press, 1932), 79.

5. Arthur Symons to Joyce, 21 Apr. 1904, in *Letters to James Joyce*, vol. 2, ed. Richard Ellmann (New York: Viking Press, 1966), 42.

6. Symons to Joyce, 4 May [1904], ibid.

7. Symons to Joyce, 5 May [1904], in Karl Beckson and John M. Munro, eds., "Letters from Arthur Symons to James Joyce: 1904–1932," *James Joyce Quarterly* 4 (Winter 1967): 93.

8. Symons to Joyce, 23 Sept. 1904, ibid., 94.

9. Symons to Grant Richards, 13 July [1904], ibid., 93.

10. Richards to Joyce, 21 Sept. 1905, quoted in Robert Scholes, "Grant Richards to James Joyce," *Studies in Bibliography* 16 (1963): 142.

11. Symons to Joyce, 23 Sept. 1904, in Beckson and Munro, "Letters," 94.

12. Symons to Joyce, 14 Nov. 1904, ibid., 94–95.

13. Symons to Joyce, 5 Oct. 1905, ibid., 95.

14. Symons to Joyce, 2 Oct. 1906, ibid., 96.

15. Ibid.

16. Symons to Mathews, 9 Oct. 1906, ibid., 96–97. Symons' reference to the *Chamber Music* manuscript as "A Book of Thirty Songs for Lovers," reflects Joyce's doubts about the title (which Stanislaus had given the book) during the months before publication. In a letter to Stanislaus, 18 Oct. 1906 (*Letters*, 2:182), Joyce wrote: "The reason I dislike *Chamber Music* as a title is that it is too complacent. I should prefer a title which to a certain extent repudiated the book, without altogether disparaging it."

17. Mathews to Symons, 11 Oct. 1906, Cornell. Symons in his reply, post-marked 13 October 1906, thanked Mathews for his letter, adding: "I am asking Joyce to send you the ms. I am sure you will like it." Princeton.

18. Joyce to Stanislaus Joyce, 18 Oct. 1906, in Joyce, *Letters*, 2:181.

19. Joyce to Mathews, 25 Oct. 1906, Texas.

20. Mathews to Joyce, 30 Oct. 1906, Cornell.

21. Ibid.

22. Herbert Gorman, *James Joyce* (New York: Rinehart, 1948), 175.

23. See advertisement in *Publishers' Circular* 85 (6 Oct. 1906): 113.

24. Mathews to Joyce, 11 Jan. 1907, Cornell.

25. The agreement, which Joyce dated and signed on 17 January 1907 and returned to Mathews, is in the Joyce Collection, Beinecke Library, Yale.

26. Joyce to Stanislaus Joyce, [?1 March 1907], in Joyce, *Letters*, 2:219.

27. Joyce to Mathews, 1 March 1907, ibid., 216–17.

28. Mathews to Joyce, 15 March 1907, Cornell.

29. Joyce to Mathews, 28 March 1907, in Joyce, *Letters*, 2:221.

30. Stanislaus Joyce, *Recollections of James Joyce* (New York: James Joyce Society, 1950), 26.

31. Joyce to Stanislaus Joyce, [?1 Mar. 1907], in *Letters*, 2:219. Cf. Joyce to Stanislaus Joyce, 18 Oct. 1906, ibid., 182.

32. Ellmann, *Joyce*, 260.

33. Mathews to Joyce (postcard), 1 May 1907, Cornell; Joyce to Mathews (postcard), 4 May 1907, Texas.

34. Joyce to Constantine P. Curran, 10 May 1907, in *Letters of James Joyce*, vol. 1, ed. Stuart Gilbert (New York: Viking, 1957), 65; Joyce to Stanislaus Joyce [?10 May 1907], in *Letters*, 2:223.

35. Gorman, *Joyce*, 191. However, all of Mathews' accounts of the sales of the book that I have seen list 500 copies. For a complete bibliographical description of *Chamber Music*, see John J. Slocum and Herbert Cahoon, *A Bibliography of James Joyce* (New Haven: Yale UP, 1953), 5–6. The most up-to-date analysis of the binding variants of *Chamber Music* is in "Miscellany Five, English Books and Manuscripts" *New Series*, Bulletin 19, Bernard Quaritch, London (1984), item 47.

36. *Publishers' Circular* 86 (4 May 1907): 543; *Book Monthly* 4 (June 1907): 641; *Athenaeum* no. 4150 (11 May 1907): 577.

37. *Bookman* 32 (June 1907): 113.

38. *Publishers' Circular* 86 (15 June 1907): 744.

39. *Nation* 1 (22 June 1907): 639, reprinted in *James Joyce: The Critical Heritage*, ed. Robert H. Deming, vol. 1 (New York: Barnes & Noble, 1970), 38–39.

40. *Freeman's Journal*, 1 June 1907, n.p.; an extract of Kettle's review appears in Deming, *Joyce: Critical Heritage*, 1:37. For a discussion of the reviews of *Chamber Music*, see Ellmann, *Joyce*, 260–61.

41. Ellmann, *Joyce*, 261.

42. Joyce to Mathews, 9 Sept. 1907, Huntington.

43. Gorman, *Joyce*, 146–58; see also Scholes, "Richards to Joyce."

44. Joyce to Mathews, 24 Sept. 1907, in Joyce, *Letters*, 2:224.

45. Ibid., 224–25.

46. Mathews to Joyce, 23 Oct. 1907, Cornell.

47. Mathews to Joyce, 29 Oct. 1907, Cornell.

48. Mathews to Joyce, 6 Feb. 1908, Cornell. Maunsel agreed to publish *Dubliners* in August 1909, but after having set the book in type and run off proof, the firm reneged on its agreement. See Ellmann, *Joyce*, 328–35.

49. Joyce, *Letters*, 2:225, n. 2.

50. Joyce to Mathews, 26 Feb. 1913, in Joyce, *Letters*, 2:323; Mathews to Joyce, 20 March 1913, Cornell. The proof sheets Joyce sent to Mathews were those provided him by Maunsel. Just as Mathews in rejecting the book in 1908 had asked Joyce to allow him to send *Dubliners* to Maunsel, so once again in 1913 Mathews concluded this letter of rejection by asking Joyce to

allow him to pass on *Dubliners* to the publisher John Long, for whom, he wrote, "this book should make a strong appeal. . . . Let me do this for you."

51. Arthur Symons, review of *Chamber Music, Nation* 1 (22 June 1907): 639, also in Deming, *Joyce: Critical Heritage*, 1:39.

52. Joyce to Mathews, Easter Day, 1913, in Joyce, *Letters*, 1:73.

53. Mathews to Joyce, 25 March 1913, Cornell.

54. Joyce to G. Molyneux Palmer, 19 July 1909, in *Letters*, 1:67.

55. Joyce to Stanislaus Joyce, [?1 Mar. 1907], in *Letters*, 2:219.

56. Stanislaus Joyce to Mathews, 19 July 1907, in *Letters*, 2:223–24; Joyce to G. Molyneux Palmer, 19 July 1909, ibid., 1:67.

57. Joyce to Mathews, 4 April 1910, in Joyce *Letters*, 1:68.

58. Mathews to Joyce, 18 May 1910, Cornell; Mathews to Joyce, 24 May 1910, Cornell.

59. See Mathews' account sheet for musical rights to *Chamber Music* dated 24 May 1910, Cornell. Also see Mathews' postcard to Joyce, 3 June 1910, Cornell.

60. Mathews to Joyce, 23 Oct. 1907, Cornell.

61. Joyce to Mathews, 10 July 1908, in Joyce, *Letters* 2:225; Mathews to Joyce, with accompanying statement, 24 July 1908, Cornell.

62. Joyce to Mathews, 13 Feb. 1909, in Joyce, *Letters*, 2:228; Mathews to Joyce, 27 Feb. 1909, Cornell.

63. In a postcard dated 9 July 1909, Cornell, Mathews told Joyce that "'Chamber Music' has been selling very little during the last year. I will let you know shortly how many have been sold."

64. Joyce to Mathews, 4 April 1910, in Joyce, *Letters*, 1:68.

65. Joyce to Mathews, 15 May 1910, ibid.

66. "A Chat with Mr. Elkin Mathews," *Publisher and Bookseller* 2 (24 Feb. 1906): 418.

67. Mathews to Joyce, 18 May 1910, Cornell.

68. Joyce to Mathews, 21 May 1910, in Joyce, *Letters*, 2:283.

69. Mathews to Joyce, 24 May 1910, Cornell. As we know, Joyce had little reason to expect help from his fellow countrymen, especially men like George Roberts of Maunsel, who treated Joyce so shabbily over *Dubliners*.

70. Mathews to Wilfrid Meynell, quoted in *James Joyce: Chamber Music*, ed. William York Tindall (New York: Columbia UP, 1954), 17.

71. Mathews to Joyce, 1 May 1907, Cornell.

72. Joyce to Mathews, 21 May 1910, in Joyce, *Letters*, 2:283; leaflet reprinted in Joyce, *Letters*, 2:332, n. 3.

73. Joyce to Mathews, 19 May 1914, EMA.

74. Mathews to Joyce, 24 May 1910, Cornell; Mathews to Joyce, 21 May 1914, Cornell.

75. See Mathews' account of *Chamber Music* sales, dated 21 Feb. 1913, Cornell.

76. Joyce to Mathews, 30 May 1912, in Joyce, *Letters*, 2:296.

77. Mathews' account of *Chamber Music* sales, dated 21 Feb. 1913, Cornell. Actually, more copies had been sold, but Mathews' figure of 177 reflects the fact that for royalty purposes, 13 copies counted as 12 (as per agreement).

78. Joyce to Mathews, 26 Feb. 1913, in Joyce, *Letters*, 2:323.

79. For example, in his postcard to Mathews of 15 July 1915 (SIU), and through his literary agent. See James B. Pinker's letter to Joyce, 29 March 1920, in John Firth, "James Pinker to James Joyce, 1915–1920," *Studies in Bibliography* 21 (1968): 223.

80. Joyce to Mathews, 8 July 1915, Buffalo.

81. See Harriet Weaver's letter to Joyce, 10 Nov. 1916, in John Firth, "Harriet Weaver's Letters to James Joyce, 1915–1920," *Studies in Bibliography* 20 (1967): 165, and B. W. Huebsch's letter to Weaver, 16 June 1916, in Joyce *Letters*, 1:91.

82. Heubsch to John Quinn, 9 July 1917, quoted in Ann Catherine McCullough, "A History of B. W. Huebsch, Publisher" (Ph.D. diss. Wisconsin, 1979), 135.

83. See, for example, Nora Joyce to Quinn, 1 Oct. 1917, quoted in McCullough, "History of Huebsch," 142 and Joyce to Harriet Weaver, 29 July 1918, in Joyce, *Letters* 1:116. Later Huebsch in his oral history said: "I see now that Joyce was right and I was wrong." Quoted in McCullough, "History," 204.

84. For an account of Joyce's relations with Huebsch, see McCullough, "History of Huebsch," ch. 3.

85. Slocum and Cahoon, *Bibliography*, 9.

86. *Pound/Joyce*, ed. Forrest Read (New York: New Directions, 1967, 136–37.

87. Ibid., 139. Although they did not find his prose disagreeable, Lady Gregory and James Stephens "valued *Chamber Music* highest in Joyce's work." See B. L. Reid, *The Man from New York: John Quinn and His Friends* (New York: Oxford UP, 1968), 530–31.

88. *Egoist* 5 (June–July 1918): 87, also in Deming, *Joyce: Critical Heritage*, 1:13.

89. James B. Pinker to Joyce, 29 March 1920, in Firth, "Pinker to Joyce," 223.

90. *Letters to James Joyce*, vol. 3, ed. Richard Ellmann (New York: Viking, 1966), 49.

91. Joyce to Weaver, 6 Nov. 1921, in Joyce, *Letters*, 1:176.

92. Symons to Grant Richards, 2 Oct. 1906, in Beckson and Munro, "Letters," 96. Scholes, "Richards to Joyce," 139, refers to Joyce as one of the two "most difficult" of Richards' authors.

93. Joyce and Mathews never met, although Joyce stopped by Mathews' shop in Vigo Street on his way to Ireland in late July 1909, hoping to see the publisher, who unfortunately was out. Joyce to Mathews, 2 Sept. 1909, Texas.

CHAPTER 5. EZRA POUND'S FIRST PUBLISHER

1. Ezra Pound to Patricia Hutchins, 7 April 1954, quoted in her *Ezra Pound's Kensington* (London: Faber & Faber, 1965), 58.

2. For a history of the partnership, see my *Early Nineties: A View from the Bodley Head* (Cambridge: Harvard UP, 1971).

3. Pound's preface to *Poetical Works of Lionel Johnson*, in *Literary Essays of Ezra Pound*, ed. T. S. Eliot (New York: New Directions, 1954), 367.

4. "A Chat with Mr. Elkin Mathews," *Publisher and Bookseller* 2 (24 Feb. 1906): 417.

5. Quoted in William Reese Co., catalogue 54, entry 378. Information based on author's conversations with Nest Elkin Mathews, and Hutchins, *Pound's Kensington*, 59.

6. Noel Stock, *The Life of Ezra Pound* (New York: Pantheon, 1970), 55.

7. Donald Gallup, *Ezra Pound: A Bibliography* (Charlottesville: University of Virginia Press, 1983), A2.

8. Pound to Mathews, n.d., Yale. George Wyndham, to whom Pound refers, was a prominent politician and author of a recent essay on Ronsard. A cousin of Lord Alfred Douglas, he had in 1895 attempted to prevent Oscar Wilde's trial and to befriend the play-wright. There is a letter in the University of Victoria library from Wyndham's secretary which thanks Mathews for allowing Wyndham to see "the poems [*Personae*?] by Ezra Pound" and declines what C. G. Petter takes to be a request from Mathews that Wyndham serve as reader for *Personae*. See Petter, "Pound's *Personae*: From Manuscript to Print," *Studies in Bibliography* 35 (1982): 123.

9. [T. S. Eliot], preface to *Ezra Pound, His Metric and Poetry* (New York: Knopf, 1917), 5. See Pound's account in "How I Began," *T. P.'s Weekly* 21 (6 June 1913): 707, and that of Homer Pound in "Ezra Pound's Father Tells How Son Went to London with a Shilling and Found Fame," by Mary Dixon Thayer in *Philadelphia Evening Bulletin*, 20 Feb. 1928, 12.

10. Pound's letter appeared in the "News and Gossip of the Literary World" section, *Boston Evening Transcript*, 14 July 1915, 21. Also quoted in *The Letters of Ezra Pound, 1907–1941*, ed. D. D. Paige (New York: Harcourt, Brace, 1950), 62.

11. Eliot, *Ezra Pound*, 6.

12. Louis L. Martz, Introduction, *Collected Early Poems of Ezra Pound*, ed. Michael John King (New York: New Directions, 1976), viii.

13. Pound probably was referring to Mathews' visit to "The Pines" in January 1900, of which he wrote "a very interesting account." See Messrs. Hodgson and Company's catalogue of the sale of Elkin Mathews' library, 26–28 April, 1922, item 521.

14. Pound, letter to William Carlos Williams, 3 Feb. 1909, in Pound, *Letters*, 7.

15. Petter, "Pound's *Personae*," 117–19, 122.

16. Michael Reck, *Ezra Pound: A Close-up* (New York: McGraw- Hill, 1967), 12.

17. *Personae* is listed in both the announcements column of *Publishers' Circular* 90 (6 March 1909): 363, and in a large Mathews advertisement, ibid., 364. *Personae* was also included in Mathews' spring announcements in *Academy* no. 1925 (27 March 1909): 930.

18. Add. Mss. 50,923, vol. 14, Oct. 1908–Sept. 1910, 393, BL, and Mathews' account of sales sheet dated 3 March 1910, which lists total cost as £31.2.0.

19. Eric Homberger, Introduction, *Ezra Pound: The Critical Heritage*, ed. Eric Homberger (London and Boston: Routledge & Kegan Paul, 1972), 6. See Homberger's review of the critical response to *Personae*, ibid., 5–6.

20. Reck, *Pound: A Close-up*, 12.

21. See Yeats's letter to Lady Gregory, 10 Dec. 1909, in *The Letters of W. B. Yeats*, ed. Allan Wade (London: Rupert Hart- Davis, 1954), 543.

22. *Punch* 136 (23 June 1909): 449, quoted in Homberger, *Pound: The Critical Heritage*, 6.

23. Hutchins, *Pound's Kensington*, 59.

24. Stock, *Life*, 61; Peter Ackroyd, *Ezra Pound and His World* (New York: Scribners, 1980), 19. Also Gallup, *Pound Bibliography*, B1; see Alun R. Jones, *The Life and Opinions of T. E. Hulme* (London: Gollancz, 1960), 25–37, for a history of the Poets' Club.

25. Pound to Mathews, n.d., Yale.

26. *Publishers' Circular* 90 (19 June 1909): 928.

27. Quoted in Gallup, *Pound Bibliography*, A3.

28. Mathews' account of sales, 3 March 1910, Yale. Mathews' letter to Pound of 19 November 1912 (Yale) indicates that 600 copies were now bound.

29. As Stock writes (*Life*, 66), Mathews "inserted a note [in *Exultations*] by which he hoped to convey to readers that inclusion of the poem in its present form was not his doing but the poet's: "The Publisher desires to state that the *Ballad of the Goodly Fere*—by wish of the Author—is reproduced exactly as it appeared in *The English Review*.'"

30. Agreement between Mathews and Pound to publish *Exultations*, Yale.

31. Pound to Mathews, 16 Sept. 1909, Yale.

32. Add. Mss. 50,923, vol. 14, Oct. 1908–Sept. 1910, 393–94, BL, and Mathews' account of sales, 3 March 1910, Yale, which lists total cost for *Exultations* as £24.8.9.

33. See reviews by Flint and Thomas in Homberger, *Pound: The Critical Heritage*, 61–62, 64–66.

34. Account of sales, 3 March 1910, Yale. The account of sales for 18 Nov. 1912 (Yale) indicates that another 150 copies had been bound.

35. Mathews to Pound, 4 March 1910, Yale.

36. Mathews, account of sales, 3 March 1911, Yale.

37. Mathews to Pound, 29 April 1910, Yale. In a postcard from Italy [21]

Ma[y] 19[10], Pound told Mathews: "Yes, I shall be in London in June & can cast my bardic eye on the printer's misdeeds," presumably meaning that he would be able to read proof for "The Dawn," which already had been prepared for the press. Ezra Pound Collection, Ms. 54, Victoria. While in London, Pound took the manuscript of "The Dawn" around to Mathews, who, having decided not to publish it after all, mailed it back to Pound in Hammersmith. Unfortunately, the manuscript was lost, and Pound was furious: "'The Dawn' has not been heard of at this end of the line, and it seems to me to have been about the acme of carelessness to have sent it unregistered, the more especially as I could quite easily have taken it away myself, as I brought it to you, if you had sent me a note to that effect." Having been rejected by both Dent and Mathews, "The Dawn" was never published. Pound to Mathews, [1910], Yale.

38. Quoted in Gallup, *Pound Bibliography*, A6.

39. Pound to Mathews, 30 Nov. [1910], Ezra Pound Collection, Mss. 55/57, Victoria. Anthony George Shiell's *Agapë and Other Poems* was privately printed in 1908.

40. Pound to Mathews, 23 Jan. 1911, Ezra Pound Collection, Mss. 65/66, Victoria.

41. Pound to Mathews, 13 Feb. 1911, Ezra Pound Collection, Mss. 67/68, Victoria.

42. Stock, *Life*, 97; Gallup, *Pound Bibliography*, A7a.

43. Pound to Mathews, 15 July 1911, Ms. 392/l, fol. 925, EMA.

44. Add. Mss. 50,924, vol. 15, Oct. 1910–June 1912, 323, BL; Mathews to Pound, 19 Nov. 1912, Yale.

45. See Homberger, *Pound: The Critical Heritage*, 77–85.

46. Brita Lindberg-Seyersted, ed., *Pound/Ford: The Story of a Literary Friendship* (New York: New Directions, 1982), 8.

47. Pound to Mathews, 30 May 1916, quoted in *Pound/Joyce: The Letters of Ezra Pound to James Joyce*, ed. Forrest Read (New York: New Directions, 1967), 285.

48. Mathews to Pound, 19 Nov. 1912, Yale; Mathews' account of sales, 18 Nov. 1912, Yale.

49. Gallup, *Pound Bibliography*, A8a.

50. Pound to Mathews, [Nov. 1912], Yale.

51. Mathews, account of sales, 18 Nov. 1912, Yale; Mathews to Pound, 19 Nov. 1912, Yale.

52. Add. Mss. 50,925, vol. 16, July 1912–, BL.

53. Gallup, *Pound Bibliography*, A3b, A7b.

54. Mathews to Pound, 19 Nov. 1912, Yale.

55. Memorandum from Matthew Bell & Co. of London to Mathews, 16 May 1916, Berkeley.

56. Mathews to Pound, 19 Nov. 1912, Yale.

57. Pound's presentation copy is in the Ransom Humanities Research Center Library, Texas.

58. Harriet Monroe, *A Poet's Life: Seventy Years in a Changing World* (New York: Macmillan, 1938), 223. As John Tytell writes in *Ezra Pound: The Solitary Volcano* (New York: Doubleday, 1987), 61, Mathews by recommending the poet's works to Monroe "may have done more than anything else for Pound."

59. Moore to Pound, 9 January 1919, Yale (published in Charles Tomlinson, *Marianne Moore: A Collection of Critical Essays* [Englewood Cliffs, N.J.: Prentice-Hall, 1969] 16–19). Mathews seems not to have recognized the note of dissatisfaction with the poetic mode of the nineties which emerged from time to time in such poems as "Revolt: Against the Crepuscular Spirit of Modern Poetry" in *Personae* and similar expressions in *Exultations* and *Canzoni*.

60. Mathews to Sir Arthur Quiller-Couch, 8 Oct. 1912, in my possession.

61. In *The Autobiography of William Carlos Williams* (New York: New Directions, 1951), 134, Williams wrote: "It was then, 1913, that Ezra in London, got my small book, *The Tempers*, published by Elkin Matthews [sic]."

62. Yale. In August 1912, Harriet Monroe wrote Pound, inviting him to contribute to *Poetry*. Having received a positive reply of 18 August from the poet, she wrote asking him to serve as foreign correspondent, which he did. Stock, *Life*, 119; Pound to Monroe, [18] Aug. 1912, in Pound, *Letters*, 9.

63. See Mathews' 1910 catalogue. Mathews knew Noguchi personally; his diary entries during 1913 and 1914 list luncheon engagements with Noguchi, who was in England at the time.

64. Stock, *Life*, 172.

65. Add. Mss. 50,926, vol. 17, entry for 24 March 1915, BL.

66. See the survey of criticism in Homberger, *Pound: The Critical Heritage*, 108–17. Commenting on the number of translations of Chinese and Japanese poetry which had appeared recently, one critic observed that the translators had "sought to contain the volatile spirit of this Oriental poetry in all kinds of forms—Omarian quatrains, rhymed and unrhymed couplets, and stanzas of various kinds." "One feels," he wrote—turning his attention to Pound's *Cathay*—"that [Pound] has, at any rate, sought for an honesty of method. His translations are not mere excuses, as is so often the case with this kind of work, to irradiate with a little of someone else's spirit a blameless but dull technique." Having commented on Pound's use of *vers libre*, the reviewer concluded that Pound "often gives us little poems in which the rich yet fastidious colours of Chinese art are admirably reproduced." *Bookman* 48 (July 1915): 112.

67. Pound to Mathews, 13 March 1913, Texas.

68. Pound, Preface to *Poetical Works of Lionel Johnson*, in *Literary Essays*, 362.

69. Pound to Lord Alfred Douglas, 18 May 1935, quoted in Gallup, *Pound Bibliography*, B9.

70. Ian Fletcher, ed., *The Collected Poems of Lionel Johnson*, 2nd, rev. ed. (New York and London: Garland, 1982), xiii–xiv.

71. Pound to Mathews, 16 Oct. 1914, Yale.

72. Pound to Floyd Dell, 20 Jan. 1911, quoted in G. Thomas Tanselle, "Two Early Letters of Ezra Pound," *American Literature* 34 (March 1962): 118.

73. Pound, Preface to *Poetical Works of Johnson*, in *Literary Essays*, 362–63.

74. Louise Imogen Guiney to Mathews, 4 Nov. [1915?], Princeton.

75. Guiney to Mathews, 9 Nov. [1915?], Princeton.

76. Pound, portion of a letter to Ifan Kyrle Fletcher, n.d., inside front cover of *Poetical Works of Lionel Johnson*, Houghton.

77. Fletcher, letter dated 8 April 1930, inside front cover of *Poetical Works of Lionel Johnson*, Houghton.

78. Pound to Harriet Monroe, March 1915, in Pound, *Letters*, 55.

79. Stock, *Life*, 184. According to Chiswick Press records (Add. Mss. 50,926, entry for 5 Nov. 1915, p. 301, BL), the cost of composing and printing *Catholic Anthology* plus extra for small type and corrections in the proofs, totaled £16.5.0. Printing 500 copies of the wrapper in black ink with Caledonian gray paper, amounted to a further £1.0.6.

80. See, for instance, "Elkin Mathews' Announcements" in *Academy* no. 4590 (16 Oct. 1915): 256, which also pointed out that the anthology was "neither Futurist nor Vorticist," showing "both the progress and the *stasis* of verse since the appearance of the anthology *'Des Imagistes'* in February 1914."

81. Pound to Douglas Goldring, [22?] Nov. 1915, in Pound, *Letters*, 65. Meynell's threats may have been responsible for Mathews' listing the anthology in later advertisements headed: "W. B. Yeats, and Others" with no mention of Pound's name. See, for instance, *Bookman* 49 (Dec. 1915): 135.

82. Pound to Kate Buss, 9 March 1916, in Pound, *Letters*, 73.

83. Stock, *Life*, 191.

84. Pound to Buss, 9 March 1916, in Pound, *Letters*, 73.

85. *Publishers' Circular* 104 (29 Jan. 1916): 85; *Athenaeum* no. 4602 (Feb. 1916): 73.

86. Pound to Joyce, 27 Nov. 1915, in Read, *Pound/Joyce*, 60–61.

87. *Athenaeum* no. 4602 (Feb. 1916): 73.

88. Gallup, *Pound Bibliography*, B10. Waugh's review appeared in the *Quarterly Review* for Oct. 1916.

89. Pound to Iris Barry, May 1916, in Pound, *Letters*, 81.

90. Quoted in B. L. Reid, *The Man from New York: John Quinn and His Friends* (New York: Oxford UP, 1968), 281.

91. Stock, *Life*, 194; Mathews' diary, entry for 12 Dec. 1915, EMA.

92. Estimate dated 4 May 1916, Berkeley.

93. Stock, *Life*, 194.

94. W. B. Clowes, *Family Business, 1803–1953*, rpt. (London: William Clowes & Sons, 1969), 74. Pound later wrote John Quinn that Mathews had told him that "Wm. Archyballed [*sic*] Clowes"—W.C.K.'s first cousin and also

a managing director in the firm—"was responsible for the trouble over Lustra." Pound to Quinn, 2 Dec. 1918, in John Quinn Memorial Collection, Rare Books and Manuscripts Division, New York Public Library.

95. Text in Homberger, *Pound: The Critical Heritage*, 121–22, and in Read, *Pound/Joyce*, app. A, 277.

96. Pound to Mathews, 3 June 1916 (postmark), Berkeley.

97. Pound to James B. Pinker, 30 Jan. 1916, in Read, *Pound/Joyce*, 66. Read (*Pound/Joyce*, 12) sees Pound's struggle with Mathews over *Lustra* as "the simultaneous counterpart of Pound's battle for *A Portrait*" and says that it "elicited from him his most forcible statements against publishers' and printers' censorship."

98. Pound to Mathews, [c. 29] May 1916, in Read, *Pound/Joyce*, 278–79.

99. Pound to Mathews, 30 May 1916 (postmark), Berkeley.

100. Pound to Mathews, 30 May 1916, in Read, *Pound/Joyce*, 282. The note Pound refers to is a statement included in his letter to Mathews, [c. 29] May 1916 (ibid., 280–82), which Pound insisted be included in *Lustra* if it were published in a censored version.

101. Pound to Mathews, 30 May 1916, in Read, *Pound/Joyce*, 283–85.

102. Stock, *Life*, 194. In a letter of May 1916 to Iris Barry, Pound in a postscript wrote: "Elkin Mathews—called in Yeats to mediate and Yeats quoted Donne at him for his soul's good. I don't know what will come of it." Yeats, *Letters*, 81.

103. Augustine Birrell to Mathews, 31 May 1916, Berkeley. Birrell was a lawyer and essayist who had been chief secretary for Ireland from 1907 to 1916, when he resigned after the Easter Rebellion. Birrell's statement regarding *The Rainbow* was reported by Pound in a letter to Mathews, 30 May 1916, in Read, *Pound/Joyce*, 283.

104. Mathews to Birrell, 31 May 1916, Berkeley.

105. Birrell to Mathews, 9 June 1916, Berkeley.

106. Mathews to Pound, 31 May 1916, Yale.

107. "Lustra of Ezra Pound": List of Emendations & Omissions to be made," dated 31 May 1916, Yale. There are two drafts of this list in the Bancroft Library at Berkeley, one of which contains a draft of Mathews' letter of 31 May 1916 on the verso. The other draft, almost identical with the former, contains on its verso a fragment of a draft agreement for the publication of *Lustra* which reads: "Memorandum of Agreement made this _____day of June 1916 Between E.P. (hereinafter called the Author) of the one part and E.M. (hereinafter called the Publisher) of the other part, whereby it is mutually agreed as follows. — 1 The Author hereby agrees to allow the Publisher the exclusive right during the legal term of copyright of printing and publishing in Great Britain, Ireland, the British Colonies and Dependencies the work intended to be entitled Lustra[.]. 2 The author hereby agrees [. . .] 3 The author will hold the Publisher harmless [. . .] 4 The Publisher having as a preliminary had a proof of the Ms."

It is from these two draft lists and the draft documents on their versos at Berkeley that Homberger in *Pound: The Critical Heritage*, 123–24, draws his list of emendations for *Lustra*.

108. Pound to Mathews, [c. 1 June 1916], Berkeley. In a letter to Iris Barry written in May 1916, Pound wrote: "The idiot Mathews has got the whole volume [*Lustra*] set up in type, and has now got a panic and marked 25 poems for deletion." Pound, *Letters*, 80–81.

109. Mathews to Pound, 10 June 1916, Yale. The draft of this letter in the Bancroft Library at Berkeley excepts only "The Temperaments," "Ancient Music," and "The Lake Isle." Presumably written in the hand of one of Mathews' clerks, the draft is found on the verso of one of the two draft copies of the list of emendations and omissions drawn up for *Lustra* and discussed in note 107, above. No mention is made of "Pagani's, November 8."

110. Although in his letter to Mathews, [c. 1 June 1916], Berkeley, Pound had offered to reimburse the publisher for the costs of *Lustra* and take over the edition himself, there is no reason to believe that Pound was serious. He wrote Iris Barry in June that Harold Monro's being "called up" stifled my shifting the book [*Lustra*] to the Poetry Bookshop," but there is no evidence that such a shift would have been possible. Pound, *Letters*, 83.

111. Pound to Monroe, 5 June 1916, in Pound, *Letters*, 81. After Mathews' death in 1921, Pound asked his London literary agent, Miss Agnes Bedford, to secure "the documents re/ Mathews fuss over Lustra. Shall use that as appendix to one of my own booklets." Quoted in a letter from Lawrence S. Rainey to the author.

112. Pound to Barry, June 1916, in Pound, *Letters*, 82–83. Looking back on the *Lustra* affair, Pound thought that it might one day "make a part of his 'Reveries over Asshood and Imbecility' or whatever else my reminiscences of a happy life are to be entitled." Reid, *The Man from New York*, 281.

113. Pound to Iris Barry, August 1916, in Pound, *Letters*, 92.

114. Gallup, *Pound Bibliography*, A11a.

115. Quoted in Stock, *Life*, 196.

116. Ibid., 204.

117. Mathews to Pound, 13 April 1918, Yale.

118. Pound to Quinn, 2 Dec. 1918, Quinn Collection, New York Public Library.

119. Quoted in Homberger, *Pound: The Critical Heritage*, 196.

120. Pound to Mrs. Mathews, 23 Dec. 1921, Ms. 392/1, fols. 1051–53, EMA. To Pound—who, according to Lawrence Rainey, was in desperate financial circumstances in late 1921—Mathews' death brought the prospect of money in the form of possible royalties due on sales of *Lustra* and *Umbra*. On 17 December 1921, he wrote his London agent, Agnes Bedford, to ask "what is to become of [Mathews'] business; and if there is any chance of its continuing, or the estate paying the royalties due." Quoted in a letter from Lawrence S. Rainey to the author.

EPILOGUE

1. Lily Yeats to J. B. Yeats, 5 Dec. 1921, National Library of Ireland.

2. Percy Muir, *Minding My Own Business: An Autobiography* (London: Chatto and Windus, 1956), 122.

3. Ibid., 13.

4. Ibid., 40.

5. Barbara Kaye (Mrs. Percy Muir), *The Company We Kept* (London: Werner Shaw; also Blakeney, Holt; Norfolk: Elkin Mathews, 1986).

APPENDIX A. ELKIN MATHEWS AND THE DANIEL PRESS

1. For a history of the Daniel Press, see Falconer Madan, *The Daniel Press: Memorials of C.H.O. Daniel with a Bibliography of the Press, 1845–1919* (Oxford: Oxford UP, 1921).

2. Ibid., 44.

3. P. M. Handover, "British Book Typography," in *Book Typography, 1815–1965, in Europe and the United States of America*, ed. Kenneth Day (London: Ernest Benn, 1966), 153.

4. Madan, *The Daniel Press*, 92. It appears that Daniel priced at least one of his books much earlier, i.e., *A New Sermon of the Newest Fashion* (1876), which according to Plomer was priced at 6/–. Henry R. Plomer, "Some Private Presses of the Nineteenth Century," *Library* 2nd ser. 1 (1900): 424.

5. Madan, *The Daniel Press*, 95. Daniel's willingness to supply dealers with copies of his books is indicated in his reply to Archibald Constable of Edinburgh, who had written to inquire about them: "I here with enclose advertisements of books printed by me," he wrote, "any of which, if not exhausted, I shall be pleased to send you. There is a 'trade' deduction of 10 p.c. on the price affixed." Daniel to Constable, 21 April 1887, EMA.

6. *Academy* 33 (April 1888): 290.

7. Daniel to Mathews, 6 March 1889, EMA.

8. Daniel to Mathews, 13 May 1889, EMA.

9. Falconer Madan, *Addenda and Corrigenda* [to *The Daniel Press*] (Oxford: Oxford UP, 1922), 6.

10. Daniel to Mathews, 7 Oct. 1890, EMA.

11. It appears that Mathews went further than merely advertising Daniel's books in his catalogues: he placed his catalogues in Daniel's books! At least one such instance has been called to my attention by Stephen Corey, Special Collections librarian, University of San Francisco, whose fine collection of Daniel Press books contains a copy of Bourdillon's *Ailes d'Alouette* with Mathews' book list for October 1890 tipped in.

12. Daniel to Mathews, 7 Oct. 1890, EMA.

13. Daniel to T [James Thursfield?], 28 Oct. 1890, ms. 328. WCL.

14. Daniel to Mathews, 13 May 1889, EMA.

15. Madan, *The Daniel Press*, 104; Daniel to Mathews, 26 Sept. 1890, EMA.

16. Bridges to Daniel, 7 Oct. 1893, Ms. 354, WCL.

17. That Bridges, too, was willing to speculate about *The Growth of Love* is suggested in a letter to Daniel, dated 27 September 1890, in which he wrote: "You ask about reserve copies of G of L. I think that I do not wish my nearer acquaintance to have any privilege. But I shd. think that if the bk is certain to rise in price that you might with-hold some copies for the advanced market." Ms. 354, WCL.

18. In his letter of 6 March 1889, EMA, Daniel mentioned a 10 percent discount. However, in his letters thereafter—e.g., that to Mathews of 13 May 1889, EMA—he allowed a 15 percent discount.

19. Daniel to Mathews, 13 May 1889, EMA.

20. Daniel to T[hursfield], 28 Oct. 1890, Ms. 328, WCL.

21. Bridges to Daniel, 19 Nov. 1889, Ms. 354, WCL.

22. Bridges to Daniel, 7 Oct. 1893, Ms. 354. WCL. Actually the listing of Bridges' *The Growth of Love* among the "New and Forthcoming Books" of the Bodley Head had occurred in a much earlier catalogue, that dated May 1891 bound in with Walter Crane's *Renascence*. Bridges observed the listing to which he objected in a catalogue dated July 1893 bound in a copy of A. C. Benson's *Poems*, which Lane had sent him as a compliment. See Bridges to Lane, 23 Oct. 1893, Ms. DON.d. 113, Bodleian.

23. Bridges to Lane, 23 Oct. 1893, Ms. DON.d. 113, Bodleian.

24. Bridges to Daniel, Ms. 354, WCL.

25. The phrase "Not published" had, in fact, been appended to the listing of *The Growth of Love* in a Bodley Head catalogue dated 1892–93 bound in with John Addington Symons' *In the Key of Blue*.

26. Bridges to Lane, 14 Feb. 1894, Ms. DON.d. 113. Bodleian.

27. Mathews to Daniel, 25 Sept. 1894, WCL.

APPENDIX B. ELKIN MATHEWS AND GORDON BOTTOMLEY

1. In a letter to Mathews, 24 March 1919, EMA, Bottomley penned this description of *The Gate of Smaragdus* for publication in one of Mathews' forthcoming catalogues. Replying to an inquiry as to the origin of the word "smaragdus," Bottomley wrote that it was "no more than a Latinate synonym for Emerald. I always thought it a beautiful word, and I used it just for its lustre and picturesqueness." Letter to Thomas B. Mosher, 12 Dec. 1909. Houghton.

2. Bottomley to Mosher, 12 Dec. 1909, Houghton. Although the imprint of the Unicorn Press remained on the title page, "an additional leaf" (Bottomley later wrote) bearing Mathews' imprint and an illustration by Balmer was "inserted opposite the title-page, without any excision being made to accom-

modate it." Bottomley, "Note" to *Poems of Thirty Years* (London: Constable, 1925), v, vi. In addition to publishing *The Gate of Smaragdus*, Mathews also purchased a number of the publications of the Unicorn Press at the sale mentioned by Bottomley. See Mathews' advertisement in *Publishers' Circular*, Christmas issue, 1904, 129.

3. Claude C. Abbott, Introduction to Bottomley's *Poems and Plays* (London: Bodley Head, 1953), 13.

4. Bottomley was referring to his *Poems at White-Nights: A Book of Verse* (London: Unicorn Press, 1899).

5. Bottomley to Mathews, 8 March 1907, in my possession.

6. Bottomley to Mathews, 12 Jan. 1916, EMA.

7. Bottomley to Mathews, 19 April 1907, in my possession.

8. Bottomley to Mathews, 8 March 1907, in my possession.

9. Bottomley to Mathews, 19 April 1907, in my possession.

10. Bottomley to Mathews, 7 May 1907, in my possession.

11. Bottomley to Mathews, 16 May 1907, in my possession.

12. Bottomley to Mathews, 11 July 1910, in my possession.

13. Bottomley to Mathews, 29 Feb. 1912, in my possession.

14. Reviewing Mathews' statement of his accounts, Bottomley in a letter to his publisher dated 12 Jan. 1916, EMA, pointed out: "In your charges for Publisher's commission on sales, I note you charge this on all the books alike at 33 1/3%. This is, of course, right and according to agreement on both the 1st and 2nd Series of 'Chambers of Imagery'; but I believe the case is different with regard to 'The Gate of Smaragdus.' You will remember that when I approached you first, on the collapse of The Unicorn Press, with regard to this book, it was already manufactured and ready for publication. The clause about advertising was more restricted than in the case of the later books: so that, all things considered, you agreed to publish it on a 25% commission, and that figure was embodied in the agreement. I hope you will find I am right in this."

15. Bottomley to Mathews, 29 Feb. 1912, in my possession.

16. Bottomley to Mathews, 17 April 1912, in my possession.

17. Bottomley to Mathews, 1 May 1912, in my possession.

18. Bottomley to Mathews, 12 Jan. 1916. EMA.

APPENDIX C. MAKING ENDS MEET

1. Binyon to an unidentified recipient, 22 Feb. 1916, in my possession.

2. "The Late Mr. Mathews," *Publishers' Circular* 115 (26 Nov. 1921): 531.

3. See R. D. Brown, "The Bodley Head Press: Some Bibliographical Extrapolations," *PBSA* 61 (1967): 39–50.

4. A practice on the part of printers which lasted until about 1917, when Chiswick Press records indicate Mathews began to be charged at the rate of

2/6 per week for printed sheets of various volumes held "to your order." Add. Mss. 50,927, dated 31 Dec. 1917, BL.

5. Add. Mss. 50,916, BL. All further references to the Chiswick Press records will be cited in parentheses in the text.

6. Clowes' estimate, n.d., Berg.

7. Clowes' estimate dated 17 Mar. 1914, Princeton.

8. Clowes' estimate dated 4 May 1916, Berkeley.

9. Mathews and Lane to the Editor, *Pall Mall Gazette* 57 (31 July 1893): 4.

10. Walter Crane to Mathews, 17 Aug. 1890, EMA.

11. Ian Fletcher, Introduction to *The Archives of Elkin Mathews, 1811–1938, Published on Microfilm* (Bishops Stortford: Chadwyck-Healey, 1973), n.p. Monro's quotation is in Joy Grant, *Harold Monro and the Poetry Bookshop* (London: Routledge and Kegan Paul, 1967), 16.

12. Bottomley to Paul Nash, 7 July 1912, in *Poet and Painter: Being the Correspondence between Gordon Bottomley and Paul Nash, 1910–1946*, ed. Claude Colleer Abbott and Anthony Bertram (Oxford: Oxford UP, 1955), 38.

13. Anne Chisholm, *Nancy Cunard: A Biography* (New York: Knopf, 1979), 83.

14. Herbert Read, *The Contrary Experience: Autobiographies* (London: Faber & Faber, 1963) 163.

15. John Drinkwater to Mathews, 12 Jan. 1907, quoted in Argosy Catalogue no. 42 (July 1972), item 149. "Graven Images," a short verse play, appeared in 1908 in Drinkwater's *Lyrical and Other Poems*, published by the Samurai Press at Cranleigh.

16. Lord Dunsany to Mathews, 8 Feb. 1912, Yale.

17. Mathews to John Mavrogordato, 14 July 1906, Texas. Mackenzie's "stuff" was probably the manuscript of *Poems*, published in 1907 by B. H. Blackwell in Oxford and by Simpkin, Marshall in London.

18. Inserted in a copy of Corbin's *The Elizabethan Hamlet* in the Colbeck Collection, University of British Columbia.

19. *The Letters of Ernest Dowson*, ed. Desmond Flower and Henry Maas (Rutherford, N.J.: Fairleigh Dickinson UP, 1967), 437.

20. Symons to Joyce, 2 Oct. 1906, in "Letters from Arthur Symons to James Joyce: 1904–1932" by Karl Beckson and John M. Munro, *James Joyce Quarterly*, 1967, 93.

21. Agreement between Mathews and Joyce dated 17 Jan. 1907, Yale.

22. Agreement between Mathews and Pound, 16 Sept. [1909], Yale.

23. Memorandum of Agreement between Mathews and Jack B. Yeats, 17 Sept. 1902, in my possession.

24. Ibid., 13 Sept. 1909, Yale.

25. Typed carbon copy of a pencilled note written on a slip of paper by Mathews, 27 May 1921, Texas. In his note of thanks to Mathews for the check, dated 31 May 1921, Yeats wrote: "'Flaunty' was the favourite. Perhaps just because it was the first." Texas.

26. Agreement between Mathews and J. M. Synge, 22 March 1905, TCD. Also transcribed in *John Millington Synge: Some Unpublished Letters and Documents* (Montreal: Red Path Press, 1959), 7–8.

27. Mathews received no income from 145 copies. Five of these went to public libraries, 6 to Synge, and 63 to reviewers, etc., totaling 74 copies. Another 71 copies were supplied to the trade free of charge under the 13 copies as 12 provision.

28. See Mathews' account-to-date sheet re *Shadow of the Glen and Riders to the Sea*, 21 June 1907, TCD.

29. "Michael Field" to Mathews, [July 1895], Columbia.

30. Mathews to "Michael Field," 9 July 1895, Columbia.

31. W. H. Davies to Mathews, 31 July 1913, in my possession.

32. Mathews to Henry Newbolt, 15 and 22 Dec, 1897, in the possession of Peter Newbolt.

33. Drinkwater in a letter to Mathews, 18 May 1917, in my possession, thanked the publisher for the draft agreement, stating that "the conditions are satisfactory with the exception of one point in clause 3. In your letter of July 24th last you mention the advance royalties as being payable on the signing of agreement, but in the draft as being payable on delivery of manuscript. As a matter of fact, I will undertake to let you have the copy, by, say, the middle of July (or earlier if you need it for printing to ensure early publication in the autumn) but I should wish the arrangement as to date of payment to stand as originally defined."

34. Dunsany to Mathews, 13 Aug. [1916?], Texas. Although Dunsany refers to four publishers in his letter, he lists only the three noted in the text.

35. Mathews to Dunsany (draft), n.d., Berg. (Another and apparently earlier draft is dated 5 July 1916.) For a table of prices at which publishers offered their books to the trade in the 1890s, see *Bookselling* 1 (Feb. 1895): 34.

36. Mathews to Reginald Hallward, 2 May 1906, in possession of Eric and Joan Stevens. The Pear Tree Press, on which Hallward's Woodlands Press was to some extent modeled, was founded in 1899 by James Guthrie. Although Mathews published only one Pear Tree Press Book,—Edward Blakeney's *The Angel of the Hours* (1907) he acted as London agent for the press. See Mathews' statement to that effect in *Elkin Mathews List, Forthcoming and Recent Books, Season 1906–7* (p. 8) in the back of Edith Escombe's *Phases of Marriage* (1907).

37. Mathews to Hallward, 11 May 1906, in possession of Eric and Joan Stevens. Among the Woodlands Press books Mathews distributed were *Vox Humana, Wild Oats, Apotheosis, Flower of Paradise*, and *Granny's Workbox*.

INDEX

A. E. (George William Russell): role in Celtic movement, 109

Abbott, Dr. Conrad: *Travels in a Tree-Top*, 195

Addison Road, London: Mathews move to no. 13, 21

Addleshaw, Percy. *See* Hemingway, Percy

Albany: John Lane's residence in, 74

Aldington, Richard: *Images of Desire*, 3, 24

"Anodos." *See* Coleridge, Mary E.

Anthologies of Verse: vogue for, 63

Archer, William: review of Newbolt's *Admirals All*, 47, 51

Arnold, Matthew: influence on Lionel Johnson, 88

Augusta, Lady Gregory: role in Synge's career, 100–103; valued Joyce's *Chamber Music*, 275n87; mentioned, 190

Balfour, Reginald: contributor to *Garland of New Poetry*, 53; mentioned, 55

Balmer, Clinton: illustrator of Bottomley's *Gate of Smaragdus*, 17, 179; influenced by Ricketts and Shannon, 179–80

Barry, Iris: Pound's letter to *re Lustra*, 164

Baudelaire, Charles: *Flowers of Evil* in translation, 62; *Les Petits Poèmes en Prose* trans. by Symons, 62, 114

Beach, Sylvia: buys books from Mathews, 25

Beardsley, Aubrey: as art editor of the *Yellow Book*, 16; caricatures Elkin Mathews, 251n23; controversy over "Black Coffee" drawing, 253n30; correspondence with Leonard Smithers, 253n30; mentioned, 4

Bedford, Agnes: as Pound's literary agent, 282n110, 283n120

Bedford Park, London: residence of Mathews at 1, Blenheim Rd. in, 9–15; described, 10; residents of, 10; social life in, 11; Mathews as neighbor of the Yeats family in, 10, 74

Begbie, Agnes: *Christmas Songs and Carols* illustrated by Edith Calvert, 21, 60–61; mentioned, 58

Bell, Matthew (bindery of): Pound's stock of books stored at, 148; fire on premises of, 27

Binyon, Laurence: on publishing costs during WWI, 27; early career of, 32; ideas on publishing poetry, 32; originated idea for Shilling Garland series, 32; role in publishing Shilling Garland series, 33–34, 38–40; protégé of Robert Bridges, 34; experiments in meter, 46; designs cover for *Garland of New Poetry*, 52; relations with Mathews, 52; on Mathews as a small-time publisher, 55, 184; introduced to Pound, 139; royalties paid to by Mathews, 259n88; mentioned, 24, 45, 47, 55

—*The Cause*, 27

—*England and Other Poems*: production costs of, 186

—*First Book of London Visions*: publications of, 36–37; reviews of, 38

—"For the Fallen": popularity of, 28

—*London Visions*: Chiswick Press bill for, 186; production costs for, 186

—*Lyric Poems*: mentioned, 32, 36, 177, 195

—*Praise of Life*: publication of, 46

—*Second Book of London Visions*: publication of, 51

—*Winnowing-Fan*: contains "For the Fallen," 28

Birnbaum, Martin: production costs for *Oscar Wilde*, 187

Birrell, Augustine: consulted *re Lustra* controversy, 161–62

286

T. S. Eliot's early poems, 29; death of, 30; response of to sales of Newbolt's *Admirals All*, 49–50; relations with Laurence Binyon, 52–53, 55; tastes and interests of, 55, 58; preface to *Vigo Verse Anthology*, 63; authorship of *The Views of Christopher* attributed to, 65; appeal of Pre-Raphaelite poetry for, 72; publisher of the Rhymers' club books, 73–74; close ties of with Yeats family, 74; role in publishing Johnson's *Poems*, 89–93 *passim*; purchases stock and copyrights for Johnson's poetry, 96; promoted Johnson's work, 96–97; role in publishing Johnson's *Poetical Works*, 98–99; published Synge's works, 101–9 *passim*; sympathy with young authors, 102, 114, 135, 166; as publisher to Lord Dunsany, 109–11; on market for poetry, 125–26; joint imprints of, 131–32; admiration for Swinburne, 136; considers publishing Monroe's *Poetry* in England, 152; threatened by Francis Meynell, 157; Lily Yeats on death of, 167; private library of sold, 167; disposal of estate of, 167–68; flair of as a collector of books, 168; correspondence with Bottomley, 179–83; fame of, 184; as publisher and distributor of Woodlands Press books, 192–93; "ghosts" in catalogues of, 195; transfers in catalogues of, 195; style of C. Elkin Mathews, 250n5; close relationship with Thomas George Mathews, 251n15; refers to John Butler Yeats's "charming persiflage," 251n24; asked to publish Wilde's *Mr. W. H.*, 252n29; and controversy over Beardsley's "Black Coffee" drawing, 253n30; burial of, 255n54; obituaries for, 255n54; visits "The Pines," 276n13; purchases publications of Unicorn Press, 285n2; imprint of: *see* Appendix D. *See also* Binyon, Laurence; Joyce, James; Pound, Ezra; Yeats, W. B.; Elkin Mathews, Ltd.; Elkin Mathews and Marrot
—Business premises. *See* Cork Street,

London; Exeter, Devon; Vigo Street, London
—Career as publisher: publishing aspirations, 4, 250n3; early years of, 5–6; continues early Bodley Head tradition, 16–17; published children's books as a specialty, 21; desire to publish poetry inexpensively, 24; production strategies, 27, 184–86; problems to posed by WWI, 27–28, 191–92; retrospective review of, 29; limitations in, 29–30; publishing resources, 55, 184–85; tastes in publishing, 122, 152; predilection for poetry and poetic fiction, 122, 253n32; business documents and correspondence, 167–68; royalties, 184–95 *passim*, 259n88; production costs, 185–87, 191–92; agreements (contracts), 187–89 *passim*
—Personality: described as "cross little man," 19; conservative nature of, 132; described as "monkish, medieval," 133; satirized in *Punch*, 137–39; as reflected in relations with authors, 253n35, 254n41; described, 255n54
—Physical appearance of: described by J. Lewis May, 11–12; described by Newbolt, 12; caricatured by Beardsley, 251n23
—Residences: *See* Addison Road, London; Bedford Park, London; Chorleywood, Herts.; Cley, Norfolk; Stoke Newington, London
—Series publications of: Mathews' opinion of, 31; problems with, 38–40; success of, 62, 67; appeal of, 67; Bottomley's response to, 67–68, 71; production costs for, 187; mentioned, 24, 31–71 *passim*. *See also* Burlington series; Satchel series; Savile series; Shilling Garland series; Vigo Cabinet series

Mathews, Elkin and John Lane: partnership between 5–6, 131, 250n7; created vogue for beautiful books, 9; and the economics of book publishing, 9; problems between, 15–16; dissolution of partnership between, 16, 74, 91; battle over Bodley Head authors, 74; as